Space, Time, and Stuff

Space, Time, and Stuff

Frank Arntzenius
with a contribution by Cian Dorr

OXFORD
UNIVERSITY PRESS

OXFORD
UNIVERSITY PRESS

Great Clarendon Street, Oxford, OX2 6DP,

Oxford University Press is a department of the University of Oxford.
It furthers the University's objective of excellence in research, scholarship,
and education by publishing worldwide.

Oxford is a registered trade mark of Oxford University Press
in the UK and in certain other countries

© Frank Arntzenius 2012

First published 2012
First published in paperback 2014

Published in the United States of America by Oxford University Press,
198 Madison Avenue, New York, NY 10016, United States of America

British Library Cataloguing in Publication Data
Data available

Library of Congress Cataloging in Publication Data
Data available

ISBN 978-0-19-969660-4 (Hbk)
ISBN 978-0-29-870591-8 (Pbk)

Contents

Preface

I originally intended this book to be accessible to anybody who is interested in the structure of space and time and knows a bit of calculus. I failed. Parts of Chapters 3, 6, 7, and 8 require a certain amount of knowledge of quantum mechanics and differential geometry. Still, I have tried to write even those chapters in such a manner that one can understand the gist of what is being said while skipping over the technical details. Consequently, I will maintain the conceit that more than a dozen people will actually get something out of this book.

In writing this book I learned a lot from David Albert, Caro Brighouse, Hartry Field, John Hawthorne, Tim Maudlin, Oliver Pooley, Laura Ruetsche, Ted Sider, Brad Skow, Brian Skyrms, and David Wallace. Special thanks go to Gordon Belot and Carl Hoefer for their extremely insightful comments on the whole manuscript, to Hilary Greaves, who should have written Chapter 7, and much more besides, and to Cian Dorr for co-authoring Chapter 8, as well as being an all-purpose oracle.

Finally, I am deeply indebted to Dada, Linda, Michael, and Mummy for their help and suffering during the long gestation period of this book.

Introduction

This book is, by and large, a book about the structure of space and time. It is not a linear progression towards some over-arching conclusion. Rather, each chapter focuses on an independent idea. Consequently, each chapter can be read on its own. However, along the way two overarching themes do emerge. Let me sketch these two themes, and then briefly outline the content of each chapter.

In the first place, much of this book can be seen as an attempt to reduce all of physics to geometry—an attempt to characterize the structure of the world solely by means of a very small stock of geometrical predicates. Part and parcel of this project is the introduction of more spaces than just our familiar four-dimensional spacetime. Tangent-bundle spaces, in which things such as velocities and vector fields live, fibre-bundle spaces, in which gauge fields live, scalar-value spaces, in which things such as mass densities and scalar fields live; at various points in the book I suggest that these spaces are existing physical objects—indeed, that they are the only physical objects that there are.

The other theme is that our knowledge of the structure of the world derives from one basic idea: the idea that the laws of the world are simple in terms of the fundamental objects and predicates. In particular, what we can know and do know about the way things could have been—what we can know and do know about the metaphysical, and physical, possibilities—derives from our knowledge of what the fundamental objects and predicates are, and what the fundamental laws are in which they figure. I argue that it is bad epistemology to infer what the fundamental objects, predicates, and laws are on the basis of intuitions as to what is, and what is not, possible. In writing this book I have been surprised to find how often philosophers of physics, myself included, have used intuitions about what the possibilities are in order to draw conclusions as to what the fundamental objects, predicates, and laws of physics are. One would have thought that philosophers of physics would be the last people on earth to make choices between rival theories of physics based on intuitions concerning what is possible. And yet they do. Standard arguments against the existence of space and time are based on intuitions as to whether there is a possible world which differs from the actual world only in that every physical object is shifted five metres to the right of where it is in the actual world. Arguments for realism about non-local quantities (loop holonomies) in gauge theories rely on analogous intuitions about the distinctness of gauge-transformation-related possible worlds. And so on. This kind of reasoning strikes me as suspicious, to say the least. It is not the use of *intuitions* that I object to. Logic and experience alone do not dictate which theories are true, or, more precisely, experience does not by itself rationally compel a unique epistemic attitude towards theories. So all of us will have to make use of intuitions, or something akin to them (plausibility judgments, priors . . .), in order to arrive at an opinion as to the relative merits of various theories. No, what I object to is using intuitions about what is and what is not *a genuine possibility* as a crucial premise in an argument concerning the relative merits of theories. If we have learned something from the history of science, surely we have learned that our best estimate as to the relative merits of theories should be based on judgments concerning the simplicity (or perhaps naturalness, or something like that) of theories (which are compatible with the phenomena), not on judgments regarding the genuineness of the possibilities that are (arguably) associated with each theory.

Enough of overarching themes. This book, in the end, is not primarily concerned with overarching themes. Its main goal is an examination of some loosely related topics. So let me now outline these topics, chapter by chapter.

In the first chapter I discuss the radical idea that, fundamentally, time has no structure whatsoever. The picture here is that time just is a collection of snapshots, that there are no fundamental facts about the length of temporal intervals, no fundamental facts even about the order in which events occur. Why did I use the word 'fundamental' here? Well, the snapshots have certain features: namely, the pattern of the events in the snapshot, which one can use to order the set of snapshots in a particular way and to infer a temporal distance between them. In this way one can make sense of the apparent order of events and of the apparent length of the temporal interval between events. But these order and distance facts are not fundamental; they derive entirely from the patterns of events in each snapshot. Julian Barbour, quite remarkably, has formulated theories along these lines. In the end, remarkable as his achievement is, I argue that it is not plausible that time has no structure.

In the second chapter I argue that while one cannot give the state of the contents of a classical world—that is, matter and fields—spacetime point by spacetime point, one can give it neighbourhood by neighbourhood, where these neighbourhoods can be as small as one likes. I also argue that one can give the geometric structure of spacetime neighbourhood by neighbourhood.

In Chapter 3 I discuss what quantities one should take to be fundamental in quantum mechanics, especially in relativistic quantum mechanics. I consider five views: 'configuration space realism', 'wave-function amplitude realism', 'density operator realism', 'Heisenberg operator realism', and 'flash-realism'. I argue in favour of 'Heisenberg operator realism' which, contrary to perceived wisdom, makes quantum mechanics an entirely local theory.

In Chapter 4 I discuss an idea that is much more radical than the idea that one cannot specify the state of spacetime point by point: I discuss the idea that there simply are no such things as spacetime points, that every part of spacetime is a finitely extended region. I will present a number of arguments in favour of this view, and then sketch a somewhat non-orthodox mathematical account of pointless spaces. But I will have to admit that, in the end, pointy spaces look better.

In Chapter 5 I discuss whether space and time exist, or there merely exist particles and fields standing in certain spatial and temporal relations. At first blush this might seem an abstruse topic: what exactly is it for space and time to exist as opposed to there being spatial and temporal relations? But, as soon as you try to manufacture a theory that only makes use of spatial distance relations, and not of space itself, you get a better grip on the issue. For instance, it is hard to see how the material universe as a whole could be rotating if there only are distance relations between bits of matter, while it seems to make obvious sense if there is such a thing as space in addition to the matter that is placed in it. I will defend the view that space and time exist.

In Chapter 6 I discuss the implications of so-called 'gauge theories' for our conception of properties, and for the reality of so-called 'fibre-bundle spaces'. Gauge theories are theories according to which the phenomena are invariant under certain transformations—so-called 'gauge transformations', which can vary from location to location. One way of understanding such theories is to claim that the only way in which properties at different locations can be compared is to 'drag' these properties to one and the same location, and then locally compare them. A gauge transformation can then be understood as a transformation which does not affect these comparison facts. Since how one property at one location compares to another property at another location generally depends on the paths by which they were brought together, it follows that no path-independent sense can be made of identity and difference of such properties at different locations. Tim Maudlin has argued that this means that we have to throw out the standard conception of what properties are: features that objects at different locations either share or do not share. I will argue that, in the end, no such radical revision is justified: once we realize that fibre-bundle spaces are just as real as spacetime we will find that all fundamental properties and relations will be such that path-independent sense can be made of their identity and difference at distant locations. Other people—so-called 'gauge relationists'—have drawn quite different conclusions from gauge theories; namely, that the relevant fundamental quantities are non-local properties of paths in spacetime (holonomies) rather than states of fields at points in spacetime. I will argue that they are mistaken.

In Chapter 7 I develop an idea of Richard Feynman's: namely, the idea that anti-particles are nothing but particles travelling back in time, and the related idea that what is standardly called the CPT theorem is really a theorem which shows that spacetime has neither a direction in time nor a spatial handedness structure. I end up conceding that while Feynman's idea is fascinating and coherent, it may not be true.

Finally, in Chapter 8 Cian Dorr and I consider whether calculus—the theory of differentiation and integration that permeates almost everywhere in the sciences—can be understood as a purely geometric theory. We suggest various ways to 'geometrize' modern calculus (differential geometry) by the introduction of one or more of the following spaces: 'scalar-value space', 'fibre-bundle space', and 'tangent-bundle space'. These geometrical theories of ours are 'nominalistic' in the sense that we do not need to assume the existence of mathematical objects such as sets. Hence 'indispensibility arguments' for the existence of mathematical objects have no purchase, at least not in the context of the theories of physics that we discuss in Chapter 8.

I have one more remark before we proceed. Much of this book is concerned with false theories; for I take it that we have good reason to believe that classical mechanics is false, that non-relativistic quantum mechanics is false. Indeed, I take it that we even have good reason to believe that General Relativity is false, and that Special Relativistic quantum mechanics is false, for we are still awaiting a satisfactory unification of General Relativity and quantum mechanics. So, what is it that I am doing when I discuss what the structure of space and time is according to classical mechanics, according to quantum mechanics, and so on? What I am doing is discussing what we should take the structure of the world to be if the phenomena were as classical mechanics, or quantum mechanics, or . . . says they are. But why care about this if these theories are false? Well, in the first place, this enterprise might have some intrinsic interest: puzzles are fun, especially the kind of hard puzzles that have been thrown at us by nature. Secondly, there is an awful lot that is right about General Relativity and about quantum mechanics. These theories, in certain circumstances at least, yield unbelievably accurate predictions. Moreover, we do not yet know of any circumstances in which either produces clearly false predictions. That is quite something. On the other hand, it has to be said that while it seems quite reasonable to expect that future science will have a huge predictive overlap with current science, it is not so obvious that it will have a huge overlap concerning the kind of fundamental structure that is the concern of this book. After all, there is a large amount of predictive overlap between classical physics and relativistic physics, and yet the fundamental structure of the world is quite different according to classical mechanics from what it is according to relativity theory. And even if it is not completely clear what the fundamental structure should be taken to be if quantum mechanics were true, it is very plausible that it is very different from what it should be taken to be if classical mechanics were true. So it may turn out to be that most of the discussion in this book will be made irrelevant by future developments in science. So be it. In the meantime, let us enjoy ourselves.

1

It's just one damn thing after another

The future ain't what it used to be

Yogi Berra

1.1 Introduction

Actually, it's not just one damn thing after another. There are always more damn things in between. And if there are always more damn things in between, then, for any given damn thing there is no damn thing that comes right after it. Which gets us into the thick of things. What, exactly, is the structure of time? In this chapter I will sketch the standard picture of the structure of time. But I will also discuss a radical alternative picture: namely, that the idea that time, fundamentally, has *no* structure at all. The idea that time, fundamentally, has no structure at all is the idea that there are no fundamental facts such as one instant being earlier or later than another, or one instant being between two other instants—no fundamental facts about the lengths of time intervals nor about the continuity of time intervals. The idea is that the history of the world is just a set of snapshots, one snapshot for each instant.

Why did I use the word 'fundamental' in the above? Why did I not just say that the idea is that time has no structure, simpliciter? Well, I did this because it would be pretty crazy to claim that no sense *whatsoever* can be made of the idea that certain instants occur between certain other ones, that no sense *whatsoever* can be made of the idea that some temporal intervals are longer than some other ones. It would not be plausible to claim that we are utterly and completely wrong when we make assertions about temporal structure. A much more plausible idea is that in so far as one can make sense of temporal structure it derives from non-temporal structure. Julian Barbour, our main protagonist in this chapter, has said exactly this: namely, that the non-temporal facts determine the temporal facts; that, at bottom, the world has no temporal structure whatsoever.[1]

There is one issue I briefly want to discuss before we proceed with the business of the structure of time. For the most part in this chapter I will speak as if instants, and time intervals, are objects—things like tables and chairs. To most non-philosophers, this sounds strange and mistaken. Surely time is not an object like a table or a chair. If it is an object it is a strangely fleeting one. We only get acquainted with it bit by bit. We never have a chance to become reacquainted with any bit once it has whizzed by. We never see time itself, just the things that take place in time. We do not seem to be able to affect time, just the things taking place in time. And so on. We will see in Chapter 5 that none of this deters me from thinking that time, or rather, spacetime, is an object. But nothing in this chapter hinges on this. For current purposes it matters not whether one thinks that time is an object, a relation, or a what-not. As long as one understands temporal talk—as long as one understands claims like 'Elizabeth Taylor married Richard Burton before she married John Warner but after she married Richard Burton' and 'He spent most of his time inebriated'—one can wonder what the structure of time is, and whether it is fundamental or derives from an underlying structure. And that is all we need for this chapter. So let us get on with business. What structure does time have?

It sounds like a funny question: what structure does time have? Buildings have structure, molecules have structure, but time? Time surely does not consist of some glued-together parts, does it? But if you think about it a bit more, you will realize that some sense can be made of the idea that time has structure. Here are some facts about the structure of time that are standardly assumed. Longer periods of time can be decomposed into smaller periods of time. Time is ultimately composed of instants, where these instants are zero-length periods of time. These instants are 'glued together' by the 'betweenness' relationship: for any pair of times t_1 and t_2 there are instants that occur between those two instants, and there are instants which are not between those instants. One can represent all the betweenness relations between times by thinking of the instants as points on a line; that is, time has a linear order. Indeed, there is much more to be said about the structure of time. I will begin this chapter by highlighting some features of standard accounts of the structure of time and space—first within classical Newtonian physics, then within modern relativistic physics.

---

[1] See Barbour (2000). Some philosophers would express Barbour's view this way: the temporal structure 'supervenes' on the non-temporal structure. Or: there is no 'world like ours' in which the temporal structure differs from the temporal structure in our world but the non-temporal structure does not differ. Indeed, there are yet other ways by which one might try to spell out what it is for some structure to be non-fundamental, to derive from other, more fundamental structure. See, for example, Skow (2010). However, I take it that it is intuitively fairly clear what it means to say that time, fundamentally, has no structure, and that this understanding suffices for this chapter.

1.2 The structure of time and space in Newtonian physics

Let us begin with the structure of time according to standard Newtonian physics. According to standard Newtonian physics time is composed of instants. But, as I have said, it is not just an unordered collection of instants, but has structure. In particular, time has *topological structure* and *metric structure*.[2]

The topological structure of a space is the structure of that space which is invariant under any stretching and squeezing of (parts of) that space, as long as that stretching and squeezing does not involve any cutting or tearing. This is why topological structure is often referred to as 'rubber sheet' structure: when one stretches and squeezes a rubber sheet, one does not alter its topological structure.

Time, according to standard Newtonian physics, can be pictured as a one-dimensional line, consisting of an infinite sequence of instants, all lined up in order of occurrence. Since the order of these instants is invariant under all possible stretchings and squeezings of this line, this order is part of the topological structure of time. More precisely: the topological structure of time determines for any instants t_1, t_2, and t_3, whether t_1 lies between t_2 and t_3, whether t_2 lies between t_1 and t_3, or whether t_3 lies between t_1 and t_2.[3] The topological structure of time does not determine which of a pair of distinct instants occurs *earlier* and which *later*, for one does not need to make any cuts or tears in the line in order to 'flip it over'. Nor does the topological structure of time determine the magnitude of the time interval between any two instants—the temporal distance between two events—for such distances are not invariant under squeezings and stretchings of the time line.

The topological structure of time includes the fact that time is 'dense': between any two distinct instants there is always at least one other instant. Saying that there is at least one instant between any two instants is really a bit coy, since that assumption immediately entails that between any two instants there are infinitely many instants! Take any two times t_1 and t_2. There must be an instant between them. Call it t_3. There must also be an instant between t_1 and t_3. Call it t_4. There must also be an instant between t_1 and t_4. Call it t_5. And so on. This process cannot end after finitely many repetitions, since there must always be a further instant in between. So there must be infinitely many instants between t_1 and t_2.

A note for the timid: this reasoning is really correct. Some people are squeamish about infinity. They say things like: 'Infinity does not really exist, it is only an idealization, we cannot really imagine infinity, we could never really understand infinity, talk

---

[2] It has other structure too: mereological structure, differential structure, measure-theoretic structure, and so on. Including accounts of this structure would lengthen and complicate this chapter, without in any essential way altering the content.

[3] It is only because time is one-dimensional and simply connected that the topology of time amounts to the betweenness relations that hold between instants. More generally, the topological structure of a space is given by designating a collection of sets of instants, the *open sets*, which is closed under union and finite intersection. This is discussed in a little more detail in Chapters 2 and 4.

of infinity is not really coherent . . .' Well, these are all excuses and prevarication. If you accept that there are instants, and that there is an instant between any two distinct instants, then you had better get used to the idea that there are infinitely many instants. No amount of hemming and hawing is going to get you out of it.

Another thing you had therefor better get used to is that there is no such thing as the instant that immediately follows a given instant. For, as I have said, there are always more instants squeezed in between. This non-existence of consecutive instants takes some getting used to. Our intuitions seem to militate against it. Let me illustrate this with an argument that Zeno presented, more than 2,000 years ago, against the possibility of motion.

Achilles is going to race a tortoise on a beach. To make it fair, Achilles starts 16 cubits behind the tortoise. Achilles runs twice as fast as the tortoise. Before the race starts the tortoise draws a line in the sand. He challenges Achilles: 'To get here is your first task'. When Achilles gets to the line, the tortoise has staggered half the distance that Achilles has run, and so is 8 cubits ahead. He draws another line: 'Next task, Achilles', he blurts. When Achilles gets to this next line, the tortoise draws another line, now 4 cubits ahead. Every time Achilles reaches another line, the tortoise draws yet another one, while staying in motion. As the race continues, the tortoise needles Achilles: 'After every task you complete, there is another task waiting, so you will never complete the last task, so you will never catch up. You may as well give up.' Common sense tells us that the tortoise is wrong. The puzzle is to figure out where his reasoning goes wrong. Some will notice that the times between the task completions get shorter and shorter. For instance, if it took Achilles 1 second to complete the first task, then the second task will take him $\frac{1}{2}$ a second, the third $\frac{1}{4}$ of a second, and so on. The mathematically sophisticated will quickly figure out that Achilles will therefore carry out infinitely many tasks in 2 seconds, and might think they have thereby solved the puzzle. A slightly more straightforward response to the puzzle—one which does not involve summing infinitely many numbers—consists simply of noting that after two seconds the tortoise will have run 16 cubits, and Achilles will have run 32 cubits, so that Achilles will have caught the tortoise after 2 seconds. While both of these responses are correct, neither of them answers the puzzle, for they do not diagnose where the tortoise made an error in his argument. The correct diagnosis is that while the tortoise was right in claiming that Achilles would never complete the last task, this is not so because there is some last task and Achilles never completes it. No. There just is no last task, just as there is no last instant immediately before another instant.[4]

The topology of time includes more than its denseness. The easiest way to summarize the classical topological structure of time is to say that the topology of time is

---

[4] You might worry that the tortoise will draw a line in the sand 16 cubits after the first one that he drew. And you might worry that if that is so, then there is a last task after all, and that Achilles does complete it. However, if we assume that the tortoise only draws lines in the sand when he is strictly ahead of Achilles, then it follows that the tortoise does not draw one 16 cubits ahead of the first one, for he does not get to that location before Achilles.

exactly the same as the topology of the (real) numbers. That is to say, one can match each instant of time with a (real) number such that the betweenness relations among instants is exactly the same as the betweenness relations among the matched (real) numbers.

The *metric structure* of time determines the magnitude of the time intervals between instants—the number of seconds that separate any pair of instants. Since there are infinitely many instants between any two instants, it had better be the case that each instant has 0 duration, or else there would be an infinite amount of time between any two instants (assuming that each instant has the same, finite, duration). Even though it seems pretty straightforward that any finite period of time is composed out of instants which have duration 0, it is still a bit strange. If something consists solely of finitely many instants, finitely many things of duration 0, it must have duration 0. (After all, finitely many 0s add to 0.) But, apparently, if you put infinitely many instants, infinitely many things of duration 0, together, you can get a period of time which has finite duration! That is odd. But there is more. Not only can you, on the standard view of time, make something that has finite duration just out of things that have 0 duration, you can in fact make periods of differing finite durations out of the very same number of instants of 0 duration: namely, out of infinitely many such instants. That is odd. This last fact also makes it clear that the metric structure of time is really structure over and above topological structure of time: the order and the number of instants in a period do not by themselves determine the length of that interval.[5] And there are even more oddities to the standard account of the structure of time. Consider a light bulb that can be switched on and off. Suppose that on one day—say a Monday—one switches the light on and off a number of times. One can then surely ask: on Monday, what was the total amount of time that the lamp was on? Bizarrely enough, one can show that on the standard account of time there exist sequences of switchings such that one cannot coherently answer this question. That is to say, according to the standard view of time there must be sets of instants which do not have a well-defined total duration. That is *very* odd. In Chapter 4 I will discuss whether there are nice ways out of these oddities; but for now let us just accept them as oddities, and soldier on.

There is one bit of structure of which it is unclear whether it is part of the structure of time in standard Newtonian physics: namely, a 'direction of time'—a 'before–after' relationship which determines for any pair of instants which of the two is the earlier one and which is the later one. The reason why it is unclear whether it is part of the standard account of time in classical physics is that textbooks on classical physics usually do not discuss this issue explicitly. In Chapter 7 we will discuss whether it is reasonable to assume that time has this structure, but for the duration of this chapter we will set this issue aside.

---

[5] The metric structure of time does determine its topological structure: t_2 is between t_1 and t_3 if the distance between t_1 and t_2 is smaller than that between t_1 and t_3 and the distance between t_3 and t_2 is smaller than that between t_3 and t_1.

Now let me briefly discuss the structure of space according to standard Newtonian physics. According to standard Newtonian physics, space, too, has topological structure and metric structure. The topological structure in this case cannot be characterized by betweenness relations. The reason for this is that space is three-dimensional, and in a three-dimensional space whether or not one point is between two other points is not determined by the topological structure of the space. Betweenness facts are not invariant under squeezings and stretchings of a three-dimensional space. For instance, imagine having a three-dimensional blob of translucent rubber in one's hand, where points *a*, *b*, and *c* in the blob are coloured blue, red, and yellow, and *a* lies exactly between *b* and *c*. By stretching and squeezing the three-dimensional blob of rubber, one can make point *a* move elsewhere. Indeed, if one squeezes hard, one can even get *c* to lie exactly between *a* and *b*. So in the three-dimensional case, betweenness structure is not determined by topological structure.

What kind of structure of a blob of rubber is not affected by squeezing and stretching? Well, for instance, whether or not a curve drawn in the rubber is continuous. When one squeezes and stretches the blob of rubber, the location and shape of a curve drawn in the rubber will alter. But if the curve is a continuous curve—a curve without gaps or jumps—it will remain a continuous curve under any squeezing and stretching that does not involve cutting or tearing. Similarly, whether two parts of the blob of rubber are connected (share a boundary) is determined by the topological structure of the blob. This should produce a serviceable idea of the topological structure of a blob of rubber. The topological structure of space, according to Newtonian physics, is just like the topological structure of a three-dimensional blob of rubber that stretches to infinity in all directions. That is it.

How about the metric structure of space according to Newtonian physics? Well, according to Newtonian physics that is just the distance structure of an infinite, three-dimensional, Euclidean space. Perhaps the simplest way to characterize the distance structure of space according to Newtonian physics is to say that one can lay down coordinates x, y, z on space such that the square of the distance between two locations which have coordinates (x_1,y_1,z_1) and (x_2,y_2,z_2) is $(x_1-x_2)^2+(y_1-y_2)^2+(z_1-z_2)^2$.

There is still one more issue that needs to be addressed. According to Newtonian physics, space exists at all times, and is unchanging ('immutable' is the word Newton used). But does the structure of space and time in Newtonian physics include a notion of identity of location in space at different times? That is to say, according to Newtonian physics, does it make sense to ask whether a material object occupies the very same location in space at two different times? Well, Newton himself thought that there were such facts. And, from now on, when I talk about Newtonian spacetime, I mean a spacetime which includes such facts; that is, Newtonian spacetime includes identity-of-spatial-location-across-time structure. But there is a closely related spacetime which does not include such structure: so-called 'neo-Newtonian spacetime'.

According to neo-Newtonian spacetime it is also true that space exists at all times and does not change. Does that not just mean that the very same spatial locations exist at different times, and hence that it makes sense to ask whether or not an object occupies the very same location at different times? No. By saying that space is unchanging one might just mean that *a* (Euclidean) space exists at all times, and that that space is unchanging only in the sense that at any time the space that exists has exactly the same structure (three-dimensional, infinite, and flat) as the space that exists at any other time. And then one could deny that one can make any sense of the idea of being at the same location at two different times.

Now, if one takes this view—that is, if one denies that there are facts about identity or non-identity of locations at different times—then there also will be no facts about the distance that an object has traversed during a period of time. For if there were facts about distances traversed during periods of time, then one could identify locations across time by saying that one is at the same location at two different times if one has traversed no distance, 0 distance, during the intervening time. But this means that in a neo-Newtonian spacetime there are no facts about rates of change of locations; that is, speeds. And if that is so then one might worry that one cannot formulate even the simplest theory of motion. However, this is not right. One can formulate standard Newtonian theories of motion in neo-Newtonian spacetime. The reason one can do so is that neo-Newtonian spacetime, while it has no notion of identity of location across time, does have cross-time structure that determines how fast any object is accelerating at any time. Let me explain.

Start with a Newtonian spacetime which has two spatial dimensions and one temporal dimension. Picture this spacetime by stacking all the spaces-at-times on top of each other. Then one can picture the identity-of-location-across-time structure by imagining vertical struts running through this spacetime (see Figure 1.1.)

Next imagine adding struts corresponding to all possible straight lines which intersect each space-at-a-time (see Figure 1.2). The set of all possible straight lines corresponds to all developments of positions with constant velocity; that is, all unaccelerated motions.

Now imagine that there is no fact of the matter as to which of these struts are the vertical struts. Then the strut structure that we have distinguishes the unaccelerated motions from the accelerated ones, but it does not distinguish being at rest—remaining at the same location—from being in motion. This is the structure of neo-Newtonian spacetime. In neo-Newtonian spacetime there are no facts about identity of location, no preferred set of parallel vertical struts, but there are facts about accelerations. And this suffices for a standard Newtonian dynamics, a standard Newtonian theory of particle motions. The reason that this suffices is that the central law of Newtonian dynamics is $F=ma$, which says that acceleration of a particle is proportional to the force applied to it (and is in the direction of the applied force) and inversely proportional to its mass. Now, as long as the magnitude (and direction) of the force applied to an object does not depend on the velocities of any objects—and indeed it does not according to standard Newtonian laws of motion—the structure of neo-Newtonian spacetime suffices to determine whether a given set of trajectories satisfies this law. So we can set

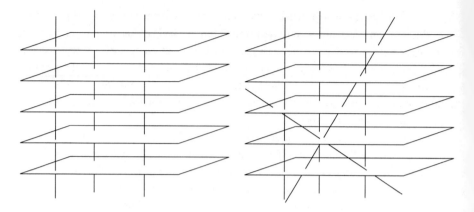

Figure 1.1 Newtonian spacetime.

Figure 1.2 Neo-Newtonian spacetime.

Newtonian dynamics in neo-Newtonian spacetime. In fact, *prima facie* neo-Newtonian spacetime seems preferable as such a setting because it has less structure than Newtonian spacetime. Newtonian spacetime has 'identity of location across time' structure which is not needed for Newtonian laws of motion, and not detectable by any direct observational means. Now, what I just said is not completely uncontroversial. One might argue that Newtonian spacetime is a more natural structure than neo-Newtonian spacetime. One could even come up with suggestions that would allow one to infer the identity of location facts from the phenomena; for example, by suggesting that the total momentum of the universe has to be 0 relative to the true standard of rest. But in this chapter I am mainly interested in the idea that time has no structure. So I will set this issue aside, and now turn to the structure of space and time in relativistic physics.

1.3 The structure of time and space in relativistic physics

First let me discuss the structure of time and space in Special Relativity, according to which, time is no longer an entity that can be neatly separated from space. There is just a single entity called spacetime, which has some temporal and some spatial features. Let me explain this in a bit more detail, by means of a parable.

In the sixteenth century in Holland, the Mondriaan Society decided to paint a square grid over all Holland, with Amsterdam at the centre of the grid. The north–south lines were painted in yellow, the east–west lines in blue. The distance that any city was to the north of Amsterdam they called the 'yellow-location', in 'yellow-space', of that city. (The 'yellow location' of a city was a negative number if it was south of Amsterdam). The distance that a city was east of Amsterdam they called the 'blue-location', in 'blue-space'. Towards the end of the sixteenth century the Great Schism occurred. The Doesburg Society broke from the Mondriaan Society. The Doesburg Society proceeded to lay down its own square grid, in red and white, which was angled at 45 degrees to the Mondriaan grid, and had the Hague at its centre. The Mondriaan Society then tried to gain the upper hand with the Dutch populace by printing a useful booklet which tabulated all the yellow-distances, the distances in yellow-space, between the cities in Holland, and also tabulated all the blue-distances, the distances in blue-space. The Doesburg Society of course responded with a booklet of its own, listing the red-distances and white-distances between the cities. Great confusion ensued among the populace, since none of the distances agreed. But then, early in the seventeenth century the great Dutch farmer Cow Minski noticed that there was something that the Mondriaan Society and the Doesburg Society always agreed on. For any two cities, if you squared the yellow-distance between them and squared the blue-distance between them, and added these numbers, you would always obtain exactly the same number as you obtained by squaring the red-distance and the white-distance and adding these up. This was a revelation. Travellers subsequently reported that this number was in fact always equal to the square of the distance measured along a straight path between the two cities. From then on only these numbers were published as the true distances between cities, and the Dutch Golden Age ensued.

OK, enough lame parable. You get the point. There are no separate spaces called 'yellow-space' and 'blue-space', or 'red-space' and 'white-space'. The surface of Holland is a single (pretty flat) two-dimensional space, with unique distances between its points which completely characterize the geometry of the Dutch landscape. One can use different coordinate systems to coordinatize this space (the yellow–blue coordinate system, or the red–white coordinate system, or . . .), but none of them is more 'correct' than any other. The essence of Special Relativity is that exactly the same is true of space and time. According to Special Relativity there is a single four-dimensional entity—Minkowski spacetime—in which all events occur. One can lay different coordinate systems, consisting of three spatial coordinates and one temporal coordinate, on this spacetime. People using different coordinate systems will disagree as to the temporal distances (time intervals) between events, and will disagree as to the spatial distances between events. However, there is a number that all coordinate systems will agree upon: namely, the so-called spacetime interval I between events. The set of all such spacetime intervals completely characterizes the (flat) geometry of Minkowski spacetime. Let us go through this in a bit more detail.

I will start by indicating a method that someone—let us call him Harry—could have for assigning temporal and spatial locations to events. To keep things very simple indeed, I will assume that Harry lives in a one-dimensional infinite space; that is, a line that has no ends. There is no force acting on Harry: he is just floating around in his one-dimensional space. He has available to him a very long ruler and many friends, each of whom has a video camera which comes equipped with an internal clock. Harry and his friends first get together and synchronize all the clocks in their video cameras. Harry then assigns each friend a specific location along the ruler by labeling each video camera with the intended location. The friends then go to their assigned places, very slowly, so that they do not jostle their video cameras and clocks. When each friend arrives at his designated location he starts video-taping the local events, while superimposing the spatial label and the internal clock-time on the image. Thus each taped event is assigned a temporal and spatial coordinate in a simple visual way. By consulting his vast library of video-tapes Harry can see the times and spatial locations at which events occurred. Of course, Harry realizes that there is no special significance to the time at which he set his clocks to 0, nor to the location that corresponds to the 0 on his ruler. And he realizes that the units by which he has marked his ruler and the units of time that his clocks use are also just a matter of convention. But he does believe that with his clocks and ruler he can measure the true time intervals between events, and the true spatial distances between events.

Meanwhile, Sally, who for the early part of her life was moving at constant speed relative to Harry, has done exactly the same with her friends, with a bunch of video cameras and rulers that were supplied by the very same store that provided Harry and his friends with rulers and video cameras. As Sally moves by Harry she falls in love with him, and stops and joins him. They recount their past adventures but discover that their respective video libraries completely disagree about the spatial distances, and about the time intervals, between events; they even disagree as to whether or not events occurred simultaneously! This is rather unexpected, and for a while each accuses the other of doctoring their video tapes. However, they then discover that there is a quantity on which their video libraries always agree. Take any two events A and B. According to Harry's video library these will have occurred a certain time dt_H apart, and a certain spatial distance dx_H apart. According to Sally's video library the same two events will have occurred some time dt_S apart, and some distance dx_S apart. They discover that they can pick a particular constant c such that for any two events the value of $c^2dt_H^2-dx_H^2$ always equals the value of $c^2dt_S^2-dx_S^2$. This is remarkable. What they have discovered is the spacetime distance, or spacetime interval, $I=c^2dt^2-dx^2$, which completely characterizes the geometry of the two-dimensional Minkowski spacetime in which they live. They now realize that there is no such thing as the true temporal distance dt between events; nor is there a true spatial distance dx between events. Rather, they live in a two-dimensional spacetime whose geometry is characterized by a spacetime distance I, on which they each were putting different coordinate systems.

Next they examine the constant c a bit closer. It has to have units of velocity (distance per time interval) to make sure that one is subtracting the same units from each other in the expression $c^2dt^2-dx^2$. They then notice that although their respective video libraries generally disagree about the velocities of objects—that is, although generally dx_H/dt_H is unequal to dx_S/dt_S—nonetheless, when dx_H/dt_H happens to equal c, then dx_S/dt_S also equals c! This can actually be derived from the fact that they always agree on the spacetime interval $I=c^2dt^2-dx^2$. For if $dx_H/dt_H=c$, then $I=c^2dt_H^2-dx_H^2=c^2dt_H^2-c^2dt_H^2=0=c^2dt_S^2-dx_S^2$, so $dx_S/dt_S=c$. Harry and Sally are intrigued by this. They go on to

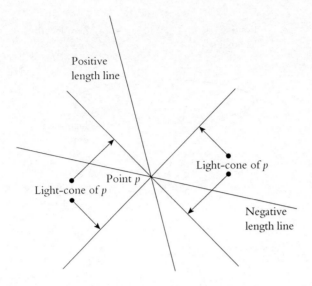

Figure 1.3 Two-dimensional Minkowski spacetime.

check the exact value of c (the value they needed to insert in order to have $c^2dt^2 - dx^2$ come out the same for different coordinate systems), and they find that it is a rather large number, which on closer inspection turns out to be the speed of light. And indeed, when they use their respective video libraries to measure the speed of light in their respective coordinate systems, they always find the same value: approximately 300,000 kilometres per second. Having discovered this, Harry and Sally decide from then on to use units in which $c{=}1$. The invariant spacetime interval then is given by the gloriously simple formula $I{=}dt^2 - dx^2$ (for any coordinate system $<x,t>$ associated with a bunch of unaccelerated clocks and rulers that are not moving relative to each other).

OK, we have now encountered some of the main features of the structure of spacetime according to Special Relativity. Notice that one of the things that is strange about it is that the spacetime interval I can be negative, as well as positive or zero. In fact, this distinction between positive and negative spacetime intervals is about all that remains of the distinction between space and time in Special Relativity. Let me draw a picture of a small part of a two-dimensional Minkowski spacetime in order to illustrate this (see Figure 1.3).

If one takes any point p in a two-dimensional Minkowski spacetime, then the set of points that are distance zero removed from p form two lines through p in the shape of an X. This is the so-called light-cone of p. It has this name because in a three-dimensional Minkowski spacetime the set of points that are distance zero removed from p form a figure that looks exactly like a double cone (see Figure 1.4).

In general, if a curve between two points lies entirely on a light-cone then the length of that curve between those points is zero. Any curve between two points that

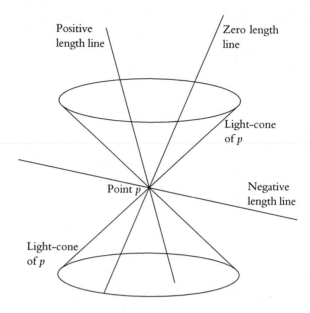

Figure 1.4 Three-dimensional Minkowski spacetime.

everywhere points in a direction inside the local light-cones has positive length, and any curve that everywhere points outside the local light-cones has negative length.[6] One can plot the points in spacetime that an object occupies throughout its history. Assuming that the object does not jump about discontinuously, these points will form a continuous line, known as the world-line of that object. The world-line of an ordinary object—an object of positive mass—will everywhere point in a direction inside the local light-cone. Such a line is known as a time-like line. Light (and anything else of rest-mass zero) will always travel in a direction parallel to the surface of the local light-cone. Lines that are parallel to the surface of the local light-cone are called light-like lines. Lines that everywhere point outside the local light-cones are called space-like lines. No objects travel along space-like lines.[7]

Let us now return to Harry and Sally, except that we now imagine them living in a two-dimensional space rather than a one-dimensional space. Recall how Harry used a bunch of video cameras equipped with clocks in order to assign space and time coordinates to events. Events that according to Harry all occur simultaneously will all lie on a surface in three-dimensional Minkowski spacetime. Such surfaces are everywhere space-like and flat. That is to say, that if one stays on such a surface the distances

[6] It is actually a matter of convention which distances count as positive and which as negative. Many textbooks adopt the opposite convention: namely, that curves inside the light-cones have negative length, and curves outside the light-cones have positive length. It is not a matter of convention that there are curves with lengths of the opposite sign. Indeed, this is of the essence of Special Relativity.

[7] At least no known objects do so. It is a contentious issue as to whether Special Relativity forbids the existence of objects that do so. We have no need to go into this issue.

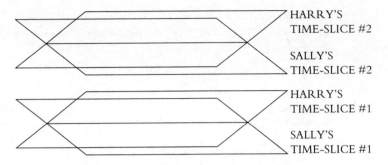

HARRY'S
TIME-SLICE #2

SALLY'S
TIME-SLICE #2

HARRY'S
TIME-SLICE #1

SALLY'S
TIME-SLICE #1

Figure 1.5 Relativity of simultaneity.

according to the Minkowski metric are everywhere negative, and in fact are identical to minus the distances on an ordinary two-dimensional flat—Euclidean—surface. These surfaces are so-called time-slices—the time-slices of Harry's coordinate system. The same things goes for events that are simultaneous according to Sally, except that her time-slices will lie at an angle to Harry's time slices (see Figure 1.5). This means that they disagree about which events occur simultaneously.

It is rather useful to note that clocks are good instruments for measuring the spacetime intervals between events that happen close to those clocks. Consider two events A and B that happen very close to some clock. If that clock is part of some coordinate system, then in those coordinates the spatial distance dx between those two events is close to 0. Thus, in those coordinates the spacetime *interval* between A and B is very close to dt^2: clocks, in effect, directly measure the spacetime interval between events that happen close to those clocks.

So far we have mostly been discussing the metric structure of Minkowski spacetime. (The spacetime interval I determines the distances—the metric structure—of spacetime.) What about the topology? The topological structure of Minkowski spacetime—the structure that is invariant under all possible stretchings of Minkowski spacetime—is quite mundane: it is just the same as the topological structure of an ordinary flat space. That is to say, the topology of three-dimensional Minkowski spacetime is just the same as that of the topology of ordinary flat three-dimensional space, and the topology of four-dimensional Minkowski spacetime is the same as that of the topology of a flat four-dimensional space.

Now let us turn to Einstein's theory of General Relativity. According to this theory, spacetime, again, is a single four-dimensional entity. But now it can be curved. Whether space is curved, in a given region of space, can be read off the metric in that region. For instance, in a flat space—a Euclidean space—the circumference of a circle of radius r equals $2\pi r$. But for a curved surface the circumference of a circle of radius r can be smaller or greater than $2\pi r$. For instance, consider the surface of a sphere. On this two-dimensional surface a circle of radius r around a point p is just the set of points which are a distance r from point p, where one measures this distance as the length of the shortest path *on the surface of the sphere* (see Figure 1.6).

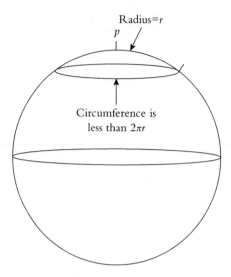

Radius=r

p

Circumference is
less than $2\pi r$

Figure 1.6 Measuring the curvature of
space

Now, the length of the circumference of such a circle on the surface of a sphere will
be somewhat less than $2\pi r$, since the surface of the sphere curves 'inwards' as one moves
away from point p. Such curvature is called positive curvature. A surface can also be
curved such that the circumference of a circle is greater than $2\pi r$, which is called negative curvature. A saddle-shaped surface has negative curvature. Imagine drawing a
closed curve on a saddle that remains at a fixed distance (as measured along the surface
of the saddle) from the point where one sits on a saddle. This line will bend upwards
as it crosses the front and back of the saddle, and bends downwards as it crosses the
sides of the saddle, thus making it longer than it would be if the surface were flat.
Spacetime can be curved in various ways in various places. Whether it is, or is not, is
determined by its metric structure.

Since spacetime can be curved in many different ways, there are many different
general relativistic spacetimes. According to General Relativity, the curvature of spacetime depends on the way matter is distributed in it: the more matter (mass–energy) in
a region, the more curved spacetime is in that region. But *locally*, on a small enough
scale, any relativistic spacetime looks just like Minkowski spacetime. That is to say, as
you consider smaller and smaller regions of any relativistic spacetime, it will appro-
ximate better and better (a portion of) flat Minkowski spacetime. In particular, at
every point in any relativistic spacetime there are local light-cones which determine
which directions are the 'positive length directions', which are the 'zero length directions', and which are the 'negative length directions' from that point. By the way, it is
not very surprising that relativistic spacetimes are locally flat. Just about any curved
surface imaginable is such that if you look at it on smaller and smaller scales, it will
start to look more and more like a flat surface. Only rather bizarre surfaces that have
'crinkles' at arbitrarily small scales will not be locally flat.

When spacetime is curved one can (typically) no longer slice spacetime into parallel, flat, time-slices. One can still introduce the notion of 'time-slice' in General Relativity: an everywhere space-like surface such that every world-line of every permanent object must pass through that surface exactly once. But almost any relativistic space-time that can be sliced into such time-slices can be sliced in infinitely many different ways.

Just as general relativistic spacetimes can be curved in different ways—can have different metric structures—they can also have different topological structures. For instance, according to General Relativity spacetime can be closed and finite, like the surface of a sphere, or open and infinite, like an infinite flat plane. These have different topological structure, since you cannot deform the one into the other by merely stretching it appropriately. You would have to *tear* a hole in a sphere (and then do a lot of stretching) in order to deform it into an infinite flat plane.

1.4 The idea that time has no structure

Now we know enough about standard views of the structure of time in order to discuss whether time might have less structure than standardly assumed. Julian Barbour has made the radical proposal that there is no fundamental temporal structure. Actually, this is not quite the way that he expresses it. He says things like 'time does not exist'. He also makes radical claims about the non-existence of space, some of which we will discuss in Chapter 5. (See Barbour, 2000, for a popular account of many of his ideas.) I do not want to claim that I am representing his views accurately or completely. In this chapter I just want to discuss the idea that there is no fundamental temporal structure, while crediting him with all the insights and arguments that can be used to defend this idea.

Suppose that each process in the world suddenly, tonight at midnight, were to speed up, say, to ten times its normal speed but otherwise would develop as it normally would have. Baseball games would last less than 20 minutes, sex would be over in a jiffy, and gales would blow. The world would become a hectic place indeed. Or would it? After all, clocks too would run at ten times their normal rate, so each process would still go at the same rate as measured by a clock. Indeed, it is fairly clear that it would be impossible for us to notice that the world had sped up. For, by assumption, our mental processes would also speed up, but *otherwise remain the same*. Hence it could not be that in such a speedy world we would arrive at a mental state that we would not have arrived at had the world not sped up. Hence we could not, at any moment, mentally detect it if the world were in fact to so speed up.

Well, that argument is not quite right. For there is a way in which it does not really make sense to suppose that *everything* remains the same except that it happens at ten times the speed. For one thing, the speeds of things will not be the same. And could not it be that our mental state depends on the speeds with which certain parts of our brain are moving? Well, in a sense it could. If some parts of our brain were to speed up relative to the rest of our brain, this could alter our mental state. Or, if my brain were to speed up compared to yours, or compared to a clock, that could alter my mental state. But it does not make much sense to suppose that if everything in the world were to speed up uniformly it would change my mental state. You might think that it would. You might think that how we feel is *directly affected* by the rate of goings on in our brain. Well, I grant that this is possible. But note that whatever change occurred in how things feel to us, it would not result in any change in any spatial arrangement of things, so not, say, in any letters that I would write down. It could alter *when* I would write them down, but not *what* I would write down. And it is hard to take seriously the idea that there could be some mental changes which are so epiphenomenal that they never result in a change in what we would write down, even, say, when we are reporting our own mental state. So it seems plausible that we would not notice it if every process in the world were to speed up uniformly.

Now, according to Barbour, not only would we not notice such a uniform speeding up of all processes, but the whole supposition makes no sense whatsoever, since there exists no time beyond the rate at which processes occur relative to each other. Time, according to Barbour, does not come equipped with a fundamental metric—an external standard relative to which all processes could speed up or slow down. Time is merely a measure of change.

The story I have painted above suggests a reason for believing that there is no fundamental temporal metric. How about the idea that there is no fundamental temporal topology? Well, imagine that one paints the state of the world at each instant on a card, and one then stacks the cards in the order in which the instants occur. Barbour's idea now is that it would not make any difference to the states that are confined to these cards if one subsequently shuffled these cards. The order in which the states, and the corresponding experiences, would occur would change, but the states themselves, the experiences themselves, would not change. Thus one could not tell by the experiences themselves whether the order in which they occurred were shuffled, as long as such a shuffling leaves intact the intrinsic character of the experiences. Now, shuffling the cards amounts to changing the topological structure of time. Thus one might claim that any supposed fundamental topological temporal structure is irrelevant to our experiences, and, indeed, that there is no fundamental temporal topological structure.

Whatever one thinks of these arguments, it gives one some understanding of the idea that time has no structure whatsoever.[8] Now let us examine Barbour's ideas in more detail.

---

[8] As will become clear, I do not put much stock in the given arguments, since they use intuitions (beliefs) about what (distinct) possiblities there are in order to infer what the fundamental structure of the (actual) world is.

1.5 Ridding time of structure in Newtonian particle physics

To start off we need to know a little bit about Newtonian particle dynamics; that is, about Newtonian theories of the development of the state of particles. Let us consider a very simple case: two point particles that interact only through an attractive Newtonian gravitational force $F=km_1m_2/r^2$, where k is a constant, m_1 and m_2 are the masses of the respective particles, and r is the distance between them. By Newton's Second Law, $F=ma$, particle 1 will always accelerate towards particle 2 with acceleration $a_1=km_2/r^2$, and particle 2 will always accelerate towards particle 1 with acceleration $a_2=km_1/r^2$. Roughly speaking, there are only two types of motion possible for such a two-particle system:

a) Each of the two particles for ever orbits around an ellipse (each of which has a focus at the centre of mass).
b) Each of the two particles travels, for ever, along a hyperbola (each of which has a focus at the centre of mass), so that they recede further and further from each other, both towards future infinity and past infinity.

I said 'roughly speaking' because there is a caveat. We have to worry about what happens if the two happen to meet at one exact point at some time, because their relative velocity at some other time points exactly along the straight line between the two particles. Let us start on this problem by assuming that there are no 'collision forces'; that is, that the two particles can occupy the same position in space at some time. Even then it is not plain sailing, because the gravitational force between the two particles diverges to infinity as their distance converges to 0, so that, strictly speaking, we cannot make sense of the force acting on them when they occupy the same location. We can fix this problem by making a continuity assumption: namely, that the trajectories in such a case are the limit of the trajectories as we 'line up' the initial velocities closer and closer. One might naturally think that this will have the consequence that they will pass through each other when they meet, but actually it follows that they will 'bounce off each other' when they meet. For as one considers orbits for initial velocities that are 'lined up' closer and closer, these orbits will become ellipses, or hyperbolae, that have tighter and tighter 'bends' when the particles are closest to each other. Given such a continuity assumption, which implies 'bouncing' in the case of perfectly aligned initial velocities, we have a theory which is deterministic: the trajectories will be uniquely determined given positions, velocities, and masses at any time t.[9]

But now suppose that time, fundamentally, has no metric. Could one still have two particles interacting in the way I have just described? It would seem not. For if time has no fundamental metric then there is no matter of fact as to how fast any particle is

---

[9] Well, not quite for every initial condition: initial co-locations do not have unique well-defined evolutions.

moving at any given moment. This also brings out how radical Barbour's idea really is. If processes are not situated in time which comes equipped with its own metric, then it makes no sense to ask how fast those processes are evolving. So, for example, there is no fact of the matter as to the velocity of a particle—no fact of the matter as to what distance the particle traverses *per unit time*. But if there is no matter of fact regarding the velocities of the particles—if the states of these particles at a given time do not include such things as their velocities—then what on earth could determine how far they will travel, whether they will orbit in ellipses or will keep receding? It seems that if time does not come equipped with a metric we could not have a decent theory of even the simplest kind of interaction.

But let us not be too hasty. If we cannot speak of the velocities of particles, given that time does not come equipped with a metric, what can we speak of? Well, we *can* speak of the directions in which the two particles are traveling, and *the speed ratio* with which they are doing this. By *the speed ratio* I mean how fast one particle is moving when the other particle's motion is taken as the standard. This quantity makes perfect sense even if time does not come equipped with its own metric, since one can speak of the distance that particle 1 travels during the time interval that particle 2 travels a given distance, without knowing anything about the *magnitude* of that time interval. Note that the existence of such speed ratios depends on there being facts about identity of location across time. For instance, suppose that during some interval particle A travels twice the distance that particle B travels. Now suppose that there were no facts about identity of location across time. Then it would be equally correct to look at this development from the point of view of a frame of reference in which particle A is standing still. In this frame, B is still moving (though at a different speed from the frame with which we started). But that means that in this frame of reference the speed ratio of B to A is infinite: a finite number divided by 0 is infinite. (In fact, it is better to say that it is an ill-defined ratio, since infinity is not a number; but this does not matter for present purposes.) The main point here is not that this ratio becomes infinite (or ill-defined) in a different frame of reference; the main point is that speed ratios are different relative to different frames of reference. Therefore, if there is no single, true, frame of reference, then speed ratios, simpliciter, are not well-defined quantities. For now I will therefore assume that there are facts about identity of location across time, and I will sketch how one can then construct a Barbourian version of a Newtonian dynamics set in a spacetime in which time has no structure. I will later return to the issue as to how one can construct a Barbourian version of Newtonian dynamics when one does not assume that there are facts about identity of location across time.

OK, let us define the *Barbour state* of the two particles to consist of the masses, positions, directions of travel, and speed ratio of the particles. *Barbour states* contain less information than standard states, since they do not include speeds, just speed ratios. However, notice that even if there were a large number of particles, once the *Barbour states* are given, you would need only one more quantity in order to fix each of the speeds. For instance, the total kinetic energy $T = \sum \frac{1}{2} m_i v_i^2 = \frac{1}{2} m_1 v_1^2 + \frac{1}{2} m_2 v_2^2 + \ldots$ of a collection of particles would suffice to determine all the speeds, given the *Barbour state*. And, what will turn out to be more relevant, the total energy E, defined as the kinetic energy T plus the potential energy V, will also determine the speeds. In the case of two gravitating particles, the potential energy $V=-km_1m_2/r$, so that in this case $E=\frac{1}{2}m_1v_1^2+\frac{1}{2}m_2v_2^2-km_1m_2/r$.

Barbour now assumes the existence of a constant of nature, E, which from the perspective of standard Newtonian theory is naturally understood as the total energy of the universe. It is important, however, that E in Barbour's theory is *not* defined as $E=\frac{1}{2}m_1v_1^2+\frac{1}{2}m_2v_2^2-km_1m_2/r$. For there are no such things as the velocities, v_1 and v_2, of particles in a universe in which time does not have a metric. Now let me give Barbour's dynamics for *Barbour states*, the rule for how a *Barbour state* at any given time determines the *Barbour state*s at all other times, where time does not have a metric. I will first do this in a rather inelegant and indirect way, and then indicate how it can be done in a more elegant and direct manner.

A dynamics is simply a rule for how the states develop in time. Here is the rule. Suppose that at time t the two-particle system is in *Barbour state B*. Use the value of E to translate the Barbour state into a unique Newtonian state S, by pretending that the quantity E equals $\frac{1}{2}m_1v_1^2+\frac{1}{2}m_2v_2^2-km_1m_2/r$. Then use the standard Newtonian dynamics for the development of standard states, set in a universe in which time does have a metric, in order to find the standard state at all times. Then translate these standard states back into *Barbour state*s, ignore the metric on time, and *voila*, we have the *Barbour states* at all times, set in a universe in which time does not have a metric, given only the *Barbour state* at time t. That is all there is to it.

Now, you might reasonably object that this dynamics, and the idea that time does not have a metric, is really ugly and implausible, since it relies on a detour through standard dynamics set in a universe in which time does have a metric. But there is an answer to this objection, for one can formulate a dynamics of *Barbour states* set in a universe in which time does not have a metric, which makes no detour through standard states, or standard dynamics. The way in which this can be done is by formulating the dynamics as a rather natural and simple so-called 'action' principle on *Barbour configuration space*.

First let me say something about action principles in general. Often one states a dynamical law—a law for the evolution of states—by stating a law which determines for any given initial state the rate at which this state will change towards the future. For instance Newton's law $F=ma$ says that the acceleration of a particle at a time—the rate of change of its velocity—is determined by the force acting on the particle at the time, and its mass. If the force acting on a particle is determined by its position—because, for example, it is in a force-field whose magnitude and direction depends on the location of the particle—this means that the rate of change of its velocity is determined by its position and its mass. And, assuming that its mass does not change in time, this in turn means that given the initial mass, position, and velocity of the particle, all its future positions (and velocities, accelerations, and so on) are uniquely determined. Note that the notion of state that we needed in order to obtain a deterministic evolution from a given initial state was one that included the velocity of the particle (as well as its position and mass).

Interestingly, such laws of evolution can (typically) also be stated in a slightly different way, by means of a so-called 'action' principle. Here is how. We start by assuming that the state of a particle at a time consists of just its mass and its position; that is, its velocity is not included. (In the next chapter I will say more about which of the two is the more appropriate notion of state.) Next we define for any finite history of states—that is, for any time-indexed path in state-space—the so-called 'action' associated with this path. For instance, for a single free particle in Newtonian space the action is $S=\int^{1}/_{2}mv^{2}dt$, the integral of the kinetic energy, where we integrate over time from the beginning to the end of the history in question. Note that this action S is defined for *any* history of positions whatsoever (provided it is sufficiently smooth that the velocity, the derivative of position with respect to time, is well defined.) The dynamics is then specified by saying that the only allowed histories are ones such that the action along the history is a local minimum; that is, it is a history such that if you consider small changes to it, while holding the initial and final states fixed, the action gets larger. In the case of a single free particle, the only histories allowed by the minimum action principle are the constant velocity histories—the paths whereby it travels in a straight line with constant velocity from the initial location to the final location of the history in question. Of course, this coincides with the paths that we get when we demand that the acceleration $a=0$. In the case of a particle subject to a force field that is constant in time, we can represent the effect of the force-field by a potential $V(x,y,z)$, and the action then becomes $S=\int(^{1}/_{2}mv^{2}-V(x,y,z))dt$. The histories that minimize this action are those such that the acceleration is proportional to $-\nabla V$; that is, the gradient of the potential V. So this action principle is equivalent to the law that $F=ma$, when we set $F=-\nabla V$.

Now we can state Barbour's theory of a pair of gravitating particles by means of an action defined on *Barbour configuration space*. The *Barbour configuration* of the pair of particles at a time consists of their positions and masses at that time. (Note that I am still assuming that there are facts about identity and non-identity of location across time.) Now define the action S of a trajectory in *Barbour configuration space* (the space of all possible *Barbour configurations*) as $S=\int d\lambda ((E+km_1m_2/r)(\Sigma_i m_i(dx_i/d\lambda)^2)^{1/2}$, where λ is an arbitrary (smooth) parameterization of this trajectory.[10] Then, as usual, we say that the only allowed trajectories are those that minimize the action. Now, this action is invariant under reparameterizations; that is, the value of the action S does not change when we switch to using a different parameterization λ' of the trajectory, where λ' is any (smooth, monotonically increasing) function of λ. So this dynamics does not depend on a temporal metric. The dynamics, for a given value of E, is deterministic. That is to

[10] A parameterization of a trajectory is an assignment of real numbers to each point on the trajectory where these real numbers increase (or decrease) monotonically (and smoothly) along the trajectory.

say, there is a unique path between any given initial and final Barbour configurations. Relatedly, any initial configuration plus initial 'direction in configuration space' determines a unique history, for a fixed value of E. An initial 'direction in configuration space' at a point in configuration space is exactly what you would think it is. One can specify it by drawing an arrow in configuration space which starts at the point in configuration space in question and points in a direction in configuration space. The length of the arrow here is immaterial: a direction in configuration space at a point in configuration space just specifies the direction in which one is going, but does not specify a 'speed' with which one is going in that direction. If you think about this for a moment you will see that an initial configuration plus direction in configuration space corresponds to what I have called a *Barbour state*: namely, positions, masses, directions of motion, and speed ratios. So, Barbour's theory is such that any *Barbour state* at any time, for a given value of E, determines a unique history of configurations, and is equivalent to the Newtonian gravitational particle theory with the corresponding total energy E. And the obvious generalization of Barbour's theory to any finite number of particles is also equivalent to the corresponding Newtonian theory.[11]

So we can formulate a fairly simple theory set in a universe in which time does not have a metric, which predicts exactly the same phenomena as the standard gravitational theory set in a universe in which time does have a metric.

So far I have not talked about the topology of time. Could one go even further and also deny that time has any fundamental topological structure? Can one deny that there is *any* fact of the matter as to the way in which instants are ordered, and can one deny that there are *any* facts about which times occur between which other times? Indeed one can. One can claim that there simply is a set of instants, and that this set has no further fundamental structure whatsoever. But what about the dynamics? Well, one can give it by just demanding that the *Barbour* states of the particles at each instant in the set must be such that one *can* order those states in such a way that they satisfy the dynamics that I described above. If we picture the states of the world at instants as paintings on a set of cards, then Barbour is suggesting that the history of the world corresponds to an unordered set of cards. Barbour's dynamics for such a set of states at instants then amounts to the demand that the set of cards must be such that the cards can be ordered in such a way so as to satisfy a particular rule for ordered cards; that is, stacks of cards. This rule is such that it corresponds to exactly the same possible stacks of cards as standard dynamics allows.

---

[11] There is a problem for infinite universes (universes with infinitely many particles), basically because in such a universe, total energy is ill-defined. Barbour does not solve this problem, and is content to deal only with finite universes. There is a somewhat analogous problem that occurs in standard Newtonian theory due to the fact that on standard formulations of Newtonian gravitational theory the force on a particle in a universe with infinitely many particles is ill-defined. This is so because that force depends on how one sums (integrates) the gravitational force on that particle due to the infinitely many other particles in the universe. One can avoid this problem by adopting a so-called Newton–Cartan theory. (See Malament (1995)). But it is not obvious how to make a Barbourian version of a Newton–Cartan theory, and Barbour (personal communication) is not in favor of attempting this.

OK. Let me now raise some worries about Barbour's idea that there is no funda-mental temporal structure. Here is an obvious worry: it certainly *seems* to us as if time has fundamental structure. So why deny it? Here is the natural response. Even though time in fact does not have any such fundamental structure there is a perfectly good explanation of why it seems that way. For the laws dictate that the states *can* be linearly ordered in such a way as to satisfy the laws that we think they satisfy relative to the linear order that we mistakenly think time itself supplies. That is to say, the laws dictate that it will *seem* as if the events occur in a linearly ordered time.

It remains hard to rid oneself of the nagging feeling that Barbour's theory amounts to a somewhat conspiratorial explanation of the phenomena. If in fact there is no fundamental temporal ordering of instants, why would God choose a set of laws that make it seem as if there is? To put it less religiously: one feels that the fact that time is ordered and that temporal intervals have lengths is a better explanation of why time seems to be linearly ordered and temporal intervals seem to have lengths, than the fact that they do not, but the laws are such that they entail that it will seem that way. In the end, I do not put much stock in this worry. It does not strike me as sound methodo-logy to demand that the fundamental structure of reality must correspond closely to the *prima facie* structure of reality. As long as one has a simple theory which explains why the world appears the way it does to us, I see no reason to impose a further demand of similarity to our pre-theoretic picture of the fundamental structure of the world.

Here is another worry. According to the 'no-temporal-structure' view there is just a set of snapshots—instantaneous states—which do not come equipped with any fundamental temporal structure. In so far as we can speak of the correct ordering of these snapshots, it is derived from the non-temporal features of each snapshot. Now, surely, the character of the experiences which are the building blocks of our mental lives are not determined by the configuration of the particles in our brain *at a single instant*. Surely the character of our basic experiences will generically depend on how the particle configurations evolve over a short, but non-zero length, period of time. However, if there is no fundamental temporal order to the instants, then how can the features of the instants alone determine the mental life that we actually have? If one way of ordering the instants, fundamentally, is as good as any other, then how can we explain that our experiences are the way they are rather than experiences that corres-pond to some higgledy-piggledy reshuffling of the ordering of the instantaneous particle configurations? Indeed, presumably on most such reshufflings there would not be any mental states at all. There would just be a bizarre discontinuous sequence of unrelated arrangements of elementary particles. Some of these arrangements at some instants would take the shape of a human being, but that surely is not enough to have instantaneous human beings with instantaneous mental lives. The obvious, and plaus-ible, response is to say that the experiences that we have correspond to the ordering of the snapshots which makes the particle configurations on them develop smoothly and according to the usual laws of physics along that ordering. The fact that this ordering is not a fundamental temporal one, but an ordering that derives from the non-temporal features of the states on each snapshot, does not disbar this ordering from supporting and explaining the existence and the character of temporally extended phenomena.[12]

Here is another worry. It is fairly natural to think that things might have been different from the way that they are—different even in ways that violate the actual laws of nature. For instance, one might think that in principle everything that in fact happened in the year 1945 could have happened in the year 1256, and vice versa. Of course, if that had happened the development of the world would not have been in accord with the actual laws of physics; indeed the development of the world would have been highly discontinuous at the stroke of midnight on the New Years' Eves of 1255, 1256, 1944, and 1945. Nonetheless, one might reasonably insist that things *could* have happened that way; one might think that while this obviously is not a physical possibility, since it is not consistent with the actual laws of physics, it is a possibility in a wider sense of 'possibility': namely, a 'metaphysical possibility'. Now note that this 'year-switched-world' does not appear to be even a metaphysical possibility on the 'no temporal structure' view. For, by hypothesis, the 'year-switched-world' contains exactly the same set of temporal snapshots as the actual world. So, on the 'no temporal struc- ture' view, it just is the same world. So, if one is convinced that the 'year-switched' possibility is a genuinely distinct possibility, then one should presumably reject the 'no temporal structure' view.[13]

Again, I am not inclined to think much of this worry. Using intuitions about what is and what is not metaphysically possible in order to decide which theories of physics are right, strikes me as putting the cart before the horse. It seems to me a better tactic to first figure out what our best theory is, and then use that theory in determin- ing what the metaphysical possibilities are. Whether or not this tactic can be made to work is a contentious issue. Be that as it may, the reverse enterprise strikes me as clearly a bad idea: arguments which start with *prima facie* intuitions as to what is and what is not metaphysically possible, and end with conclusions as to what the best theories in science must be like, do not make for sound methodology, and would hamper scientific progress.

---

[12] Barbour does appear to believe that our experiences are determined by 'instantaneous experiences' which in turn are determined by instantaneous particle configurations. See Barbour (2000), Chapter 2.

[13] Of course, in order to say anything about what is and what is not metaphysically possible one will have to use some intuitions, or some theory, concerning what the metaphysical possibilities are. In the main text I have used the working assumption that something akin to a combinatorial account of metaphysical pos- sibility is correct. The combinatorial idea, roughly speaking, is that something is a metaphysical possibility if it can be constructed by recombining the fundamental objects and quantities of the actual world, and if not, it is not a metaphysical possibility—or at least, it is not a 'non-alien' possibility. Such a combinatorial account of metaphysical possibility is contentious. However, since in the main text I end up claiming that arguments from premises concerning what is and what is not metaphysically possible to conclusions about the viability of certain scientific theories are not to be trusted, there is no need for me to defend such a combinatorial account of metaphysical possibility.

Another worry is that Barbour's theory is, in a particular sense, not local. Here is the worry. Suppose that one has two particles orbiting each other somewhere in empty space, and two other particles, very far away, orbiting each other. If these two pairs are very far from each other, they are effectively isolated, since the gravitational force diminishes with the square of the distance. If one wants to consider a case in which they are truly completely isolated, one could, for instance, consider two pairs of particles where the two particles in each pair are attached to each other by a spring, but the two pairs are not coupled to each other in any way. But let us stick to the gravitational case, since that is the case on which we have concentrated. Suppose that one specifies the local Barbour state; that is, the masses, positions, directions of motion, and the speed ratio for one of the two pairs of particles. This will not determine the future (or past) states of this pair, since the energy of the isolated pair is not determined by the quantities that we have specified. Even if one additionally specifies the value of the global energy, the global quantity E, the future and past state of the isolated pair will still not be determined. For the global E plus the Barbour state that isolated pair does not pick out the effective energy of that pair. Now, this type of local indeterminism can be quite severe. Let me describe a simple case where standard Newtonian physics is 'locally deterministic'; that is, where the future evolution of the state of an isolated system is determined by its state and the Newtonian laws, but where Barbourian local physics is badly indeterministic.

Suppose we have two particles of identical mass, isolated from the rest of the universe, which initially are moving away from each other with equal and opposite velocities, where these velocities are in the direction of the line between the two initial particle positions. If the initial velocities are below a certain value ('escape velocity') the particles will move away from each other for a while, then come to a halt, and then start to move back towards each other. Where the 'turnaround point' for each particle will be depends on the initial velocities. Because of the symmetry of the set-up the turnaround point for each of the two particles will be equally far from the point that it started. Now consider two such possible scenarios which differ only in terms of the magnitude of the initial velocities that the particles have. The turnaround point in the case of the lower initial velocities will be less far away than in the case of the higher initial velocities. Now think of what this looks like in Barbourian physics. Note that until the turnaround point corresponding to the lesser velocities is reached, the trajectory in configuration space will be exactly the same for both cases. That is to say, if we cannot avail ourselves of a metric in time—if, as in Barbour's theory, all we have is a trajectory in configuration space (parameterized by some smooth parameter in configuration space if you wish, as long as it does not come with a metric)—then we have a bad violation of local determinism: even a complete finite history of particle configurations will not determine subsequent development of those particle configurations. They may turn around at any time after the given history, or never turn around. In order to determine the future evolution we need either a metric on time, or we need something like the local, effective, energy E of the pair in question. It seems no good to assume that in addition to the Barbour states there are many additional facts: namely, values of all the 'local Es'. Would each of these be another constant of nature? What happens when systems cease to be isolated? A more promising response would be to say that, in fact, no systems of particles are ever truly isolated from the other particles in the universe, so that the idea of 'local' determinism is a lost cause anyhow. Well, one could indeed say that. But note that it removes flexibility from Barbour's theory. What if it turned out that there are truly local interactions, analogous to a pair of particles being connected by a spring? In that case one can make sense of local determinism in a Newtonian theory, but it would fail for a Barbourian theory.

One can ameliorate the worry about locality by pointing out that the case which I discussed—namely, identical mass particles moving with equal speeds in opposite directions—is not generic. For instance, suppose that the two initial velocities are not both in the direction of the line connecting them. Then the particle trajectories will be ellipses, hyperbolae, or parabolae. Now, just the initial masses, positions and speed ratios—that is, just the initial location in configuration space and direction in configuration space—will in this generic case still not determine the future evolution in configuration space for an isolated subsystem. We still, as it were, do not know what the velocities of the particles are, or what the effective energy of the isolated pair is. However, any *finite temporal development* of the configuration, no matter how short, will, in the generic case, determine a unique future. For such a finite history gives us a finite trajectory, a finite bit of a pair of ellipses, hyperbolae, or parabolae, and these finite bits determine unique complete pairs of ellipses or hyperbolae; that is, unique evolutions of the configuration as long as the system remains isolated. So, while generically the data needed to determine evolutions of isolated systems are not the same for a Newtonian theory and a Barbourian theory, cases of severe difference—cases in which even a finite Barbourian history does not determine future development—are non-generic.[14] Still, the fact remains that the 'initial value data'—the data one needs in order to determine a unique future evolution, given the laws of nature—are not as nice for isolated systems in Barbourian theories as they are in Newtonian theories. In Newtonian theories the initial value data are the same for the entire universe as they are for an isolated system. In Barbourian theories, because of the constant E that occurs in the laws, the initial value data are not the same for the entire universe as they are for an isolated system.

Next, let me discuss worries that one might have about whether one can know the value that the constant E in fact has. Consider a solution to the Barbourian action principle with a particular value of E. One can 'translate' such a solution into a standard Newtonian spacetime with particle trajectories in it by pretending that E equals the total energy. Now, suppose we put coordinates x, y, z, t on this Newtonian spacetime where these coordinates are moving with a constant velocity. That is to say,

---

[14] They have measure 0 in the space of initial-configurations-plus-directions-of-evolution-of-configurations.

suppose we have coordinates x, y, z and t such that if one considers any fixed triple of values for x, y, and z for all values of t—for example, $x=5$, $y=3$, $z=2$ for all t—this determines a line in Newtonian spacetime which moves with constant velocity according to the identity of location structure of the Newtonian spacetime. Will now the evolution of the coordinate values of all the particle trajectories relative to this coordinate system also satisfy a Barbourian action principle? Yes, it will, but, generically it will satisfy an action principle with a value of E different from the one that governs the evolution relative to a coordinate system that is not moving. This is so for the simple reason that the value of total energy is frame dependent in Newtonian physics. Suppose now that we are living in a Barbourian universe. One might worry that there is then no way of telling what the true law is that governs our universe, since there is no way of telling what the true value of E is. And then one might worry that Barbour's theory is objectionable because it postulates an ineffable fact.

The obvious thing to say about this worry is that people who postulate a standard Newtonian spacetime are in exactly the same bind. They are supposing that there are facts about identity of location across time. But, for exactly the same reason, there appears to be no way of telling what this identity of location across time structure is. Of course, this is exactly the reason why many people prefer to set Newtonian dynamics in a neo-Newtonian spacetime, in which there is no such ineffable structure. So the thing to examine is whether Barbour can make an analogous move.

Neo-Newtonian spacetime has 'straight line' structure; that is, 'inertial' structure. There are facts of the form: locations a, b, and c at times t_1, t_2, and t_3 lie on a straight line. Can Barbour assume the analogous structure? No. Barbour denies that time has any structure, so he cannot postulate such cross-time facts. But he has an interesting way out of this problem (which he likes for independent reasons: see Chapter 5). Here is what he does.

He assumes that the history of the universe amounts just to a set of configurations at instants, where a configuration at an instant is specified by all the masses and all the distances between particles at that instant. There are no facts as to identity and non-identity of configurations at different times, nor are there facts about triples of configurations lying on straight lines, or anything like that. Now stack all the instantaneous configurations on top of each other in such a way that the distances vary smoothly. Next, assign triples of numbers—one triple x^i_t, y^i_t, z^i_t for each particle i at each time t, such that at each time t the distance between particle i and particle j equals $\sqrt{((x^i_t - x^j_t)^2 + (y^i_t - y^j_t)^2 + (z^i_t - z^j_t)^2)}$; that is, such that the triples behave exactly as if they are Cartesian coordinates for each particle at each time. Now, of course, there are lots of different ways of assigning triples subject to this constraint. Given only this constraint, the triple of numbers associated with a given particle, say particle j, could vary quite arbitrarily, even discontinuously, in time. But we are going to impose a constraint which will fix the triples almost uniquely. The idea is that we want to make sure that the triples, in a precise sense, vary minimally when we compare the triples at one time to the triples at another time. In particular, let us define the magnitude M of the difference between the sets of triples at one time s and the sets of triples at another time t as follows;

$$M=\sqrt{1/2}\Sigma_i m_i((x^i_s-x^i_t)^2+(y^i_s-y^i_t)^2+(z^i_s-z^i_t)^2)$$

Now we demand that the triples be assigned in such a way that the values of M are as small as they can possibly be. Barbour calls this minimization principle a 'best match-ing' principle.

Intuitively speaking, what we have done is the following. We started with sets of distances at instants, and no cross-time relations of any sort. We then assigned triples of numbers subject to the above minimization constraint. The minimization constraint can be pictured in the following way: embed the distances in a fully coordinatized spacetime such that the total kinetic energy is minimal and the total (centre of mass) angular momentum is 0 and total momentum is 0. This embedding is unique up to a global spatial shift, a global spatial rotation, and arbitrary temporal dilations. That is to say, take any such embedding, and shift all particles at all times by a fixed (time inde-pendent) distance in a fixed direction, and you obtain another allowed embedding. Similarly, take any such embedding and rotate the positions of all particles at all times by any fixed angle around any fixed spatial axis and you obtain another allowed embedding. Finally, take an allowed embedding and change it by stretching and shrink-ing it in the temporal direction by a factor that varies arbitrarily, but smoothly, across time, and you obatin another allowed embedding.

Given that this is what we have done it should be clear how to finish our Barbourian theory: now demand that our previous Barbourian action principle is satisfied; that is, demand that the action $S=\int d\lambda\,((E+km_1m_2/r)(\Sigma_i m_i(dx_i/d\lambda)^2)^{1/2}$ is mimimal for allowed histories of configurations, where the x_i denote the triples of numbers we obtained after we subjected them to the above minimization constraint, and λ denotes an arbi-trary smooth coordinatisation of the instants. The sets of configurations allowed by this theory correspond to the solutions of the corresponding neo-Newtonian theory sub-ject to the constraint that the total angular momentum of the universe is 0. Moreover, we can in principle figure out the value of E: it is the total energy of the universe relative to the frame of reference in which the total momentum of the universe is 0.[15] So, one can, after all, formulate a Barbourian particle that is analogous to standard Newtonian dynamics set in a neo-Newtonian spacetime. The only difference between this and the previous case is that the current Barbourian theory additionally predicts that the total angular momentum of the universe equals 0. Interestingly, observational data suggest that the angular momentum of the universe is, in fact, either 0 or very close to it. So, if anything, Barbour fares even better in this context!

There is a worry that the Barbourian tactic here is a little too flexible. In essence, Barbour's 'best matching' procedure is a way to infer inertial structure from histories of

---

[15] This presupposes that the total energy of the universe is finite. But that had better be the case anyhow, in order for Barbour's theory to work.

distances. The worry now is that whenever one can infer some structure—some features F of the world—from the history of other features G of the world, one can then go on to deny that features F are fundamental features of the world by incorporating into one's theory the formula, or formulae, that spell out how F is determined by G. But it surely is not right that whenever one can do this it is indeed correct to infer that features F are not fundamental. For instance, just because one can infer all mass values from the histories of accelerations in a Newtonian (purely gravitational) universe, this surely does not mean that masses are not fundamental quantities. On the other hand, I would not want to claim that any reduction in the stock of fundamental objects and fundamental properties of some theory is always misguided. No, the important question, as always, is the relative simplicity of the two theories in question. And in this particular case, I do not find it obvious what the verdict is.

Finally, let me raise a worry concerning the specific claim that time has no *topological* structure. Recall that we managed to form a theory according to which time does not even have topological structure by having our theory simply assert that there exists a way of ordering the instants so that certain dynamical laws (which presuppose such an ordering) are true relative to that ordering. Now, this seems a strange kind of theory to me. Indeed, it seems to me that in the relevant sense of 'simple' or 'plausible' it is not a simple or plausible theory. One way to see this is to realize that if such a theory is counted as simple, then we can easily manufacture lots of 'simple' theories which get rid of just about any objects, quantities, or properties that one wishes to get rid of for whatever reason. For instance, we could get rid of the quantity 'electrical charge' by adopting a theory which says: 'There is no such quantity as electrical charge, but there is a way of assigning (make-believe) electrical charge values to all the objects in the universe such that the usual laws (of electromagnetism) hold relative to that assignment'; or 'There are no protons, but there is a way of assigning (make-believe) proton trajectories to the history of the universe such that the usual laws hold relative to that assignment'. It is not easy to make precise exactly in which sense such theories are not simple. Cian Dorr (2010) has started on the project of making this precise, and in particular argues that it is a 'bad' feature of a theory if it includes formulae which are governed by (non-negated) existential quantifiers, as in 'there exists a function from objects to real numbers (make-belief charge values) such that . . .'.[16] But even without a compelling and precise account of the epistemologically relevant sense of simplicity, it seems clear to me that eliminating topological structure in the suggested manner

---

[16] One can also use this criterion to argue that a Barbourian theory which includes a 'best-matching' principle is not simple, for the logical form of the relevant part of such a theory is as follows: for any coordinate system CS, either the usual laws hold relative to it, or there are coordinate systems which are 'better matching' than CS. So, such a theory includes a formula governed by an existential quantifier (that is, 'there are coordinate systems which are "better matching" than CS'), and hence it has a 'bad' feature by the 'existential quantification criterion'. However, a lot more work regarding the precise details of, and defence of, this proposed measure of simplicity is needed before I would regard this as a very telling argument against such Barbourian theories.

does not yield a plausible theory. The proposed manner of eliminating topological structure is theft rather than honest toil.

All in all, in the context of Newtonian physics we have found no utterly compelling arguments against the Barbourian view that time has no structure. I am most perturbed by the 'non-locality' worry when considering the elimination of metric structure, and the 'theft rather than toil' worry when considering the elimination of topological structure. But I would not want to claim that these are conclusive objections.

1.6 Ridding time of structure in Special Relativity

I have previously explained that according to Special Relativity, space and time are not separate entities—that instead there is one entity: spacetime. So how are we then to interpret the idea that time has no structure? We should not understand it as the idea that spacetime has no structure, for then we would just be left with a set of spacetime points, each with some individual features perhaps, but otherwise not connected to each other in any way, and that is just not going to be enough to allow a plausible representation of anything like our world. Rather, one should claim that, contrary to what Special Relativity says, space and time actually are separate entities, and that there is a unique set of different states at different times. Then one can go ahead and claim that time has no structure, and see whether one can formulate a plausible theory which predicts the same phenomena as Special Relativity does.

Indeed, as Julian Barbour has shown, one can follow exactly the same strategy as in the non-relativistic case, and one obtains almost exactly the same results. Let me be a little more precise. In the Newtonian case I distinguished two different Newtonian theories, and two corresponding Barbourian theories—ones in which one assumed facts about identity of location across time, and ones in which one did not. In fact, there are also two distinct versions of Special Relativity. When I presented Special Relativity above, I presented the standard 'Einsteinian' Special Relativity, according to which there are no facts about identity of spatial location across time. Einsteinian relativity does assume the existence of cross-time structure; for example, the assumed metric is a spacetime metric rather than a purely spatial metric. Indeed, according to Einsteinian relativity, spacetime is a four-dimensional manifold with a four-dimensional structure, rather than a collection of three-dimensional spaces at times connected by cross-time relations. But there is a rival theory—so-called 'Lorentzian' Special Relativity, according to which there are facts about identity of location across time. These facts, of course, determine (up to a choice of origin and orientation) preferred coordinate systems, frames of reference: namely, those that always assign the same spatial coordinates to identical locations at different times. Now, Lorentzian relativity seems less plausible than Einsteinian relativity, exactly because it assumes more structure than does Einsteinian relativity, especially since those facts are empirically inaccessible. Still, let us ask both in the case of Lorentzian relativity and Einsteinian relativity whether one can formulate Barbourian analogues.

Let us start with Lorentzian theory. Indeed, one can do so in a manner that is quite analogous to the Newtonian case. That is to say, given a Lorentzian particle or field theory, one can write down a corresponding Barbourian action principle, which includes a constant E, which determines which sets of (particle or field) configurations are allowed to occur on the set of all instants. This action principle makes use of the cross-time identity of location structure, but it makes no use of any other cross-time structure. Solutions to this Barbourian action principle—sets of configurations on instants—are equivalent to solutions of the Lorentzian theory with which we started, in the following sense. One can form a spacetime out of these instants by stacking the instants on top of each other in a manner that makes the development of the configurations in the stacking direction (time) smooth, and so that identical spatial locations are put on top of identical spatial locations. One can then assign a temporal coordinate t in the stacking direction such that the spacetime (with particles and/or fields in it) corresponds to a solution of the Lorentzian theory with which we started, and E corresponds to the total energy of the universe. (See the appendix to Pooley (2001). The relevant action principle is his equation A.4.)

There is one issue that in the Lorentzian case is slightly different from the Newtonian case. In the Newtonian case we found that the Barbourian could not tell, by observation, what the value of E in fact was, nor what the true frame of reference was; that is, what the true cross-time identity of location facts were. The same thing is true in the Lorentzian case: the Barbourian cannot, by observation, tell what the true value of E is, nor what the true rest frame is. However, in the Newtonian case this did not mean that the Barbourian could not tell what the true decomposition of history into instants was, for that decomposition was the same no matter what the cross-time identity of location facts were. However, in the Lorentzian case the slicing of history into instants is different depending on what the true rest frame is. As a consequence the Barbourian cannot tell how history decomposes into the true instants. Still, while this may be a problem, the Barbourian is no worse off than the Lorentzian. The Lorentzian, after all, also accepts that there is a unique preferred slicing of spacetime into spaces-at-times, and it also cannot tell which this correct slicing is. So, once again, the Barbourian is not at disadvantage.

Now let us turn to Einsteinian relativity. Once again it turns out that one can formulate a corresponding Barbourian theory—this time in a manner that is analogous to the neo-Newtonian case. Here is how. One first stacks all the instants, with their configurations, in such a manner that the variation of the distances and/or the variations in the field configurations is smooth. One then puts 'best matching' spatial coordinates on all the instants in the stack; that is, coordinates such that total spatial momentum and total angular momentum of the universe is 0 at all times. Then one imposes the same action principle as in the Lorentzian case. Any stack formed in this way will then correspond to an Einsteinian solution in the following sense. One can assign a temporal coordinate t (in the stacking direction) such that the evolution of the field/particle configurations relative to the 'best matching' spatial coordinates and the temporal coordinate t will be exactly the same as they are relative to an inertial coordinatisation of an Einsteinian solution which has total energy = E, total angular momentum = 0, and total spatial momentum = 0 relative to that inertial coordinate system. (See the appendix to Pooley (2001). The relevant action principle is his equation A.5.)

There is, however, an important difference between the Einsteinian case and the neo-Newtonian case. Suppose we take a Barbourian solution. As I said, this will correspond to an Einsteinian solution—a history of configurations in Minkowski spacetime—together with an inertial coordinate system $\{x,y,z,t\}$ relative to which total spatial momentum = 0. Now suppose we look at this Einsteinian solution from the point of view of a different inertial coordinate system $\{x',y',z',t'\}$—one that is moving relative to the coordinate system $\{x,y,z,t\}$. In particular, let us look at the history of configurations on the time-slices $t' = r$ of this new coordinate system. Since this is a set of smoothly varying configurations, we can ask: does this set satisfy Barbour's theory? The answer is that if we started with a Barbourian action principle in which $E = 0$ it will, and if we started with a Barbourian action principle in which $E \neq 0$, it will not.

Before discussing the implications of this fact, let me briefly sketch why this is so. According to Special Relativity, total energy and total spatial momentum have frame-dependent values. Consider for instance (ordinary, spatial) velocity in Newtonian physics. Relative to a spatial coordinate system x,y,z we can speak of the x-component of velocity, the y-component of velocity, and the z-component of velocity. But of course, the magnitude that each has depends on which coordinate system one uses. Velocity itself is a three-dimensional vector, whose components have values only relative to a coordinate system. Similarly, according to Einsteinian relativity, total energy and spatial momentum (three components) form a four-dimensional vector, whose components only have values relative to a coordinate system. Now, if relative to some inertial coordinate system all the components have value zero, then it is the 'null four-vector', and its components have value zero relative to any coordinate system. But if relative to some inertial coordinate system the momentum components are all zero, but the energy component is non-zero, then relative to any inertial frame which moves relative to the original coordinate system the value of the momentum components will be non-zero. Now, from the Barbourian perspective this means that this coordinate system is not a 'best matching' coordinate system. But if one then adjusts one's coordinates so as to get a 'best matching' coordinate system, one will find that the evolution of the configurations relative to that 'best matching' coordinate system no longer satisfies Barbour's (Lorentzian) action principle. (Again, see the appendix to Pooley (2001) for details.)

Let us now turn to the implications of the above. One can take two attitudes. One attitude is that there is no problem—in fact, that the above is a good thing. If, as a matter of fact, E is (finite and) non-zero, then we can, in principle, figure out what the correct decomposition of world history into instants is (and, consequently, what the true value of E is): it is the one relative to which total momentum of the universe is zero. The other attitude one can take is that there is something objectionable about the idea that the Barbourian action principle is not valid relative to all 'frames of reference'; one might think that Barbour's action principle ought to have the same invariances as Einsteinian relativity has. In that case one should add the demand that $E = 0$. However, this, to me, seems a strange attitude. Why should one wish to postulate that there is in fact a unique way in which world history is composed out of instants, and then go on to demand that one's laws of evolution should be such that one cannot tell how in fact world history is composed out of instants?

All in all, it appears that no significant new problems arise in the case of Special Relativity. So, again, we have found no compelling reason to reject the idea that time has no structure.

1.7 Ridding time of structure in General Relativity

Finally, let us turn to General Relativity. Again, we should interpret the idea that time has no structure as the idea that space and time are quite separate entities, and that time has no structure. And again, it is Barbour who has argued that one can indeed have a theory in which time has no structure which makes the same predictions as General Relativity. According to Barbour's theory, the state of the world at an instant consists of a three-dimensional space, with a spatial metric on it, which determines the way in which space at that instant is curved, and particles and/or fields distributed in it.[17] Barbour gives his dynamics for these states, as before, by means of an action principle.[18]

His dynamics is such that given a state at an instant, and a direction in the space of possible instantaneous states, in which this state is developing, but of course not a *rate* at which it is developing in this direction, it predicts a set of possible developments of this state.[19] Before explaining the sense in which the predictions of Barbour's dynamics are the same as those of General Relativity, let me emphasize that Barbour's dynamics is radically indeterministic: given any initial state and direction in which that state is developing, there are infinitely many different possible developments of this state according to Barbour's dynamics. To understand why this is the case, and to understand the sense in which Barbour's theory makes the same predictions as General Relativity, let us first examine the sense in which General Relativity is deterministic.

According to General Relativity, space and time form a single four-dimensional entity: spacetime. One can (generically) slice such a spacetime into three-dimensional time-slices (inextendible space-like surfaces); and (generically) there are many—indeed infinitely many—different ways of doing this, just like there are many ways to slice an

---

[17] Well, to be precise, it is an equivalence class of such states under the 'spatial diffeomorphisms'. This issue is not important for current purposes.

[18] For details, see Barbour (1994), Pooley (2001), and Barbour, Foster, and O Murchadha (2002).

[19] There is no constant E which occurs in Barbour action principle. One can, but need not, introduce a constant that plays the same role as that of the cosmological constant in Einstein's equation.

apple. The metric of spacetime determines the distances along all lines in spacetime, and in particular, therefore, it determines all the distances in any given time-slice. Since each time-slice is space-like and has three dimensions, these distances amount to spatial distances in a curved, three-dimensional space. The equations of General Relativity now are such that if one gives the spatial metric on any such time-slice, and one states how that metric changes as one 'pushes away' from that time-slice, at some rate and in some direction in spacetime, then there is a unique spacetime with a unique spacetime metric into which that time-slice fits.

Now we can diagnose the source of the indeterminism of Barbour's theory, and see the sense in which it predicts exactly the same as General Relativity. The different possible developments that Barbour's dynamics allows from a given initial state and initial direction of development correspond exactly to the different ways in which one can slice the unique General Relativistic spacetime determined by the corresponding General Relativistic initial state and initial direction of development. Barbour's set of possible different developments of three-dimensional spatial states, from a given initial spatial state and direction of development, can always be fitted into a unique four-dimensional spacetime with a unique four-dimensional metric, in such a way that the spatial metric of each spatial state is exactly the one entailed by the spacetime metric, and these possible developments always correspond exactly to *all* the possible ways of slicing that unique spacetime into spatial states. Of course, from Barbour's point of view this construction of a four-dimensional spacetime, and subsequent construction of all possible slicings of it, is a peculiar thing to do. There is, according to his theory, fundamentally just one unique set of instants, each with their unique spatial metric and particle/field configuration on them. One can, if one wishes, pretend that there is a four-dimensional spacetime, and then one can imagine slicing this four-dimensional spacetime in various ways. But none of this corresponds to what there fundamentally is according to Barbour's theory. Unfortunately, from the Barbourian perspective, since all of the 'reslicings' satisfy exactly the same Barbourian action principle, we will never know which the fundamentally correct one is. But that does not mean that there is not a unique fundamentally correct slicing. According to Barbour's theory, whether or not we can know it, there is a fact of the matter as to which the fundamentally correct way is to slice the history of our universe into instants.

At this point I have to say that it seems more plausible that there is a single four-dimensional spacetime which can be sliced in many fundamentally equally correct ways. The Barbourian alternative is that there is a unique set of instants which have no fundamental temporal structure, which can nonetheless be stacked so as to look exactly like a four-dimensional spacetime with spatiotemporal structure, and, when this is done, they fit so perfectly that it is impossible to figure out which where the 'seams' are; that is, how in fact the world decomposes into fundamentally unrelated instants. This Barbourian theory just seems a bit too conspiratorial to be plausible. Indeed, it seems that Barbour himself is sympathetic to this verdict: 'If the world were purely classical I think we would have to say . . . that the unity that Minkowski proclaimed so confidently is the deepest truth of spacetime. The three-spaces out of which it can be built up in so many different ways are knitted together by extraordinarily taut interwoven bonds'. (Barbour (2000), p. 180.) In his book, and in various papers, Barbour goes on to explain why he thinks that when one combines General Relativity with quantum mechanics one has good reason to believe that time has no structure. He also suggests getting rid of even more structure by resorting to so-called 'conformal theories' in which cross-time comparisons of distances are not possible, only cross-time comparisons of relative distances—shapes—are possible, and he suggests that such theories might allow one to infer from the phenomena what the uniquely correct decomposition into temporal instants is. However, these ideas of his are rather unfinished, and too technical, for me to discuss them here and now. (If you want to know more, check out his website at http://www.platonia.com/.) The upshot of this chapter is that the radical idea that time has no structure whatsoever is surprisingly viable.

2

There goes the neighbourhood . . .

I marvel how Nature could ever find space
For so many strange contrasts in one human face:
There's thought and no thought, and there's paleness and bloom
And bustle and sluggishness, pleasure and gloom.

William Wordsworth

2.1 Introduction

How did God forge Being? He wove a cloth, and on it lay a pattern. An assassination here, a protein there, a path cleared in a forest, a love wasted away. All this buzzing and blooming is but stillness on the fabric of space and time.

I could go on, but I am no poet. So let us get more prosaic and quote an influential contemporary philosopher, David Lewis, who is perhaps the best-known proponent of the idea that the world is painted on the cloth of space and time: 'All there is to the world is a vast mosaic of local matters of fact, just one little thing and then another . . . We have geometry: a system of external relations of spatiotemporal distances between points . . . And at those points we have local qualities: perfectly natural intrinsic properties which need nothing bigger than a point at which to be instantiated. For short, we have an arrangement of qualities. And that is all. There is no difference without difference in the arrangement of qualities.'[1]

Lewis's picture is that spacetime is the fundamental backdrop against which all events occur, and that everything that happens in spacetime is entirely determined by what is the case at each point in spacetime. On his view the geometric structure of spacetime is given by the distance relations between points in spacetime; that is, the spatiotemporal distances that exist between all spacetime points.[2] According to Lewis

---

[1] This quote is from David Lewis (1986b), page ix.

[2] Spatiotemporal distances can factor into separate spatial and temporal distances as they do in Newtonian physics, or not, as in relativistic physics. Whether it does or does not so factor does not matter for the discussion in this chapter.

this geometric structure is highly non-local, since it consists of distance relations between distinct, distant, points. But other than this distance structure, the structure of the history of the world is entirely local according to Lewis. For, given the backdrop of spacetime, one can specify *every* feature of the history of the world by specifying all the *local* features of each point in spacetime. Or, to put it less operationally, the set of all local features determines all features of the history of the world, given the geometry of spacetime.

It is widely accepted that in quantum mechanics one cannot give the state of the world location by location, and even David Lewis was, grudgingly, willing to countenance this possibility. However, in this chapter I am going to argue that Lewis' picture is already mistaken in classical physics. (In the next chapter I will discuss, among other things, what happens with Lewis's picture in quantum mechanics.) One might think that my disagreement with Lewis is yet another example of the kind of pedantic philosopher's fight over details that is of no real interest or consequence. Well, perhaps so, but it concerns a very general and fundamental issue. Our understanding of the world by and large derives from breaking it down into its constituent parts, and figuring out what the properties of those parts are. Now, in this chapter I will not deny that the world is composed out of ultimate parts (I will attempt to deny even this in Chapter 4). In particular, for the purposes of this chapter I am quite happy to accept that the ultimate parts of the world are spacetime points. What I am going to deny in this chapter is that the properties of the world are determined by the properties of each of its ultimate parts. I am going to claim that according to classical physics the world has irreducibly 'holistic' properties. That, if you think about it, is a fairly general and radical view. So much by way of advertising. Now let me present a little more detail regarding Lewis's atomistic view.

First let me distinguish the idea that all features of world history are determined by the features at each point in spacetime—the idea that the state of the history of the world is 'separable'—from the idea that the laws of evolution (in time) are such that the (temporal) evolution of the state of a system confined to some spatial region is determined by local features; that is, the idea that dynamics is local. In this chapter we are primarily concerned with the first idea, not with the second idea. When Lewis claims that all features of the history of the world are determined by the features at each spacetime point, he means to include the claim that the laws of the world are determined by all features at each spacetime point, but he does not mean to include the claim that the laws themselves must be local; that is, that the laws must be such that how the state of a system confined to a spatial region develops according to those laws is determined by features local to that region. For instance, the idea that the history of a Newtonian particle world is completely given once you have given the positions and masses of all particles at all times is quite compatible with the idea that according to the Newtonian laws the acceleration of a particle at a time depends on the position of all masses throughout the universe at that time. So the idea that states are separable is quite distinct from the idea that laws of evolution are local.

Next let me discuss what Lewis means by 'perfectly natural intrinsic properties'. They are what I called 'fundamental properties' in Chapter 1. A good working idea of what the fundamental properties are, and what the fundamental relations are, is that they are the properties and relations that occur in the fundamental laws of physics. Note that this should *not* be understood as the idea that the fundamental properties are *defined* as the properties that occur in the fundamental laws of physics. No, the distinction between fundamental and non-fundamental properties, and relations, is basic— not to be analysed, explained, nor understood in terms of other, more basic, concepts or distinctions.[3]

Why assume that there is such a distinction? Because armed with such a distinction we can attack a number of otherwise vexing puzzles. Let me briefly sketch a few such puzzles and how one might go about solving them by making use of the distinction between fundamental and non-fundamental properties and relations.

Why is it that the predicates that we use have the referents that they do? When we use a predicate, such as 'green', we take it that even though we have only applied the predicate in a finite number of cases, it has an objective (and fairly definite) extension among the cases to which we have not applied the predicate: among all the objects-at-times to which we have not yet applied the predicate 'green' (because they are in the future, or we did not see them, or we saw them but we did not describe their colour, and so on). There are many objects that belong to the extension of 'green' (that is, many objects are green), and many that do not belong to that extension. To be sure, in some cases it will be vague as to whether an object at a time belongs to the extension of 'green', but it is not the case that it is completely indeterminate as to what the extension of 'green' is. What determines what the extension of 'green' is? David Lewis's idea is that the extension of a predicate is determined by the 'use' of that predicate and by the 'eligibility' of each of the candidate extensions. The idea that our 'use' of the predicate matters is a generalization of the idea that it matters to which objects-at-times, so far, we have applied the predicate. The idea of 'eligibility' is that an extension is more 'eligible' than another if it is more fundamental. Of course, a lot of details have to be filled in here. One needs to give an account of what it is for one extension to be *more* fundamental than another; one needs to give some account of something like *degrees* of fundamentality; and one needs to give an account of which aspects of usage matter, how, and how much. Still, armed with a distinction between fundamental and non-fundamental properties one can at least see how one can get started on the project of explaining why it is that our words refer to certain things and not to other things.

Another puzzle which, armed with the distinction between fundamental properties and non-fundamental ones, one can see how to attack is Nelson Goodman's 'new riddle of induction'. Goodman defined the predicates 'grue' and 'bleen' in the following

---

[3] The fundamental laws of physics, according to Lewis, are the simplest strongest expression of the patterns in the distribution of the fundamental properties and relations.

manner. An object is grue if, and only if, it is first examined before the year 2050 and is green, or it is not examined before 2050 and is blue. An object is bleen if, and only if, it is first examined before 2050 and is blue, or is not examined before 2050 and is green. Now suppose that all emeralds that we have examined so far are green. It seems, then, that we are justified in inferring that, most likely, all emeralds are green, including the ones that will not be examined before 2050. However, note that it is also the case that all emeralds that we have examined so far are grue. So, if there were no relevant distinction between the predicates 'green' and 'grue', we would also be warranted in inferring that all emeralds are grue, including the ones that will not be examined before 2050. But if both inferences are justified, then we are both justified in believing that the emeralds that we will first examine after 2050 are green, and that they are 'grue', hence, blue. But we cannot be justified both in believing that these emeralds are blue and that they are green. So we have a problem.

Let us make use of our distinction. If green is a fundamental property then grue, presumably, is not. Now let us claim that one should only expect fundamental properties and relations to be distributed in simple patterns. If, then, being an emerald is a fundamental property, we can reasonably expect all emeralds to be green rather than grue. Of course, this is only a sketch of an argument; there remain details to be sorted out. For instance, presumably the predicate 'is an emerald' is not totally fundamental. So, once again, we will need an account of something like degrees of fundamentality, and an account of how such degrees relate to inductive inferences. Here is another worry: what reason do we have to think that 'green' is a more fundamental predicate than 'grue'? I suggest that the correct answer is along the following lines. Which predicate is more fundamental depends on how we introduce the predicates. Suppose we were to introduce 'green' by pointing at certain things, and then take it that things like those that we pointed at are also in the extension of 'green'. Then, given our previous idea about reference fixing, the extension of 'green' should be a fairly fundamental one—as fundamental as it can be given only the constraint of what we pointed at. If we were to then introduce the term 'grue' not by pointing at things, but by defining it, as Goodman did, in terms of 'green' and 'examinations' and '2050', then its extension should be less fundamental than that of 'green'. So we have reason to believe that our term 'green' refers to a more fundamental property than our term 'grue'. And we can see how the distinction between fundamental and non-fundamental properties can be used to attack Goodman's new riddle of induction.

Here is yet another puzzle we can try attacking, armed with our distinction. Other things being equal, scientists—and ordinary folk, for that matter—will prefer simple theories to complex theories; that is, think that the simple theories are more likely to be true. But, *prima facie*, whether a theory is more or less simple depends on the terms that one uses to state the theory. If one is allowed to use any predicate P, no matter how natural or unnatural its extension, then any theory whatsoever can take the sublimely simple form, 'Everything is P'. On the other hand, if we have a preferred set of predicates—the fundamental ones—then one can start thinking about how to define the simplicity of a theory; for example, in terms of the complexity of an expression of that theory in a language that uses only fundamental predicates.

Here is another case—the most important case for purposes of this chapter—in which we can make use of the distinction between fundamental and non-fundamental properties: namely, the issue of separability. Above, I said that the state of the history of the world is separable if that state is determined by the features, the properties, of each spacetime point. Now, if we place no restriction on what counts as a property of a spacetime point, then every world is separable, for one of the properties of any space-time point p whatsoever is that it is surrounded by a world with such-and-such features. The obvious response is that we should restrict ourselves to the genuine properties that belong just to that point p—p's 'intrinsic' properties—and that we should disbar as irrelevant properties that just code up what the world around p looks like. The problem is that it is not obvious how to present a non-question-begging account of what the intrinsic properties of a point (or a region, or an object, or a system) are. Lewis's answer to this conundrum was to define the notion of a duplicate of an object (region, system, point) as follows: A is a duplicate of B if and only if there is a one-to-one mapping of all parts of A onto all parts of B which preserves all funda-mental properties and relations. And then he said that something is an intrinsic property of an object if it shares that property with every possible duplicate. Given this account of the intrinsic properties of an object, we now have a pretty clear notion of what it is for all features of the world to be determined by the intrinsic features of each spacetime point; that is, what it is for the world to be separable.

2.2 How separable is the geometric structure of spacetime?

It seems obvious that Lewis is correct when he says that the geometrical structure of world history is not determined by the geometric structure intrinsic to each of its spacetime points. In fact, though he does not explicitly say so, Lewis presumably thinks that spacetime points do not have any (non-trivial intrinsic) geometrical structure; they are the smallest, ultimate, parts of the history of the universe, and have no further, internal, geometrical structure. Now, at various points in this book I will be suggesting that spacetime points are in fact not the smallest, ultimate, parts of the geometrical structure of the universe. Be that as it may, it still seems clear that the geometrical structure of spacetime is not determined by the geometrical structure of each of the spacetime points in it. Surely the distances between spacetime points are not deter-mined by whatever internal geometrical structure each of these points may, or may not, have. Having sided with Lewis on this matter let me nonetheless enter into a little more detail, mainly in order to clarify the analogies and disanalogies with the non-geometrical features of the world.

Let us begin with the topological structure of spacetime. As we saw in Chapter 1, the topological structure of a spacetime determines which sets of points are connected to each other to form a single, connected, region, and which sets of points form two or more disconnected regions. It determines which regions have holes in them, and which regions do not. It determines which curves are continuous, and which are discontinuous.[4] Indeed, as I said in Chapter 1, it determines any structure that is invariant under all stretching, shearing, and squeezing.

The standard way to specify the topological structure of a set of points S is by specifying which subsets of that set are 'open', subject to the following axioms:

1) the intersection of finitely many open sets is open,
2) the union of any collection of open sets is open,
3) the set consisting of all points in S is open, and
4) the set that has no points in it—the empty set—is open.

Intuitively speaking, the open sets are those such that none of its points lie on the boundary (the edge) of the set in question; you get an open set by taking any old set, and taking away all of the points that lie on its boundary. 'Closed' sets are the complements of open sets; they are, intuitively speaking, sets which include all their boundary points.

A simple, and important, example is the standard topological structure of the real number line. According to the standard topology of the real number line, any set (a,b) consisting of all the real numbers that lie strictly between any pair of distinct real numbers a and b is an open set. The rest of the open sets are determined by our axioms. So, the union of any set of open intervals is an open set. And the intersection of any finite collection of open intervals is an open set. However, now consider the intersection of all sets of the form $(-a, a)$, where a can be any real number other than 0. Of course, the only number common to all these sets is the number 0. We denote the set consisting only of the number 0 as follows: [0]. (A square bracket indicates that the number next to it is included in the set, and a round bracket that the number next to it is not included.) We are here taking the intersection of infinitely many sets, so this procedure is not guaranteed to produce an open set. In fact, [0] is not an open set. Intuitively this is fairly obvious: this set includes the one boundary point that it has, namely 0. More formally, it is not open because it is impossible to form [0] by taking unions and finite intersections of sets of the form (a, b). In fact [0] is a 'closed' set: it is the complement of the open set that you obtain by taking away the number 0 from the set of all numbers.

Another important topology is the standard topology of n-tuples of real numbers; that is, of the 'Cartesian product' of n real lines. You can picture this as a space spanned by n real lines, all lying orthogonal to each other and crossing each other at the 0-point on each real line. The standard topology of, for example, the set of all triples of real numbers can be given in the following way. Any set of triples consisting of all the

---

[4] A curve is a set of points 'parameterized'—indexed or labelled—by (an open segment of) the real numbers.

points that lie 'within distance d' of some given triple $<r_1,r_2,r_3>$ is an open set. That is to say, for any real number d, and any triple of real numbers $<r_1,r_2,r_3>$, the set of all triples $<x,y,z>$ such that $\sqrt{((x-r_1)^2+(y-r_2)^2+(z-r_3)^2)}<d$ forms an open set (often called an open ball). That is all there is to specifying the topology of all triples of real numbers. And this generalizes to n-tuples of real numbers, for any finite n.

How about the topology of spacetime? Well, the topology of Newtonian, neo-Newtonian, and Special Relativistic spacetime is the same as that of the set of all quadruples of real numbers. Note that this does not mean that these spacetimes have *all* structure in common with that of the set of all quadruples of real numbers. For instance, real numbers can be added and multiplied; there are facts as to which real number is the sum of two other real numbers and which is the product of two real numbers. But these facts are not determined by the *topological* structure of the real numbers. And spacetime does not have such an addition and multiplication structure. To be clear: I used the addition and multiplication structure of the real numbers to define the topological structure of real numbers (and that of n-tuples of real numbers), but the *topological* structure of the real numbers does not encode the addition and multiplication structure. The topological structure of the real numbers is a weaker structure than the addition and multiplication structure, and it is this topological structure that is identical with the topological structure of Newtonian, neo-Newtonian and Special Relativistic spacetime.

It is, incidentally, a bit annoying that the simplest way to give the topological structure of spacetime is via the topological structure of real numbers. For one thing, if one does not think that numbers exist (because, for example, one thinks that only physical entities like tables and electrons exist), then one might hope that one could give the topological structure of spacetime directly, without making recourse to the real numbers. We will return to this issue in Chapter 8.

How about the topological structure of spacetime according to General Relativity? Well, as we saw in Chapter 1, according to General Relativity there are many different possibilities for the topological structure of spacetime. It can be an infinite four-dimensional space; that is, it can have the same topological structure as that of the set of all quadruples of real numbers, but it can also be of finite extent; for example, the four-dimensional analogue of the surface of a sphere, or some weird four-dimensional knot. Indeed, there are many possible topological structures of spacetime according to General Relativity, but one thing has to be the case: *locally* it has to have the same topology as that of quadruples of real numbers. That is to say, for any spacetime point p in any General Relativistic spacetime there is an open set R containing p such that the topological structure of R is the same as that of an open ball in the space of quadruples of real numbers.

Now, it is rather remarkable that all the topological features of any space (including spacetime), which include all facts about connectedness and continuity of any parts of that space, are determined by a mere designation of a collection of subsets as being the 'open sets'. It is quite enlightening to look at the first few pages of a topology textbook to get an idea of why this is so. For the sake of brevity let me here just give you a brief glimpse, by defining the continuity of functions in terms of the openness of sets. Consider a function f from a space X to a space Y. The 'inverse image' $f^{-1}(V)$ of a subset V of points in Y is the subset U of X that consists exactly of all the points in X that get mapped to a point in V. A function f from X to Y is defined to be continuous if whenever $f^{-1}(V)=U$ and V is open, then U is open. To get some feel for this definition let us consider the case where both X and Y have the topology of the real number line. Consider then, for instance, the function $f(x)=x$, which maps every number to itself. Clearly it is a continuous function by our definition, since the inverse image of any set is just that same set. Now consider instead the function $g(x)$ where for all x smaller than 0 we have $g(x)=x$, and for all x greater than or equal to 0 we have $g(x)=x+2$. This function jumps in value at $x=0$. And, indeed, according to our formal definition of continuity this function is not continuous. For instance, the inverse image of the open set $(1, 3)$ is the set $[0,1)$, which includes the number 0 and hence is not open. The problem is that the numbers that are just below 2 do not have inverse images at all, because of the jump. Hence the inverse image of the open set $(1,3)$ 'cuts off' at the number 0, in a manner so as to include 0, and nothing below 0.

OK, now that we have some idea as to what the topological structure of a spacetime is, let us return to the question as to whether it is separable. To answer that question we first have to decide what the fundamental topological properties of points and sets of points (regions) are. Given the axioms that we stated above, the obvious suggestion is that the only fundamental topological property is that of 'openness'.[5] Later in this section I will briefly sketch a reason to think 'openness' should not be taken as a fundamental topological property, but for now let us work with the assumption that it is. It immediately follows that topological structure is not separable. For the topological properties of any two points are just the same: each point is not an open set. That is all there is to be said about the intrinsic topological properties of a point. So any two sets whatsoever consist of points each of which has exactly the same topological properties. But not all sets have exactly the same topological properties (some are open and some are not open). So it cannot be that the topological properties of sets of points are determined by the topological properties of the points in the set. Of course, this is hardly surprising: at some point early on in the game of adding structure the points will have to be 'tied together' to create a space, or a spacetime, rather than a set of unrelated points.

However, there is also a clear sense in which topological structure is 'almost separable'. Let me explain. Suppose that we have a spacetime T and any collection of open subsets S_i such that the union $\cup S_i$ of all these subsets is the whole spacetime T.[6] The

---

[5] The relations 'union', 'intersection', 'complementation', 'being an element of', and the property 'being empty' are set-theoretic, and, plausibly, 'is an element of' is the only fundamental one among them.

[6] This can always be done, since it is one of the axioms of topology that the total space T must be open. There are pathological cases in which the only open sets are the entire space and the empty set, but these are not viable spacetimes.

topology of the entire spacetime T is in fact completely determined by the topology of each of the subsets S_i. The proof is trivial. We know that the topology of T is determined once we know exactly which the open subsets of T are. Well, consider some subset O of T which in fact is open. Let O_i denote the intersection of O with S_i, i.e. $O_i = O \cap S_i$. Since the intersection of any two open sets is open, each such O_i is open. Since each O_i is entirely contained in the corresponding S_i, the topology of the corresponding S_i determines that O_i is open. Since the union of open sets is open, the topology of each of the S_i determines that $\cup O_i$ is open. But $\cup O_i = O$, and thus the topology of each of the S_i determines that O is open, for arbitrary open O. Thus, the topology of any collection of open sets entirely determines the topology of the union of those sets. So topology is separable in the sense that given any division of the total space into open neighbourhoods, the topology of each of the neighbourhoods determines the overall topology. Let us call this sense of separability 'neighbourhood-separability'. Neighbourhood-separable is just about as separable as one could possibly have hoped topological structure to be. Given that the spacetime has to somehow be glued together, we see that topological structure ties it together with extremely local ties.

Before turning to metric structure, let me state my previously promised worry about taking 'openness' to be the fundamental topological property. As we have seen, one of the jobs that we can do armed with a distinction between fundamental and non-fundamental properties is that we can define what it is for something to be a duplicate of another thing. Imagine a two-dimensional purely spatial world and a three-dimensional purely spatial world, where both spaces are flat infinite Euclidean spaces. Consider a circle in the two-dimensional world, and consider all the points that lie inside that circle. This is an open set, an open disk, since it is a set of all points that are within a certain distance (the radius of the circle) from a certain point (the centre of the circle). Now let us think whether there are topological duplicates of this disk in the three-dimensional world. *Prima facie*, one would think so: there are plenty of two-dimensional disks to be found in the three-dimensional world whose topological structure appears to be exactly the same as that of the disk in the two-dimensional world. However, none of the two-dimensional disks in the three-dimensional world are open according to the (standard) topology of the three-dimensional world. For just as one cannot form a point on the real line by taking finitely many intersections of finite intervals on the real line, one cannot form a two-dimensional disk by taking finitely many intersections of three-dimensional open balls. In fact, the three-dimensional world contains no topological duplicates whatsoever of the two-dimensional open disk in the two-dimensional world. This seems strange and objectionable: surely the two-dimensional disks in the two-dimensional space and the three-dimensional space are intrinsically identical. For this reason, and many others reasons besides, Tim Maudlin has developed a quite different, and quite fascinating, alternative way of doing topology (and much more besides): see Maudlin (manuscript); it is well worth reading. (Note also that in Chapter 8, views will be considered according to which openness is not a fundamental property.)

Let us now turn to the metric structure of a spacetime. Lewis suggested that the metric structure of spacetime is given by facts about the distances between all pairs of points. That is to say, his suggestion is that there is one fundamental metric relation—namely, the distance relation—and that the fundamental distance facts consist of all the distances between all the points in spacetime. There are a couple of reasons for not liking this approach to the metric structure of spacetime. In the first place this collection of facts is highly redundant and highly constrained: one can delete lots of facts from this collection, and still have enough to determine distance relations. Hence the distance facts are highly constrained: one cannot vary the facts about distances between points p and q while keeping fixed all other distance facts. One might hope that one's collection of fundamental facts could be more sparse and less constrained. Secondly, as it stands, it is not clear how one could specify the structure of a relativistic spacetime in this way. As we have seen, in relativistic spacetimes, paths can have negative lengths. So one cannot say that the distance between two points equals the length of the path with the least length. One might instead suggest that it should equal the length of the unique straight line running between the two points. But this will not do in General Relativity, in which there are 'geodesics' between pairs of points—lines that are 'as straight as possible given the curvature of spacetime'—but there need not be a unique geodesic between a given pair of points. All of this is not to say that one could not do something along the lines that David Lewis suggests. One can in fact divide up any General Relativistic spacetime into small patches so that in each patch there is a unique geodesic between any pair of points in that patch. One could then assume that there are unique distances between pairs of points in the same patch, subject to certain constraints. And one could then let these distances determine the metric structure of the whole of spacetime. But if distance between points is the fundamental metric relation then it would seem that General Relativity should count as a rather complicated theory, for the laws of General Relativity are rather complicated when stated in terms of a distance relation between pairs of points.

So let me briefly turn to the question as to how one standardly characterizes the allowed distance structures in General Relativity. A distance structure in General Relativity is determined by a 'metric tensor field'. I will introduce the notion of a tensor field later in this chapter. For now, just say that the metric structure of a spacetime in General Relativity amounts to a specification of the lengths of all (smooth) paths in spacetime. Since paths are extended objects, it may seem that this will be a highly non-separable structure. However, if one has a collection of open subsets, the union of which is the entire space, then the lengths of all the paths confined to these subsets determine all lengths in the entire space. For consider an arbitrary path from a to b. Suppose this path passes through a bunch of the open subsets. To determine the length of the path, simply add up all the lengths of all the paths in each subset, and then subtract all the lengths in the overlaps of the open subsets (subtract it twice for any triple overlap, and so on). Thus the length of an arbitrary path is determined by the lengths of paths in each of the open subsets. So all path lengths in the spacetime are determined by all path lengths in each of a collection of open subsets that cover the manifold, no matter how small these subsets. Thus, the metric structure of spacetime is also 'neighbourhood-separable'.

Having seen how separable the geometric structure of spacetime is, let us now see how separable the non-geometric structure of spacetime is, how separable the structure of the contents of spacetime is.

2.3 How separable is classical particle structure?

Let us begin with the most obvious feature of classical particles: namely, their positions. The 'position structure', or 'occupation structure', of spacetime consists just of the facts as to which spacetime region are occupied by particles (partially or wholly) and which are not. By the occupation structure of a spacetime I simply mean which regions are occupied (partially or wholly) and which are not; I do not mean this structure to include any of the features of the particles (masses, charges, velocities, and so on). It seems intuitively clear that the occupation structure of spacetime is separable: the list of which points are occupied and which are not obviously determines which regions are occupied (wholly or partially) and which are not. The fly in the ointment here is that on Lewis's account of intrinsic properties the occupation of a spacetime point by a particle is not an intrinsic property of that point—at least, not if one assume that particles are objects and spacetime points are objects. If that is so, then 'occupation' is presumably a fundamental *relation* between two objects, and then 'being occupied by a particle' is, presumably, not a fundamental property of spacetime points, and hence not an intrinsic property. But it would be rather uninteresting to end here and just say that the world is not separable because of this problem. What to do? One solution would be to claim that the only objects are spacetime points, and that 'being occupied by a material object' is, after all, an intrinsic property of spacetime points: what we intuitively think of as a relation between an object and a spacetime point could be conceived of as a fundamental property had just by the spacetime point (where occupation by different types of objects naturally can be assumed to correspond to different fundamental properties). While I am sympathetic to the idea that the only objects are spacetime regions, I would not wish to predicate the possibility of separability on it. So, let me instead stipulate that something is to count as an intrinsic property of a region if, and only if, it is a property of all duplicates *of that region plus its occupants*.

OK. Let us turn to a paradigm fundamental feature of classical particles: their mass. If the particles are point particles then it seems plausible that the value of the mass of such a particle at a given point in spacetime is a fundamental property of that point in spacetime. And if that is right, then the mass structure of the world is separable, since one can then give all the mass facts of the world spacetime point by spacetime point. But we immediately face a worry analogous to the worry that occupation relations are fundamental rather than occupation properties. Here is the worry. Because there are lots of mass values there are lots of mass properties, as many as there are (positive) real numbers. Since one needs (some of) the arithmetical properties of mass values in the laws of physics, and one needs them when making claims such as 'this object is twice as heavy as that object', it seems plausible that mass values are not fundamental properties of spacetime points, but rather the relation 'r is the mass value of x' is the fundamental mass relation, which is a relation between numbers and spacetime points. (Even better: 'r is the mass of x relative to unit y'. More on that below.) *Prima facie* this means that mass values are not intrinsic to locations, or objects, after all, but rather, relations between objects and real numbers. Well, just as in the case of particle positions, in order to give separability a fair shot, I am just going to stipulate that an object, or a location, having some mass value counts as an intrinsic property of that object, or that location.

Even though the above seems the obvious view to have, there are alternatives. An important alternative is that mass values are not fundamental properties, but instead there are fundamental relations—'mass ratios'—which obtain between pairs of particles (pairs of points in spacetime), which are of the form 'the particle located at p is 3.41 times as massive as the particle located at q'. Suppose now that these mass ratios satisfy the following two constraints:

a) Whenever a is x times as massive as b and b is y times as massive as c, then a is $x.y$ times as massive as c, and

b) the mass ratio between a particle and itself is always 1.

Then one can, by convention, designate a particular object to have mass=1, and then the mass relationships will determine unique numerical masses for each object. Note that if one wants to allow the possibility of particles whose mass is zero, then we need to introduce two special mass ratios: 'infinity', which holds between particles of non-zero mass and particles of zero mass, and 'ill-defined', which holds between two particle of zero mass. In any case, on this view the mass structure of the universe is neither separable nor neighbourhood-separable.

Is there a compelling reason to favor either of the above two views? Here are three arguments favoring the intrinsic property view. In the first place, no matter how much we isolate an object from its environment, and no matter how much we change the environment around an object, the way in which it responds to an applied force depends on its mass, where this mass does not appear to depend in any way on what we do to the environment of the object in question. Surely the most plausible explanation is that mass is an intrinsic property of objects, rather than that its mass is a convenient representation of a multitude of mass relations in which it stands. Secondly, if mass relations are fundamental, then why do they happen to satisfy the two above constraints which allow them to be represented as ratios of real numbers? Thirdly, one might have the intuition that things could have been different from the way they actually are in that everything might have had, say, twice the mass that it actually has. But this is not a distinct possibility on the mass ratio view, since all mass ratios are invariant under such a doubling of mass values.

What can we say in defence of the mass ratio view? The first two arguments are *prima facie* good arguments. However, later in this chapter we will find reasons to think that they are not compelling. The third argument seems dubious right from the start. Let me distinguish two versions of the third argument. On the first version one is imagining a world that is completely identical to the actual world, including the trajectories of all particles, except that all mass values are doubled. Well, my 'intuitions' leave it utterly unclear whether that is a genuinely distinct possible world. Moreover, it seems obvious that consulting one's intuitions as to whether or not certain putative possibilities are 'genuinely distinct' is hardly going to provide one with reliable evidence as to the whether masses or mass ratios are fundamental. So the first version of the argument seems no good. On the second version one is imagining a world which is exactly like the actual world at some moment in time, except that all masses are doubled. Both before and after this moment the trajectories of particles in this world are different from what they are in the actual world, intuitively speaking, because the same forces produce different accelerations in the different worlds. Now, of course, since the trajectories are different this will be a genuinely distinct possibility on the mass ratio view, so there is no problem in accounting for the distinctness of this possibility on the mass ratio view. A mass ratio adherent may, or may not, go on to make identifications of mass values in the two different possible worlds on the basis of the trajectories (the accelerations in particular) in the two possible worlds, but all of this is neither here nor there when it comes to judging the plausibility of the mass–ratio view versus the plausibility of the mass–value view.

Having agreed that there are two good *prima facie* reasons to prefer the mass–value view, let me now give a good *prima facie* reason to prefer the mass–ratio view. The mass–ratio view explains why the numerical values of masses are conventional to the extent that they are: namely, up to a choice of unit. On the mass–ratio view there is no fundamental fact as to whether the mass of some object is 1 or 2.343 or π: its value is only determined up to a conventional choice of unit. One might respond that this conventionality can also be understood when one carefully formulates the intrinsic mass–value view. For one might claim that the proper way to understand a mass–value attribution is as a relation between a particle (at a location in spacetime), a unit (such as kilograms), and a (real) number. However, this hardly helps. If a unit here is taken to refer to some (conventionally chosen) physical object, then one is back at having a fundamental non-local relation. To say that an object has a mass of, say, 3.4 kilograms would just be to say that that object stands in a particular fundamental relation to some other (conventionally chosen) object. If, on the other hand, one claims that a unit should not be identified with some (conventionally chosen) object, then what is it: some abstract object that is not located in spacetime? That might alleviate the worry about having a fundamental relation that is non-local in spacetime, but it replaces it by a relation to some strange object that has no spatiotemporal location.

The above brings out another worry. Both the mass–value view and the mass–ratio view postulate the existence of fundamental relations between particles and (real) numbers. If one is inclined to think that numbers do not exist, this would be very worrying. But even if one thinks numbers do exist, it seems rather strange that the mass structure of the physical world consists in certain relations holding between physical objects (particles) and certain abstract objects (numbers). This issue will be discussed more extensively in Chapter 8. For now let me sketch how one can characterize the mass structure of the world such that it does not involve any relations to abstract objects. Assume the existence of two fundamental three-place relations: 'massbetweenness', and 'massaddition'. Intuitively, the idea is that the massbetweenness relation holds between particles a, b, and c if, and only if, the mass of b is strictly between that of a and c, and the massaddition relation holds between particles a, b, and c if, and only if, the mass of a plus the mass of b equals the mass of c. Now, if we assume that the massbetweenness relation and the massaddition relation satisfies certain constraints—that is, certain axioms—then the set of all massbetweenness and massaddition facts will fix the mass value facts up to a choice of unit. Let me give two examples of constraints that these relations must satisfy—one purely illustrative, and one that matters for present purposes.

Associativity axiom. If massaddition(a,b,c) and massaddition(c,d,e) and massaddition(b,d,f), then massaddition(a,f,e). Intuively speaking, this says that mass addition is associative: $(a+b)+d=a+(b+d)$.

Richness axiom. Given any particle a there is a particle b such that massaddition(b,b,a). This axiom intuitively says that for any particle a there is another particle b which has half the mass of a.

Now note that the Richness axiom immediately entails that there are infinitely many different particles of different mass, for one can keep on halving masses, starting from any particle. But, if it entails the existence of infinitely many particles, which may not be true, then why introduce it? Well, we need the Richness axiom (or a similar axiom) in order to make sure that we have enough massaddition facts in order to fix the mass values up to a choice of scale. Imagine, for instance, that there were just a finite number of particles. If, intuitively speaking, the masses of these particle were random it could easily be the case that all massaddition claims would be false; it could easily be the case that no particle has a mass that is exactly equal to the masses of two other particles. And if that were the case, then the massaddition facts and massbetweenness facts could not possibly determine all the mass values up to a choice of unit. For, any change in the putative mass values that only keeps fixed the massbetweenness facts—that is, any reassignment that merely keeps fixed the order in which the mass values lie on the real line—would be an equally good numerical representation of the massbetweenness and massaddition facts, so they could not possibly determine all mass values up to a choice of unit (up to *linear* rescalings). The Richness axiom gets rid of this problem: if the Richness axiom is satisfied then the mass values are determined up to a choice of unit; that is, up to linear rescalings. How does this work? Well, one can determine the mass ratios of any two particles a and b by picking smaller and smaller masses c, and seeing how many such masses c one needs to add together in order to get a total mass that is bigger than that of a, and how many one needs to add together in order to get a total mass that is bigger than that of b. The ratio of the numbers of masses c that one needs to get above the mass of a and of b respectively, as one chooses a smaller and smaller mass for c, will converge to the mass ratio of a and b. So the Richness axiom is essential for the massaddition and massbetweenness approach.

But what of this approach if there are not enough particles, say, if there are only finitely many particles in the universe. Well, in that case one could assume that massbetweenness and massaddition are relations between *mass properties* rather than relations between *particles*, and assume that there are infinitely many distinct mass properties—indeed, assume that there are just as many mass properties as real numbers. Then the betweenness and addition relations between these mass properties will again determine that these mass properties can be represented by real numbers which are unique up to linear rescalings. So this approach is still viable even if there are only finitely many particles. The crux of this view is that it assumes the existence of further entities which one quantifies over and applies fundamental predicates to. Whether one calls these entities 'mass properties' as I have done here, or 'locations in mass-space', as in chapter 8, is neither here nor there. (For more detail, see Chapter 8.) What is nice about this approach is that real numbers are not needed, and that there is a neat explanation why they can nonetheless be fruitfully used in representations of physical states of affairs, and why in this representation the choice of unit is conventional.

One might think that there exists a further reason to prefer the view that massaddition and massbetweenness are fundamental to the idea that mass values are fundamental (or the idea that mass ratios are fundamental). For one might wonder why mass values are unique; that is to say, one might wonder why one cannot have an object such that its mass is 5 kilograms and its mass is also 7 kilograms. Why can the fundamental mass–value relation not hold between an object x, the unit kilogram, and the number 5, as well as between object x, the unit kilogram, and the number 7? (And one can ask the analogous question about mass ratios). And one might think that if one takes massbetweenness and massaddition as fundamental one can do better, since one can then explain this uniqueness, since one can prove that when the relevant axioms are satisfied the massbetweenness and massaddition relations can be represented by attaching a *single* number to each object (its mass value), where the set of all these numbers are unique up to linear rescalings. Well, I agree that one can explain that in this manner, but the explanation relies on the axioms that we assumed to hold of the massaddition and massbetweenness relation. And we can, of course, similarly assume axioms concerning mass values which imply that each object has only one mass value (relative to a unit). This also provides a response to the earlier argument that I gave against the mass ratio view on the grounds that it needed to assume that the mass ratios satisfied certain constraints in order for them to be represented as ratios of real numbers. What we now see is that each account will have to impose certain axioms; the only question is, which axiom systems are simpler and more natural. In so far as the axiom systems in question seem to be roughly equally natural and simple, the arguments based on constraints appear to be a wash.

Let me summarize. Taking mass values as fundamental implies that the mass structure of the world is separable. But on that view the fundamental relations are ones between a particle, a number, and a unit. Taking mass ratios to be fundamental implies that there are no units occurring in the fundamental relations, but there are still numbers in the fundamental relations, and the mass structure of the world is highly non-separable. Taking mass betweenness and massaddition to be fundamental implies that there are neither numbers nor units in the fundamental relations, but, of course, the mass structure of the world is highly non-separable. It is not obvious what the correct view is.

Let us now see what happens if all particles are extended; that is, if there are no point particles. To be precise, let us assume that mass is distributed in the world in a 'non-singular' way; that is, that any 0-sized volume of space (at a time) has 0 mass. This, of course, immediately entails that the mass of a region cannot be determined by the mass of each point in that region: each point has exactly the same fundamental mass property—namely, 0 mass—so one cannot account for the different masses of different regions of the same volume in terms of their fundamental mass properties. So separability fails if one assumes that what is fundamental is mass values. And, of course, if one takes mass ratios, or massbetweenness and massaddition, as fundamental, then separability fails too.

However, *neighbourhood* separability still holds if one takes mass values as fundamental. The mass of any region R is determined by the masses of all parts of each of a collection of open regions $\{O_i\}$ which covers all of spacetime: just take the intersection of R with each of the O_i, add all the masses of all these intersections, then subtract the masses of regions that you double counted (and subtract analogously for triple counted, and so on), because it was in the overlap of distinct O_i. This will determine the total mass of R.[7]

Does *neighbourhood* separability hold if one takes mass ratios, or massbetweenness and massaddition relations to be fundamental? That depends. Suppose that there are three disjoint regions A, B, and O, the union of which is spacetime, such that the (total) mass of A is non-zero the (total) mass of B is non-zero, the (total) mass of O is 0, and O is an open region which 'separates' A from B. By saying that O 'separates' A from B, I mean that any continuous path from anywhere in A to anywhere in B must pass through O. Now consider a collection of open regions O_i, the union of which is all of spacetime, such that it divides into three subcollections

1) The single region O.
2) A collection of regions each of which overlaps with A or with A and O, none of which overlaps with any of the region in the next subcollection: namely ...
3) A collection of regions each of which overlaps with B or B and O, none of which overlaps with any of the regions in the previous subcollection.

[7] Note that I am assuming that mass is countably additive, and that spacetime has the Lindelof property; that is, that any open cover has a countable subcover. Both of these are standard assumptions.

In this case the mass ratios confined to each of the regions O_i tell us nothing about the mass ratios between (any parts of) A and (any parts of) B. So they do not determine all mass ratios. So neighbourhood separability fails. And the same thing, of course, holds for the massbetweenness and massaddition relations. On the other hand, suppose that every open region has non-zero mass. Then the mass ratios confined to each of a collection of open regions O_i do determine all mass ratios: one can get from any open region to any other open region via open overlaps that do not have mass 0, and this will fix all mass ratios. The same is true if one assumes that massbetweenness and massaddition are fundamental: there will be 'enough' mass addition and massbetweenness facts in each overlap region, since each such overlap region must be open and have finite mass, and the masses of the collection of all subregions of any given massive region R must vary continuously from the mass m of that region R to 0, since we assumed non-singular mass distributions. So if every open region has non-zero mass, then neighbourhood separability holds. Thus, if mass ratios, or massaddition and massbetweenness, are fundamental, then whether neighbourhood separability holds depends on how mass is in fact distributed in the world.

There is an alternative to all of the above, for one need not assume that the mass values (or the mass ratios, or the massbetweenness and massaddition relations) are fundamental. One could instead assume that so-called 'mass-density' values (or mass-density ratios, or mass-density betweenness and mass-density addition) are fundamental. What are mass-density values? They are properties of points, such that when you integrate them over all points in a region you determine the (total) mass of that region. You might think that taking mass densities to be fundamental is no different from the view that masses are fundamental, since the one is definable in terms of the other. However, that is not right. It is true (given smoothness assumptions) that the one is definable in terms of the other, but it is not true that this means that it does not matter which one takes to be fundamental. If one takes masses to be fundamental properties of regions and one defines mass-densities of points in terms of masses of regions, then mass-densities are not intrinsic to points, while if one takes mass-densities to be fundamental properties of points, then it immediately follows that they are intrinsic to points. Why is it that if one takes masses of regions to be fundamental, then mass-densities are not intrinsic to points? Well, if one takes masses of regions to be fundamental, then one can define the mass-density of a point as the limit (that is, the number to which one gets closer and closer) of the mass divided by the volume of a sequence of regions that converges to the point in question. But this does not make the mass-density of that point an *intrinsic* property of that point. The only fundamental mass property of a point, after all, is just that it has mass zero. The way we just defined the mass density of a point means that it is determined by the masses of smaller and smaller regions that converge towards that point. So the fundamental mass properties of the parts of any open neighbourhood of the point determine the mass density of the point, but the fundamental mass property just of the point itself is simply that it has mass 0, which clearly does not determine the mass density of the point.

What about separability on the mass-density view? If one takes mass-density ratios, or mass-density betweenness and mass-density addition as fundamental, then of course, separability fails, and neighbourhood separability fails in the same circumstances that it fails for mass ratios and massbetweenness and massaddition. But if one takes mass-density values to be fundamental then the mass structure of the world is indeed separable.

The upshot is that there is only one way to have it that the mass structure of the world is separable: namely, to assume that for point particles mass values are fundamental, and for extended particles mass-densities are fundamental. I am inclined to think that this is an implausible view, because the fundamental facts then consist of relations to numbers and 'units', where, in order to avoid non-separability, these 'units', whatever they are, cannot have spatiotemporal locations. But even if one does not baulk at such fundamental relations, we will later find other reasons to believe that classical worlds are not separable.

How about other properties of classical particles, such as charge? *Prima facie* charge does not bring up any significant new issues, for it seems that one faces exactly the same issues as with masses: namely, charges versus charge densities, and charge values versus charge ratios versus chargebetweenness and chargeaddition. However, there is a further issue that is more readily brought out in the case of charge than in the case of mass: namely, the issue of global symmetry and separability.

Suppose that the laws of our world are invariant under a flipping of the sign of all charges in the history of the world. One can take two attitudes towards this fact. One attitude is that despite this remarkable symmetry, nonetheless our world would have been different had all the charges had the opposite sign. The other attitude is that this symmetry indicates that things could not have been different in the manner just described; that is, that a 'charged flipped world' is not really a distinct possibility, a distinct 'possible world'. Rather, the locution 'the charge flipped world' is a somewhat confusing locution which picks out none other than the actual world. Now, this issue—the issue as to whether we should take certain invariances of our laws to indicate that certain putative differences are not real differences—is an issue that will recur in this book. And I will discuss it *ad nauseam* in other places (especially in Chapters 5 and 6). However, in this chapter I do not want to discuss whether or not a global charge flip produces a distinct possibility—a distinct possible world. Even less do I want to discuss whether there is a determinate fact as to whether it produces a distinct possible world. In this chapter I want to focus on separability, and I want to keep other issues, as much as I can, at bay. So, what I will now discuss is what we should conclude regarding the separability of the charge structure of the world *on the assumption* that a global charge flip does *not* produce a genuinely distinct possible world.

If one were to take the view that charge values are fundamental, then, *prima facie*, a global charge flip must produce a distinct possible world, since it changes the charge values of every object that has non-zero charge. But if one were to take the view, say, that charge ratios are fundamental (and that they are all the fundamental charge properties/relations that there are), then a global charge flip does not produce a distinct possible world, for charge ratios are invariant under global charge flips. Indeed, one cannot really make sense of the notion of a global charge flip if one takes charge ratios to be fundamental.[8] So it would seem that if one maintains that global charge flips do not produce distinct possible worlds, then one cannot take charge values to be one's fundamental quantities; one has to assume some fundamental charge properties/relations which are not intrinsic to points, thus making the charge structure of the world non-separable. So it would seem that if a global charge flip does not produce a distinct possible world, then the charge structure of the world cannot be separable.

But is that really right? No. One has to go to some lengths—lengths that some might consider implausible—but one can maintain that charge values are fundamental, that the charge structure of the world is separable, and deny that a global charge flip produces a distinct possible world. In particular, one can maintain that every distinct distribution of charge values corresponds to a distinct possible world, except that charge distributions that are related by a global charge flip correspond to the same possible world.

Prima facie, this does not seem a coherent position. How on earth can one maintain that charge values are fundamental while claiming that a transformation that changes *all* charge values leaves the total state the same? Surely this is just incoherent. If flipping the charge of *one* particle changes the state of that particle, and hence changes the state of the world, then surely changing the state of all particles, by flipping the charges of all particles, must, *a fortiori*, change the state of the world. As compelling as this argument may seem, one can wriggle out of it.

First let me simplify matters by supposing that every elementary particle in the actual world either has charge +1 (relative to some unit) or −1. (So, on the charge-ratio view, all charge ratios are +1 or −1.) The way in which to defend the view that charge values are fundamental against the apparently compelling argument is to claim that there are no facts about identity of charge values across possible worlds. For instance, take the actual distribution of charge values in our world, and imagine flipping the charge of one solitary particle X, where X has charge +1 in the actual world. This produces a distinct possible world. But the idea now is that there is no fact of the matter whether in this distinct possible world particle X has charge −1 (and every other particle has the same charge as in the actual world) or particle X has charge +1 (and every other particle has the opposite charge as in the actual world). So, flipping the charge of one particle does change the state of the world (and it changes the state of the world in exactly same way as flipping the charge of all the other particles), but flipping the charge of all particles does not change the state of the world. In each possible world the charge structure corresponds to a division of all elementary particles into two sets. In the actual world we have conventionally called the one set the charge=+1 set, and the other one the charge=−1 set. But there are no facts about cross-world identity of

---

[8] On the charge ratio view one can make sense of non-global charge flips—the flipping of some, but not all, charges. But there is no fact of the matter as to which charges are flipped and which stay the same.

the sets in question. For any non-actual possible world there is no fact of the matter as to which of the two sets in that world is the '+1 set', and which is the '−1 set.'

The above does not mean that there could not be an 'identity of charge sets' relation between pairs of worlds, which, for example, could be relevant in determining the truth values of counterfactuals. Consider, for instance, a possible history of some spacetime region which is very similar to the actual history of some spacetime region. There are a large number of particles which start out in exactly the same position configuration as in the actual spacetime region, and after that the positions evolve exactly as if all charges are the same as in the actual situation except for one particle which behaves as if it has the opposite charge from what it has in the actual world. Moreover, the two charge sets in that possible history differ only from the charge sets in the actual history by the addition/subtraction of that one particle. In that case one could use the similarity of the histories to identify each charge set in the actual situation with the charge set in the possible situation which differs only by this one particle (rather than with the charge set that differs in all but that one particle.)

It is important to note a couple of features of this cross-world 'identity of charge set' relation. In the first place, if two worlds are very different then presumably no cross-world 'identity of charge set' relation will hold. In the second place, the relation will not be transitive. For it is extremely plausible that one can find a sequence of possible situations, starting and ending with some actual situation S, such that following the 'identity of charge set' relation as one goes through the sequence, if one starts with the +1 charge set in S, one ends up with the −1 charge set in S.[9] Most importantly, one can therefore not use this relation in order to divide all charges in all possible worlds into two sets, the '+1' set and the '−1' set. Let me now discuss a couple of objections that one might raise against this view.

First objection. The view that charge values are fundamental combined with the view that a global charge flip does not change the state of the world just is the same as the charge ratio view: denying cross-world identity of charge properties while accepting cross-world identity of charge ratios amounts to adopting the charge ratio view. Response: no it does not. If charge values are fundamental then certain sets of objects are fundamental (perfectly natural), but if charge ratios are fundamental then certain sets *of ordered pairs of objects* are fundamental (perfectly natural). Those are different options. It is true that the charge ratio relations determine uniquely a partition into two sets corresponding to two different charge values, and vice versa. But there is still a difference between the two views. For one thing, on the charge value view the charge state of the world is separable, and on the charge-ratio view it is not.

Second objection. The view that charge values are fundamental combined with the view that a global charge flip does not change the state of the world has as a consequence that there is no fact of the matter as to whether or not particles in different

---

[9] It may additionally be the case that the relation is vague and context-dependent. It might also have been better to call it a 'similarity of charge set relation'.

possible worlds are duplicates of each other. This means that there is no fact of the matter as to what the intrinsic properties of objects are, and hence that there is no fact of the matter as to whether or not the state of the world is separable. Response: there is a fact of the matter as to whether or not objects in the same possible world are duplicates; moreover, the fundamental properties are, by fiat, intrinsic to the objects of which they are properties, and hence the charge state of the world is separable according to the charge-value view. It may seem strange to maintain that charge values are fundamental and yet maintain that there is never a fact of the matter as to whether or not particles in different possible worlds have the same charge value. However, such non-factualism regarding fundamental property identity across possible worlds must occur as soon as one allows that some redistributions of fundamental properties across objects do not generate distinct possible worlds. So, the view that charge values are fundamental and that a global charge flip does not produce a distinct possible world is neither incoherent, nor identical to the charge-ratio view.

However, I do not wish to defend the charge-value view. Far from it. In fact, my view is that it is a mistake to derive conclusions as to what the fundamental properties and relations are from intuitions about the 'genuine distinctness' of certain putative metaphysical possibilities. Making such inferences, it seems to me, is akin to having the tail wag the dog. Rather, based on the issues discussed so far I would be inclined to conclude that the mass and charge structure of a classical particle world is not separable, because I like the austerity and simplicity of having betweenness and addition as fundamental relations. But this is only a mild, subjective, preference at this point: I will develop more compelling arguments against the separability of classical states by considering other features of classical worlds: in particular, vector-field features. As a warm-up, let us consider particle velocities.

2.4 Are velocities intrinsic to spacetime points?

For most of this section I will be, for reasons of simplicity and convenience, talk about velocities as they occur in Newtonian physics, not as they occur in relativistic physics. This will not matter, since everything I say carries over to relativistic physics. However, towards the end of this section certain differences between Newtonian physics and relativistic physics will matter. At that point I will introduce relativistic physics explicitly.

Let us start with point particles. Velocities of point particles, as standardly conceived, are not intrinsic to spacetime points. On the standard conception of velocities, they are defined in terms of rates of change of position. To be precise, the velocity $v(t)$ of some particle at some time t is standardly defined as $v(t)=\lim(x(t+dt)-x(t))/dt$, where one takes the limit as the time interval dt goes to 0. This means that the velocity at a time t is determined by the position development in any open neighbourhood of t, but not by the position at instant t alone. Thus, given the standard definition of velocities, point-particle velocities are not intrinsic to spacetime points. OK, but is it worrying for Lewis's view if point-particle velocities are not point-local qualities?

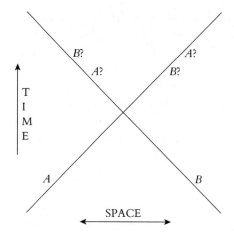

Figure 2.1 Point particle coincidence.

Prima facie, it would seem not. Lewis just maintains that the distribution of all point-local features in spacetime determines all features of the world; he does not maintain that every feature of the world is point-local. And while velocities may not be point-local, surely the distribution of positions at all times will still determine the velocities at all times. For, surely, the position distributions at all times determine a unique set of spacetime trajectories, and these in turn, surely, determine the velocities at all times.

Unfortunately, this is not so. In the first place, if a trajectory is not continuous, or not differentiable, then there is no well-defined velocity where it is not continuous or not differentiable. This, of course, is no problem for Lewis; if there is no well-defined velocity then there is no well-defined velocity. More worrying for Lewis is the following case: two point particles which encounter each other at a point in a two-dimensional spacetime (see Figure 1).

The worry here is that the position distribution in spacetime does not determine whether the two particles bounced off each other or passed through each other, and hence does not determine the velocities of the particles at the point where the two lines intersect.

Here is a similar problem involving an extended homogenous object in a two-dimensional Newtonian spacetime. Suppose we have an homogeneous object in the shape of a pencil (see Figure 2.) Now consider a point p in space inside the pencil: there will be a finite time interval during which the intrinsic properties instantiated near that point do not change. Indeed, it should be clear that for some spacetime points the position distribution in even a fairly large open neighbourhood of that spacetime point could not possibly determine a unique velocity at that spacetime point. If there is to be a velocity in the interior of the pencil that is determined by the position distribution in spacetime, then it has to be determined by extremely non-local features of that spacetime.

Yet another example would be that of an homogeneous solid sphere in a three-dimensional space which does not interact with anything and rotates at a constant rate

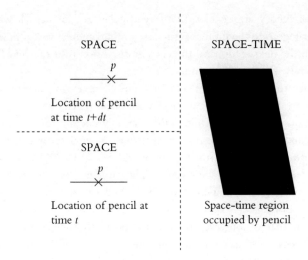

Figure 2.2 Pencil in motion.

through all of history. In this case the position distribution in the universe would have been the same had the sphere never rotated; indeed, it would have been the same no matter which axis it was rotating around, no matter at which speed. So the position distribution throughout all of history everywhere cannot determine unique velocities anywhere in the sphere.[10]

One might object to all of these examples that they are not realistic: point particles surely never meet at an exact point, and extended homogeneous matter surely does not exist, let alone in the shape of a perfect sphere. And why infer anything about the separability of the actual world from non-actual examples? Well, I grant you that the actual world is not classical, let alone that it contains classical point particles meeting at spacetime points, or extended homogeneous classical matter in the shape of an exact sphere. But much of this book—indeed much of just about *any* book about the foundations of physics—consists of investigating theories which we have good reason to believe to be false. It seems intrinsically interesting (to me at least) to investigate what the world would be like if certain theories were true, even if I have good reason to believe that they are not true. This is especially so for a theory which at some time was one of our best theories, or a theory such that one of our current best theories bears some structural similarity to it, or when we have reason to believe that certain

[10] If one becomes more realistic about the physics of spinning spheres one finds that there are certain features (such as oblateness due to rotation induced stresses) that distinguish spinning from non-spinning disks, and one might try to wriggle out of the problem by making use of these features in order to derive velocities from point-local features. However, one can block this way out by considering the question whether two spheres are rotating in the same or in the opposite direction around the same axis with the same angular speed. For more details, see Butterfield (2004). One can also consider an infinitely long pencil moving with different possible velocities in the direction in which it is lined up, so that it always occupies the same region in space.

aspects of the theory are correct. In the particular case of particle velocities, the problem is analogous to the more realistic case of fundamental vector fields, which we will discuss in the next section. So the current discussion is, at the very least, a useful warm-up exercise for the next section.

Let us return to the problem of velocities. There are several ways to maintain that the state of the world is separable in the face of the above examples.

In the first place one could maintain that the only relevant fundamental properties are positions, and that velocities, in so far as they exist, are determined by the position distribution throughout the history of the world. See Sider (2001), Chapter 6, Section 5, for a defence of such a view. One might wonder why Sider is even interested in non-fundamental, non-point-local, velocities. Well, he wants to talk about velocities for the same reason that all of us do: velocities are extremely useful when describing the phenomena that we observe, and, more importantly, they figure prominently in the laws of physics. So let us see what sense Sider can make of the velocities of objects. For non-colliding point particles he can, of course, define velocities as the temporal derivative of the position development. But how about velocities at meetings of point particles, velocities in the interior of homogeneous pencils, and velocities of rotating homogeneous spheres? Sider's basic idea is as follows. The velocities of such objects are determined, in so far as they are determinate, by the rule that their velocities should satisfy the same simple laws that the velocities of all other objects satisfy. Velocities should satisfy simple, plausible, laws, and velocities are determinate in so far as that demand fixes them uniquely. For instance, consider a solid uniform sphere that has not interacted with anything until it collides with another object, whereupon it breaks into parts which fly off exactly as if the sphere had previously been rotating (around a particular axis at a particular speed). In that case, on Sider's view it is correct to say that the sphere (and all of its parts) had the corresponding rotational velocities at all times prior to its collision. Of course, this makes velocities highly non-intrinsic. And it means that if there is a sphere which throughout the course of history does not interact with any other object, there is no fact of the matter regarding the velocity of it or any of its parts.

I do not like Sider's view. Suppose we were to discover that in fact there are homogeneous classical spheres in our world. Suppose that when such spheres interact they always interact as if they have a well-defined rotational velocity. Then suppose we find a sphere which, for all we know, has never interacted with anything else, and will never interact with anything else. I doubt that anybody would respond with the thought, 'Hm, that's interesting, this sphere may have no well-defined rotational velocity.' I submit that almost all of us would be thinking, 'Hm, this sphere has some well-defined rotational velocity, but we may never find out what it is; indeed, there may be no evidence available whatsoever as to what it is.' OK, so this is how we would react, but is that an argument? I think it is. We prefer, other things being equal, simpler theories—theories whose laws are simple in terms of the fundamental quantities that the theory postulates. Velocities are not fundamental in Sider's theory. But he wants to talk of velocities exactly because the laws are simple in terms of them. Unfortunately, the laws are not simple in terms of the fundamental quantities that he admits: positions. In terms of his fundamental quantities the laws are something like this: those position distributions are allowed which are compatible (in a sense that can be spelled out) with an assignment of velocities such that the velocities (and terms definable in terms of them such as accelerations) are part of simple laws. But such laws are patently not simple or natural—at least not in the sense that is relevant to figuring out how plausible they are.

In the second place one might take the view that velocities are well-defined at all occupied points in spacetime, even in the case of eternally isolated homogeneous spheres, since everything is made up of point particles whose identities determine unique trajectories which always have unique temporal derivatives (tangents). The idea here is that if extended objects such as solid spheres behave as if they have well-defined rotational velocities when they interact with other objects, then the best explanation of this behaviour is that extended objects are composed out of point particles whose trajectories determine unique velocities. On this view there is more to the history of the world than just a list of which spacetime points are occupied (and more than just a list of mass, charge . . . features of the spacetime points) since the intrinsic features of any point include *which* particle is occupying that point. On this view, for example, there could be a fundamental relation between point particles and locations in space-time which determines which spacetime regions (time-like lines) are trajectories of point particles and which are not. If one additionally (axiomatically) assumes that the set of points occupied by a point particle always forms a differentiable (and time-like) trajectory in spacetime which does not overlap with any other such trajectory and assumes that the set of all trajectories fills all of the occupied regions in spacetime, then there will be a unique velocity associated with each occupied spacetime point. Of course, the velocities will not be intrinsic features of the points, but they will be neighbourhood local; that is, determined by the fundamental features of any open neighbourhood of the point in question.

I should perhaps say a bit more about how this view relates to a view that is called 'three-dimensionalism' in philosophy, which will also bring out how subtle the issue is as to whether the state of the world is separable. Let us start on this enterprise by contemplating the question as to whether a point particle such as A has a part which exists only at an instant, a 'temporal part', or 'temporal stage' of A. If one is not used to these kinds of philosophical questions one might not be entirely sure what question is asked here, and one might have a feeling that one has started to engage on a somewhat unclear, perhaps even meaningless, game when one starts answering such questions. But let us set such feelings aside and see where the game leads. It seems fairly natural and innocent to answer our question with 'sure, all point particles such as A do have temporal parts, such as A-at-*t*, which exist only at an instant such as *t*.' The next seemingly innocent question then is: 'Suppose we have a bunch of distinct non-overlapping objects, is there now an object, however weird and scattered, that is composed exactly of these objects?' Again, aside from the feeling that one is playing a stupid game, a fairly natural and innocent answer is 'sure, any collection of distinct non-overlapping objects composes another object.' But if one gives these two answers, then the view that homogeneous spheres have unique rotational velocities appears to be in trouble. For if there is a bunch of point particles composing the sphere, whose trajectories determine the velocity of each spacetime point in the sphere's history, then we can construct 'new' objects, 'new' point particles, from the temporal stages of the original point particles, where the velocities of the new point particles will be quite different from the original set, so that we no longer have unique velocities. (Just 'rethread' the history of the sphere with trajectories in any way you please, and you will see that the new 'threads' are composable from the temporal stages of the point particles with which one started.) While it is not completely clear what the view called 'three-dimensionalism' exactly is (for more on this see Sider (2001), Chapter 3), there is a natural response to the above problem that is in the spirit of three-dimensionalism: namely, denying that point particles have temporal parts. Another, closely related, response would be admitting that they do have temporal parts, and admitting that these temporal parts can be composed to form other objects with other trajectories, but denying that these objects are equally natural; that is, maintaining that there is some further fundamental feature that distinguishes 'gerrymandered' objects from 'natural' objects, which serves to distinguish the 'true, causally relevant' velocities from the 'fake, impostor' velocities. Yet another closely related response would be to maintain that there is a fundamental (equivalence) relation—call it 'genidentity'—between occupied spacetime points which picks out unique trajectories which fill all occupied spacetime regions. Now notice that according to the first response the state of the world is separable, but on the second and third responses it is not. For the second response assumes the existence of a fundamental property of *extended* (that is, not point-local) objects—namely, being 'gerrymandered' or not—which is not determined by the point-local fundamental features of the extended object in question. And the third response assumes the existence of a fundamental relation between distinct spacetime points: namely, the 'genidentity' relation. Now I have no desire to enter into detailed consideration as to whether these three responses are genuinely distinct responses, and if so, which is the most plausible. As I said, this section is mainly supposed to be a warm-up exercise for the main argument against separability that will come in the next section. I will here content myself with pointing out that there is a *prima facie* coherent way of reconciling well-defined unique velocities with a separable world along the lines of three-dimensionalism.

In the third place one might claim that every occupied point has a fundamental, hence intrinsic, property: namely, an 'intrinsic velocity'. This property is not defined as the temporal derivative of a position development; it is not defined as the tangent to some trajectory. No, intrinsic velocities are just further fundamental features of the world, which are instantiated at occupied spacetime points.[11] This, in fact, is the view that David Lewis himself favored. Let me present three objections to this view.

In the first place, it seems that intrinsic velocities are bizarre, because they raise the spectre of two distinct metaphysically possible worlds with the same trajectories, where in one world the intrinsic velocities are 'lined up' with the ordinary velocities (the tangents to the trajectories), and in the other world they are not. But why admit such bizarre possibilities? As you might expect, I find this objection somewhat unpersuasive. Intuitions about distinctness of possibilities surely are no guide to the fundamental furniture of the universe: the proper epistemological route is from phenomena to simple theories, with certain fundamental quantities, to metaphysical possibilities, not the other way round.

So let me turn to a second objection. It seems unnecessarily profligate to have intrinsic velocities, because, at the very least in the case of point particles, there is no need to postulate the existence of intrinsic velocities, and, other things being equal, simpler theories with fewer fundamental quantities are preferable.

Now let me turn to a third objection to intrinsic velocities. Intrinsic velocities would be otiose if there were no (causal) connection between them and other features of the world. The obvious connection to postulate is that at any time any point particle moves in the direction that its intrinsic velocity points with a speed that corresponds to the magnitude of its intrinsic velocity, and more generally that objects behave exactly as if they are composed of point particles which have ordinary velocities equal (in direction and magnitude) to their intrinsic velocities. The most natural way to formulate such a theory would be to assume that there is a fundamental relation of 'Sameness of direction and magnitude'—'Sameness' for short—between intrinsic velocities and ordinary velocities, and then assume a law which says that particle trajectories are such that their intrinsic velocities and their ordinary velocities are always The Same. However, since ordinary velocities are neighbourhood local quantities, this notion of Sameness would be a fundamental neighbourhood local relation, so that one would need a fundamental neighbourhood local relation after all. (Whether one considers Sameness a geometrical relation or a non-geometrical relation is in my view a moot issue. I will return to this question later in this section.)

Next, let us ask what the relata of the Sameness relation would be. That depends a bit on how one conceives of intrinsic velocities. One could think of intrinsic velocities as properties of particles at points, subject to certain (vector) axioms. Or one could think of them as objects—for example, points in an additional space, the 'intrinsic velocity space', where this space has a structure given by certain (vector-space) axioms. If they are the latter, then Sameness could be thought of as a fundamental relation between points in the intrinsic velocity space, spacetime points p, and trajectories in a

---

[11] A version of this view would be that the intrinsic state of an object at a time is given by a (canonical) position q and a (canonical) momentum p. The laws of dynamics would be Hamilton's equations: $\partial H/\partial q_i = -dp_i/dt$ and $\partial H/\partial p_i = dq_i/dt$. The second of these equations should be understood as a dynamical law rather than a definition of the canonical momentum.

neighbourhood of p. If they are the former, one could think of Sameness as a fundamental (higher-order) relation between intrinsic velocities, spacetime points p, and
trajectories in a neighbourhood of p. Either way, we have a predicate (. . . is The Same
as . . . at . . .') which takes intrinsic velocities as one of its arguments. So we have committed ourselves to the existence of further entities—namely, intrinsic velocities (whether
you call them properties, or points in a space), which, other things being equal, is
a mark against a theory. (Note that my second objection and my third objection are
not identical. The second objection was an objection to the addition of unnecessary
elements to our ideology—that is, to our catalogue of fundamental predicates—while
the current objection is an objection to the addition of unnecessary elements to our
ontology; that is, the things that we quantify over and to which our fundamental predicates apply.)

However, this third objection is not quite watertight. While it is true that the most
obvious way to formulate dynamical laws will involve a fundamental relation of
'Sameness' between intrinsic velocities and ordinary velocities, one does not have
to use such a relation. One could simply assume a law which says that the intrinsic
velocities are such that for any pair of points x and y at which there are well-defined
ordinary velocities the ratio of the magnitudes of the ordinary velocities at x and y
equals the ratio of the magnitudes of the intrinsic velocities at x and y, and the angle
between the ordinary velocities at x and y equals the angle between the intrinsic
velocities at x and y. And then one can go on to give the usual laws that govern forces
and accelerations. The idea here is that one does not need a fundamental notion of
Sameness: as long as intrinsic velocities and ordinary velocities are correlated in the
right way one can state laws that are empirically equivalent to the usual laws. Indeed
so. However, notice that the demand that there is such a correlation is just the demand
that there is a vector-space isomorphism between the vector-space structure of the
ordinary velocities (at each spacetime point p) and the vector-space structure of the
intrinsic velocities (which respects the sameness of ordinary velocities at different locations in spacetime). And that means that, yet again, we have to quantify over, and have
predicates applying to, intrinsic velocities. That is to say, once again we are committed
to the existence of intrinsic velocities (whether conceived of as properties or as locations in 'intrinsic velocity space').

Matters become even worse when we consider velocities in Special and General
Relativity. In Special Relativity there is no frame-independent notion of temporal
and spatial distances, and there is no identity of locations across time, so there is no
coordinate-independent notion of the rate of change of spatial location. However,
there is still a coordinate-independent notion of the ordinary velocity of a point
particle at some point on its world-line: namely, its so-called '4-velocity', which is a
vector tangent to the world-line of the point-particle at the given point. (It is called
it a 4-velocity because it is a vector in a *four*-dimensional space.) It can be defined
in the following manner. (We will see a slightly more modern and abstract notion of
4-velocities in the next section.) Take a world-line in spacetime. Imagine that a perfect

clock traveled along this world-line and that it labeled all the points on this world-line with the time that it indicated at each point. Of course, it is arbitrary when the clock happens to read 0. But that is OK, since we are going to use this labeling in such a way that it does not matter where it reads 0. The only thing that is going to matter is that the labels indicate the spacetime distance (the spacetime interval) between any two points on the world-line, as measured along the world-line. We call such a labeling a 'parameterization by proper time'. Given such a parameterization, one can define the spacetime tangent to a world-line at a point on the world-line to be the spacetime vector whose direction indicates the direction in which the world-line is pointed at that point, and whose magnitude corresponds to the rate at which it is going in that direction according to the proper time parameterization.[12] Of course, thus defined, the 4-velocity at a point is not intrinsic to a point, since it involves taking limits in a neighbourhood of that point.

One can define 4-velocities in General Relativity in the same way. One has to be a bit careful, though, as to how one pictures them. One should not picture them as arrows lying within spacetime. There are several reasons not to do so. In the first place, the arrows would have to be 'bent' if one pictured them as lying in a curved spacetime. Secondly, if they were confined to a curved spacetime, it would not seem to make any sense to 'add up' two different 4-velocities.[13] But it does make sense to add up 4-velocities (since one can add up the relevant directional derivatives). Thirdly, 4-velocities are quantities which, though not point-local, are nonetheless extremely local: namely, neighbourhood-local. Hence it is wrong to think of them as extended over finite distances in spacetime. One should picture 4-velocities as lying in a flat space outside spacetime that is tangent to spacetime at the point in question: the 'tangent space' (see Figure 2.3).

Now consider 4-velocities in a curved space. Does it make sense to ask whether two 4-velocities at two different locations are parallel; that is, are they pointing in the same direction, and does it make sense to ask what angle there is between them? It does not. Consider a tangent vector at a point p on the equator of a sphere, where that tangent vector is pointed in the direction of the North Pole (see Figure 2.4).

Now imagine dragging it around the equator to point q, and then dragging it south to the South Pole, all the while making sure not to change the direction in which it

---

[12] In coordinate system (t, x, y, z) the components of a 4-velocity v are $(dt/d\tau, dx/d\tau, dy/d\tau, dz/d\tau)$, where τ is the proper time parameterization of the world-line in question. The (invariant) magnitude of a 4-velocity v according to relativity theory is $g(v,v)$, where g is the metric tensor. This magnitude is always -1. Note that this notion of magnitude is different from our pictorial idea of the magnitude of a vector. For in order to compute the magnitude of a 4-vector in a given frame of reference (in relativity theory), one has to *subtract* (not add) the square of the first component of the 4-vector from the sum of the squares of the last three components.

[13] Adding up of vectors can be pictured as putting the tail of one vector at the tip of the other vector, which produces a vector from the tail of the first vector to the tip of the second vector. However, if vectors are curved entities lying in a curved space, it will typically not be possible to put them tip to tail while retaining the curved shape of the vector that one is moving. And that means that it is not entirely clear what it would be to add such vectors.

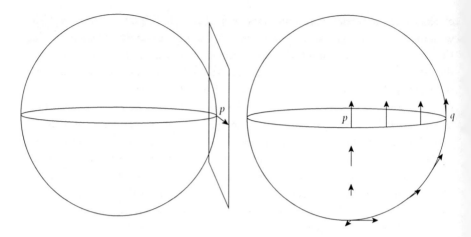

Figure 2.3 Tangent space.

Figure 2.4 Parallelhood in curved space.

is pointed. One will then end up with a tangent vector at the South Pole that points in the direction of the shortest path from the South Pole to q. However, had one instead dragged this tangent vector directly to the South Pole from p, while making sure not to change the direction in which it is pointed, one would have ended up with a different tangent vector at the South Pole—one that points in the direction of the shortest path from the South Pole to p. Therefore it does not make sense to ask which of those two tangent vectors at the South Pole is 'really parallel' to the tangent vector that we started with at p, nor does it make sense to ask what the angle is between them.

According to General Relativity, as in the above example, it does make sense to ask whether, as one 'drags' a tangent vector along a (smooth) path, this tangent vector changes its direction or remains parallel. Spacetime, according to General Relativity, includes a structure that determines what it is for a vector to be 'parallel transported' along a path. In general, when one parallel transports a given tangent vector from one point to another, which tangent vector one ends up with depends on the path that one takes. That is why according to General Relativity there is no path-independent notion of parallelism of tangent vectors at different locations. The structure that determines what it is for a tangent vector to be parallel transported along a path is known as a 'connection': for any tangent vector at any point and any direction, the connection determines what happens to that tangent vector as one parallel transports it in that direction. Of course, since it tells one how nearby tangent spaces are connected, the connection at a point is not intrinsic to a point, but it is intrinsic to arbitrarily small open neighbourhoods. In Chapter 6 I will explain in more detail what connections are, and what the most plausible fundamental structure is of spaces that include such connections. For now the most important fact is that in General Relativity, no path-independent sense can be made of the angle between ordinary velocities at different locations. Therefore, even if one assumes the existence of point-local intrinsic velocities, one will still not be able to formulate a satisfactory theory according to which the non-geometrical state of the world is separable. One can of course postulate that the structure of all intrinsic velocities at all locations in spacetime includes a parallel transport structure which is isomorphic to that of the parallel transport structure of all ordinary velocities at all points in spacetime. However, it should by now be patently obvious that if one does so one is adding an ugly, and in normal cases unnecessary, layer of structure to ones theory, and in so doing one is committed to the existence of additional entities, intrinsic velocities, which, other things being equal, one would think implausible.

Finally, let me turn to another issue that is brought up by the discussion in this section. Lewis made a distinction between the geometrical structure of the world, which he claimed to be non-separable, and the non-geometrical structure of the world which he claimed to be separable (at least in the non-quantum mechanical case). One might now try to save Lewis's claims by accepting that there is a fundamental relation of 'Sameness' between intrinsic velocities and ordinary velocities, which is neighbourhood-local rather than point-local, and then claim that this is no problem for Lewis's view since this 'Sameness' is a geometrical relation. This raises the issue as to what counts as a geometrical relation and what counts as a non-geometrical relation. For instance, if Sameness of intrinsic velocities and ordinary velocities counts as a geometrical relation, then how about mass ratios, or massbetweenness and massaddition? In Chapter 8 the view will be presented that one should regard massbetweenness and massaddition as relations that hold between points in 'mass-space', where this mass-space is just as real and physical a space as spacetime is. Does that mean that these mass relations are geometrical relations? I am not quite sure how one might argue for or against this view. More importantly, it seems to me that, at the very least with respect to the issue of separability, it is pointless to try to find some totally precise way of distinguishing between geometrical and non-geometrical relations. We have found, and will find, reasons to believe that classical worlds are not separable. But it seems to be to be a useless exercise to try to find a division into geometrical and non-geometrical structure which makes the non-geometrical structure separable.

The upshot of the current section is that the most promising way to defend the claim that the non-geometrical structure of classical worlds which include homogeneous objects is separable, is a 'three-dimensional' view according to which such homogeneous objects decompose in a unique way into point-particles which do not have temporal parts.

2.5 How separable are the properties of classical fields?

In this section I will be talking about classical fields in relativistic spacetimes. The restriction to relativistic spacetimes is for convenience only; the conclusions of this section would be no different if I also discussed classical fields in Newtonian or neo-Newtonian spacetimes.

All classical fields are 'tensor fields', which here are taken to include 'scalar fields' and 'vector fields'. I will explain what these terms mean as we go along. Before that, let me note that what I just said is not quite true. There are also classical gauge fields and classical spinor fields. I will discuss classical gauge fields in Chapter 5. With respect to separability, spinor fields are not relevantly different from gauge fields, so I will set them aside.[14] OK, let us get on with business.

A scalar field is a field whose state can be represented by a single real number for each point in spacetime. For instance, mass-density can be thought of as a scalar field, since the mass-densities of extended objects can be represented by numbers representing the mass-density at each point in spacetime. One could also think of temperature as a scalar field. And one can assume the existence of other scalar fields that are spread throughout the universe and can interact with material objects and other scalar fields. So, if one is willing to accept that mass-density values are intrinsic properties of space-time points, then one can accept that scalar field values are intrinsic properties of spacetime points, so that the structure of scalar fields is separable.

Matters, however, are not so simple when it comes to vector fields. A vector field (in spacetime) is a set of 4-vectors—one 4-vector for each point in spacetime. (Normally, the vectors are assumed to vary 'smoothly' across spacetime.) We have just seen an example of a 4-vector: namely, the 4-velocity of a particle. We defined the 4-velocity of a particle at a point on its worldline as the tangent to its worldline at that point (where we parameterize the worldline by proper time). But the 4-vectors that make up vector fields are not tangents to worldlines. So what are the 4-vectors that make up vector fields?

Here is a standard definition: a 4-vector v_p at spacetime point p is a map from smooth scalar functions (on spacetime) to real numbers, which satisfies the following constraints for all smooth scalar functions f and g and all real numbers α:

1) $v_p(f+g)=v_p(f)+v_p(g)$
2) $v_p(\alpha f)=\alpha v_p(f)$
3) $v_p(fg)=f(p)v_p(g)+g(p)v_p(f)$

Let us see, intuitively speaking, why a map satisfying these constraints can be understood to be a 4-vector. Let us begin with the notion of a 'directional derivative'. Suppose one has a scalar function f on a spacetime. Then one can pick a point x in that spacetime—a direction d pointing away from x, and a rate r—and ask the question: what is the rate of change of the function f if one starts at x and then travels away from x in direction d at rate r? The answer to that question is the 'directional derivative' of the function f in that direction at that rate. Note that a directional derivative has a

---

[14] In General Relativity, spinor fields are akin to gauge fields, in that they can be taken to correspond to a section of a particular 'fibre bundle'. See Wald (1984), Chapter 13.

magnitude as well as a direction: in order for there to be a well-defined answer to the question 'what is the rate of change of the function in that direction?', one needs to specify the rate at which one is moving in that direction, and that rate is a single, real-number-valued, magnitude. Thus, intuitively, a directional derivative at a point corresponds to a vector at that point. Now, a directional derivative at a point is a map from scalar functions to real numbers that in fact satisfies the above three constraints. (That it satisfies the first two constraints should be pretty intuitive even if you have never done calculus. The third constraint amounts to the product rule for differentiation of functions.) The converse—the claim that anything that satisfies the above three constraints corresponds to a directional derivative at p—is less obvious. Here is a sketch of a proof (but feel free to skip this).

Let x^1, x^2, x^3, x^4 be coordinate functions in an open neighbourhood of p. Let f be an arbitrary smooth function from spacetime to the real numbers. By 'Taylor's formula with remainder' (see any calculus textbook) there exist functions g_i such that

$$f(x)=f(p)+\Sigma(\partial f/\partial x^i)(p).(x^i-p^i)+\Sigma g^i(x).(x^i-p^i)$$

Here p^i are the coordinates of point p, and the summations are over i from 1 to 4. Notice that the value of the last term is 0 at when $x=p$. It is easy to show that $v_p(f)=0$ if f is a constant function, and that $v_p(fg)=0$ if $f(p)=0$ and $g(p)=0$. Now

$$v_p f=v_p \ (f(p))+\Sigma(v_p(\partial f/\partial x^i(p).(x^i-p^i)+v_p(g^i(x).(x^i-p^i))$$

So

$$v_p f=0+\Sigma(\partial f/\partial x^i(p).(v_p(x^i)-v_p(p^i))+0$$

Let us now define $v_p(x^i)=v_p^i$, and call these 'the components of v_p relative to coordinates x^i'. We then have

$$v_p f=\Sigma v_p^i \partial f/\partial x^i(p)$$

That is to say, when we apply a map v_p satisfying the above three constraints to a function f, this is equivalent to taking the directional derivative of f at point p, where the directional derivative has components v_p^i relative to coordinates x^1, x^2, x^3, x^4.

So there is a 1–1 correspondence between things that satisfy the three constraints, and directional derivatives. That is why one can take satisfaction of the above three constraints as a definition of what it is to be a 4-vector.[15]

Now, such a map v_p needs as its 'input' the behavior of a function f in a *neighbourhood* of p. Intuitively this is clear, for the value of a function at a point does not suffice to determine the directional derivative of the function at that point. More formally, it is

---

[15] It would be nice if tangents to worldlines also counted as 4-vectors according to this definition. They do. Here is how one defines the tangent to a curve in such a way that it is a 4-vector by this definition. Consider a curve $\gamma(t)$. Then define its tangent at a point to be the map that maps any function f to the value of $(d/dt)(f(\gamma(t))$ at that point.

easy to prove that any (non-null) map v_p from functions f to real numbers that satisfies the above three constraints cannot depend only on the value of the function f at point p. Here is the proof. Suppose that the map $v_p(f)$ only needed $f(p)$—that is, a single real number r, as its input—and satisfied all three constraints. By constraint 2 we have $v_p(\alpha r)=\alpha v_p(r)$. By constraint 3: $v_p(ff)=f(p)v_p(f)+f(p)v_p(f)$; that is, $v_p(rr)=rv_p(r)+rv_p(r)=2rv_p(r)$. But $v_p(rr)=rv_p(r)$, so we have a contradiction (unless $v_p(r)=0$ for all r, which is the null map). So it follows that a map v_p from functions to real numbers satisfying the above three constraints needs as its input more than just the value of the function at point p. A 4-vector at a point p is a relation between functions *in a neighbourhood of p* and real numbers. So a 4-vector v_p at a point p is *not* an intrinsic property of that point. It is a *neighbourhood-local* quantity. So the state of a vector field is neighbourhood-separable, but not point-separable.

Things are no better for the lover of locality when it comes to 'tensor fields'. What are tensor fields? Well, my account of tensor fields is going to be rather quick. Unless you have dealt with tensors before you will not derive much of an idea of what tensors are like from my account. However, my main point here is to argue that tensors are not intrinsic to points, which can be established in a quite cursory fashion.

Let me start by defining '1-forms'. A 1-form at a point p in spacetime is a linear map ω_p from 4-vectors at p to real numbers; that is, a map such that $\omega_p(\alpha v_p+\beta u_p)=\alpha\omega_p(v_p)+\beta\omega_p(u_p)$ for any real numbers α and β, and any vectors v_p and u_p. Given a set of coordinates (x, y, z, t), one can represent any spacetime vector v_p at a point p as a column of four numbers that indicate the magnitude of the vector in each of the coordinate directions:

$$\begin{pmatrix} v^1 \\ v^2 \\ v^3 \\ v^4 \end{pmatrix}$$

One can represent any 1-form ω_p by a row of four numbers $(\omega_1, \omega_2, \omega_3, \omega_4)$. The linear map ω_p from vectors v_p to numbers then corresponds to multiplication and addition of the numbers in the rows and columns; that is, the 1-form ω_p maps the vector v_p to the number $\omega_1 v^1+\omega_2 v^2+\omega_3 v^3+\omega_4 v^4$. Clearly this is a linear map. And it is not to hard to see that any linear map from vectors to numbers can be represented by such a row of four numbers. This gives us some idea of what 1-forms are. Now we can go on to define tensors.

A tensor at point p of type (m, n) is a map from m 1-forms at p and n vectors at p to real numbers, which is linear in each of the vectors and 1-forms. For instance, a tensor of type $(0,2)$ is a map T_p from pairs of vectors (u_p,v_p) to real numbers such that $T_p(\alpha u_p+\beta u'_p,\gamma v_p+\delta v'_p)=\alpha\gamma T_p(u_p,v_p)+\alpha\delta T_p(u_p,v'_p)+\beta\gamma T_p(u'_p,v_p)+\beta\delta T_p(u'_p,v'_p)$. In a given coordinate system one can represent such a tensor as a 4x4 matrix T_{ij}. The bilinear map from pairs of vectors to real numbers then corresponds to matrix multiplication: $\sum T_{ij}u^iv^j$. The so-called 'metric tensor' at a spacetime point p is a (symmetric and non-degenerate[16]) tensor g_p of type (0,2). The metric tensor field g; that is, the metric tensors g_p at all points p in spacetime, determines all distances in that spacetime. How? Well, take any curve $\gamma(t)$ in spacetime. At each point p on that curve there is a tangent v_p to that curve. The length of γ between any two points on γ is the integral $\int (g_p v_p v_p)^{1/2}$ dt between those two points. This determines all distances in spacetime.

Whether one has or has not followed all the details, it should be clear that tensors are not intrinsic to a point. Tensors, after all, are maps from vectors and 1-forms to real numbers, and since vectors (and therefore 1-forms) are not intrinsic to a point, neither are tensors. If one needs any further confirmation of this view, consider for instance the metric tensor. The metric tensors at all points in spacetime determine all distances in spacetime. Since it should be obvious that distances in a spacetime are not determined by the intrinsic properties at all points in that spacetime, it cannot be the case that metric tensors are intrinsic to points.

There is one more issue to discuss in connection with fields before I discuss how separability relates to dynamical locality and relativistic invariance. The last issue that I want to discuss in connection with field theories is the way in which quantities such as mass and charge appear in classical field theories. Classical fields are not composed out of lots of point-particles each of which have a mass and/or a charge, and so on. One might therefore think that there is no sense in which masses and charges are associated with classical fields. But that is not right. Masses and charges are associated with classical fields—or at least, they can be. In particular, quantities like masses and charges are associated with the kind of fields which, when they are quantized, give rise to 'elementary-particle-like behaviour', or, slightly more precisely, give rise to 'elementary-particle-like' behaviour in certain circumstances. The way in which quantities like mass or charge appear in field theories is as constants in the equations giving the dynamical laws that the field satisfies. For instance, consider the Klein–Gordon equation governing a scalar field φ: $(\partial^\mu \partial_\mu + m^2)\varphi = 0$. This equation tells one that at any point in spacetime the (covariant) sum of the double directional derivatives of the scalar field is proportional to the scalar field itself. The constant of proportionality is m^2, and m here stands for the mass associated with the field. Masses and charges are thus associated with entire fields, not with any parts of the fields, nor with any particular regions in spacetime. So, from the point of view of separability, they are irrelevant, or, at least, as irrelevant as any constants appearing in the laws. So if there were only fields and no particles in the world, an assumption which is quite natural in the context of General Relativity, then there is one less issue to worry about when it comes to separability.

The upshot of all of this is that classical worlds—at least ones which are fairly similar to our world—are not separable, but are neighbourhood separable. And if one wishes to draw a distinction between geometrical structure of such worlds and non-geometrical structure, then on the most plausible way of drawing such a distinction neither the

---

[16] Symmetry means that $g_p u_p v_p = g_p v_p u_p$ for all u_p and v_p. Non-degeneracy means that, if for some fixed v_p one has that $g_p u_p v_p = 0$ for all u_p, then $v_p = 0$.

geometrical structure nor the non-geometrical structure is separable, but both are neighbourhood separable.

2.6 Separability, dynamical locality, and relativity

But why is it so natural to think that the non-geometric structure of classical worlds is separable? I suggest that this is so for three reasons. In the first place, it is a remarkable fact that all the mass facts, all the charge facts, all the distance facts, and all the tensor field facts can be naturally and simply summarized in point-by-point fashion. Whether or not the values of masses, mass-densities, charges, charge-densities, scalars, vectors, and tensors at points are *intrinsic* to points, it is, quite remarkably, the case that all the facts can be stated in a simple and neat point-by-point fashion, and it is in this point-by-point fashion that we normally think of the state of a classical world. In the second place, when we think a classical world in this way there is a very natural and simple set of such properties *at an instant in time* which, given the dynamical laws, suffices to determine the history of the world: the positions, velocities, charges, charge densities, masses, mass densities, and tensor fields plus their spatial and temporal derivatives at an instant, given typical classical dynamical laws, will determine the history of the world. This also explains why we are so inclined to think that velocities are intrinsic to instants: velocities are needed in order to determine the future (and past) development of the state of the world. In fact, this notion of the 'state at a time' that suffices to determine history, given the laws, is such an important concept that it deserves its own name. If there is a natural and simple set of features of an instant which, given the laws, determines the history of the world, then, whether or not that set of features is *intrinsic* to that instant, let us call it the 'initial value state' of the world at that instant.

Let me now interject an important aside. The above also provides us with a response to the argument that I presented a while back (in Section 3) against the mass ratio view, on the grounds that, causally speaking, the world behaves as if its mass properties are local intrinsic properties. The response is that one should distinguish between 'causal locality'—the existence of initial value properties in terms of which the evolution of the world is governed by dynamically local laws—and 'fundamental locality'—separability. If one has a simple and plausible theory that is non-separable, which explains why the world behaves in a causally local manner, then the fact that the world is causally local is no argument against its being fundamentally non-local; that is, non-separable. So now we have dispensed of all arguments in favor of the mass value and mass ratio views. So, if one thinks it plausible that numbers and units are not part of the fundamental structure of physical reality, then one should think that (charge and mass) betweenness and addition relations are fundamental, rather than (mass and charge) values or (mass and charge) ratios. OK, back to the issue as to why one might be inclined to believe that classical worlds are point-local.

The third reason one might be inclined to give is that it seems evident that classical possible worlds can be generated by redistributing, as we please, point-local masses, mass-densities, charges, charge-densities, scalars, vectors, and tensors across spacetime (perhaps subject to some simple and natural constraints).[17] I find this third reason a particularly bad one. Inferring from intuitions as to what is possible to conclusions as to what is fundamental is bad practice in my view. In any case, I take it that the above gives a decent explanation of why it is so seductive to think of the non-geometric structure of classical worlds as being point-separable, even though in fact this is not so.

Let me also try to explain why Lewis, and presumably many others, had the idea that geometrical structure and non-geometrical structure are very different, in that the first is non-separable and the second is separable. In the first place, prior to General Relativity geometric features are not normally considered to be part of initial value states: prior to General Relativity the geometrical structure of the world is fixed once and for all, it does not change in time, and it is not influenced by the non-geometrical features of the world. So, prior to General Relativity there is no reason to even consider whether geometrical structure is stateable in point-by-point fashion. In the second place, geometrical structure obviously is not stateable in point-by-point fashion: distances can obviously not be stated in point-by-point fashion. And if one never has thought about the notion of 'neighbourhood separability', perhaps because one has always thought of non-geometrical structure as being 'point-separable', then all one can say about geometric structure is that it just is not separable. In the third place, if one is not accustomed to the metric tensor of relativity theory it is not at all obvious that one can state the metric facts in a nice and simple point-by-point fashion. And even if one does notice this it still remains the case that topological structure (and, as we shall see in Chapter 8, so-called 'differential structure') is not stateable in a simple and neat point-by-point fashion.

Now let me turn to dynamical locality—the idea that how the state of a system or region develops depends on conditions at, or near, the system or region. There are several ways in which to make this basic idea precise. In the first place, should we understand the notion of state here as the state intrinsic to the system, or region, in question, or should we understand it as the initial value state of that system, or region? Well, one could just define two different senses of dynamical locality. However, in the first place, physicists and philosophers typically have initial value states in mind when they are discussing dynamical locality. In the second place, intuitively speaking, even if one has the view that the non-local massbetweenness and massaddition relations are fundamental, when judging whether or not a particular theory is dynamically non-local, one surely just wants to check whether the evolution of some region depends on the mass values in, or near, that region. So surely the more interesting notion of dynamical locality is the one that asks whether the evolution of the initial value state of a system, or region, is determined by the local initial value state of that system, or region. Another question is what should one take 'conditions at or near a region' to be.

---

[17] I am leaving it rather vague as to what extent this includes the redistribution of geometric properties, because I think our intuitions are rather vague regarding this issue.

A natural answer to this question is that 'conditions at or near the region in question' should be taken to be the initial value features of any open region that includes the region in question. The reason for demanding that the region be open is to allow that the development of the state can depend on (spatial) derivatives on the boundary of the region in question. And finally one might ask what exactly should count as the 'evolution' of the state in question. A natural answer here is that by the evolution of the state one means the temporal derivative of the initial value state of the region in question.

Having made these suggestions I nonetheless do not want to fuss too much about how exactly one should define dynamical locality. Slightly different notions can be interesting in different cases. The main thing I want to get across is that even outside of relativistic contexts there is an interesting notion of dynamical locality.

Let me present a couple of examples. Newtonian gravitational theory clearly fails dynamical locality, since the evolution of a particle's initial value state (mass, position, velocity) is not determined by local conditions, since its acceleration depends on the positions of all particles in the universe at the time in question. Well, actually, that depends a bit on how one formulates Newtonian gravitational theory. For one need not formulate Newtonian gravitation theory as a theory in which particles directly cause gravitational forces on other particles, without any mediating field. One can also formulate Newtonian gravitational theory assuming that the distribution of all particles in the universe at a time determines a gravitational potential field at that time, where this gravitational potential field locally determines particle accelerations. If one formulates a Newtonian gravitational theory along those lines, then the particle accelerations are locally determined, but the evolution of the gravitational potential field is not locally determined.

On the other hand, any field theory whose dynamical equations consist of local differential equations—that is to say, equations which say that the rate of change of the initial value state of the field at a point is determined by the initial value state of the field and its spatial derivatives at that point—clearly satisfies locality. Note that this can include field equations according to which field 'disturbances' propagate at arbitrarily fast speeds.

Finally, why should we care about separability or about dynamical locality? Well, some think that there is something inherently objectionable about violations of separability and/or violations of dynamical locality; that, other things being equal, theories according to which the world is separable are more likely to be true than theories according to which the world is not separable, or that, other things being equal, theories according to which the world is dynamically local are more likely to be true than theories according to which the world is not dynamically local. For instance, Newton, in a letter to Bentley, said:

It is inconceivable that inanimate brute matter should, without the mediation of something else, which is not material, operate upon, and affect other matter, without mutual contact; as it must do, if gravitation (in the sense of Epicurus) be essential and inherent in it. And this is one reason, why I desired you would not ascribe innate gravity to me. That gravity should be innate, inherent, and essential to matter, so that one body may act upon another at a distance through a vacuum, without the mediation of anything else, by and through which their action and force may be conveyed from one to another, is to me so great an absurdity, that I believe no man who has in philosophical matters a competent faculty of thinking, can ever fall into it. Gravity must be caused by an agent acting constantly according to certain laws; but whether this agent be material or immaterial, I have left to the consideration of my readers.

Newton clearly found it nigh on impossible to believe that there could be violations of dynamical locality. I expect that his objections to violations of dynamical locality, and those of others who share his sentiment, have much to do with the fact that the world of our ordinary experiences appears not to contain violations of dynamical locality. But I see no reason to demand that fundamentally the world is similar to the way it *prima facie* appears to us.

The notion of separability, or something close to it, was, as far as I know, first introduced by Einstein. Here is a quote:

... it is characteristic of these physical things that they are conceived of as being arranged in a spacetime continuum. Further, it appears to be essential for this arrangement of the things introduced in physics that, at a specific time, these things claim an existence independent of one another, insofar as these things 'lie in different parts of space'. Without such an assumption of the mutually independent existence (the 'being-thus') of spatially distant things, an assumption which originates in everyday thought, physical thought in the sense familiar to us would not be possible. Nor does one see how physical laws could be formulated and tested without such a clean separation. Field theory has carried out this principle to the extreme, in that it localizes within infinitely small (four-dimensional) space-elements the elementary things existing independent of one another that it takes as basic. (Translation by Howard (1985).)

It has to be said that what Einstein has in mind here appears not to be exactly what I have called separability, since he emphasizes the independence of *spatially* distant things *at a time*. Even so, we have seen that violations of spatial separability at a time do not entail the impossibility of physical thought, or the impossibility of formulating and testing laws. Thus I see no compelling reason to demand separability. The only issue is what the simplest, most natural, theory is.

However, does relativity theory not give us reason to think that the world is dynamically local and is separable? Yes and no. According to relativity theory there is no fact of the matter as to which events are simultaneous with which events that occur at other locations. This has as a consequence that it is not an easy task to write down a dynamically non-local law. Suppose, for example, that one says that the gravitational force on a particle A 'now' depends on where the other particles are 'now'. Then, if the law is to be coherent it had better be the case that in any frame of reference the distribution of particles in the 'now' of that frame of reference implies the same force 'now' on particle A. That is not to say that violations of dynamical locality are not compatible with relativity theory. They are, but defending that would require a rather long and irrelevant discussion, so I will not do so here. (If you are interested, see Arntzenius (1994).) The main point is that relativity theory does give us reason to believe that the world is dynamically local—not an utterly compelling reason, but good reason. But relativity gives us little reason to believe that the world is separable. For instance, all of the violations of separability that we have considered in this chapter are fully compatible with Special Relativity and General Relativity. In any case, there is no need to think whether relativity gives us some general reason to think the world is separable and/or dynamically non-local. We can just check each candidate theory that interests us as to whether it is relativistic, whether it is separable, and whether it is simple (in terms of its fundamental quantities) and plausible. The upshot of this chapter is that classical worlds, both relativistic and Newtonian, most plausibly are neighbourhood-separable, both with respect to their geometric and their non-geometric structure.

3

The world according to quantum mechanics

'Forty-two,' said Deep Thought, with infinite majesty and calm.

Douglas Adams

3.1 Introduction

Let us start by distinguishing two questions

1) What is the fundamental structure of the world according to quantum mechanics?
2) How does the fundamental structure of the world determine the phenomena, and how do the phenomena supervene on the fundamental structure?

In this chapter I am interested in the first question, and I will discuss five different answers. I will end up advocating the co-called 'Deutsch–Hayden' account of the fundamental structure of the world which has the remarkable feature that according to it the quantum mechanical state of the world is separable and its dynamics (its law of evolution in time) is local—something which many have thought to be impossible.

One might naturally identify the second question with the question as to the correct 'interpretation' of quantum mechanics. However, when philosophers, or physicists, talk about 'interpretations' of quantum mechanics, they usually conflate the two questions which I have just separated. Of course, how one answers the second question depends on how one answers the first question. I am inclined to advocate a modern version of the 'many worlds' account of how the phenomena supervene on the 'Deutsch–Hayden' structure of the world. (See Wallace (2010) for an excellent account of a modern 'many worlds' account.) But I have nothing new to add to extant discussions of answers to the second question. Moreover, this book is mostly about the question as to what the fundamental structure of the world is, so I will not discuss the second question in this chapter.

I will start by examining whether according to quantum mechanics the world is separable. This will naturally lead to a discussion of the more general issue as to what the fundamental structure of reality is according to quantum mechanics.

3.2 An argument that the world is not separable according to quantum mechanics

It is pretty much universally accepted that according to quantum mechanics the world is not separable. Let me explain why. I will use as an example the 'spin' of an electron. According to quantum mechanics, any electron has 'spin', which, roughly speaking, means that it behaves as if it is spinning along some (internal) axis. An electron also has an electric charge. A rotating charge produces a magnetic field that is parallel to the axis of rotation. So each electron produces a magnetic field. And one can use this magnetic field to measure along which axis the electron is spinning in the following manner. One takes an electron, and sends it through an inhomogeneous magnetic field, which is produced by a pair of magnets that are aligned in some direction, which I will call the z-direction (see Figure 3.1).

The magnetic field produced by the magnets will deflect the electrons as they pass through it. In fact, quantum mechanics predicts that if one observes which path the electron takes after it has gone through the magnetic field, then one will find that there are only two possible paths that the electron can take. It will either be deflected upwards, in the $+z$-direction, or downwards, in the $-z$-direction. If it is deflected upwards, we say that the electron has $\text{spin}_z=+\frac{1}{2}$ after the measurement. If it is deflected downwards we say that the electron has $\text{spin}_z=-\frac{1}{2}$ after the measurement. (Spin_z is short for 'spin in the z-direction'.)

Quantum mechanics also says that the quantum state of the electron before it goes through the magnets does not determine whether it will subsequently be deflected

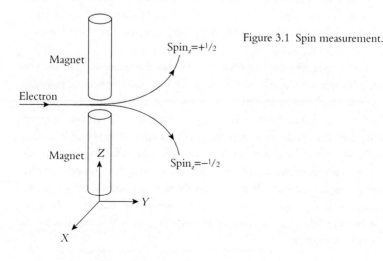

Figure 3.1 Spin measurement.

Figure 3.2 Spin Hilbert space.

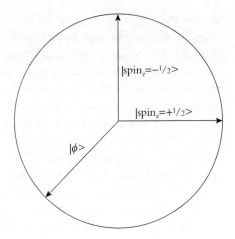

upwards or downwards; the prior quantum state only determines the probabilities for these two possible outcomes. To be precise, there are infinitely many spin-states that the electron can be in prior to the measurement, and among all of those there are only two spin-states that are such that they determine with certainty (with chance=1) what the outcome of a spin-measurement in the z-direction will be. These two states are called the $\text{spin}_z=+\frac{1}{2}$ 'eigenstate', and the $\text{spin}_z=-\frac{1}{2}$ 'eigenstate'. If the electron starts in any other spin-state, both deflections will have a non-zero chance.

It is a remarkable fact that all of these infinitely many spin-states can be constructed out of just the $\text{spin}_z=+\frac{1}{2}$ eigenstate and the $\text{spin}_z=-\frac{1}{2}$ eigenstate. This is so because quantum states can be represented as vectors. The vectors in question are not space-time vectors; they are not vectors in a space that is tangent to spacetime. Rather, they are vectors in some other vector space: a so-called 'Hilbert space'. The main thing for now is that this means that one can add such vectors together and one can multiply them by numbers, and then one obtains other vectors (in the same Hilbert space) which also represent possible quantum mechanical states. In general, the numbers that one can multiply Hilbert space vectors by are complex numbers, but I will explain why quantum mechanical states are non-separable using only the real numbers.

In the case of the spin-states of a single electron—that is, ignoring all features of the electron other than its spin—the relevant Hilbert space is very simple. The $\text{spin}_z=+\frac{1}{2}$ eigenstate and the $\text{spin}_z=-\frac{1}{2}$ eigenstate can be represented as two orthogonal vectors, each of length 1, in a two-dimensional vector space (see Figure 2). In fact, all and only the vectors of length 1 represent possible spin-states of a single electron.[1] I will therefore call the length 1 vectors 'state-vectors' and use Dirac's notation to denote them: $|\text{spin}_z=+\frac{1}{2}\rangle$ denotes the vector representing the $\text{spin}_z=+\frac{1}{2}$ eigenstate, and $|\text{spin}_z=-\frac{1}{2}\rangle$

---

[1] But note that two vectors of length 1 pointing in exactly opposite directions represent the same spin-state. More generally, if c is a complex number of length (modulus) 1, then $|\varphi\rangle$ and $c|\varphi\rangle$ represent the same spin-state.

denotes the vector representing the $\text{spin}_z = -\frac{1}{2}$ eigenstate. All the other possible spin-states are then represented by all the other vectors in this two-dimensional vector space that have length 1, such as $|\varphi\rangle$. Now we can see the sense in which all possible spin-states can be constructed out of the $\text{spin}_z = +\frac{1}{2}$ eigenstate and the $\text{spin}_z = -\frac{1}{2}$ eigenstate. Any vector in a real two-dimensional vector space can be formed by first multiplying each of two orthogonal vectors by appropriate real numbers, and then adding the resulting vectors together. That is, any spin-state-vector $|\psi\rangle$ is such that $|\psi\rangle = c_1|\text{spin}_z = +\frac{1}{2}\rangle + c_2|\text{spin}_z = -\frac{1}{2}\rangle$ for some real numbers c_1 and c_2. Note that since $|\psi\rangle$ must have length 1, it follows that $|c_1|^2 + |c_2|^2 = 1$, where $|c|$ denotes the absolute value (the modulus) of the number c. One says that $|\psi\rangle$ is a 'superposition' of the state-vectors $|\text{spin}_z = +\frac{1}{2}\rangle$ and $|\text{spin}_z = -\frac{1}{2}\rangle$, with coefficients c_1 and c_2. For instance, in Figure 2, $|\varphi\rangle = (-1/\sqrt{2})|\text{spin}_z = +\frac{1}{2}\rangle - (1/\sqrt{2})|\text{spin}_z = -\frac{1}{2}\rangle$.

But why can the spin-states of a single electron be represented in this manner? What does it mean to say that a quantum mechanical state is represented by some vector in a Hilbert space? Well, as I said, the spin-state of the electron prior to a measurement of spin_z determines the probabilities of the results of this measurement. The way in which it does this is very simple: if the prior state-vector is $|\psi\rangle = c_1|\text{spin}_z = +\frac{1}{2}\rangle + c_2|\text{spin}_z = -\frac{1}{2}\rangle$, then the probability of its being deflected upwards—that is, of finding the result that $\text{spin}_z = +\frac{1}{2}$, equals $|c_1|^2$—and the probability of its being deflected downwards—of finding the result that $\text{spin}_z = -\frac{1}{2}$—equals $|c_2|^2$. (We can now see why the length of each vector that represents a possible quantum state has to be 1: the chances of the two possible outcomes of a measurement must sum to 1, since the chance that the measurement will have either one outcome or the other is 1.)

Note that there is nothing special about the direction that I have called the z-direction. That is to say, for any direction z' other than z there are also two orthogonal state-vectors $|\text{spin}_{z'} = +\frac{1}{2}\rangle$ and $|\text{spin}_{z'} = -\frac{1}{2}\rangle$ (in the same Hilbert space), which would determine the outcome of a measurement of spin in the z' direction, were one to perform it. An arbitrary vector $|\psi\rangle$ will also be a superposition of these state-vectors: $|\psi\rangle = d_1|\text{spin}_{z'} = +\frac{1}{2}\rangle + d_2|\text{spin}_{z'} = -\frac{1}{2}\rangle$, for some numbers d_1 and d_2, and the squares of these numbers will correspond to the probabilities of the possible results ($+\frac{1}{2}$ and $-\frac{1}{2}$) of a measurement of $\text{spin}_{z'}$. Let us now turn to the spin states of a pair of electrons.

One might hope that the spin-state of a pair of electrons can be given by giving the spin-state vectors of each of the electrons. If that were so, the spin-state of the pair would be separable. However, unfortunately that is not so. It is of course true that any pair of spin-state vectors of each individual electron corresponds to a possible spin-state vector for the pair of electrons.[2] But, perhaps rather surprisingly, the pair has more possible spin-state vectors than that. Perhaps even more surprisingly, we already know enough about quantum mechanics to be able to see that this must be so.

---

[2] This is not quite right. Electrons are fermions, so pairs of electrons are restricted to anti-symmetric states. This is a complication that I will here ignore.

It is clear that there must be at least four spin-states for the pair of electrons. For, there is the state of the pair such that particles 1 and 2 are both in state $|\text{spin}_z=+^1/_2>$, there is the state of the pair such that both are in the state $|\text{spin}_z=-^1/_2>$, there is the state of the pair such that particle 1 is in state $|\text{spin}_z=+^1/_2>$ and particle 2 is in state $|\text{spin}_z=-^1/_2>$, and finally there is the state of the pair such that particle 1 is in state $|\text{spin}_z=-^1/_2>$ and particle 2 is in state $|\text{spin}_z=+^1/_2>$. Let me introduce some obvious notation for these four states of the pair: $|\text{spin}^1_z=+^1/_2>|\text{spin}^2_z=+^1/_2>$, $|\text{spin}^1_z=-^1/_2>|\text{spin}^2_z=-^1/_2>$, $|\text{spin}^1_z=+^1/_2>|\text{spin}^2_z=-^1/_2>$, and $|\text{spin}^1_z=-^1/_2>|\text{spin}^2_z=+^1/_2>$. These are the four spin$_z$ eigenstates of the pair. Now, as I have said, according to quantum mechanics, if one takes two quantum states and forms a superposition of them—that is, sums the state-vectors to form a new vector (of length 1)—then one obtains another state-vector. For example, $|\chi>=(1/\sqrt{2})|\text{spin}^1_z=+^1/_2>|\text{spin}^2_z=+^1/_2>+(1/\sqrt{2})|\text{spin}^1_z=-^1/_2>|\text{spin}^2_z=-^1/_2>$ is also a possible state-vector for the pair of electrons.[3] What are the properties of this state?

Well, one possible measurement on the pair of electrons is just to measure spin$_z$ of each of the particles. What are the probabilities of the possible results of this measurement if the pair starts in the state $|\chi>$? If the state were $|\text{spin}^1_z=+^1/_2>|\text{spin}^2_z=+^1/_2>$, both particles would be deflected upwards by the magnets, and if the state were $|\text{spin}^1_z=-^1/_2>|\text{spin}^2_z=-^1/_2>$, both particles would be deflected downwards. Since $|\chi>$ is a superposition of these states, with coefficients that are both $1/\sqrt{2}$, it follows that for initial state $|\chi>$ the probability that both electrons deflect up is $|1/\sqrt{2}|^2=^1/_2$, and the probability that both electrons deflect down is also $|1/\sqrt{2}|^2=2$.

Could $|\chi>$ be equal to some state $|\varphi>=|\alpha^1>|\beta^2>$, where $|\alpha^1>$ is some spin-state of particle 1, and $|\beta^2>$ is some spin-state of particle 2? To get a grip on this question, let us suppose we measure spin$_z$ of each particle when the pair is initially in state $|\alpha^1>|\beta^2>$. In that case, what are the probabilities of the results? Well, state $|\alpha^1>|\beta^2>$ for the pair just means that particle 1 is in state $|\alpha^1>$ and particle two is in state $|\beta^2>$. State $|\alpha^1>$, no matter what it is, can be written as a superposition of spin$_z$ states: $|\alpha^1>=c_1|\text{spin}^1_z=+^1/_2>+c_2|\text{spin}^1_z=-^1/_2>$ for some c_1 and c_2. Similarly, state $|\beta^2>$, no matter what it is, can be written as a superposition of spin$_z$ states: $|\beta^2>=d_1|\text{spin}^2_z=+^1/_2>+d_2|\text{spin}^2_z=-^1/_2>$ for some d_1 and d_2. What are the probabilities for the results of a spin$_z$ measurement on particle 1 when the pair is in state $|\alpha^1>|\beta^2>$? Since particle 1 is simply in state $|\alpha^1>=c_1|\text{spin}^1_z=+^1/_2>+c_2|\text{spin}^1_z=-^1/_2>$, the probability that particle 1 deflects upwards is $|c_1|^2$, and the probability that it deflects downwards is $|c_2|^2$. If state $|\alpha^1>|\beta^2>$ is to be identical to state $|\chi>$, these probabilities had better both be $^1/_2$; that is, $|c_1|^2=|c_2|^2=^1/_2$, since that is what the probabilities are in state $|\chi>$. Similarly, it had better be the case that $|d_1|^2=|d_2|^2=^1/_2$. So let us assume that this is so. But now what, for example, is the probability that *both* electrons are deflected upwards when we measure spin$_z$ of both particles when the initial state is $|\alpha^1>|\beta^2>$? Well, since this state just means that particle 1 is in state $|\alpha^1>$ and

---

[3] This assumes that states $|\text{spin}^1_z=+^1/_2>|\text{spin}^2_z=+^1/_2>$ and $|\text{spin}^1_z=-^1/_2>|\text{spin}^2_z=-^1/_2>$ are orthogonal. But one can easily see why this should be the case. If the pair is in state $|\text{spin}^1_z=+^1/_2>|\text{spin}^2_z=+^1/_2>$ then, if one measures spin^1_z and spin^2_z, one is certain of getting results $+^1/_2$ and $+^1/_2$. The chance of getting results $-^1/_2$ and $-^1/_2$ is therefore zero, and so $|\text{spin}^1_z=+^1/_2>|\text{spin}^2_z=+^1/_2>$ should be orthogonal to state $|\text{spin}^1_z=-^1/_2>|\text{spin}^2_z=-^1/_2>$.

particle 2 is in state $|\beta^2>$, the probability that the second particle deflects upwards is the same whether or not particle 1 deflects upwards. Since particle 1, on average, deflects upwards half of the times, and particle 2 deflects upwards, on average, half of the times no matter what particle 1 is doing, it follows that, on average, they will both deflect upwards only $\frac{1}{4}$ of the time. But that means that state $|\alpha^1>|\beta^2>$ cannot be the same as state $|\chi>$, since if the pair is initially in state $|\chi>$ the probability that both deflect upwards is $\frac{1}{2}$. So state $|\chi>$ cannot correspond to a pair of spin-states of the individual particles.

States such as $|\chi>$, which are not equal to a pair of spin-states, are called 'entangled states'. The reason one calls them entangled is that they imply that there are correlations between the results of measurements of both particles that are not possible if each particle is in some particular spin-state. Generally, if a collection of particles at some time is not in an entangled state, the only way that their state can subsequently become entangled is if the particles meet and interact. Afterwards, however, they typically remain in an entangled state no matter how far apart they drift in space.

That is all very well, but what should we say about the state of one of the electrons when it is part of a pair that is in such an entangled state? If we stick with the idea that the state of an electron must be a vector in the single-electron Hilbert space, then we have just argued that it cannot have a state at all. And indeed, that is one thing that one can say: one can say that when an electron is part of a pair that is in an entangled state, that electron just does not have a quantum state at all. All that one can then say is that it is part of a pair that is in some (entangled) state. Specifying which (entangled) state it is in will then determine the probabilities of all possible outcomes of all possible measurements on the pair of particles. In particular, it will determine the probabilities of all possible outcomes of all possible measurements on just one of the electrons.

Now, one might feel a little queasy about the idea that an electron has no definite state whatsoever. What one can then do, and what most textbooks do, is to broaden the notion of quantum state, and allow it to be something other than a vector in a Hilbert space. That is to say, in addition to the 'pure states'—the state-vectors with which we are already familiar—one assumes the existence of so-called 'mixed states'. Informally speaking, the 'mixed state' of a particle, or a system, is just a summary of all the probabilities of all possible results of all possible measurements on just that particle, or just that system. More formally speaking, mixed states can be represented by so-called 'density operators', where a density operator is a 'linear operator' on the Hilbert space of the particle, or system, in question, which is 'self-adjoint', 'positive semi-definite' and 'has trace 1'. I am not going to explain each of these terms, since I do not need to do so for current purposes. But it is useful to know that:

1) Any coherent probability assignment to all the possible results of measurements can be represented by a density operator.[4]

---

[4] By Gleason's theorem, any probability assignment which is additive over any countable set of orthogonal subspaces can be represented by a density operator.

2) There is a simple rule to go from the pure state of a larger entangled system to the mixed state of any of its subsystems.[5]

The question now is: do the mixed states of the subsystems of a system that is in a pure state determine the pure state in question? It is easy to see that they do not. Consider the following entangled state: $|\psi\rangle=(1/\sqrt{2})|spin^1_z=+^1/_2\rangle|\mu^2\rangle+(1/\sqrt{2})|spin^1_z=-^1/_2\rangle|\nu^2\rangle$, where $|\mu^2\rangle$ and $|\nu^2\rangle$ is some arbitrary pair of orthogonal states of the second electron. Clearly, the probabilities of the two possible results of a measurement of spin$_z$ of particle 1, are $^1/_2$ and $^1/_2$, *no matter what the states* $|\mu^2\rangle$ *and* $|\nu^2\rangle$ *are*. More generally, according to quantum mechanics, the probabilities for the possible results of *any* measurement solely on particle 1 do not depend on what the states $|\mu^2\rangle$ and $|\nu^2\rangle$ are. Now consider the following pair of entangled states:

$$|\chi\rangle=(1/\sqrt{2})|spin^1_z=+^1/_2\rangle|spin^2_z=+^1/_2\rangle+(1/\sqrt{2})|spin^1_z=-^1/_2\rangle|spin^2_z=-^1/_2\rangle$$

and

$$|\xi\rangle=(1/\sqrt{2})|spin^1_z=+^1/_2\rangle|spin^2_z=-^1/_2\rangle+(1/\sqrt{2})|spin^1_z=-^1/_2\rangle|spin^2_z=+^1/_2\rangle$$

The probabilities of all possible measurements on particle 1 are the same for each of those two states. And the probabilities of all possible measurements on particle 2 are the same for each of those states. That is to say, the mixed states of particle 1 and of particle 2 are the same whether the pair is in entangled state $|\chi\rangle$ or in entangled state $|\xi\rangle$. But those are 2 different entangled states. If one were to measure spin$_z$ on both particles, then, if the initial state were $|\chi\rangle$ they would always be deflected in the same direction (half of the time upwards, half of the time downwards), while the electrons would always deflect in opposite directions if the initial state were $|\xi\rangle$. Thus the mixed states of each of the electrons do not determine the entangled state of the pair. Moreover, all of this is the case no matter how far apart the electrons are. So, according to quantum mechanics the state of the world is non-separable. Moreover, such entanglement is ubiquitous: generically, once systems have interacted their joint state becomes, and remains, an entangled state.[6] And this non-separability is quite global; neighbourhood separability fails just as dramatically. This is why it is standardly accepted that separability fails miserably in quantum mechanics.

Let me try to strengthen the above argument—which, however, will not be a watertight argument, which may seem rather a shame. But actually it is just as well that it is not watertight, since we will find that there are coherent accounts according to which the quantum mechanical state of the world is separable. Still, it useful to see how hard it is to reconcile separability with quantum mechanics. So here we go.

---

[5] The operation in question is 'tracing out' over the degrees of freedom other than the subsystem in question.

[6] Indeed, in quantum field theory, due to the spin-statistics theorem, no such initial interactions are even needed to achieve such entanglement.

An arbitrary spin-state of a pair of electrons can be written in the form:

$$c_1|s^1_z=+\tfrac{1}{2}>|s^2_z=+\tfrac{1}{2}>+c_2|s^1_z=-\tfrac{1}{2}>|s^2_z=-\tfrac{1}{2}>+c_3|s^1_z=+\tfrac{1}{2}>|s^2_z=-\tfrac{1}{2}>+$$
$$c_4|s^1_z=-\tfrac{1}{2}>|s^2_z=+\tfrac{1}{2}>$$

So if the separate states of each electron, when taken together, are to determine this global state, they must determine the four coefficients c_1, c_2, c_3 and c_4 of the four spin eigenstates. As we have seen, this is more information than the local mixed states contain. So there must be further features of the local state of particle 1 and of the local state of particle 2 which, taken together, determine these four coefficients. Why not simply postulate exactly enough further features of the local states such that, taken together, they determine these four coefficients? Can this work?

It does not seem likely. Suppose that particles a, b, c, d all start in exactly the same separate pure states, and that a and b are at one end of the universe, while c and d are at the other end of the universe. Then suppose that particles a and b interact, and at the same time (relativistically, in a space-like separated region) at the other end of the universe, particles c and d interact *in exactly the same way* as a and b. After this has happened, since they have done exactly the same thing, and started out in the same state, the local state of particles a and c should be exactly the same local state, no matter what features this local state is assumed to have. For the same reason, the local states of particles b and d should be exactly the same. Now, according to quantum theory particles a and b are in an entangled joint state after they interact, and particles c and d are in an entangled joint state after they interact. But, of course, particles a and d are not in a joint entangled state, since they never interacted, nor are b and c. The problem now is that I have just said that the local states of particles a and c are exactly the same. Thus, if the two local states of particles a and b determine the entangled state that the pair is in, then the two local states of particles c and b, which are exactly the same as those of a and b, determine that c and b are in this same entangled state. But that is not true!

The problem is that the global quantum state keeps tabs on which particle interacted with which particle by putting them in an entangled state, and this entanglement is retained no matter how far apart they subsequently go. If one tries to have this entanglement determined by the intrinsic features of each particle separately, then one needs these features not only to determine the form that this entanglement takes, but also to determine with *which* other particles they are entangled. And there seems to be no natural way to do that. One might imagine doing this by assuming that the state of each particle, as it were, keeps a record of which particles it interacted with in the past. That is the sort of thing that humans often do: we remember whom we spoke with by remembering what they looked like, or sounded like, and so on. The problem, however, is that it does not seem plausible that elementary particles have distinguishing features, nor that when they interact they add a distinguishing feature so as to remember who it was that they interacted with. It therefore seems quite implausible that local states determine the global entanglements that quantum mechanics dictates. But implausible is not the same as impossible, as we shall see in Section 3.14.

3.3 Configuration space realism

David Albert (1996) has argued that the space in which quantum mechanical events occur—the fundamental space of quantum mechanics—is not the three-dimensional space (or the four-dimensional spacetime) with which we are familiar, but is configuration space (or configuration spacetime). The configuration space for a collection of N particles has 3N dimensions: a single point in this configuration space represents the positions of all N particles in three-dimensional space. Physicists often work with configuration space (perhaps even more often with 'phase space', which includes all the particle momenta as well as positions), since it can be mathematically convenient to represent the positions of N particles not by N points in three-dimensional space, but by a single point in a 3N-dimensional space. But typically, in so far as they think about such matters, they think of configuration space as a mere mathematical convenience. They do not think of configuration space as the fundamental physical space. Albert, however, thinks that quantum mechanics shows that configuration space is the fundamental physical space, and that three-dimensional space is not the fundamental physical space. Here is how he expresses his idea:

There is an arena in which the dynamics does its work, a stage on which whatever theory we happen to be entertaining depicts the world as unfolding, a space (that is) in which a specification of the local conditions at every address at some particular time amounts to a complete specification of the physical situation of the world ... The space in which any realistic understanding of quantum mechanics is necessarily going to depict the history of the world as playing itself out is configuration space.

In this quote, Albert also claims that quantum mechanical states are separable ('a specification of the local conditions at every address at some particular time amounts to a complete specification of the physical situation'). Before critically examining the idea that configuration space is the fundamental space, let me briefly explain why he claims that quantum mechanical states are separable if configuration space is the fundamental space.

We have seen that one can represent each possible spin-state $|\psi\rangle$ of an electron as a superposition of two spin-states: namely, the spin eigenstates $|spin_z=+\frac{1}{2}\rangle$ and $|spin_z=-\frac{1}{2}\rangle$ which correspond to the two possible results of a spin-measurement in direction z:

$$|\psi\rangle = c_1|spin_z=+\frac{1}{2}\rangle + c_2|spin_z=-\frac{1}{2}\rangle$$

where c_1 and c_2 are complex numbers such that $|c_1|^2+|c_2|^2=1$. In non-relativistic quantum mechanics something similar is true about the position states of elementary particles. That is to say, roughly speaking, one can represent each possible position state $|\psi\rangle$ of an elementary particle as a superposition of position eigenstates $|x\rangle$:

$$|\psi\rangle = \Sigma c_x|x\rangle$$

where the sum is over all points in space x, and $\Sigma|c_x|^2=1$. Now, this is only roughly correct, for if one works out the mathematical details (in the standard way at least) it turns out that there are, strictly speaking, no position eigenstates $|x>$. Moreover, an uncountably infinite sum of numbers such as $\sum|c_x|^2$ makes no sense. Nonetheless, what is true is that one can represent each possible position state of an elementary particle by an uncountably infinite set of complex numbers c_x—one for each location x, where $\int|c_x|^2 dx=1$. It is customary to denote these numbers as $\psi(x)$ (rather than as c_x), and to call this $\psi(x)$ the 'wave-function' of the particle in question. The (complex) value of this function $\psi(p)$ at some point p (at some time) is often called the 'amplitude' of the wave-function at location p (at that time). The square of the absolute value (modulus) of the amplitude of the wave-function at location p at time t—that is, $|\psi(p,t)|^2$—equals the probability density that the particle will be found at location p if its position were measured at time t. This means that the chance that it will be found in a (spatial) region R at time t, equals $\int|\psi(x,t)|^2 dx$, where the integral is over region R.

In the case of spin-states, we have seen that spin-states of pairs of particles correspond to superpositions of each of four possible pairs of spin-eigenstates. Similarly, the position states of pairs of particles correspond to a set of amplitudes for each possible combination of positions for the pair; that is to say, by a wave-function $\psi(x_1, x_2)$ which specifies the probability amplitude for every possible pair of positions x_1 and x_2 of particles 1 and 2 respectively. And more generally, the position state of N particles corresponds to a wave-function $\psi(x_1, x_2, \ldots, x_N)$.

Now, the vast majority of functions $\psi(x_1, x_2, \ldots, x_N)$ cannot be written as the multiplication of N separate functions: $\psi(x_1).\psi(x_1), \ldots \psi(x_N)$. Nor is there any other natural way to code up the multi-particle wave-function $\psi(x_1, x_2, \ldots, x_N)$ by N separate functions $\psi(x_1), \psi(x_2), \ldots, \psi(x_N)$, let alone that it can be coded up by N separate functions such that it is plausible that these functions represent the intrinsic features of particles at locations in three-dimensional space. So if one thinks of three-dimensional space as being the fundamental space over which the quantum mechanical amplitudes are distributed, then the state of the world is not separable. But if, as Albert claims, configuration space is the fundamental space, and the value of the multi-particle wave-function at each point in configuration space, at each time, corresponds to an intrinsic property of that point in configurations space, then the state of the world (at least the position state) is separable. So let us now evaluate the idea that configuration space is the fundamental space.

3.4 Configuration space realism in Newtonian particle mechanics

Let us start by looking at a simple non-quantum mechanical case: namely, a non-relativistic classical particle mechanics. Suppose there are N classical point particles of equal mass in a three-dimensional space where the particles repel each other, and the strength of the repulsion is a (simple) function of the three-dimensional distance between them. Let us assume that the repulsion is instantaneous, so non-relativistic, and that there is no separate repelling field with its own degrees of freedom. We can

Figure 3.3 Trajectory in configuration space.

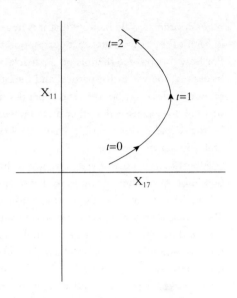

imagine this as frictionless three-dimensional space billiards where, rather than pure collision interactions, there is a repelling force between particles which is a smooth, decreasing, function of the distances. Now suppose we represent the state of such a system by a single point in configuration space. Albert pictures this single point as representing the location of the one and only thing that exists—the so-called 'world-particle'—in the multi-dimensional configuration space. What will the evolution of this single point look like?

Consider the development, say, of coordinate x_{17}, where this coordinate corresponds to the y-location of particle number 6. (I will later present a coordinate-independent picture.) Say that at time $t=1$ coordinate x_{17} has value 5 and its rate of change is 0 at that time. What will be the development of the value of x_{17}? To first approximation it is going to stay the same, since its rate of change is 0 at time $t=1$. But suppose that there is another particle, particle 2, which is close to particle 6 in three-dimensional space at $t=1$, and that all other particles are far away from particle 6 at $t=1$. Suppose, in fact, that the two particles have the same x and z coordinate values at that time, and that particle 2 is located at $y=6$ at $t=1$. Particle 2 will repel particle 6 (and vice versa), so it will produce an acceleration of particle 6's y-coordinate in the (negative) y-direction.

See Figure 3.3 for a (partial) picture of the trajectory of the state in configuration space. I have drawn in another coordinate, x_{11}, and I have assumed that that other coordinate is changing at a constant rate in time—that it is not accelerating. (I cannot draw all the other coordinates, as I do not have enough dimensions available in my picture.)

In general, the trajectory of the world-particle in configuration space will be such that how much a particular coordinate (which corresponds to the location in some direction of some particle) accelerates depends on how far away its value is from certain other coordinate values. Note that it is not simply a matter of checking its 'y-distance' in each of the coordinates that correspond to the y-coordinates of the other particles. For how much force there is on a particle in the y-direction depends not just on the 'y-distance' between that particle and the other particles. Rather, how much force the other particles exert on particle 6 depends on the 'three-dimensional distances' between them. If, for example, the other particles were 'close in the y-direction' but miles away in 'the x and z directions', then it would feel very little force in the 'y-direction'. Still, you get the picture.

Albert's view is that if you were given the development of the single point in configuration space, then, if you looked at it carefully you would realize that its evolution is such that there is a simple translation of the position of the world-particle in 3N-dimensional space to N locations in a three-dimensional space, such that the evolution of the single position can be simply characterized in terms of repulsive forces in the three-dimensional space which depend just on the inter-particle distances in the three-dimensional space. And since one can do that, Albert thinks that one has good reason to claim that the fundamental space of that world is three-dimensional—that 'the stage on which the world unfolds' is three-dimensional rather than 3N-dimensional. Since I am not quite sure what it is to be 'given' the development of a single point in configuration space, I prefer to put it this way: if the phenomena were that of classical space billiards, then one has good reason to think that the fundamental space is three-dimensional rather than 3N-dimensional.

I agree with Albert on this verdict. But I want to give some additional reasons for this verdict, since they will become important in the quantum mechanical case. Let me start by being more precise about the two theories that we are comparing: the three-dimensional theory, and the 3N-dimensional theory.

The three-dimensional theory says something like this. There is a three-dimensional space, which has a flat, Euclidean, metric, and time, which has a metric. There are N particles in this three-dimensional space, all of the same mass, which move according to Newton's law $F=ma$. There is a distance-dependent repulsive force F between all pairs of particles which is some simple function f of the distances d between the particle: $F=f(d)$.

Now let us turn to the 3N-dimensional theory. Here is a suggestion for such a theory. There exists a 3N-dimensional space, and a single 'world particle' which at all times occupies a single point in this space. One can coordinatize this space by means of 3N coordinates $<x_1,x_2,\ldots,x_{3N}>$ such that triples of coordinates $<x_1,x_2,x_3>$, $<x_4,x_5,x_6>,\ldots<x_{3N-2},x_{3N-1},x_{3N}>$ develop exactly as if they are the coordinates of particles $1\ldots N$ of equal mass which live in a three-dimensional space with repulsive forces between them that depend on the distances in three-dimensional space between them.

This theory seems ugly and implausible—but not because it uses the 'as if' locution. One can get rid of that locution by saying that there exist coordinates such that the evolution relative to those coordinates is governed by simple 'three-dimensional repelling force' equations. But this theory is still ugly and implausible. This theory says: 'There exist coordinates such that ...' However, it is implausible that coordinate systems are fundamental quantities; more importantly, it is implausible that the *existence of certain coordinate systems* is a rock bottom fact about reality. What is plausible is that the existence of these coordinate systems relative to which the laws take a certain simple form, is due to the fact that there is some fundamental structure of reality which features in the laws, so that the laws take a particularly simple form relative to coordinate systems that are adapted to that structure. Consider, for instance, a theory that says: 'There exist coordinate systems for spacetime such that the coordinates of free particles follow straight lines relative to these coordinate systems.' This does not seem a plausible fundamental law. Better would be a theory which includes the assumption that spacetime has a coordinate independent structure, affine structure, which distinguishes straight lines from curved ones, and includes the assumption that free particles travel along straight lines. Similarly: 'There exist spatial coordinate systems such that the gravitational force between pairs of particles is inversely proportional to $(x_1{}^2-x_2{}^2)+(x_1{}^2-y_2{}^2)+(z_1{}^2-z_2{}^2)$.' This does not seem a plausible fundamental law. Better would be a theory which includes the assumption that space has a coordinate-independent Euclidean metric, which in Cartesian coordinates takes the form $\sqrt{((x_1{}^2-x_2{}^2)+(x_1{}^2-y_2{}^2)+(z_1{}^2-z_2{}^2))}$.

We want a theory which postulates certain objects with certain coordinate-independent fundamental features, and some laws which can be formulated only in terms of those fundamental features. Can we formulate a theory along the lines of theory B in this way? Yes, we can.

Now, the following is not as perspicacious as I would have liked. And, God knows, I may have made mistakes. But the gist is all that matters, and the gist should become clear. Here, then, is a sketch of a 3N-dimensional theory of the desired variety.

A) There is a 3N-dimensional space, configuration space, which has a flat, Euclidean, metric.

B) Configuration space contains a unique three-dimensional, unbounded, flat subspace which I will call the 'co-location subspace'.

Intuitively speaking this co-location subspace corresponds to all N particles (in the three-dimensional picture) occupying the same location in three-dimensional space.

C) The tangent space T_p at each point p in configuration space contains a unique set of N mutually orthogonal three-dimensional subspaces, which I will call 'particle tangent spaces' and denote as $T_p{}^1,\ldots,T_p{}^N$.

Intuitively speaking, if the 'world-particle' moves in the direction of a vector that lies in $T_p{}^j$, then this corresponds, in the three-dimensional picture, to a motion just of particle j, while all other particles stay where they are. Of course, 'most' vectors in tangent space T_p do not lie in any one of the N-particle tangent spaces, but are superpositions of vectors lying in the particle tangent spaces. This corresponds to the fact that 'most' developments of the positions of N particles in three-dimensional space consist of all particles moving, rather than just 1 or 2 particles moving and the rest standing still.

D) If vector V_p is in T_p^j, and vector V_q 'points in the same direction' as V_p, then V_q is in T_q^j

Note that it makes sense to speak of vectors at different locations in configuration space 'pointing in the same direction', since we have assumed that the configuration space is a flat Euclidean space (flatness of the metric of configuration space implies that there is a path independent notion of tangent vectors at different points in configuration space pointing in the same direction). Intuitively speaking, D) ensures that the particle tangent spaces of the same particle at different locations in configuration space are all 'parallel' to each other.

E) There is a 1–1, inner-product-preserving, 'same-three-dimensional-vector' equivalence relation between vectors in any pair of distinct particle tangent spaces T_p^k and T_p^l at the same point p in configuration space.

Note that the metric on the configuration space provides us with an inner-product on the tangent spaces. Intuitively speaking, the 'same-three-dimensional-vector' relation determines whether a motion of the world-particle in configuration space corresponds to distinct particles in the three-dimensional picture moving with the same three-dimensional velocity in three-dimensional space or with different three-dimensional velocities.

F) For any point p in the co-location subspace, if one moves from p in the direction of a tangent vector V_p, where V_p is an equal weighted sum of N distinct vectors V_p^i (in N distinct particle tangent spaces T_p^i) which all stand in the 'same-three-dimensional-vector' relation, then one stays in the co-location surface.

This ensures that the 'co-location structure' and the 'three-dimensional-vector structure' harmonize. Intuitively speaking, it says that if one starts with all particles in the three-dimensional picture occupying the same location in three-dimensional space, and all particles then move with the same three-dimensional velocity, then it will remain the case that all the particles are at the same location in three-dimensional space.

Once we have all this structure in place, we can characterize what a 'good' coordinate system is for configuration space. Here is how to make a 'good' coordinate system. Pick some point p in the co-location subspace. Then pick three orthogonal vectors in particle tangent space T_p^1. The straight lines in the corresponding three directions in configuration space are going to be the first three coordinate lines x_1, x_2, x_3. Pick three real numbers as the values of the three coordinates at p. Increase these values linearly with the metric as you travel along the lines. Then find the three vectors in T_p^2 that stand in the 'same-three-dimensional-vector' relation to the three vectors in T_p^1. The straight lines that these determine are the coordinate lines x_4, x_5, x_6. Assign the same triple of coordinate values at p to x_4, x_5, x_6 as you assigned to x_1, x_2, x_3 at p. Then increase the values of x_4, x_5, x_6 in the same linear fashion as before. And so on for all N particle tangent spaces. This will produce a 'good' coordinate system for configuration space. And then one can impose the equations of the three-dimensional theory on the coordinate triples of any 'good' coordinate system.

There probably are other coordinate independent structures for a 3N-dimensional configuration space that one could postulate in order to formulate a 3N-dimensional theory which explains the phenomena of space billiards. However, since the repelling force in space billiards, by assumption, depends on a set of three-dimensional distances, one way or another, one will have to recover all the three-dimensional distances which a single point in configuration space represents from the structure of that configuration space. The most natural way that I could think of doing this was by postulating a privileged set of points which represent the configurations in which all three-dimensional distances are 0, and postulating a privileged set of directions such that moving away from one of the privileged points in one such privileged direction corresponds to moving one of the three-dimensional particles away from all the others. As a consequence the structure of the 3N-dimensional space in the 3N-dimensional theory is significantly less natural and more complicated than the structure of three-dimensional space in the three-dimensional theory. And this is precisely why the three-dimensional theory is more plausible: it is more simple and natural, when stated in terms of the fundamental quantities that it postulates, than the 3N-dimensional theory.[7]

Matters get slightly worse for the 3N-dimensional theory when we consider space billiards with balls of different masses. The three-dimensional theory in that case just needs to assume that each particle has a fundamental mass. The 3N-dimensional theory will have to postulate fundamental masses that are properties of the particle-tangent-spaces. (Other particle properties such as charge could be treated analogously.) All in all, it seems clear that in the case of classical space billiards the theory that says that there are many objects in a three-dimensional theory is a better theory of the phenomena than the theory that says there is only one thing—the world-particle—which lives in a multi-dimensional configuration space. Let us turn to quantum mechanics.

3.5 Configuration space realism in non-relativistic quantum particle mechanics

Luckily we can be pretty quick. As we have seen, one can represent the position state of a collection of N quantum particles by a wave-function, a complex valued function distributed over configuration space. The law that governs the evolution of this

---

[7] One might think that one does not need to do anything as complicated as I did if one formulates ones 3N-dimensional theory in Lagrangian form. But that is not right. One would still need the co-location structure and the three-dimensional direction structure in order to pick out the 'good coordinatisations' of configuration space—those relative to which the potential energy term in the Lagrangian takes its usual simple form.

wave-function in standard (non-collapse) non-relativistic quantum particle mechanics is the Schrödinger equation:

$$i\hbar\partial\psi(x_1,\ldots,x_{3N})/\partial t = \Sigma_i(-\hbar^2/2m_i)(\partial^2\psi(x_1,\ldots,x_{3N})/\partial x_i^2) + V(x_1,\ldots,x_{3N})\psi(x_1,\ldots,x_{3N})$$

In particular, in the quantum mechanical version of space billiards, a way to state the law that governs the evolution of the wave-function in configuration space would be to say: 'There exist coordinate systems $(x_1,\ldots,x_{3N})$ such that relative to such a coordinate system the potential energy term V takes the form $V=\Sigma_{ij}f(D_{ij})$, where the sum is over the is and js from 1 through N, and $D_{ij}=\sqrt{((x_{3i}-x_{3j})^2+(x_{3i+1}-x_{3j+1})^2+(x_{3i+2}-x_{3j+2})^2)}$, and the mass terms m_i depend only on the index i'. Again, such a law is not a plausible fundamental law because it says: 'There exist coordinate systems such that . . .' In order to formulate a good theory we will need to assume the existence of exactly the same structure in configuration space as we do in the classical case. In the classical case we concluded that therefore the three-dimensional theory was more plausible than the configuration space theory. Why not do the same thing in the quantum case? Well, if one does so, then the quantum mechanical state of the world will not be separable: the quantum mechanical state $\psi(x_1,\ldots,x_{3N})$ can be specified point by point in configuration space, but it cannot be specified point by point in three-dimensional space. So, if one takes it for granted, as Albert seems to do, that the state of the world must be separable, then one will just have to accept configuration space as one's fundamental space, and accept that it has a rather complex structure—a structure which looks as if its only purpose is to code up an underlying three-dimensional multiple-particle occupation pattern. However, there is nothing mandatory about separability, and it seems preferable to formulate the theory taking three-dimensional space as fundamental, since the structure of three-dimensional space can be assumed to be the same as it is in the classical case: namely, that of a three-dimensional flat Euclidean space. Of course, one will have to assume the existence of a non-local fundamental quantity, the wave-function, whose amplitude is a function of n locations in three-dimensional space, or perhaps better, whose amplitude is a function of the occupation pattern of three-dimensional space (since that allows particle creations and annihilations). But I do not want to claim that it is totally obvious, which is the better theory as yet. My main argument against configuration space theories is yet to come. My main argument will be that there is no plausible configuration space theory in the case of relativistic quantum mechanics, to which we now turn.

3.6 Relativistic quantum mechanics and narratability failure

Intuitively speaking, in relativistic theories time is no longer a separate entity from space; there is just a single unified spacetime. So, naively, one would expect that if there is a problem with respect to spatial separability in non-relativistic quantum mechanics, then there is a problem with respect to temporal separability in relativistic quantum mechanics. And indeed there is. The problem is nicely brought out in a manuscript by David Albert, entitled 'Physics and Narrative'.[8] I will use a slight variation on his argument in order to bring out the problem, and will then discuss a number of different possible reactions to the problem.

My main example will involve the spin-states of a pair of electrons. I will use more compact notation than before: $|\text{spin}^1_z = +\frac{1}{2}\rangle$ will be abbreviated as $|+^1_z\rangle$, and so on. Consider now the co-called 'singlet state' of the pair:

$$|\psi\rangle = (1/\sqrt{2})(|+^1_z\rangle|-^2_z\rangle - |-^1_z\rangle|+^2_z\rangle)$$

This state is such that if we were to measure the spin in the z-direction of both particles, we have a 50% chance of producing 'spin-up' for particle 1 and 'spin-down' for particle 2, and a 50% chance of producing 'spin-down' for particle 1 and 'spin-up' for particle 1. Now let us think what this singlet state looks like when written as a superposition of the spin eigenstates in a direction different from z. Let us call this direction w. You might think that what the state will then look like will depend on which direction w we pick, but we will see that for the special case of the singlet state it in fact does not depend on what the direction w is.

Whatever the direction w is, we know that we can write any spin-state of each particle, and hence also the spin eigenstates in the z-direction, as a superposition of the spin eigenstates in direction w:

$$|+^1_z\rangle = a|+^1_w\rangle + b|-^1_w\rangle$$
$$|+^2_z\rangle = a|+^2_w\rangle + b|-^2_w\rangle$$
$$|-^1_z\rangle = c|+^1_w\rangle + d|-^1_w\rangle$$
$$|-^2_z\rangle = c|+^2_w\rangle + d|-^2_w\rangle$$

for some complex numbers a, b, c, and d.

Now let us write the singlet state in terms of the eigenvectors of spin in direction w:

$$(1/\sqrt{2})(|+^1_z\rangle|-^2_z\rangle - |-^1_z\rangle|+^2_z\rangle) = (1/\sqrt{2})((a|+^1_w\rangle + b|-^1_w\rangle)(c|+^2_w\rangle + d|-^2_w\rangle) - (c|+^1_w\rangle + d|-^1_w\rangle)(a|+^2_w\rangle + b|-^2_w\rangle)$$

Multiplying the terms through we find that this equals

$$(1/\sqrt{2})((ac-ca)|+^1_w\rangle|+^2_w\rangle + (ad-cb)|+^1_w\rangle|-^2_w\rangle + (bc-da)|-^1_w\rangle|+^2_w\rangle + (bd-db)|-^1_w\rangle|-^2_w\rangle))$$

Now $(ac-ca)=0$, $(bd-db)=0$, and $(ad-cb)=-(bc-da)$, so this means that the singlet state

$$|\psi\rangle = (1/\sqrt{2})(f|+^1_w\rangle|-^2_w\rangle - f|-^1_w\rangle|+^2_w\rangle)$$

[8] As far as I know it is not published anywhere. I suggest Googling it. I hope that by the time you read this it has been published, or is available somewhere on the Web.

for some complex number f. We also know that the sum of the squares of $(1/\sqrt{2})(f)$ and $(1/\sqrt{2})(-f)$ must sum to 1. So f must be a complex number of length (modulus) 1. So, up to an arbitrary, and irrelevant, phase the singlet state takes the same form in terms of the spin eigenstates in direction w as it does in terms of the spin eigenstates in direction z.[9] Indeed, since we assumed nothing about direction w, it takes the same form relative to the spin eigenstates of *any* direction whatsoever. And, hence, the probabilities for the results of measurements of spin in *any* direction are the same in the singlet state: always opposite results for the two particles, and each individual result has a 50% chance. What this means is that the singlet state is rotation-invariant: the state, and the chances that it implies, looks the same from any angle. So, if we were to 'grab' each of a pair of particles in a singlet state and rotate each one of them around the same axis over the same angle, the pair would remain in exactly the same singlet state. Let us make use of this rotation invariance.

Consider the following evolution of the quantum mechanical state of two electrons in some inertial frame X in Minkowski spacetime. At $t=0$ the electrons are in a singlet state—one electron located at $x=0$, and the other located at $x=1$. The dynamics is such that at $t=0$, in frame X, both at $x=0$ and at $x=1$, the spins are simultaneously 'flipped'; that is

$|+^1_z>$ evolves into $|-^1_z>$
$|+^2_z>$ evolves into $|-^2_z>$
$|-^1_z>$ evolves into $-|+^1_z>$
$|-^2_z>$ evolves into $-|+^2_z>$

One can either assume that this happens through an instantaneous 'flipping' of spins, or, more realistically, through a non-instantaneous rotation of the spins during some time interval, ending in a rotation over 180 degrees, where this happens at the same rate at locations $x=0$ and $x=1$ relative to frame X. The singlet state $(1/\sqrt{2})(|+^1_z>|-^2_z> -|-^1_z>|+^2_z>)$ will then evolve into $(1/\sqrt{2})(-|-^1_z>|+^2_z>+|+^1_z>|-^2_z>)=(1/\sqrt{2})(|+^1_z>|-^2_z> -|-^1_z>|+^2_z>)$; that is, it will remain the same. Indeed, since the singlet state is rotation-invariant the pair will remain in the singlet state during the rotation, as long as the rotation occurs simultaneously, at the same rate, at both locations relative to frame X.

But now let us consider a frame X' in which the flipping of the spin at the left-hand side occurs before the flipping at the right-hand side. In this frame the state is not always the singlet state (since $(1/\sqrt{2})(|-^1_z>|-^2_z>+|+^1_z>|+^2_z>)$ is not the singlet state). It immediately follows that the history of the state in frame X, *all by itself*, cannot determine the history in frame X'. After all, in frame X the state is always the singlet state,

---

[9] The 'phase' of the complex number f is the angle that it makes with the real axis in the complex plane. Readers who have never dealt with complex numbers will not be able to follow all the details of the arguments in this chapter. Perhaps the diligent reader will want to read some more about complex numbers. T. Needham, *Visual Complex Analysis* (1997) is a great book, but it contains much more than is required for understanding what I am talking about here. The Wikipedia entry on complex numbers should suffice.

which is compatible with the dynamics always being trivial; that is, there being no interaction (in particular no interaction which flips spins), which is compatible with it always being the singlet state in frame X'.

This is surprising, and is very different from standard, non-quantum, relativistic theories, in which one determines the state at a location in spacetime in one frame of reference by performing the appropriate (Lorentz) transformation on the state at that location in another frame of reference. Indeed, it seems better to postulate a coordinate-independent neighbourhood-local state at each point, and then define coordinate-dependent representations of these neighbourhood-local states, whose transformation properties follow from the way in which one defines the coordinate representations of the coordinate-independent neighbourhood-local states. What the spin singlet example shows is that things are very different in quantum mechanics: we are presented with frame-dependent states, and we find that we cannot obtain the history of quantum mechanical states in one frame of reference from the history of quantum mechanical states in another frame of reference. We have, of course, already encountered the idea that quantum mechanical states cannot be thought of as being determined by local, or by neighbourhood-local, states. That is, we are quite used to the idea that in terms of spatial separability, quantum mechanics differs from standard classical theories. But what is new here is that we have a frame-dependent notion of state, and even when we know everything that happens at all times in one frame of reference we still do not know everything, and in particular we do not know everything that is the case in another frame of reference. Albert calls this a failure of 'narratability'.

The above suggests that temporal separability fails in relativistic quantum mechanics: the fundamental features at each instant (in a single frame of reference) do not determine all the features. However, this does not have to be so. Maybe what we are missing are not multi-time facts. Or maybe we are not actually missing any facts; maybe there is a privileged frame of reference such that if we give the wave-function at each time in that frame we have given everything, that is, maybe in some cases there is no fact of the matter as to what the evolution of the wave-function is in other 'underprivileged' frames of reference. And even if temporal separability does fail, the question remains: in what way does it fail? How should we characterize the state of the history of the world? In what sense can this be the state of a Special Relativistic world, and in what sense can it be the state of a Minkowski spacetime?

3.7 Can one use dynamics to rescue narratability?

In my example the fact that the pair of particles was in a singlet state at each time frame X did not determine whether it was in the singlet state at all times in other frames. What we saw was that if the dynamics, the law of evolution, was such that it simultaneously rotated the spins in frame X, then it would not always be a singlet state in frame X', but if the dynamics was trivial—that is, did not rotate any spins at any time in frame X—then it would always remain the singlet state in frame X'. This suggests that if in addition to the history of states in frame X we also know what the dynamical law is, then we can infer the history in one frame from the history in another frame. In fact this is correct, and we will see in subsequent sections how one can use the dynamics to go from the history in one frame to the history in another frame. But in this section I want to focus on the question as to whether this fact implies that there is no problem; that it shows that the world is narratable after all.

One might argue that since the states at each instant in one frame of reference, given the dynamical laws, allow us to infer the states at each instant in any other frame of reference, it follows that the states at all instants in one frame of reference do determine everything, and hence that the history of the world can be given instant by instant in one frame of reference, that the history of the world is narratable after all. This, *prima facie*, is a mistake. In classical theories we have local coordinate independent quantities (scalars, vectors, tensors) whose states have different representations in different frames of reference; that is, different coordinate representations. The history in a frame of reference X′ can be obtained from the history in a distinct frame of reference X by transforming the X-coordinate representation of each local quantity into the corresponding X′-coordinate representation. None of this has anything to do with the dynamics, the laws of temporal evolution. Going from the history of states in one frame to the history of states in another frame amounts to going from one coordinate representation to another coordinate representation of the distribution of the underlying coordinate independent geometric quantities, which has nothing to do with dynamical laws that may or may not govern the evolution of these quantities. A theory postulates certain fundamental objects, certain fundamental properties, and certain fundamental relations (and perhaps higher-order fundamental properties and relations), and postulates certain laws governing these relations.[10] When we ask whether according to a theory the state of the world is spatially, or temporally, separable, we are asking whether all the fundamental properties and relations can be given point by point, or instant by instant. Whether we can use the laws in order to infer certain properties and relations from other properties and relations is neither here nor there when it comes to the issue of narratability and the issue of temporal separability.

In fact, the issue runs deeper than the issues of separability and narratibility. Suppose one were to say that each time-slice in each frame of reference (or perhaps each space-like hypersurface) in Minkowski spacetime has as a fundamental feature a wave-function. And suppose that one gave a rule, involving the dynamics, for going from the wave-function associated with one time-slice to the wave-function associated with any other time-slice. Even if we were to grant that this makes the state of the history

---

[10] One can have different ideas as to the nature of these laws. Humeans think that these laws are something like simple summaries of regular features of the development of the state; they think that the dynamical laws are completely determined by the features of the states, so that there could be no difference in dynamical laws without a difference in the history of states. Non-Humeans think that the laws are something 'over and above' the features of the states, and, typically, think that there are possibilities that differ in these laws while not differing in the history of states. Either way, there is a crucial distinction between the states of the world and the laws that govern them.

of the world narratable and temporally separable, there remains the question in which sense such a theory is genuinely relativistic. What sense can we now make of the idea that different frames of reference correspond to different ways of looking at the same underlying reality? What sense can we now make of the idea that states in different frames are different coordinate representations of the same underlying reality?

3.8 There is no configuration spacetime

It would be nice if we could have a quantum theory which has fundamental local geometric quantities such as scalar, vector, tensor fields and particle trajectories whose coordinate representations entail how states transform when one goes from one frame to another. Of course we know one obstacle to this idea: the fact that quantum states are non-separable. And we have seen a suggested solution: regard the wave-function not as a scalar function in three-dimensional space, but as a scalar function on 3N-dimensional configuration space. Can we apply this idea in the relativistic case in order to obtain a theory of separable quantum states which explains how the states transform when one goes from one coordinate system to another? In the non-quantum case this was straightforward: one assumes the existence of coordinate independent particle trajectories and scalar, vector, and tensor fields in a Minkowski spacetime. One defines representations of these objects relative to the possible coordinatisations of Minkowski spacetime, and this determines how these representations change when one goes from one coordinate system to another. Can we not do the same thing for configuration spacetime? No, we cannot. There is no such thing as configuration spacetime in a relativistic theory. Let me explain.

Suppose we have an inertial coordinate system (x,y,z,t) for a Minkowski spacetime. For convenience I will abbreviate (x,y,z,t) as (x,t) in this section. We can use such a coordinate system to give a coordinate representation of every possible history of locations of a *pair* of particles: any sex-tuple of functions $(x_1(t), x_2(t))$ represents a possible history of 2-particle configurations in Minkowski spacetime. One can picture such a history as a line running in the t-direction in a seven-dimensional space coordinatized by x_1, x_2, and t. One can obviously do the same thing with some other inertial coordinate system (x',t'). But it would be a mistake to think that what is going on here is that there is a single underlying configuration spacetime which can either be coordinatized using coordinates (x_1,x_2,t) or using coordinates (x_1',x_2',t'). The reason why this would be a mistake is simple: there is no 1–1 relation between the points in the space co-ordinatized by (x_1',x_2',t') and the points in the space coordinatized by (x_1,x_2,t). For instance, suppose that at $t=0$ one particle is at $x=3$ and the other is at $x=5$ in frame X. Such an assignment of a pair of exact locations which is simultaneous in frame X picks out a unique point in the space coordinatized by coordinates (x_1,x_2,t): namely, the point with coordinates $(3,5,0)$. But a (generic) distinct frame X' has a different associated notion of simultaneity. So the point with coordinates $(3,5,0)$ in the space coordinatized by coordinates (x_1,x_2,t) does not correspond to any single point in the space coordinatized by (x_1',x_2',t'). Rather, the point with coordinates (3,5,0) in the space coordinatized by coordinates (x_1,x_2,t) corresponds to a constraint in the space coordinatized by (x_1',x_2',t') which on one time-slice restricts the possibilities to a three-dimensional subspace, and on another time-slice again restricts the possibilities to a three-dimensional subspace. In short, we do not have an underlying configuration spacetime with alternate coordinatisations. This scuppers any straightforward implementation of the idea that we can go from one frame to another by transforming wave-functions point by point according to some local rule. But all is not yet lost for the configuration space approach.

3.9 Multi-time configuration space wave-functions

Unfortunately, from this point on in this chapter there will be occasions on which I will not be able to explain things by just assuming familiarity with calculus: I will sometimes assume some familiarity with some of the details of quantum mechanics, and sometimes even some familiarity with some elementary aspects of quantum field theory.[11]

Dirac and, following him, Tomonaga and Schwinger, suggested using 'multi-time' wave-functions in order to make quantum theory a theory which is relativistic in a clear and simple sense. Let me illustrate their idea by starting with a very simple case: two particles, a and b, which (on some time-slice in some frame) are in a non-entangled product state $\psi(x_a,x_b,t)=\psi(x_a,t)\psi(x_b,t)$. Suppose that the two particles do not interact; that is, that the total Hamiltonian is a sum of two Hamiltonians H_a and H_b, where H_a is a function only of the position and momentum operators of particle a and H_b is a function only of the position and momentum operators of particle b. Then we can attach an amplitude to two-time conditions such as $<x_a$ at t_1 and x_b at time $t_2>$ by evolving $\psi(x_b,t_1)$ according to Hamiltonian H_b from time t_1 to t_2; that is, $\psi(x_a$ at t_1 and x_b at $t_2)=\psi(x_a,t_1)\psi(x_b,t_2)$. The state on a time-slice t' in a different frame of reference is then just given by the amplitudes $\psi(x_a$ at t_1 and x_b at $t_2)$ for all pairs of spacetime points $<(x_a,t_1),(x_b,t_2)>$ such that (x_a,t_1) lies on time-slice t' and (x_b,t_2) lies on time-slice t'. Now, this procedure also works for non-factorizable initial states. That is to say, we can assume the existence of a multi-time wave-function $\psi(x_a,x_b,t_a,t_b)$, which satisfies both of the following equations:

$$H_a\,\psi(x_a,x_b,t_a,t_b)=i\hbar\partial\psi/\partial t_a$$
$$H_b\,\psi(x_a,x_b,t_a,t_b)=i\hbar\partial\psi/\partial t_b$$

[11] For the more assiduous reader I can recommend D. Albert, *Quantum Mechanics and Experience* (Harvard University Press, Cambridge, 1992), as a philosophical introduction to quantum mechanics; C. Isham, *Lectures on Quantum Theory* (Imperial College Press, London, 1995), as an introduction to the formalism of quantum mechanics; P. Teller, *An Interpretive Introduction to Quantum Field Theory* (Princeton University Press, Princeton, 1995), as a philosophical introduction to quantum field theory; and R. Greiner and J. Reinhardt, *Field Quantization* (Springer, Berlin, 1996), as an introduction to the formalism of quantum field theory.

On this view the history of the world consists of coordinate independent wave-function amplitudes distributed in a multi-time configuration space.

How does this theory relate these fundamental quantities to the phenomena? The easiest way to do this is to translate the multi-time states into the single time states that we are familiar with. How does one do that? Well, we need to assume that the multi-time configuration space has quite a lot of structure. Here is a natural way to picture this structure. Two-particle multi-time configuration spacetime is the Cartesian product of 'a-spacetime' and 'b-spacetime'. Each of these two spacetimes has a Minkowski structure. And there is a notion of identity and non-identity of a location in a-spacetime and b-spacetime. Then a time-slice in Minkowski spacetime corresponds to a pair of time-slices in a-spacetime and b-spacetime. And we can ask for the state on that Minkowski time-slice: it is given by the amplitudes $\psi(x_a, x_b, t_a, t_b)$ at all points in configuration spacetime such that (x_a, t_a) and (x_b, t_b) lie on that time-slice. The theory is relativistic in a fairly straightforward sense: each particle spacetime is a Minkowski spacetime, and the laws of evolution only make use of this structure plus the identity of location structure.

Let me now look at our spin singlet example to see what this looks like from the current perspective. On the current view the fundamental features of the world are the amplitudes for all points in two-time configuration spacetime. Now, consider the amplitudes for all points in two-time configuration spacetime which correspond to some single time-slice t in Minkowski spacetime. For simplicity let me work with a 'Minkowski' spacetime with one spatial dimension and one temporal dimension. Then the set of points in two-time configuration spacetime that correspond to time-slice t forms a two-dimensional surface in the four-dimensional two-time configuration spacetime. Now consider the surfaces corresponding to two time-slices t and t' in different frames. Each of these surfaces is two-dimensional. Since the whole space is four-dimensional, these two surfaces intersect at a single point. In fact, they will intersect at a point that corresponds to both particles having exactly the same location in space and time. Now consider all the time-slices $\{t\}$ in some frame of reference and consider a single time-slice t' in another frame of reference. Each time-slice t intersects with exactly one point of t'—a point that corresponds to the two particles being at the same spacetime location. The set of all the intersection points forms a line on t'—the line consisting of all the co-location points on t'. So if one knows the amplitudes for all pairs of points on all the time-slices $\{t\}$, one thereby merely thereby knows the amplitudes for a complete set of co-location points on t'; one knows the amplitudes $\psi(x_a, x_b, t')$ for the set of points on t' restricted to $x_a = x_b$. Small wonder that one cannot directly infer the state on t'; that is, $\psi(x_a, x_b, t')$ for all pairs (x_a, x_b). So, from the current perspective it is not surprising that knowing all the amplitudes in one frame of reference does not directly determine the amplitudes in other frames of reference. What is surprising is that the dynamics allows one to infer what they are. The dynamics in two-time configuration space just happens to be such that giving the data on a time-slice—that is, on such a two-dimensional surface—does determine the amplitudes everywhere in configuration spacetime. But from the current perspective, this is a lucky fact about the dynamics.

This all seems fairly nice, but the theory encounters some trouble when we consider interactions. In order to deal with interactions, Tomonaga (1946) considered the interaction representation in quantum field theory. In the interaction picture both the field operators and the quantum state evolve in time. The interaction picture field operators $\hat{\varphi}^I(x,t)$ evolve according to the free field Hamiltonian H_F:

$$\hat{\varphi}^I(x,t) = \exp(i\hbar H_F)\hat{\varphi}^S(x)\exp(-i\hbar H_F)$$

The quantum state $\psi(t)$ evolves according to the interaction Hamiltonian H_I:

$$H_I\psi(t) = i\hbar\partial_t\psi(t)$$

What Tomonaga then suggests is to take some coordinate system, (x,y,z,t) and to introduce a separate time coordinate t_{xyz} for each location in space. So the wave-function now becomes $\psi(t_{xyz})$, where for any smooth function t_{xyz} from locations in space to times; that is, any smooth surface that extends to all of space which does not 'double back' relative to the given coordinate system, $\psi(t_{xyz})$ gives the amplitude for a field configuration on that surface. Now consider the Interaction Hamiltonian. It is the integral of the Interaction Hamiltonian density H_I. The Interaction Hamiltonian density $H_I(x,y,z,t)$ at a location (x,y,z,t) in space and time is a function of the field operators at that location in space and time. Since these field operators, in the interaction representation, evolve in time (according to the free field equations), $H_I(x,y,z,t)$ is a spacetime-dependent operator. Tomonaga now assumes that the infinitely multitime wave-function simultaneously satisfies infinitely many equations of the form—one for each time t_{xyz}:

$$H_I(x,y,z,t)\psi(t_{xyz}) = i\hbar\partial\psi(t_{xyz})/\partial t_{xyz}$$

More precisely, the right-hand side should be a 'functional derivative':

$$H_I(x,y,z,t)\psi(t_{xyz}) = i\hbar\delta\psi(t_{xyz})/\delta t_{xyz}$$

This equations says that when one considers any ψ on any surface, and one takes the limit of small (smooth) variations of that surface in the t direction at (and near) a point (x,y,z), the rate of change of ψ is proportional to H at that point acting on ψ.

Unfortunately, there is a problem with equation. Double derivatives commute:

$$\partial(\partial\psi(t_{xyz})/\partial t_{xyz})\partial t_{x'y'z'} = \partial(\partial\psi(t_{xyz})/\partial t_{x'y'z'})\partial t_{xyz}$$

So, for the set equation to be consistent, it should be the case that

$$H_I(x,y,z,t)H_I(x',y',z',t) = H_I(x',y',z',t)H_I(x,y,z,t)$$

But this is not generally true. It is true if (x',y',z',t) and (x,y,z,t) are space-like related. But so far we have put no restriction on the form of the function t_{xyz}—that is, on the shape of the surface on which we are assuming the wave-function to be defined. So we have a problem. In fact, we should not be that surprised that we encountered trouble. By allowing surfaces corresponding to any (smooth, total) functions t_{xyz} in some frame, we thereby allowed surfaces that can be crossed multiple times by time-like trajectories. And one would expect it to be a bit hard to have a proper initial value problem for such surfaces; one would expect that simple-minded equations might not have global solutions for all initial value states. OK, so Tomonaga said, fine, but we can still assume that for each (smooth) space-like surface we have a wave-function which develops according to the equation,

$$H_l(x,y,z,t)\psi(t_{xyz})=i\hbar\delta\psi(t_{xyz})/\delta t_{xyz}$$

It is time to take stock. How can we understand the relativistic nature of Tomonaga's theory? Well, to begin with, note that we do not have amplitudes for locations in a number of copies of Minkowski spacetime. In the n-particle case we, in effect, introduced a separate Minkowski spacetime for each particle. But in the field case we did not introduce a Minkowski spacetime for each field, or anything like that. Rather, we introduced a separate temporal space for each location in space. We then assumed that if we picked any (smoothly varying) set of temporal locations for all spatial locations, there was a unique amplitude associated with any combination of local field states at these locations. (And we assumed that these amplitudes satisfied the above evolution equation.) But, other than that we now have states for arbitrary space-like surfaces, this does not seem much better than the previously mentioned idea that we have states attached to time-slices, where the states on different time-slices are related by rules that involve the dynamics. We do satisfy the constraint that probabilities for local field states at a given point in spacetime (modulo worries about fields at exact points making sense) are the same in all frames of reference. But that is also satisfied according to the previously mentioned idea. All that we, in effect, have done is make precise the dynamics-involving rule for going from the state on one space-like hypersurface to the state on any other space-like hypersurface.

Let me express another worry about Tomonaga's theory. In the interaction picture the field operators evolve in time as well as the quantum state. It is therefore not plausible to think of the state of the world on a time-slice (or on a space-like surface) as being given just by the quantum state on this time-slice. One also needs to know which operators represent the fields; one has no idea what consequences a particular quantum state on a time-slice has in the interaction picture has for the phenomena unless one also knows what the operators are that correspond to the fields on that time-slice. So one needs a dual ontology in Tomonaga's theory: one both needs operators at spacetime points, and quantum states attached to space-like surfaces.

All of this does not seem to give us a very simple and nice theory, nor a nice and simple account of the sense in which the theory is relativistic.

3.10 Indeterministic relativistic theories in general

If one thinks of a wave-function, the quantum mechanical amplitudes, as some field distributed in Minkowski spacetime, then it seems puzzling that one cannot give the

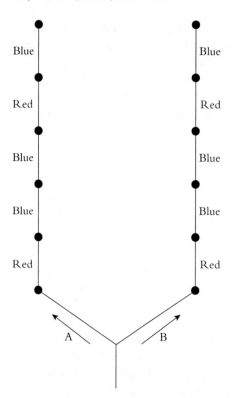

Figure 3.4 Example of relativistic indeterminism.

state of the world at a time by giving the state of this field at each location in space at that time. We have examined trying to remedy this by saying that the real arena of events is configuration space. But we discovered that we then had to postulate some fairly unnatural structure for this configuration space, and that it was unclear, at best, how to extend this to relativistic theories, since there is no configuration spacetime.

In this section I want to examine the idea that quantum mechanical amplitudes are not akin to classical fields, but are akin to probabilities. Perhaps then the puzzlement about non-separability will disappear. After all, the probability of <state S at location (x,t)> and the probability of <state S′ at location $(x′,t)$> does not generally determine the probability of <state S at (x,t) and state S′ at $(x′,t)$>. Similarly, the probability of <state S at location (x,t)> and the probability of <state S at location $(x,t′)$> does not generally determine the probability of <state S at (x,t) and state S′ at $(x,t′)$>. (I am using the brackets '<' and '>' just in order to make clear exactly what the probabilities are probabilities of.) And, finally, even the history of probabilities of states on all the time-slices of one frame of reference does not generally determine the history of probabilities of states on the time-slices of another frame of reference. Since the truth of this last claim may not be obvious, let me illustrate it with an example (see figure 3.4).

Suppose that there is a particular type of particle, which always does the following. Once it comes into existence it always moves on an inertial trajectory (it never accelerates). Ten seconds proper time (along its trajectory in spacetime) after it has come into existence it always explodes into two particles. These two particles—let us call them A and B—always move away from the explosion with equal speed and opposite direction relative to the trajectory of the original particle (which now no longer exists) until they are 5 feet apart (in the frame of reference corresponding to the motion of the original particle). At this point they both stop moving relative to the trajectory of the original particle, and they acquire a colour: either red or blue. Each colour is equally likely, but the probability is 1 that they acquire the same colour. From then on, every time a second has elapsed (as measured along their trajectories) they have a 50% chance of switching colour, and a 50% chance of remaining the same colour, but always either both switch or neither switch. That is, in a frame of reference (x,t) associated with the trajectory of the original particle there is always probability 1 that they have the same colour, and with probability 0.5 this colour is red and with probability 0.5 it is blue. Now consider a frame (x',t') in which the *first* colour-switching time of particle A occurs simultaneous with the *second* colour-switching time of particle B. In this frame there is no correlation between the simultaneous colours of A and B. Notice the following. The actual probabilities in frame (x',t')—namely, uncorrelated probabilities of 0.5 for each colour of each particle—are not only compatible with the actual probabilities in frame X—namely, totally correlated probabilities of 0.5—but are also compatible with totally uncorrelated probabilities of 0.5 in frame (x,t). So, in general, the probabilities in one frame do not determine the probabilities in another frame. And there is nothing mysterious about this non-narratability of probabilities. It is as unmysterious as the fact that the probability of X and the probability of Y does not determine the probability of X and Y.

Furthermore, if we include the transition probabilities, the dynamics, in one frame, then we *can* infer the probabilities and transition probabilities in any other frame. Take the case of correlated colour switches in frame (x,t). Suppose that in fame (x',t') at time $t'=1$ particle A is red and particle B is blue. Then the transition probability

Pr(A is blue at $t'=2$/A is red and B is blue at $t'=1$)=1

This is so because if B is blue at $t'=1$, then B is blue at $t = 2$ (since this is one and the same spacetime point), so (with probability 1) A is blue at $t = 2$, so A is blue at $t' = 2$. More generally, the probabilities plus transition probabilities in one frame determine the probabilities of (all finite features of) histories, which in turn determine probabilities and transition probabilities in any other frame.

So we have a nice analogy in order to understand as to why quantum mechanical amplitudes are non-separable, and why it is that dynamics is needed to go from amplitudes on time-slices in one frame to amplitudes on time-slices in another frame. Let us see how far this analogy gets us. Before turning to quantum mechanics, let me quickly sketch how one could generally construct relativistic indeterministic theories.

Let us start by discussing non-relativistic indeterministic theories. One can specify such a theory just by specifying transition probabilities—Markovian ones, for example—such that the transition probabilities over longer times are determined by shorter time transition probabilities:

$$\Pr(s_3 \text{ at } t_3/s_1 \text{ at } t_1) = \Sigma i \, \Pr(s_3 \text{ at } t_3/s_2{}^i \text{ at } t_2)\Pr(s_2{}^i \text{ at } t_2/s_1 \text{ at } t_1)$$

A state at a time t, or a probability distribution at a time t, together with such transition probabilities, will generate probability distributions at all later times; that is, an evolving probability distribution. Indeed, it will generate a probability distribution over histories of states after t. Alternatively, one could take as fundamental a probability distribution over histories, and from it generate transition probabilities and probabilities at times. If the history is infinite in time, or if there are infinitely many possible states at each time, matters are not quite this simple. For in that case probabilities of complete histories will generically be 0, and such probabilities of complete histories cannot by themselves generate any transition probabilities or probabilities of states at times. The most natural and common way to deal with this problem is to specify probabilities for (measurable) sets of histories.

Now let us turn to relativistic indeterministic theories. One way to give such a theory is to give transition probabilities from earlier states on time-slices to later states on time-slices. Such a theory is relativistic if the transition probabilities are the same in all frames of reference.[12] But there is now a consistency demand. Suppose one takes an initial distribution on some time-slice t in some frame X, and evolves it to future time-slices in frame X according to the given transition probabilities. This gives rise to probabilities of histories of states after t. Consistency now demands that these probabilities of histories are compatible with probabilities in frame X' evolving according to the same transition probabilities. The natural way to check for this would be to find the evolving probability distribution in X' from the probabilities of histories in X, and then see whether it is evolving according to the given transition probabilities. However, the probability distribution on a time-slice t' in X' is not determined by the given probabilities of histories. The problem is that any time-slice t' in X has a portion that lies prior to any time-slice t in X, so we cannot infer probabilities of states on X' given probabilities of histories after some time-slice t in X.

Another way to give a relativistic indeterministic theory—one that is better from the point of view of the above problem—is to give a rule for the transition probabilities from states on earlier space-like surfaces t to states on later space-like surfaces t', where these space-like surfaces need not be flat. Consistency then demands that the rule for the transition probabilities is such that

$$\text{Prob}(s_3 \text{ on } t_1/s_1 \text{ on } t_1) = \Sigma_{s2}\text{Prob}(s_3 \text{ on } t_3/s_2 \text{ on } t_2)\text{Prob}(s_2 \text{ on } t_2/s_1 \text{ on } t_1)$$

---

[12] One might think that my toy colour theory is not relativistic, because the transition probabilities are not the same in different frames of reference. However, the transition probabilities are not different in different frames of reference. Rather, in each frame of reference what the transition probabilities depends on the velocity of the particles relative to that frame of reference. But it is the same velocity-dependence in each frame of reference, so the transition probabilities are the same in each frame of reference.

for any surface t_2 lying between t_1 on t_3. That is, the rule should be such that evolving the probability distribution from one surface to another yields the same result no matter what sequence of intermediate surfaces one uses to evolve it.

Consistency also demands the following. Suppose space-like surfaces t_1 and t_2 have a region R in common. Then, in so far as one can speak of properties intrinsic to region R, the probabilities for such properties should be the same on surfaces t_1 and t_2.

The main point of this section is to point out that probabilities of states are quite different types of quantities from quantities such as positions and momenta, or local field values, which characterize the states themselves. Probabilities generically are 'non-separable' in the sense that probabilities of states at two locations are not determined by the probabilities of the states at each of the locations. Also, generically, in order to go from probabilities on the space-like surfaces of one foliation to those on the space-like surfaces of another foliation one needs dynamics; that is, transition probabilities. Now let us attempt to understand the relativistic nature of relativistic quantum mechanics by taking it that quantum mechanical amplitudes are quantities akin to probabilities.

3.11 Amplitude realism

Let us begin with a non-relativistic (non-collapse) quantum mechanics of particles in the position representation. According to such a theory there are amplitudes for complete position configurations x at times t, and the dynamics of the theory specifies transition amplitudes between different configurations at different times. Squaring the absolute value of the amplitudes of complete configurations gives the probabilities of complete configurations at times. Squaring the absolute values of the transition amplitudes between complete configurations gives the transition probabilities. Unfortunately we do not get coherent probabilities of histories. The quantum mechanical *amplitudes* $\psi(x$ at $t)$ and transition *amplitudes* $\psi(x'$ at t'/x at $t)$ satisfy the rule:

$$\psi(x' \text{ at } t') = \int \psi(x' \text{ at } t'/x \text{ at } t)\psi(x \text{ at } t)dx$$

So the quantum mechanical probabilities, which we get by squaring the modulus of these amplitudes, generically, do not satisfy the rule; that is:

$$\Pr(x' \text{ at } t') \neq \int \Pr(x' \text{ at } t'/x \text{ at } t)\Pr(x \text{ at } t)dx$$

This is one reason why in this attempt to understand the non-separable nature of quantum mechanical states, we are going to take it that quantum mechanical *amplitudes*, and transition *amplitudes*, are fundamental quantities akin to classical probabilities, rather than taking it that quantum mechanical *probabilities* are fundamental quantities akin to classical probabilities.

The path integral formalism tells us that the transition amplitudes can be derived from amplitudes associated with histories—so-called 'path amplitudes'—in the way that one would expect if the amplitudes were probabilities. In particular, associated with any finite history h, starting with configuration x at t and ending with configuration x' at t', there is the (classical) action $S(h)=\int Ldt$, where L is the (classical) Lagrangian. The path amplitude $\psi(h)$ associated with a history h satisfies the law:

$$\psi(h)=\exp(iS(h))$$

(Note that each path amplitude is a complex number of modulus 1—a 'pure phase'.) And then the transition amplitudes $\psi(x'$ at t'/x at $t)$ satisfy the law:

$$\psi(x' \text{ at } t'/x \text{ at } t)=\Sigma\psi(h)$$

where the 'sum' is over all histories that begin with x at t and end with x' at t'.[13] One can then show that the amplitudes $\psi(x,t)$ will evolve according to the Schrodinger equation.

Note that the path amplitudes play the role of 'conditional amplitudes', not the role of 'joint amplitudes'; that is, they are analogous to conditional probabilities, not analogous to joint probabilities. Note also that now we do not have the problem that amplitudes of individual histories have to be 0. Even though we are summing infinitely many such amplitudes, and all of them are non-zero, they can still 'sum' to something finite, because they are complex numbers, not real numbers.

The picture I now want to consider is this. The fundamental quantities are amplitudes of configurations at times and path amplitudes. Configurations at times are geometrical features of Newtonian spacetime. Paths—histories of configurations—are geometrical features of Newtonian spacetime. Amplitudes are quantities that attach to these geometrical features. Everything else, including the phenomena, supervenes on the amplitude facts. Could we make do with even less? Could we have 'joint amplitudes' analogous to joint probabilities, which determine both the amplitudes at times and path amplitudes? Yes.

Suppose we start with the picture in which we have both path amplitudes and amplitudes of states at times. Then let us define joint amplitudes

$$j(h)=\psi(x \text{ at } t)\psi(h)$$

where x at t is the starting configuration of h. If all we have is the joint amplitudes $j(h)$, can we recover the amplitudes at times $\psi(t)$ and path amplitudes $\psi(h)$? We can. For,

$$\psi(x' \text{ at } t')=\int\Sigma\psi(h)\psi(x \text{ at } t)dx$$

where we 'sum' over all histories starting at x at t and ending at x' at t'. But

$$\psi(h)\psi(x \text{ at } t)=j(h)$$

So $\psi(x'$ at $t')$ is just the 'sum' of all joint amplitudes of all histories starting at some time t, and ending at x' at t'. So we can recover $\psi(t)$ from the $j(h)$, and do so in the way that

---

[13] This is a 'sum' over uncountably many paths. So we need a measure over such sets of paths. This is mathematically non-trivial (and obviously must make use of a measure on spacetime).

one would expect if they were probabilities of states at times and joint probabilities of histories. We can also recover the $\psi(h)$ from the $j(h)$ and the $\psi(t)$: it is just the phase you need to go from $\psi(t)$ to $j(h)$ by multiplication.[14]

However, the joint amplitudes $j(h)$ might not plausibly be taken to be the fundamental quantities. For the best way to state the laws of the world in terms of the joint amplitudes is to say that the joint amplitudes can be factored into amplitudes of histories and amplitudes at times, where these two amplitudes satisfy the laws that I specified above. For instance, let history h just be history h_1 follow by history h_2. Then $\psi(h)=\psi(h_1).\psi(h_2)$. But the joint amplitudes $j(h)$, $j(h_1)$ and $j(h_2)$ do not satisfy this rule, indeed $j(h_1)$ and $j(h_2)$ do not determine $j(h)$. Also note that one would get quite different joint amplitudes for histories if one were to multiply the path amplitude (or even its complex conjugate) with the amplitude at the endpoint of h. So, just as in the classical case, it might be better to think of the joint amplitudes to be composed of two fundamental quantities: the contingent amplitudes at times, and the nomic path amplitudes.

Now let us turn to relativistic quantum mechanics. There are problems in understanding relativistic quantum theory as fundamentally being a theory of particles. A quantum theory of particles should include a local particle number operator. However, one can prove, given certain plausible assumptions, that local number operators cannot exist in a relativistic quantum theory (see, for example, Halvorson and Clifton (2001)). And there are some additional problems (see, for example, Wallace (2001)). While it still seems plausible that in certain circumstances one will encounter particle-like behaviour in relativistic quantum theories, it also seems plausible that, fundamentally, relativistic quantum theories are not theories of particles. So let me now turn to relativistic quantum theories formulated as path integrals over field configurations.

Just as one can define the action associated with a path in particle configuration space, one can define an action associated with a path h in field configuration space. Let history h have initial configuration c on space-like surface t, and final configuration c' on space-like surface t'. Then the action associated with h is

$S(h)=\int Ldxdydzdt$

where L is the classical Lagrangian density and the integral is over the spacetime region between s and s'.[15] Then let us assume that

$\psi(c' \text{ on } t'/c \text{ on } t)=\Sigma\exp(iS(h))$

where the 'sum' is over all histories that start with c on t and end with c' on t'. Now if one assumes that

[14] One might even conjecture that there is just a single nomic joint, which corresponds to the idea that the initial amplitude distribution is a special one that is fixed by law—say the vacuum state, or a low entropy big bang state.

[15] Not all actions S are the integral of the classical Lagrangian density. Sometimes one has an 'effective action' S_{eff} instead. But the transition amplitudes are still the sums over all paths of $\exp(iS_{eff}(h))$.

$$\psi(c' \text{ on } t') = \Sigma \psi(c' \text{ on } t'/c \text{ on } t)\psi(c \text{ on } t)$$

where the 'sum' is over all configurations c, this will induce the same evolution of the field-configuration-wave-function as the theory of Tomonaga that I mentioned above. (See Burton (1955) for a proof.)[16]

Do these amplitudes behave like the probabilities of relativistic theories? Well, they satisfy the constraint that the evolution of amplitudes of complete states from one space-like surface to another is independent of the sequence of surfaces that one chooses to evolve along.

For instance, consider space-like surfaces t_1, t_2, and t_3. Let me denote a history that starts with configuration c_1 on t_1 and ends with configuration c_2 on t_2 as $h(c_1 \rightarrow c_2)$. The path integral formalism tells us that the transition amplitude from c_1 on t_1 to c_2 on t_2 equals the sum of the amplitudes of all histories $h(c_1 \rightarrow c_2)$. That is,

$$\psi(c_2 \text{ on } t_2/c_1 \text{ on } t_1) = \Sigma \psi(h(c_1 \rightarrow c_2))$$

So

$$\psi(c_2 \text{ on } t_2) = \Sigma \psi(c_1 \text{ on } t_1)\Sigma \psi(h(c_1 \rightarrow c_2))$$

where the first summation is over configurations c_1 and the second over histories from c_1 on t_1 to c_2 on t_2. Similarly

$$\psi(c_3 \text{ on } t_3) = \Sigma \psi(c_2 \text{ on } t_2)\Sigma \psi(h(c_2 \rightarrow c_3))$$

where the first summation is over configurations c_2 and the second over histories from c_2 on t_2 to c_3 on t_3. Inserting the one expression into the other, we obtain

$$\psi(c_3 \text{ on } t_3) = \Sigma\Sigma \psi(c_1 \text{ on } t_1)\Sigma \psi(h(c_1 \rightarrow c_2))\Sigma \psi(h(c_2 \rightarrow c_3))$$

where the first summation is over all configurations c_2, the second over all configurations c_1, the third over all histories from c_1 on t_1 to c_2 on t_2, and the forth over all histories from c_2 on t_2 to c_3 on t_3. Since amplitudes of concatenated histories equal the multiplication of the amplitudes of the histories the above expression is equal to

$$\Sigma \psi(c_1 \text{ on } t_1)\Sigma \psi(h(c_1 \rightarrow c_3))$$

where the first summation is over all configurations c_1 and the last one is over all histories from c_1 to c_3. But this equals $\psi(c_3$ on $t_3)$ calculated by the path integral rule going directly from t_1 to t_3. So we have met the first consistency constraint: in this respect amplitudes in relativistic quantum field theory behave in exactly the same way that probabilities behave in a relativistic indeterministic theory.

---

[16] Sidenote: any classical field distribution $\phi(x,y,z,t,)$ over any spacetime region R has an associated action $S=\int Ldxdydzdt$, where the integral is over region R. Hence it has an associated amplitude $\exp(iS)$, which one can think of as the amplitude associated with the set of classical histories that satisfy the constraint that they equal ϕ on R. What significance this number has—what its connection to probabilities, for example—is unclear to me.

Figure 3.5 A consistency constraint.

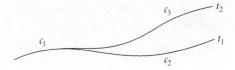

How about the second consistency constraint? First let me discuss something simpler. Consider two space-like surfaces t_1 and t_2. In a relativistic indeterministic theory

$$\Pr(s_1 \text{ on } t_1) = \Pr(s_1 \text{ on } t_1)\Sigma\Pr(s_2 \text{ on } t_2/s_1 \text{ on } t_1)$$

where the summation is over all states s_2. But in a quantum theory it is not true that

$$\psi(s_1 \text{ on } t_1) = \psi(s_1 \text{ on } t_1)\Sigma\psi(s_2 \text{ on } t_2/s_1 \text{ on } t_1)$$

where the summation is over all states s_2. It is true that $\Sigma|\psi(s_2 \text{ on } t_2/s_1 \text{ on } t_1)|^2 = 1$. But it is not true that $\Sigma\psi(s_2 \text{ on } t_2/s_1 \text{ on } t_1) = 1$. Moreover, generically it is not true for different initial states s_1 and $s_{1'}$ that $\Sigma\psi(s_2 \text{ on } t_2/s_1 \text{ on } t_1)$ and $\Sigma\psi(s_2 \text{ on } t_2/s_1 \text{ on } t_1)$ differ merely by a phase, which is what would be necessary for

$$|\psi(s_1 \text{ on } t_1)\Sigma\psi(s_2 \text{ on } t_2)/s_1 \text{ on } t_1)|^2 / |\psi(s_{1'} \text{ on } t_1)\Sigma\psi(s_2 \text{ on } t_2/s_{1'} \text{ on } t_1)|^2$$

to give the correct ratio of probabilities of s_1 and s_2 on t_1.

So this is a way in which amplitudes do not behave like probabilities. Now this may not be much of a surprise. After all, the amplitudes of all possible states on a space-like surface do not sum to 1. Only the squares of these amplitudes do that. So, this might seem no big deal. Still, this difference between amplitudes and probabilities has as a consequence that our second constraint is violated by amplitudes. Let me explain why.

Recall that the second constraint was the constraint that if two space-like surfaces t_1 and t_2 have a region R in common, then, in so far as there are properties intrinsic to R, the probabilities of those properties must be the same according to the probability distribution of states on t_1 and the probability distribution of states on t_2. Applying this constraint to amplitudes is the demand that, in so far as there are properties intrinsic to R, the amplitudes of those properties must be the same according to the amplitude distribution of states on t_1 and the amplitude distribution of states on t_2. What could we mean by the amplitude of a property that is not maximal? Well, since we are attributing amplitudes to complete field configurations, the natural notion of properties intrinsic to a region R would be the features that are determined by field configuration on R. What could we mean by the amplitude of such features? Well, I will end up arguing that one should not countenance such quantities, but the natural suggestion in the meantime is that the amplitude of a feature in a region R equals the sum of the amplitudes of all complete configurations that have that feature.

OK, now suppose that on space-like surface t_1 the probability amplitude is 1 (times some phase) that we have configuration c_1 on R and configuration c_2 on the rest of t_1 (see Figure 3.5). Then, of course, the amplitude of configuration c_1 on t_1 is just 1 (times some phase). What, then, is the probability amplitude of a configuration on t_2 consisting of c_1 on R and some configuration c_3 on the rest of t_2? Of course, it is just the transition amplitude:

$$\psi(c_1 \text{ on } R, c_3 \text{ on rest of } t_2/c_1 \text{ on } R, c_2 \text{ on rest of } t_1)$$

That is:

$$\psi(c_1 \text{ and } c_3 \text{ on } t_2)=\psi(c_1 \text{ and } c_3 \text{ on } t_2/c_1 \text{ and } c_2 \text{ on } t_1)$$

So the amplitude of configuration c_1 on t_2 is:

$$\psi(c_1 \text{ on } t_2)=\Sigma\psi(c_1 \text{ and } c_3 \text{ on } t_2)=\Sigma\psi(c_1 \text{ and } c_3 \text{ on } t_2/c_1 \text{ and } c_2 \text{ on } t_1)$$

where the summations are over all configurations c_3. Now, for the same reason as before, this need not sum to 1 (up to a phase), and therefore the amplitude of c_1 on R will depend on which hypersurface one considers R to be a part of. I.e. there is no such thing as the amplitude of a configuration on R per se. One might insist in talking about amplitudes of features of regions relative to space-like surfaces, but it does not seem likely that talk of such space-like surface dependent features is going to be of any use when it comes to given an account of the phenomena in R. In short, I suggest not paying any attention to such amplitudes when it comes to giving an account of the relation between the amplitudes that there are and the phenomena that there are.

What then of our second constraint? Well, we can still apply it to squares of amplitudes at times, i.e. probabilities at times (rather than to amplitudes.) The demand then is that the probability of configuration c_1 is the same on t_2 and t_1. And this constraint, of course, is satisfied. For the rule for going from amplitudes of complete states to probabilities of features is that the probability of a feature is the sum of the square of the amplitudes of the configurations that have that feature:

$$\text{Prob}(c_1 \text{ on } t_2)=\Sigma|\psi(c_1 \text{ and } c_3 \text{ on } t_2)|^2=\Sigma|\psi(c_1 \text{ and } c_3 \text{ on } t_2/c_1 \text{ and } c_2 \text{ on } t_1)|^2=1$$

where the summations are over configurations c_3.

OK, let us take stock again. The view that I have been examining in this section is the view that amplitudes and transition amplitudes (or perhaps just the joint amplitudes) are the fundamental quantities. As with probabilities, the amplitude for a complete state s' on a space-like surface t' equals the sums of the products of amplitudes of complete states s on an earlier space-like surface t times the transition amplitudes between these complete states. As with probabilities, the amplitude of a complete state s' on a space-like surface t' equals the sum of the joint history amplitudes of histories beginning on an earlier surface t and ending with state s' on t'. Unlike probabilities, the transition amplitudes to all future states do not sum to 1. As a consequence the amplitudes for configurations on parts of space-like surfaces depend on the space-like surface of which one considers them to be a part. The natural response is to deny that talk of such amplitudes makes sense, or, more mildly, is of any interest. The relativistic nature of relativistic quantum mechanics lies in the fact that the amplitudes are coordinate-independent quantities that attach to coordinate-independent states on space-like surfaces and to coordinate-independent histories of states. One can then picture a relativistic quantum history as a huge set of Minkowski world histories, each with an amplitude attached to them, where these amplitudes satisfy a very simple rule: the 'path integral rule'. But I admit that it is not entirely clear how much this helps our understanding of the relativistic nature of relativistic quantum mechanics. Let us briefly discuss a variation on amplitude realism, before going on to other views.

3.12 Liberal amplitude realism

On the view that I have just discussed, the histories were histories of particle positions, and/or of field configurations. That is, the histories were histories of a preferred configuration basis. But what, one might object, is so special about histories of position configurations and/or histories of field configurations?[17] After all, the path integral formalism can also be applied in momentum representation or indeed in any representation whatsoever, including time-dependent ones. For the path integral formalism just relies on the fact that the amplitude to go from a state $|\phi>$ to a state $|\psi>$ must equal the sum of the amplitudes of going from $|\phi>$ to $|\psi>$ via each of a set of intermediate states $|i>$, where the intermediate states can be any set of basis vectors in the relevant Hilbert space.

The obvious response to this plea for equality is to say that all bases are indeed equal. That is, there exist a vast multitude of histories of bases, for each such history of bases there is a vast multitude of histories of base vectors, and the fundamental facts consist of amplitudes for each of such history of base vectors.

However, this equality of bases brings a cost with it. In the first place, the path integral laws governing the amplitudes are typically most simply and naturally stated in the particle configuration and field configuration representations, not in any of the huge infinitude of other representations that there are. Secondly, the task of relating what there fundamentally is to the world as it appears to us, is made a bit more daunting by adding such a vast multitude of histories—especially so since these additional histories generically amount to a (temporal) series of values for some bizarre (temporal) series of non-local observables which bears no obvious relation to the history of appearances. Thirdly, this view is not very austere. The amplitudes and transition amplitudes in one basis determine those in all other bases. So we are adding a lot of redundant information when we add facts about amplitudes and transition amplitudes in all bases other than a particular, privileged, basis. So liberal amplitude realism does not seem to be a very attractive view.

3.13 Density-operator realism

David Wallace and Chris Timpson have suggested a more traditional view (see Wallace and Timpson (forthcoming)), which is basically the standard view that the (intrinsic)

---

[17] One might even worry that there no unique field configuration basis.

state of any object can be represented by a density operator (which determines the expectation values of all observables of that object), combined with the idea that the fundamental objects just are spacetime and its parts; that is, regions of spacetime. That is to say, rather than that time-slices have quantum mechanical states, or that systems of particles and/or fields have quantum mechanical states at times, spacetime regions (which includes time-slices if one is not too mathematically rigorous, but also temporally extended regions) have quantum mechanical states. And rather than that these states are wave-functions, or vectors in a Hilbert space, the states are density operators, or, algebraically, positive linear functionals on the algebras of operators which represents the observables of the regions. A density operator associated with a spacetime region, or a positive linear functional on the algebra of observables associated with a region, determines the expectation values of all the observables associated with that region, so that one can also think of the state of a region as amounting to the set of all expectation values of all observables associated with a region. Now the density operators ρ_A and ρ_B (or the algebraic state, or set of expectation values) representing the states of regions A and B generically do not determine the density operator ρ_R (the algebraic state, the set of expectation values) representing the state of the union of these regions R=A∪B. This is why, according to Wallace and Timpson, spatial and temporal separability are violated.

Temporal non-separability shows up in the following way when one has the Wallace–Timpson conception of quantum mechanical states. Suppose that in the Heisenberg picture, A is the operator associated with some observable on a time-slice t_1, and B is the operator associated with some observable on a time-slice t_2. Then the density operators associated with these time-slices, ρ_{t1} and ρ_{t2}, do not determine the expectation value of the observable associated with operator AB+BA, while the density operator associated with the union of the time-slices, $\rho_{t1∪t2}$, does determine this expectation value. (One has to consider operator AB+BA rather than just operator AB, or just operator BA, since AB might not be self-adjoint, while AB+BA will be as long as A and B are self-adjoint, which they are, since they correspond to observables.)

How does one transform states in one frame of reference to states in another frame on the Wallace–Timpson view? Suppose, for example, that one knows all the density operators associated with all the time-slices in one frame of reference. How does this relate to the density operators associated with the time-slices in another frame of reference? Well, there is a representation of the Poincaré group by operators U on the relevant Hilbert space, such that the density operator D′ on time-slice t' is related to the density operator D on time-slice t as follows:

$$\rho_{t'}=U^\dagger_{tt'}\rho_t U_{tt'}$$

More generally, there is a representation of the Poincaré group, such that for any Poincaré transformation P, if PR is the Poincaré transform of region R, then

$$\rho_{PR}=U^\dagger_P\rho_R U_P$$

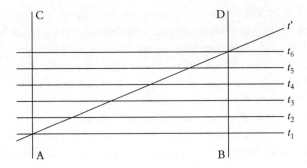

Figure 3.6 Transforming non-separable states.

Now, of course, which operator U_P is depends on the dynamics. In particular, when the Poincaré transformation is just a temporal shift, the operator U_P is just the unitary operator that corresponds to the Hamiltonian evolution of quantum states. So one might think that this is not much of an improvement on the idea that one transforms states from a time-slice in one frame to a time-slice in another frame by a rule that incorporates the dynamics.

However, let me now argue that, in the first place, it is quite explicable why the dynamics is needed here, and in the second place, the transformation rule is as local and natural as it can be.

Once one accepts that there is spatial non-separability, one can explain why dynamics is needed to transform states from one frame to another. Suppose we have two particles in a non-separable spin-state, where the world-line of particle 1 passes through spacetime points A and C, and the world-line of particle 2 passes through B and D (see Figure 3.6). Because of failure of spatial separability one cannot give the spin-state of the two particles on time-slice t_1 by giving the state at A and the state at B, nor the state on time-slice t_2 by giving the state at C and the state at D. So, of course, one cannot figure out the state on time-slice t' by looking at the state at A on time-slice t_1 and the state at D on time-slice t_6. There is a state at A (represented by a density operator which determines the expectation values of all observables of particle 1), but that state is entangled with the state at B. In order to know the state at A and D on t', one needs to know how these entanglements evolve as one evolves the intrinsic state of particle 2 from B to D. And of course, that depends on the dynamics.

Given that this is the case the Poincaré transformation rules for the density matrices are as simple and natural as they can be, the expectation values of *local* observables transform exactly as do their classical analogues. The expectation value of a local scalar field transforms as a classical scalar field, and the expectation value of a local vector field transforms as a classical vector field. That is to say, the expectation value of local fields transform exactly as the corresponding local fields do in classical relativistic theories. What more could one want?

In short, we have a clear relativistic notion of the state of spacetime regions. The only thing that is strange about relativistic quantum mechanics is that temporal and spatial separability fails. Since we have already become accustomed to the failure of spatial separability, it should not be too hard to get used to the failure of temporal separability. And it should come as no surprise that failure of spatial separability is accompanied by failure of temporal separability in a relativistic theory.

It seems to me that all of this indeed is quite acceptable. And I would accept it without much hesitation if it were not for the fact that, surprisingly—shockingly, even—there exists an account of quantum mechanical states that makes them entirely separable, and makes their dynamics entirely local. Let us see how this miracle can happen.

3.14 Heisenberg-operator realism

Deutsch and Hayden (2000) exploit the Heisenberg picture of quantum mechanics in order to arrive at a separable notion of quantum state evolving according to a local dynamics. Their basic idea is this. In the Heisenberg picture the quantum state does not change. So one can, by convention, take this quantum state to be some fixed vector (or ray) $|0>$. One uses it as part of a fixed algorithm to calculate the expectation values of operators. But one does not regard this vector $|0>$ as representing some property of the world—as some feature of the world that could have been different. Rather, the temporally evolving operators alone, which in the Heisenberg picture represent the observables of a system, represent the temporally evolving state of the system—the temporally evolving properties of the system. This state is separable, and evolves according to a local dynamics. Let me now present a bit more detail.

Deutsch and Hayden take as their example a system of n interacting qubits.[18] A qubit is a system whose state-space is two-dimensional Hilbert space, such as the spin-states of a spin-$\frac{1}{2}$ particle. They take the state of qubit i at any time to be given by the Heisenberg operators S^i_x, S^i_y, and S^i_z that represent the three spin observables of that qubit at that time; and they take the state of a collection of N qubits to be given by the 3N Heisenberg operators that represent the spin observables of the N qubits. The reason why they need only these three operators per qubit is that one can show that every Hermitian operator on the total system Hilbert space is a weighted sum of products of these qubit operators, and the dynamics of any observable of the total system is determined by the dynamics of these qubit observables.[19] The dynamics of the qubit observables is

---

[18] Technicalities aside, Deutsch and Hayden could equally well have taken the Heisenberg picture in quantum field theory and used the field states at locations in spacetime in place of qubits.

[19] Just as there are austere and liberal versions of the amplitudes-of-histories view, there are austere and liberal version of the Deutsch–Hayden view. The austere version assumes the state of a system to be given by a minimal set of Heisenberg operators, while the liberal one assumes that they are given by all sets of Heisenberg operators.

$$\frac{d}{dt}S^k_{\ 1} = -i[H(S^1_{\ x}, S^1_{\ y}, \ldots, S^N_{\ z}), S^k_{\ 1}]$$

where H is the Hamiltonian operator. This dynamics is local if one assumes a Hamiltonian with only local interaction terms. Since on the Deutsch–Hayden conception, states are separable (the state of the total system is determined by the state of each qubit), and the dynamics of states is local, we have a formulation of quantum mechanics that makes the theory entirely separable and local. The Deutsch–Hayden theory is relativistic in the following sense: the fundamental field operators transform as their classical analogous do—as scalars, vectors, tensors, and spinors. The transformations of all operators follow from the transformations of the fundamental field operators.

Finally, before turning to objections to the Deutsch–Hayden view, let me indicate how it avoids Albert's narratability problem. Consider again the example of a pair of spin-$\frac{1}{2}$ particles in a singlet state, whose spins are simultaneously rotated in some frame of reference. As we have seen, given such a Hamiltonian, the Schrödinger state of that pair of particles does not change in that frame of reference. However, the same is not true of the Heisenberg state! Consider, for example, the temporal development of the operator which represents the observable 'spin in direction z of particle 1'. At each time it has two eigenvectors, and those eigenvectors will change as time progresses (representing the 'rotating' action of the Hamiltonian). Of course, at each time its expectation value will be 0 (given the total system singlet state). Indeed, the expectation values of all observables on time-slices of the frame of reference in which the rotation is simultaneous will be invariant in time. However, that does not mean that the Heisenberg state does not change in that frame of reference. It does.[20]

All in all, we have a completely local and completely separable theory which is relativistic in a straightforward sense, and which, moreover, avoids narratability problems. This seems too good to be true, so let us consider some worries.

First let me discuss the worry that by regarding the history of the world as entirely given by the history of the evolving operators, one has left something out: the state vector |0>. One way in which one might try to explicate this worry is to say the following. The history of the world could have been different, not only in that the laws of dynamics could have been different, so that in the Heisenberg representation the evolution of the operators would have been different, but also in that the state vector, which does not evolve in time in the Heisenberg representation, could have been different. That is, it might not have been |0>.

The response is to go on the counter-offensive: if one assumes that the state vector in the Heisenberg picture corresponds to a feature of the world that could have been

---

[20] After the 180-degree rotation, the eigenvector corresponding to the $+\frac{1}{2}$ value has 'rotated' to the place where the eigenvector corresponding to the $-\frac{1}{2}$ value was at the start. So the operator representing spin-z observable is different after the 180-degree rotation (or the 'flip').

different one is adding otiose redundancy to the theory. Of course, if one imagines that such a state vector corresponds to such a further feature of the world, then by imagining that one varies the state vector while not varying the history of operator states, one will arrive at a different history of expectation values of observables. And this different history of operator states does indeed correspond to a different world history. However, that different world history simply amounts to a different history of operator states, not to an identical operator history but different state vector. That is to say, there is a redundancy of representation. The very same history of expectation values of observables can be represented in many different ways: state vector X together with operator history X, or state vector Y with operator history Y, or . . . ; that is, there is an unnecessary redundancy if one takes it that the state vector in the Heisenberg representation corresponds to some feature of the world. In fact, the different possible histories of the world correspond 1–1 to different possible operator histories. Of course, one can represent the possible world histories in different ways, depending on which state vector one conventionally uses to translate operator histories into expectation values of observables. But given a conventional choice of state vector, there is a 1–1 correspondence between operator histories and world histories. There is no further degree of freedom in the world that corresponds to a state vector degree of freedom.

Now let me discuss an objection that Wallace and Timpson (2007) have given to the Deutsch–Hayden view. They claim that the Deutsch and Hayden's notion of state contains an unwanted gauge freedom, that there is a many-to-one relation between Deutsch–Hayden states and physical states, and that when one removes this gauge degree of freedom from Deutsch–Hayden states, one arrives at the Wallace–Timpson notion of the state of a system (or region): namely, the density operator notion. Here is their argument.

Consider any time-dependent unitary operator $V(t)$ (map from times to unitary operators), such that at each time,

$$V(t)|0\rangle = \exp(-i\theta(t))|0\rangle$$

That is, a unitary operator which at each time is such that when it acts on state vector $|0\rangle$ it, at most, changes its phase. Note that there are many such unitary transformations: any 'rotation' of vectors 'around' vector $|0\rangle$ in the Hilbert space which leaves $|0\rangle$ invariant is such a transformation. Now suppose we transform the operator states with such a (time-dependent) unitary operator:

$$S^i_k(t) \Rightarrow S'^i_k(t) = V^\dagger(t)S^i_k(t)V(t)$$

This will change the dynamics to:

$$\frac{d}{dt}S'^k_1 = -i[H(S'^1_x, S'^1_y, \ldots, S'^N_z), S'^k_1] - i[V^\dagger\frac{d}{dt}V, S'^k_1]$$

But the expectation values are not changed at all:

$$\langle 0|S'^i_k|0\rangle = \langle 0|V^\dagger(t)S^i_k V|0\rangle = \langle 0|S^i_k|0\rangle$$

Since the expectation values are not changed at all, Wallace and Timpson point out that the situation here is analogous to that of electromagnetism: that the transformation induced by V(t) is a gauge transformation. They conclude that just as one should regard states of the electromagnetic potential A that are related gauge transformations as corresponding to the same physical state, one should regard Duetsch–Hayden states that are related by the V(t)-induced gauge transformations as representing the same physical state. But this notion of state just is the Wallace–Timpson density matrix notion of states, since Deutsch–Hayden states are related by a gauge transformation just in case they determine the same expectation values.

This seems a strong argument. Still, I will demur. On the Deutsch–Hayden view it is true that if one applies an active gauge transformation to the actual Deutsch–Hayden world-history, one ends up with a world history with exactly the same history of expectation values as in the actual world. However, the accompanying changes that one needs to make in the dynamics, for generic gauge transformations, leave the dynamics less natural. Indeed, such changes appear designed to make sure that the operators in that world develop in such a way that they correspond to the same history of expectation values as in the actual world. Consider, for example, the following, putatively analogous, case. One could claim that flipping the sign of the (electrical) charge of some subset of the set of all charged particles does not change the physical state of the world, as long as one alters the dynamics in such a way that the flipped charges dynamically behave as if they had the opposite sign of charge. The expectation values in this case will also be the same in that the development of positions will be the same in any possible situation, including any possible charge measurement situation. But it surely does not seem plausible that flipping the sign of some subset of the set of all particles does not change the physical state of the world.

However, how about the time-independent gauge transformation; that is, transformations V(t) which change the phase of |0> but are the same at all times. These require no change in the dynamics. The situation here is analogous to the situation with respect to the global charge flip transformation (the transformation which flips the sign of all charges in the history of the universe) discussed in Chapter 2. The only difference is that there are many transformations V which change the phase of |0>, while there is only one global charge flip transformation. Well, just as in the case of a global charge flip there are three attitudes that one can take. In the first place, one can capitulate; that is, accept that all transformations V(t), including the time-dependent ones, leave the state of the history of the world invariant, and accept Spacetime State Realism. In the second place one can claim that the time-dependent transformations change the state of the history of the world, but the time-independent ones do not. This is compatible with Heisenberg-operator realism, if one accepts that there are no facts about identity of Heisenberg operators across possible worlds, or across possible situations. Finally, one can claim that possible worlds, or possible situations, that are related by time-independent transformations V are not identical, and maintain Heisenberg-operator realism. As I have said on a number of previous occasions, it strikes me as a bad idea to use intuitions regarding distinctness of possibilities as a guide for what the fundamental structure of reality is. Rather, one should prefer theories that are simpler in terms of their fundamental quantities, and one should prefer theories that have a sparser collection of fundamental quantities. Consequently, while I do not find it completely obvious which of the three canvassed views is the best, it seems to me that it is clear that the first option is the least attractive. Surely, other things being equal, a conception of fundamental state according to which the world is separable and the dynamics is simple and local, is preferable to one according to which this is not the case.

Let me end by briefly discussing how on earth it can be that conventional wisdom is so wrong. How exactly did Deutsch and Hayden manage to achieve the miracle of making quantum mechanics separable? Well, we know that we can always take a non-separable theory and manufacture an empirically equivalent separable theory by means of an obvious trick. Just maintain that the state at any point in spacetime encodes the state everywhere in spacetime (like Leibniz's monads); for example, by adding a local, but not locally detectable, property corresponding to each global property. Of course, this is a silly trick: nobody would think that a theory which postulates an enormously rich and complex local state, which is not locally detectable, solely for the purpose of having a theory which makes the state of the world separable is *ipso facto* more plausible than a theory according to which the state of the world is non-separable. What Deutsch and Hayden have shown is that in the particular case of quantum mechanics one can manufacture a theory according to which the quantum mechanical state of the world is separable in a very simple and natural way—simply by taking the Heisenberg representation seriously! The trick is that identifying which operator (in the Heisenberg representation) corresponds to a given observable O_x at some location x in spacetime contains much more information than just the expectation value of that observable. In particular, when one is given the operator corresponding to some observable O_x at location x, and one is given the operator corresponding to some other observable P_y at some other location y, then one *ipso facto* knows, given the conventionally fixed, constant, quantum state of the universe, the correlations between those two observables—the joint expectation values. (By contrast, the local expectation values by themselves do not determine these correlations.) Thus there is a very simple and natural conception of the local quantum mechanical state: namely, a set of local Heisenberg operators, such that the state of the world is separable and dynamically local.[21] I like this theory!

3.15 Flash realism

So far I have talked about standard non-collapse quantum mechanics, according to which the evolution of the quantum state is unitary—theories according to which

---

[21] Note that, of course, this is only so if the full state of the world is given by the standard quantum mechanical state. That is to say, I am assuming there are no 'hidden variables'.

Figure 3.7 Relativistic collapse?

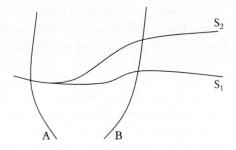

there are no 'collapses' of wave-functions. But there are versions of quantum mechanics according to which the wave-function undergoes probabilistic 'collapses' at times. An example of such a theory is one that says that if an object initially is in a state $\Sigma c_i |O_i\rangle$, where O is a (maximal) observable and the $|O_i\rangle$ its eigenstates, and one measures O, then it will 'collapse' onto one of the $|O_i\rangle$, and the probability that it will 'collapse' onto state $|O_i\rangle$ equals $|c_i|^2$.

Suppose now that one has two particles A and B in a singlet state which are far apart in space (see Figure 3.7). Suppose one measures the spin of particle B between space-like surfaces S_1 and S_2. If one's notion of the local state is the local density operator, then the state of particle A on S_1 is a mixture of spin-up and spin-down states, and the state of A on S_2 is either the pure spin-up state or the (pure) spin-down state. These local states differ, and they differ in the local expectation values associated with the states. No such problem occurred for the various non-collapse theories that we examined. This problem makes it even harder to understand in which sense relativistic collapse theories are relativistic than it is to understand the sense in which relativistic non-collapse theories are relativistic.

There is also another problem with collapse accounts. So far I have assumed that collapses occur when one makes a measurement. But, what exactly, physically, determines whether or not a measurement occurs? As yet, this is not a very satisfactory theory.

However, Roderick Tumulka (2006) has recently attempted to find a solution to both of the above problems. The basic idea is this. There is an initial wave-function of the universe on some time-slice. It defines probabilities for future collapses of wave-functions which are centred on precise points in spacetime. If a collapse occurs, then the collapsed wave-function provides probabilities for future collapses. And so on. The centres of the collapses are called 'flashes', and provide the supervenience basis for the phenomena. However, it is not quite as simple as that. If one does the above in a simple-minded way, even ignoring the problem that wave-functions will be hyper-plane dependent, one will not arrive at a frame-independent rule for the probabilities of future flashes. What Tumulka instead does is use a set of so-called 'seed flashes'—a set of initial centres of collapse, one for each particle in the universe—together with the initial wave-function of the universe, in order to produce a relativistically invariant formula which determines the probabilities of all possible histories of flashes. His theory is not yet fully general: it allows neither particle creations and annihilations, nor particle interactions (though it does allow entangled states). And, of course, it is not empirically equivalent to non-collapse theories. But it is still worth examining, since it seems to be an example of a fully relativistic collapse theory.

Let me first discuss the status of the wave-function in this theory. You may have noticed that in the end I only mentioned an 'initial wave-function', which together with an initial set of flashes, determines the probabilities of histories of flashes. I did not speak of collapsed wave-functions. Tumulka does define a 'collapsed wave-function' in terms of an initial wave-function and a sequence of flashes. Indeed, he does so in two different ways. But he regards these collapsed wave-functions as an inessential auxiliary device: the collapsed wave-functions are not part of the fundamental history of the world. Indeed, he regards even the initial wave-function as not being part of the fundamental history of the world. Let me discuss both of these claims in turn.

First let me argue that it is indeed better to not regard the collapsed wave-functions as part of the fundamental history of the world. Since the initial wave-function plus the flashes uniquely determine the history of collapsed wave-functions, and the phenomena can be taken to supervene on the history of flashes only, it seems one has no real need for fundamental facts about collapsed wave-functions. Since wave-functions which collapse make it hard to make sense of states on parts of time-slices, and make it hard to understand transformations from one frame to another frame, it seems best to do without them. Consequently, it no longer seems appropriate to call it a 'collapse' view. Rather, it is view in which there is a single 'initial wave-function' and a stochastic law which specifies how this 'initial wave-function' determines the probabilities of flashes.

Now let me turn to what Tumulka calls the 'initial wave-function'. Do we need to regard it as specifying some feature of the world, one which could have been otherwise, or can we regard it otherwise, as in the Deutsch–Hayden view? Well, on the Deutsch–Hayden view the history of certain Heisenberg operators represent the history of the world. But there is no analogue of Heisenberg operators in Tumulka's theory. We do have a history of flashes. But the flashes by themselves do not specify the probabilities of future flashes; for that we need the initial wave-function. So it seems that if we do not regard the 'initial wave-function' as specifying some feature of the world, then the Tumulka theory has a problem.

One could try to wriggle out of this problem. One could claim that there is no fact about the 'initial wave-function', but postulate a law of the following form: the probabilities of flashes are deduced by giving a particular 'initial wave-function' plus Tumulka's law for how this determines the probabilities of histories of flashes. However, such a view would only be plausible if such a law could be stated in a natural and direct way, rather than via a reference to this non-existent quantity. Moreover, only if the particular 'initial wave-function' needed to state the law would be simple and natural (the vacuum state, for example) does it seem that such a theory would be half-plausible.

Even then, it would seem strange to deny the metaphysical possibility that the world could have been different in a way that corresponds to a change in initial wave-function. So, as it stands, this does not seem a plausible view.

It therefore seems better to assume that there is quantity—a fundamental property of the world, call it the 'initial wave-function', or simply the 'world-vector'—such that it, together with any initial condition (namely, a set of initial flashes), determines all probabilities for all histories of flashes. (There is only one actual history of flashes, not multiple histories as in the amplitudes of histories view.) This view is relativistic in the sense that there is a global, coordinate-independent quantity, the 'world vector', which determines probabilities of coordinate independent histories in a Minkowski space-time. On this view then, there is one object: Minkowski spacetime. It has two types of properties. One of them is a global property: the world-vector. The other properties are local properties, which specify at which spacetime points flashes occur. And there is one law, which determines the probabilities of flash distributions in terms of an initial set of flashes and the world-vector. The only problem is that Tumulka's theory cannot (as yet) handle interactions.

3.16 Tentative conclusions

In this chapter I have examined what the fundamental structure of the world is according to quantum mechanics. I have considered five views.

According to configuration space realism, the state of the world is (neighbourhood) separable. But it requires configuration space to have a fairly unnatural structure, and it suffers from the problem that there is no relativistic configuration spacetime. Attempts, by Tomonaga and others, to overcome this problem by postulating a multi-time configuration spacetime amounted to a rather tortured version of the fairly standard view that quantum mechanical states attach to space-like hypersurfaces in a Minkowski spacetime, together with a dynamical rule for going from the state on one space-like hypersurface to the state on another space-like hypersurface.

Amplitude realism is relativistic in that it assumes the existence of fundamental coordinate-independent quantities: namely, amplitudes and transition amplitudes, which attach to coordinate independent states on space-like surfaces and coordinate-independent histories of such states. On this view the transformations between states on different space-like surfaces can be understood in terms of (dynamical) transition amplitudes between such states, but cannot be understood in terms of amplitudes for states on common parts of space-like surfaces.

Density-operator realism is relativistic in that it assumes fundamental coordinate-independent quantities associated with spacetime regions: namely, density operators. The density operator associated with the union of two regions is not determined by the density operators associated with each of the regions. So, according to the density-operator realism the state of the world is non-separable. The relativistic transformations between these states on different space-like surfaces correspond to a representation of the Poincaré group—a representation which depends on the dynamics. But in each case this representation is simple and natural in that the expectation values of local fields transform exactly as the corresponding classical local fields.

According to Heisenberg-operator realism, the state of any system is given by a set of operators which correspond to a set of observables of that system. The operators characterizing the state of the union of two systems is determined by the operators characterizing the state of each of the systems, so the state of the world is separable on this view. The transformations of the operators are simple and natural in that they transform just as their classical analogues. One could argue that the representative operators over-represent the physical states of systems on the grounds that many different operator states correspond to the same expectation values, but such arguments do not seem compelling.

Finally, flash realism assumes that there is a global quantum state—the 'world vector' —as well as a set of flashes at points in spacetime, and a law relating the world vector to probabilities of flash distributions. As yet it cannot handle general interactions, and it is not empirically equivalent to standard (non-collapse) quantum mechanics.

All in all, I favour Heisenberg-operator realism. But I expect that the future will bring new options and new arguments which will change my view.

4

Pointlessness

Glory be to God for dappled things
For skies of couple-colour as a brinded cow
For rose-moles all in stipple upon trout that swim
Fresh-firecoal chestnut-falls; finches' wings
Landscape plotted and pieced—fold, fallow, and plough
And all trades, their gear and tackle and trim.
All things counter, original, spare, strange;
Whatever is fickle, freckled (who knows how?)
With swift, slow; sweet, sour; adazzle, dim
He fathers-forth whose beauty is past change
Praise him

Gerald Manley Hopkins

4.1 Introduction

In Chapter 1 we questioned whether there was anything more to time than a set of instants, a set of points in time. In Chapters 2 and 3 we questioned whether the structure of the world can be given spacetime point by spacetime point; whether God is a pointillist painter. In this chapter we will question whether such points even exist, whether there are instants of time, points of space, points in spacetime available as God's canvas.

It is standardly assumed that space and time consist of extensionless, zero-sized, points. It is also a standard assumption that all matter in the universe has point-sized parts. We are not often explicitly reminded of these very basic assumptions. But they are there. For instance, one standardly assumes that one can represent the states of material objects, and of fields, by functions from points in space and time to point values. Electric fields, mass densities, gravitational potentials, and so on, are standardly represented as functions from *points* in space and time to *point* values. This practice would seem to make no sense if time and space did not have points as parts.

There is an alternative that has not been much explored—at least not in the physics literature The alternative is that space and time and matter are 'pointless', or 'gunky'. The idea here is not that space and time and matter have smallest finite-sized bits, that space and time and matter are 'chunky'. Rather, the idea is that every part of space and time and matter has a non-zero, finite, size, and yet every such part can always be subdivided into further, smaller, parts. That is to say, the idea is that every part of space and time and matter has a non-zero size, and yet there is no smallest size.

Let me emphasize how radical this idea is. It is very natural to think that any thing decomposes into some ultimate collection of fundamental parts. And it is very natural to think that the features of any object are determined by the way that object is constructed from its ultimate parts, and by the elementary features of these ultimate parts. Indeed, much of the history of science can be seen as an attempt to break down complex objects and processes into ultimate parts, and to find the laws that govern these ultimate parts. But if there are no smallest regions, and if there are no smallest parts of objects, then a spatial or temporal decomposition of a region, or of an object, cannot bottom out at an ultimate level. The idea that the features of large regions and large objects are determined by the features of minimal-sized regions and minimal-sized objects cannot work if space and time, and the objects in it, are gunky; that is, pointless. Space, time, and objects would simply not have ultimate parts. There would just be an infinite descending chain of ever-smaller parts—a somewhat dizzying prospect.

Well, let us not get ahead of ourselves. Not only would it require a fairly radical revision of our atomistic intuitions, it would also require a fairly radical and extensive re-working of standard mathematical methods for doing physics. If we cannot use real numbers to coordinatise locations in space and time, what can we use? If we cannot use ordinary functions to describe the states of things, what can we use?

All things in good order. We will get started on the business of rewriting physics a bit later. First we will consider arguments for undertaking this seemingly mad enterprise. To preview: we will find no utterly compelling arguments against the existence of points. But we will find non-compelling reasons to explore the mathematics of gunky space and time.

4.2 The possibility of motion and determinism

Zeno argued that if time consists of instants of zero duration, then during each such instant an object cannot move. But if time consists entirely of a series of such instants then objects can never move. In view of this problem Aristotle proposed that there are no instants, no 0-sized intervals of time—indeed, no smallest-sized, atomic, intervals of time. Rather, time consists of smaller and smaller intervals. To put it another way: the world is a true movie, not a sequence of snapshots. To put it even more suggestively: becoming is not reducible to being.

One may not be impressed by Zeno's argument. One may for instance respond, as did some commentators in the Middle Ages, that to be in motion is just to be at different locations at different times, so that it simply is not true that just because one occupies only one location at one time one never moves.

Indeed, this is a perfectly coherent way to respond to Zeno's problem. However, one can then formulate a new worry, which is closely related to Zeno's worry. For if motion is just a matter of being at different locations at different times, then the intrinsic state of an object at an instant does not include its velocity. How, then, does an object at an instant 'know' in which direction to continue, and at what speed? Less anthropomorphically: if the instantaneous states of objects do not include their velocities, then how could the instantaneous state of the world determine its subsequent states? That is, how could determinism hold? The world may in fact develop in a deterministic fashion, and it may not, but surely whether it does, or does not, should depend on the character of the laws of evolution of the world, rather than that the atomicity of the structure of time alone should imply that the world cannot be deterministic.[1]

One might attempt to respond to this argument by claiming that even if time consists of 0-sized instants, nonetheless the intrinsic state of an object at a time does include a velocity. Such an 'intrinsic velocity' would not be defined (as in ordinary calculus) in terms of (limits of) the position development of an object. Rather, it would be a primitive intrinsic feature of an object at a time, which *causes* the object to subsequently move in the direction in which the intrinsic velocity is pointing. In Chapter 2 we discussed this idea and found it unappealing, since it was not clear how to reconcile this idea with the fact that there is no path-independent notion of the parallelhood of velocities in curved spacetimes.

A more plausible response to Zeno, however, can be made on behalf of points. For one could simply claim that determinism should not be understood as the idea that the state at an instant determines states at all other times. Rather, it should be understood as the idea that *any finite history* of states determines states at all other times. So Zeno's arrow provides no compelling argument against point-sized instants. Let us turn to another argument.

4.3 Cutting things in half

If space consists of points then one cannot cut a region exactly in two halves. For if one of the two regions includes the point on the cutting line—if it is topologically closed at the cut—then the other does not include the points on the cutting line; that is, it is open at the cut (see Figure 4.1).

Imagine, for instance, that we have x and y coordinates which are parallel to the sides of a rectangle. Suppose that the horizontal x-coordinate of the rectangle runs from 0 to 2, and suppose that we cut the rectangle at $x=1$. The question then arises: do the points that have x-coordinate=1 belong to the left-hand side after we have made

---

[1] Well, it could still be deterministic if the equations of motion were first order, as they are in quantum mechanics. Still, one might like to think that even if the equations of motion are second order, as they are in classical mechanics, the world could be deterministic.

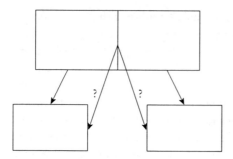

Figure 4.1 Halving a rectangle.

our cut, or to the right-hand side? If they belong to the left-hand side, then the left half is closed at the cut, and the right half is open. If vice versa, then the left side is open. So the two parts would not be identical. Even if one were to make some of the points of the $x=1$ line belong to one side after the cut, and some to the other side, what to do with the mid-point on the $x=1$ line? Perhaps surprisingly, it is an inescapable fact that one simply cannot cut a region into two halves which have completely identical structure if regions are composed out of points. One might reasonably conjecture that such an impossibility is an artefact of our mathematical representation of regions. One might conjecture that in physical reality there are no differences between regions that amount to differences only on their 'edges'. *Prima facie*, I find it hard to believe that there really are distinctions between topologically open and topologically closed regions in nature. Still, I agree that this is not a knock-down argument.

4.4 Paradoxes of size

If there exist points in space, and space is continuous, then it can be shown that there must be regions that have no well-defined size. For instance, there will be a part of any wall in any room such that it has no well-defined size. If you wanted to paint such a part of a wall in your house blue, there would be no possible answer to the question: 'How much paint will I need to paint that part of my wall blue?' The problem is not that you would not know how much paint you would need, nor that you would need 0 litres of paint. Rather, the problem is that there just exists no quantity r of paint such that you would need that quantity to paint that region. Let me be a little more precise.

One can prove that in a space that contains continuum many points—that is, that contains as many points as there are real numbers—there must exist regions that have no well-defined 'measure'. At least, this is so if one assumes the 'axiom of choice' and one assumes that the 'measure' is 'countably additive'. A 'measure' is a numerical assignment of sizes to regions, which is 'finitely additive'. A measure is 'finitely additive' if the measure of the union of two regions that do not overlap is the sum of the measures of each of the two regions. (It immediately follows that measure of a finite collection of non-overlapping regions equals the sum of the finitely many measures.) A measure is countably additive if the measure of the union of countably many non-overlapping regions is the sum of the countably many measures of all the regions; that is, if it equals the limit of the sum as one sums the measures of more and more of the regions in the countable set of regions. The 'axiom of choice', in this context, says that given any collection of regions there is a region that contains exactly one point from each region in the collection.

One can also prove that in a continuous pointy space of three or more dimensions there must exist regions that have no well-defined measure, if one assumes the axiom of choice and one assumes that the measure is invariant under (distance-preserving) translations and rotations.[2]

Let me prove a version of such theorems: what is known as the 'Vitali paradox'. Consider the points on the circumference of a circle, where the total length of that circumference is 1 metre. Let us suppose that there is a rotation invariant measure m on the regions of that circumference. Since we can represent each point on the circumference by a real number between 0 and 1 (0 included, 1 excluded), the regions correspond to sets of real numbers between 0 and 1. So the measure is a measure on sets of numbers between 0 and 1. Consider the relation R that holds between two points on that circumference if the distance along the circumference is a rational number. Consider now some point x on the circumference and the set S_x of all other points that stands in relation R to x. Each of the points in S_x will also stand in relation R to each other: a rational plus or minus a rational is another rational. So the relation R divides the set of points on the circumference into equivalence classes S_i. Now pick one point from each such equivalence class S_i and form a set C. Because of the axiom of choice we know that C exists. So each element in C is an irrational distance from each other point in C. (If they were a rational distance apart they would have been in the same equivalence class, but we have picked only one representative from each equivalence class). What is the measure of set C? Well, let us assume that C has some measure $m(C)$, where $m(C)$ can be any real number, including 0. Now let us rotate the set C by a distance r around the circumference, where r is a rational, to obtain set C_r. How many such sets are there? Countably many, since there are countable many rationals r. They must each get equal probability by our assumption of the rotation invariance of the measure. Now each such set is mutually exclusive. For suppose there is some point q that is both in C_r and in $C_{r'}$. Since you obtain $C_{r'}$ by rotating C_r by a rational distance (namely distance $r'-r$) and q is in $C_{r'}$, there will be some point p in C_r such that if you rotate p by a rational distance you land on point q. But q by assumption is also in C_r, so there are two points in C_r which are a rational distance from each other. But we have constructed C_r so that this is false. So the sets are mutually exclusive. The sets C_r are also jointly exhaustive, for the set C with which we started had a representative from each equivalence class S_i of points that are a rational distance away from each other. So we can reach any point by taking some point in C and rotating it a rational distance. So the collection of sets that are the rational rotations of C are jointly exhaustive. So now we have a countable collection of sets C_r such that each of

---

[2] See, for example, Skyrms (1983) and Wagon (1985).

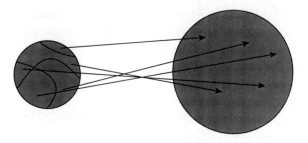

Figure 4.2 Banach–Tarski paradox.

them must get the same measure, and the sum of their measures must be the measure of the whole circumference, which is 1. But if we assume countable additivity then we have a contradiction, for there exists no number x such that the sum of countably many xs equals 1. (If $x=0$ then the countable sum is 0, and if x is non-zero then the countable sum diverges to infinity.)

There is even more weirdness about points and sizes: Banach and Tarski have shown that the existence of points implies cost-free increases in size. That is to say, they showed that in a continuous pointy three-dimensional space one can take, for instance, a sphere, break it into a finite number of pieces, move those pieces around rigidly (while preserving distances between the parts of the pieces), and rearrange those pieces to form a sphere that is double the size of the sphere that one started with (see Figure 4.2). (See, for example, Wagon (1985) for the fascinating details.)

There is, in fact, a close relationship between this result and the fact that there are regions which have no well-defined size. Some of the parts into which we must break the sphere must have no well-defined sized. It is not hard to see that this must be so, for rigid motions preserve size, and the size of an object that consists exactly of finitely many non-overlapping parts is just the sum of the sizes of those parts. So Banach and Tarski's result depends essentially on the existence of sizeless regions.

How might one respond on behalf of points? Well, in the first place, one might deny the axiom of choice. This is an issue that could take us deeply into an area of philosophy of mathematics and mathematical physics to which I have nothing new to contribute. I merely wish to point out that denying the axiom of choice implicitly commits one to (being part of) a large project: namely, that of rewriting that part of mathematics and mathematical physics that one wants to retain, in such a way that it makes no use of the axiom of choice. My only comment on this project is that I am interested in a different project in this chapter: doing physics without points. The project of this chapter has several independent motivations, only one of which concerns the measure theoretic paradoxes.

A second possible response to the measure theoretic paradoxes is: who cares? Surely we will not actually be able to get our hands on measureless parts of objects.

Surely size-altering decompositions and recompositions are not practically achievable. So why worry? Well, indeed, one cannot have explicit constructions of measureless regions. (One can show that one really needs the axiom of choice to guarantee the existence of the non-measurable regions; but there can be no constructive proof of the existence of such regions. One can also show that the regions in question must have a very strange shape; for instance, they will not have smooth boundaries; they will be extremely bizarre scattered sets of points.) Nonetheless, the mere existence of regions and/or parts which have no measure, and the mere possibility of size-altering de-compositions and recompositions, remains bizarre, and *prima facie* implausible.

A third possible response to the measure theoretic paradoxes (on behalf of points) is to claim that not all sets of points correspond to genuine physical regions. In particular one could claim that all physical regions have a well-defined size (are measurable), and that sets of points which are non-measurable are mathematical artefacts which do not exist as physical regions. (One might, for example, claim that only 'Borel' regions exist. I will define 'Borel' regions a bit later.) However, as long as one admits the existence of physical points this seems an implausible stance to take. In the first place, it seems a rather innocuous and natural assumption that if two (non-overlapping) regions exist, then there is an object that is composed of both these regions. For instance, that the left half of my room exists and that the right half of my room exists is surely just as plausible as that my room exists. Similarly, that there is region composed exactly of the interior space of the White House plus the interior space of 10 Downing Street surely is plausible. It may be a somewhat strange region in that it is a disconnected region (since it has two parts which are widely separated). But to deny that it exists at all seems rather implausible. Where would it then be that the Iraq war was devised? OK, I admit I am being a bit glib here. Some philosophers, for instance, have argued that only points exist, that regions consisting of more than one point do not exist. They have claimed, more generally, that only certain elementary constituents of reality ('simples') exist, and that no composites exist at all. *Prima facie* this seems to me a confusion between what is fundamental and what exists; surely the composites exist, even if they may not be the fundamental constituents of reality. Be that as it may, the denial of the existence of anything other than points is not what is going on when one denies the existence of non-measurable physical regions. In that case one still wants there to be measurable physical regions that are not just single points. For one thing one wants to be able to attach quantities such as size and mass to at least some regions that are not point-sized, for if not there seems to be no plausible way to formulate an adequate theory of physics. Slightly more formally, the objection that I am raising to the current attempt to escape the Banach–Tarski paradox is that one plausibly needs a non-nihilist mereology (mereology: the theory of parts and wholes) in order to set one's physics in, and that, other things being equal, one would prefer a standard mereology, which, for example, allows arbitrary composition of regions (arbitrary fusion). Still, I agree that once again we have found no utterly devastating argument against points. Let us look at yet another argument against points.

4.5 Quantum mechanics and points

In non-relativistic quantum mechanics one can represent the state of a single particle by a wave-function. The probability that a particle will be found in a particular region upon measurement is given by the integral of the square of this wave-function in this region. If one has two functions whose values differ on a set of points of measure 0, then integrating them over any region will always yield identical results. Thus, as far as probabilities of results of measurements are concerned, functions that differ on a set of points of measure 0 are equivalent. This provides motivation for the claim that functions that differ on a set of points of measure 0 correspond to the same wave-function—the same quantum state.

A more formal motivation for this derives from the fact that in a Hilbert space there is a unique null vector, a unique vector whose inner product with itself is 0. Thus, if one wishes to represent vectors in a separable Hilbert space (with a countable infinity of dimensions) by (complex) functions on space (or configuration space), and one wishes to represent the inner product of vectors by integration of the corresponding functions, then one has to represent vectors not by functions but by equivalence classes of functions whose values differ on up to (Lebesque) measure 0 points. Indeed, although it is not often brought to the fore, it is a standard assumption in quantum mechanics that wave-functions correspond to equivalence classes of (square integrable) functions that differ up to Lebesque measure 0.

This ignoring of measure 0 differences between regions in space suggests that quantum mechanics should be set in a gunky space, not in a pointy space. (I will flesh out this claim in more detail when I examine the measure theoretic approach to gunk.) But, as always, there are responses possible on behalf of the point-lover.

One might simply claim that what I have said is false; one might claim that quantum mechanics does make use of wave-functions that differ only on a measure 0 set of points from each other. Quantum mechanics, for example, uses wave-functions that are eigenfunctions of position—so-called 'delta functions'—which differ from each other only on measure 0 sets of points. However, 'delta functions' are not functions at all. Indeed, position operators, on the standard separable Hilbert space approach to quantum mechanics, simply cannot have eigenstates. Nonetheless, it is true that there are (non-standard) ways of rigorizing the notion of an eigenstate of position, thereby sanctioning states that, in a clear sense, are confined to a single point, while departing from the standard formalism of separable Hilbert spaces (see, for example, Böhm (1978) and Halvorson (2001)). Not only does one have to depart from the standard formalism of separable Hilbert spaces in order to do so, but position eigenstates also have the feature that observables such as momentum and energy have no well-defined expectation values in such position eigenstates. In Arntzenius (2004) I discuss whether it is worth paying this price for the acquisition of position eigenstates, and argue for a cautious 'no'. Let me here merely say that it is far from clear that it is worth paying this price; and leave it at that.

Similar considerations apply in relativistic quantum field theories. There are various theorems that show that there cannot be field operators associated with individual spacetime points. Rather, there are operators ('smeared field operators', or the operators in a 'local algebra of operators') associated with open regions in space or spacetime. This again suggests that relativistic quantum field theory is most naturally set in a gunky spacetime. However, once again the argument is far from watertight. In the first place one would have to be precise about the fundamental objects and quantities in relativistic quantum field theory (which we tried to do in the previous chapter), and then one would have to go about showing that these fundamental objects and quantities can be plausibly represented in a gunky spacetime. In the second place, there are non-standard approaches to relativistic quantum field theory in which point-local objects ('sesquilinear forms') play a fundamental role, which may or may not be representable in a gunky spacetime. (For more detail, see Halvorson and Müger (2006)).

Quite apart from the technical details, there is another response that can be made on behalf of the point-lover. One could simply accept that quantum mechanics happens not to make use of measure 0 differences, and argue that this is all good and well, but this does not mean that such differences do not exist. Not every theory needs to make use of all the features that Nature has on offer.

Once again I agree that the current argument against points is not compelling. Nonetheless, it seems to me that Nature is piling up the hints that there just might be no points out there in space and time. Let us look at one more problem with points before trying to make do without points.

4.6 Contact between objects

In the nineteenth century some people started worrying about the possibility of contact between solid objects if space consists of points. Here is a sketch of such worries. Let us suppose that solid objects cannot interpenetrate—that solid objects cannot occupy overlapping regions. Now consider two solid objects which always occupy closed regions; that is, regions which include their own boundary. Such objects can never be in contact, for closed regions either overlap or are a finite distance apart. In order to avoid interpenetration such objects must decrease their velocities when they are still a finite distance apart, so some kind of action at a distance would have to occur. It seems strange and objectionable that the mere existence of solid objects should imply action at a distance. Alternatively, suppose that solid objects occupy open regions. Then there must always be at least one point separating them; so they still cannot be in genuine contact, and they still must change their velocities without ever being in genuine contact.

The impossibility of genuine contact seems to provide an objection to the existence of points. However, there are a couple of adequate responses that one can give on behalf of points.

In the first place, one could respond that in any case one would not want such 'genuine contact', since collisions would lead to sharp, undifferentiable, kinks in the trajectories of objects. One could plausibly argue that a more realistic physics has objects interacting through fields. Then there will never be 'genuine contact', so there is no 'problem of contact'. One could amplify this line of thought by claiming that it is even more realistic to suppose that quantum mechanics, with an ontology of wave-functions (or perhaps wave-functions plus point particles), is correct, and that given such an ontology there is no problem of contact.

Secondly, one could argue that even if one wants to countenance solid objects which interact by contact, one could just have a slightly different account of what it is to 'be in contact' and what it is to 'interpenetrate'. One could, for example, just say that two objects are 'in contact' if and only if the boundaries of the regions that they occupy overlap. (A point p lies on the boundary of region R if any open set containing p intersects both R and the complement of R.) And one can say that objects do not 'interpenetrate' unless they overlap on more than just their boundaries. Physics can then proceed as usual. Of course, this would mean that objects occupying open regions (in a three-dimensional space) that are separated by a two-dimensional surface are in contact, and that bodies occupying closed regions which overlap on a two-dimensional surface do not interpenetrate. But so what? It does not lead to any trouble in formulating physics, or any trouble with experiment. It only leads to trouble with philosophers who think that it is *a priori* that 'genuine contact' is possible, where 'genuine contact' means having not even a single point in between, and who think it is *a priori* that 'interpenetration' is not possible for solid objects, where 'interpenetration' means not overlapping even on a single point. I do not know whether to respond to such philosophers that in a Newtonian collision world there are, in their sense of 'solid', no solid objects, or whether to respond that in their sense of 'genuine contact' there is no genuine contact, and in their sense of 'interpenetration' there is interpenetration. But one can do Newtonian collision physics when one defines contact as having overlapping boundaries, and interpenetration as overlapping on more than a boundary.

Both of the above responses on behalf of points seem adequate. Nonetheless, note that neither of the responses requires a physics that makes essential use of points, or, more generally, of measure 0 differences. So one is still left with the suspicion that points, and measure 0 differences, are artifacts of the mathematics, and do not exist in reality.

In general, it appears that every problem associated with the existence of points can be overcome; there appears to be no single devastating argument that space and time have to be gunky. Nonetheless, it remains of interest to examine the possibility of doing physics in gunky space and time in more detail.

There are two main approaches to the mathematics of pointless spaces: the measure theoretic approach (see especially Skyrms (1993)), and the topological approach (see especially Roeper (1997)). Let us start with the topological approach.

4.7 The topological approach to pointless spaces

My strategy for constructing a pointless topological space will be as follows. I will start with an ordinary pointy topological space. I will then 'put on blurry spectacles' which

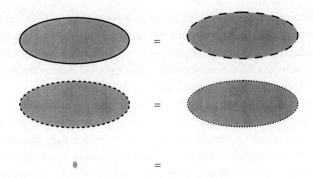

Figure 4.3 Differing on a boundary.

wash out differences in regions which, intuitively speaking, are differences in the (pointy) mathematical representation of space that do not correspond to differences in actual physical space. This will yield a pointless topology. Once I have a pointless topology, I, of course, no longer have ordinary (pointy) functions. But there are still maps from pointless regions to pointless regions. We will see that a rather natural set of such maps corresponds 1–1 to pointy functions that map regular closed regions to regular closed regions. Unfortunately this does not include functions which are constant on a finite region, so that we do not appear to have enough materials with which to do physics. Furthermore, one would like to be able to put a measure on a pointless topological space. We will find that there is also a problem in putting a measure on a pointless topological space. I will therefore advocate switching to the measure theoretic approach. Now for some of the details.

Let us start with an ordinary pointy topological space which is a 'locally compact T_2 space'. A topological space is a 'T_2 space' if and only if for any distinct points x and x' there are disjoint open subsets O and O' containing x and x' respectively. (This is a very mild 'separability' condition.) A topological space is 'locally compact' if and only if for every point x there exists a 'compact' closed set C such that x lies in the 'interior' of C. A set S is 'compact' if and only if for every collection of open sets $\{O_a\}$ such that S is a subset of the union of these open sets, $S \subseteq U\{O_a\}$, there is a finite subcollection of these open sets such that S is a subset of the union of that subcollection: $S \subseteq O_{a1} U O_{a2} U \ldots U O_{an}$. The demand that a space be locally compact is satisfied by just about any space that arises in physics.

Now let us put on our blurry spectacles, and ignore differences between sets that 'differ only on their boundaries'. (See Figure 4.3. The black lines indicate points on the boundary that are not included in the grey regions. The dot on the bottom left represents a single point, which, when we wear our spectacles looks the same as a completely empty region on the bottom right.)

We will say that two sets A and B 'differ only on their boundaries' if and only if the closure of the interior of A is equal to the closure of the interior of B; that is, if $\mathrm{ClInt}(A)=\mathrm{ClInt}(B)$. (The interior of a set consists of the points of that set that do not lie on its boundary.) Here are a couple of examples of sets that, by this definition, differ only on their boundaries. Any set and its interior differ only on their boundaries. (ClIntInt(A)=ClInt(A).) Any set consisting of finitely many points and any other set consisting only of finitely many points differ only on their boundaries, since the closure of the interior of each of them is the empty set.

Now, let us partition all pointy regions (all sets of points) into equivalence classes R of regions that differ only on their boundaries. The motivation for doing this is that our 'blurry glasses' cannot distinguish regions that are in the same equivalence class, so we can regard these equivalence classes as corresponding to pointless regions. (From here on the symbols 'R' and 'R$_i$' will be denote pointless regions rather than pointy regions.)

Now let us give these equivalence classes R mereological structure; that is, 'part–whole' structure. (This mereology will be standard except that it will include a 'null region'; it will be a complete Boolean algebra.) In order to do this, let me first note that every equivalence class of pointy regions will include exactly one 'regular closed' pointy region. (A pointy region S is said to be 'regular closed' if and only if ClInt(S)=S.) Take pointy region S in some equivalence class. Now consider ClInt(S). It will be in the same equivalence class as S, since ClInt(S)=ClIntClInt(S). For the same reason, ClInt(S) is regular closed. It is also the *only* regular closed pointy region in that equivalence class. For suppose S' is regular closed and in the same equivalence class as S. Then ClInt(S)=ClInt(S')=S', so S' is the same as ClInt(S). So there is a 1–1 correspondence between pointless regions R and regular closed pointy regions PR. We can therefore define a mereological structure on the equivalence classes R by defining a mereological (Boolean) structure ($\leq$, $\neg$, $\wedge$, $\vee$) on the corresponding regular closed pointy regions PR. ($\leq$ denotes the 'part of' relation, $\neg$ denotes the 'complementation' operation, $\wedge$ denotes the 'meet' operation, and $\vee$ denotes the 'fusion' operation.) Now we define the mereological structure in the following way:

1) The empty set is the null region.
2) PR$_i\leq$PR$_j$ if and only if PR$_i\subset$PR$_j$.
3) $\neg$PR=Cl(Co(PR)). (Co(PR) is the set theoretic complement of PR.)
4) PR$_i\vee$PR$_j$=PR$_i\cup$PR$_j$.
5) PR$_i\wedge$PR$_j$=Cl(IntPR$_i\cap$IntPR$_j$).
6) If S is a set of regular closed pointy regions, then $\vee$S=Cl$\cup$\{PR|PRεS\}.
7) If S is a set of regular closed pointy regions, then $\wedge$S=ClInt$\cap$\{PR|PRεS\}.

Next let us give the pointless regions' topological structure, which, however, cannot be given in the same way that we gave pointy spaces topological structure—that is, in terms of a distinction between open and closed regions, for that is exactly the kind of distinction that we do not believe exists if reality is pointless. Instead, we will give the topological structure of pointless regions in terms of the primitive notions of 'part of', 'connectedness', and 'limitedness'. And again, we will use the 1–1 correspondence with regular closed pointy regions to determine the topological structure of the pointless regions. In particular, we stipulate that

1) Two pointless regions are 'connected' if and only if the closed regular pointy regions that they correspond to have non-empty intersection.
2) A pointless region is 'limited' if and only if the closed regular pointy region that it corresponds to is compact.

Now we can make use of a result that Peter Roeper (1997) proved. He has shown that any collection of pointless regions that is constructed in the above way (by taking equivalence classes of pointy regions in a locally compact T_2 space which differ only on their boundaries) will satisfy the following axioms of pointless topology:

A_1 If pointless region A is connected to pointless region B, then B is connected to A.

A_2 Every pointless region that is not the pointless 'null region' is connected to itself. (The pointless 'null region' corresponds to the equivalence class of regions which differ only on their boundaries from the null set.)

A_3 The null region is not connected to any pointless region.

A_4 If A is connected to B, and B is a part of C, then A is connected to C.

A_5 If A is connected to the 'fusion' of B and C, then A is connected to B, or A is connected to C.

A_6 The null region is limited.

A_7 If A is limited, and B is a part of A, then B is limited.

A_8 If A and B are limited, then the fusion of A and B is limited.

A_9 If A is connected to B, then there is a pointless limited region C such that C is a part of B, and A is connected to C.

A_{10} If A is limited, B is not the pointless null region, and A is not connected to the 'complement' of B, then there is a pointless region C which is non-null and limited, such that A is not connected to the 'complement' of C, and C is not connected to the 'complement' of B. (The 'complement' of a pointless region A is the pointless region −A such that A and −A have no parts in common, and every non-null pointless region has some part in common either with A or with −A.)

Roeper also proved that any complete Boolean algebra of pointless regions which satisfies the above axioms will correspond 1–1 to equivalence classes of pointy regions in the unique corresponding locally compact T_2 pointy topological space.

From a philosophical point of view it would have made more sense to start with the axioms of pointless topology, and then to show that any complete Boolean algebra of pointless regions which satisfies these axioms will correspond 1–1 to equivalence classes of pointy regions in the unique corresponding locally compact T_2 space. After all, I certainly do not want to say that pointless regions *just are* equivalence classes of pointy regions, for that would mean that pointless regions just are mathematical constructions out of entities (pointy regions) which I believe not to exist. And that would not make much sense. No, the pointless view that I am here exploring is that pointy regions really do not exist, let alone that equivalence classes of them exist. The things that really exist are pointless regions, the primitive predicates and relations that are needed are the 'part of' relation, the 'limitedness' predicate and the 'connected to' relation, and the axioms that characterize the true topology of space are A_1 through A_{10}. However, not only is it much easier to introduce the machinery of pointless topologies via a construction out of pointy topologies; it is also important to see that pointless regions behave exactly the way that our blurry spectacle motivation wants them to behave. That is why I constructed pointless topologies in the way that I did. OK, on to the next tasks: placing material objects and fields in such a pointless topological space, and giving this space more structure than topological structure.

4.8 Objects in a pointless topology

If space is pointless then one cannot specify the locations of material objects by indicating for each point in space whether or not that object occupies it. So how should we conceive of the locational properties of objects in a pointless space? Well, here is a suggestion. We specify the locational state of a material object by specifying for every pointless region whether or not the object is entirely contained in that region.

This suggestion is problematic. The problem is that, despite the fact that space is pointless, one could nonetheless have point particles if one followed this suggestion. How? Well, imagine that a material object is such that it is entirely contained in each of a collection of smaller and smaller pointless regions. Now, if for any pointless region within which the object is contained there is an arbitrarily small pointless subregion within which the object is contained, the object could not have any finite size. So it must have size zero.[3] This is surprising. For it means that one can have pointless space containing point particles! However, allowing such a thing seems to defeat most of the reasons we started on this whole business of gunk. We wanted neither points in space nor point particles.

Moreover, allowing such point particles also leads to a formal feature that seems objectionable: namely, a violation of 'countable additivity'. Here is what that means in this context, and why it fails. Consider the following plausible looking principle: if an object is wholly outside each of a countable collection of regions R_i, then it is also wholly outside the fusion of these regions. Now consider our example. If a particle is entirely contained in each of a collection of converging regions, then it is wholly outside the complements of these regions. Now consider the fusion of the complements of these regions. Intuitively speaking, the only thing that this fusion does not contain is the point to which the converging collection is converging. But remember that we are in a pointless space, and there exists no such point. So one should expect that the fusion of this countable collection is the whole space, for there is no pointless region that it misses out on, as it were. And indeed, this is correct: the fusion of these complements is the whole space. But a material object cannot lie entirely outside the whole of

---

[3] This does not quite mean that it has to be a point particle, since it could still be a line, or an infinitely thin surface. But one can define a notion of 'a converging set of regions' in such a way that the particle does indeed have to be a point particle if it is entirely within each of the regions in the 'converging set of regions'.

space. So we have a countable collection of regions such that the object lies wholly outside each one of the regions in the collection, but is wholly contained in their fusion. This is a failure of countable additivity, and seems bizarre and objectionable. So it seems that one should not allow a specification of the locational properties of a material object by specifying for each region whether or not it is entirely contained in it.

The obvious alternative is the following. One specifies the locational properties of a material object by specifying which region the object exactly fills. It will then, of course, be entirely contained in any region that includes this region, and so on. But it could not be entirely contained in a converging collection of regions, for there is a minimal region, such that it is not contained in anything smaller than that region. So far so good.

4.9 Fields in a pointless topology

How about the states of a field such as the electric field in a pointless topology? Here is a very natural suggestion. We specify the state of a field by specifying for each pointless region in space the exact range of values that the field obtains in that region. This brings up a further issue. Should we think of the possible ranges of values of the field as pointless ranges or as pointy ranges? Should we think that fields can have exact point values, or that the value spaces of fields are as gunky as the physical space that they inhabit? Well, the most natural assumption here surely is that the value space also is gunky: why would nature burden value spaces with distinctions that it does not burden space and time with? So in what follows I will assume that value spaces are gunky too. But it is important to note that this assumption does not make much difference: if one were to assume that the value space is pointy one would be able to recover exactly the same pointy functions as one does if one assumes that the value space is gunky.[4]

Following Roeper (1997), let us call a map h from a pointless physical space S to a pointless field value space VS a 'bounded continuous mereological' map, if it satisfies the following constraints:

1) $h(R)$ is the null region in VS if and only if R is the null region in S.
2) If R_1 is part of R_2, then $h(R_1)$ is part of $h(R_2)$.
3) If V is non-null and part of $h(R_1)$, then there exists a non-null R_2 such that R_2 is part of R_1 and $h(R_2)$ is part of V.
4) If R_1 is connected to R_2, then $h(R_1)$ is connected to $h(R_2)$.
5) If R is limited, then $h(R)$ is limited.

One can prove (see Roeper (1997)) that there is a 1–1 correspondence between bounded continuous mereological maps (between two pointless spaces) and continuous pointy

---

[4] At least, this is so if one assumes that the bounded mereological mappings map pointless regions into closed regular pointy regions in the pointy value space.

functions (between the two corresponding locally compact T_2 spaces) which map regular closed sets of points to regular closed sets of points. That is to say, if we specify the state of a pointless field in a pointless space by means of a bounded continuous mereological map h, then this is equivalent to specifying the corresponding pointy field in the corresponding pointy space by means of a function f from points in space to pointy field values, where f must satisfy the constraint that it maps regular closed sets of points in space to regular closed sets of field values. So on the topological approach to gunk we can recover all field states that correspond to pointy functions which map regular closed sets to regular closed sets. That is a lot. But is it enough?

4.10 Problems for the topological approach to gunk

No, it is not enough. Consider a pointy function f that has a fixed constant value v over some non-null regular closed pointy region PR. It will map every subset of PR, and hence every regular closed subset of PR, to the singleton set $\{v\}$. And a singleton is not a regular closed set. So a function that is constant over some regular closed region PR does not preserve the property of being regular closed. But clearly such functions can occur in physics. For instance, an homogeneous object will have a mass density that is constant over the region that the object occupies.

Another problem is that operations that are quite simple and natural on pointy functions are not that simple or natural on the corresponding bounded continuous mereological maps. For instance, in physics one will often want to do something such as multiply two pointy functions $f_1(x)$ and $f_2(x)$ to form $f_3(x)=f_1(x).f_2(x)$. The value of f_3 at each point p of space is just the multiplication of the values of f_1 and f_2 at that point. But the corresponding bounded continuous mereological map h_3 between the corresponding pointless spaces is not equal to the 'multiplication' of the corresponding bounded continuous mereological maps h_1 and h_2. Indeed, no straightforward sense can be made of 'multiplying' mereological maps.

To make the problem vivid let me consider a very simple example. Consider the pointy functions $f_1(x)=x$, and $f_2(x)=1-x$. Multiplying these two together we obtain $x-x^2$. Let us denote the mereological maps that correspond to f_1 and f_2 as h_1 and h_2. How can we determine h_3 from h_1 and h_2? Not straightforwardly. For instance, $h_1[0,1]=[0,1]$ and $h_2[0,1]=[0,1]$. But this tells us very little about $h_3[0,1]$. In fact, $h_3[0,1]=[0,1/4]$, since $x-x^2$ takes on value 0 for $x=0$ and $x=1$, and reaches its maximum value of $1/4$ at $x=1/2$. But this cannot be inferred from $h_1[0,1]=[0,1]$ and $h_2[0,1]=[0,1]$. Knowing what some region R gets mapped to by mereological maps h_1 and h_2 tells us next to nothing about what that region gets mapped to by the map h_3 which corresponds to the multiplication of the corresponding pointy functions. The features of mereological maps that determine what the 'product' of two mereological maps is are quite 'global' or 'holistic'. The simplest way to figure out what the 'product mereological map' h_3 is, is to translate h_1 and h_2 into pointy functions, then multiply these pointy functions, and then translate this back into the corresponding mereological map. And the same goes for other operations on pointy functions, such as addition. The problem now is that operations such as addition and multiplication of pointy functions occurs all over the place in our laws of physics (which typically take the form of *local* differential equations).

To compound matters: multiplication and/or addition of functions can easily take one from two functions that are not constant over any closed regular region to one that is. The addition of $f_1(x)=x$ and $f_2(x)=-x$ is $f_3(x)=0$. So the set of pointy functions that we can represent in a pointless space is not closed under the operations of 'pointy-addition' and 'pointy-multiplication'.

One might attempt to shrug one's shoulders—at least with respect to the problem that operations that are simple on pointy functions are not simple with respect to mereological maps. One might say 'So what? OK, so we will do our calculations with pointy functions, but we can still maintain that these pointy functions are just convenient representations of the true underlying mereological maps'. Well, as you might expect by now, I do not approve of this attitude. A good theory is a theory such that its laws are simple when stated in terms of the fundamental objects and quantities that it postulates. To believe that space is pointless is to believe that the fundamental spacetime objects are pointless regions, and that the fundamental quantities include mereological maps from pointless spacetime regions to pointless (or perhaps pointy) value spaces. If in terms of those objects and quantities (what we take to be) the laws are much more complicated and unnatural than they are in terms of pointy spacetime and pointy functions, then this argues strongly in favour of pointy spacetime and pointy functions.

There is even more trouble. It seems clear that we will need to put a measure on pointless regions, for how else are we going to able to talk of the sizes of regions, and how else are we going to be able to do the pointless analogue of the integration of functions—something that we surely have to be able to do. Unfortunately, when one tries to put a measure on a pointless topological space one will run into difficulties that appear to be nigh on insurmountable.

Let me start on the project of putting a measure on a pointless topological space by considering a very simple case. We know that there is a 1–1 correspondence between pointless topological spaces and pointy locally compact T_2 spaces. Let us now consider the pointless topological space that corresponds to the pointy one-dimensional continuum; that is, the real number line. We know that there is a 1–1 correspondence between the pointless regions R in the pointless one-dimensional continuum and the regular closed sets of real numbers. Given this fact, the obvious way to try to put a measure on the pointless regions in the pointless continuum is to identify the measure of any pointless region R with the standard (Lebesque) measure of the corresponding closed regular set of real numbers PR. The problem now is that this will turn out to yield a non-additive measure. We can see this by looking at a so-called 'Cantor set'; or rather, the complement of a Cantor set (see Figure 4.4).

Start with the set [0,1]. Call this set S_0. It is a regular closed set with Lebesque measure 1. Now consider the middle quarter of this set; that is, the set [3/8, 5/8]. It is the

Figure 4.4 The Cantor Archipelago.

big grey 'island' in the middle of Figure 4.4. Call this set S_1. S_1 is a regular closed set with measure 1/4. Now consider the set S_2, which has consists of two parts, two islands, which fill the middle of the gaps left by S_1, where S_1 has total measure 1/8 (each of its islands has measure 1/16). That is to say, S_2=[7/32,9/32]∪[23/32,25/32]. Keep on doing this. That is, set S_n consists of islands which are slotted in the middle of all the gaps left by the previous islands, and S_n in total has half the measure of set S_{n-1}. (In Figure 4.4 I have drawn sets S_1, S_2, and S_3.) Since each set S_n is a regular closed set, each such set corresponds to a pointless region R_n in the pointless one-dimensional continuum. Let us now ask what the fusion $\vee\{R_n\}$ of all these pointless regions—the 'Pointless Cantor Archipelago'—is. Well, by our account of the mereology of pointless regions, this is going to be the unique pointless region that corresponds to the regular closed pointy region ClU$\{S_n\}$. Now, the union of all pointy regions S_n is dense on the set [0,1]: one keeps slotting 'islands' in halfway between all previous islands, so that for any point p and any distance d, no matter how small d is, there will be an island within distance d of point p. So every point whatsoever will either lie on one of the islands, or on the boundary of the union of the islands. So the closure of the union of all the islands is just the whole region [0,1]. So the pointless region $\vee\{R_n\}$ corresponds to the equivalence class of regions that differs by measure 0 from the whole pointy region [0,1].

Now we can see why we are in trouble if we assign measures to pointless regions by assigning them the Lebesque measure of the unique regular closed regions to which they correspond. For $\vee\{R_n\}$ will be assigned measure 1 by this method, while the sum of the measures of the R_n equals 1/4+1/8+1/16+1/32+...=1/2. That is to say, this measure will not be countably additive. In fact, the problem is even worse. (The argument in the following paragraph is essentially from Russell (2008).)

Let us split the Pointy Cantor Archipelago into two: the Pointy Odd Archipelago, S_1∪S_3∪S_5∪S_7∪ ..., and the Pointy Even Archipelago, S_2∪S_4∪S_6∪S_8∪ ... Any point in [0,1] lies either in the interior of one of the Pointy Odd Islands, or in the interior of one of the Pointy Even Islands, or lies both on the boundary of the Pointy Odd Archipelago and on the boundary of the Pointy Even Archipelago. For if a point does not lie in the interior of any island, then both the Pointy Odd Archipelago gets arbitrarily close to it and the Pointy Even Archipelago gets arbitrarily close to it. Now let us consider the Pointless Odd Archipelago; that is, the fusion of the Pointless Odd Islands. According to our mereology this corresponds to regular closed pointy region ClU$\{S_o\}$—the closure of the union of all the Pointy Odd Islands. Similarly, the Pointless Even Archipelago corresponds to ClU$\{S_e\}$, the closure of the union of all Pointy Even Islands. The Lebesque measure of the Pointy Even Archipelago is 1/8+1/32+1/128 + ...=1/6. This implies that the Lebesque measure of ClU$\{S_o\}$=5/6, since ClU$\{S_o\}$ includes everything that does not lie in the interior of one of the Even

Islands. And that means that the measure of the Pointless Odd Archipelago is 5/6. Similarly, the Lebesque measure of the Pointy Odd Archipelago is $1/4+1/16+1/64 +\ldots=2/6$. This similarly implies that the Lebesque measure of $ClU\{S_e\}=4/6$. So the measure of the Pointless Even Archipelago is 4/6. Now the Pointless Even Archipelago and the Pointless Odd Archipelago have no overlap: there is no non-null pointless region that is both part of the Pointless Odd Archipelago and the Pointless Even Archipelago. (One might think that they must overlap, since their 'boundaries' overlap. Well, the pointy regions $ClU\{S_e\}$ and $ClU\{S_o\}$ do overlap, but their overlap is a region that consists of a set of disconnected points, which corresponds to the pointless null region. In a pointless space there are no regions that are boundaries of other regions. Boundary regions disappear—become null—when we put on our blurry spectacles. Moreover, the fusion of the Pointless Even Archipelago and the Pointless Odd Archipelago is the whole pointless region [0,1]. So, if the measure is additive 5/6 plus 4/6 should equal 1. But that is not true, so the measure in question is not additive; that is, it is not a measure at all.

One might conjecture that the problem here is that I suggested the wrong rule for assigning measures to pointless regions. Well, while one can show that one can assign a finitely additive measure to all pointless regions (more about that below), one can also prove that there does not exist a countably additive measure over all pointless regions. The reason that one cannot do this is that the mereology of pointless regions violates a condition called 'countable weak distributivity', and one can prove that one cannot put a countably additive measure on any mereology that violates this condition. For the sake of precision let me state countable weak distributivity, while noting that one can skip over this if one wishes, since I will not prove the relevant results (they are too mathematically involved), but will indicate where you can find the relevant proofs.

Let $\{R_{ij}\}$ be a collection of pointless regions indexed by pairs of integers i,j. Let f be a function from the integers to finite non-empty sets integers. Let F be the collection of all such functions. Define

$$R_{if}=\vee_{j\in f(i)}R_{ij}$$

The mereology (Boolean algebra) of pointless regions is now said to be weakly countably distributive if and only if:

$$\wedge_i\vee_jR_{ij}=\vee_{f\in F}\wedge_iR_{if}$$

(There are some further conditions to be satisfied in case the Boolean algebra is not complete, and one can also generalize to cardinalities higher than countability. See Sikorski (1964), p. 127.)

One can then prove that one cannot put a countably additive semi-finite positive measure on the elements of a Boolean algebra that violates countable weak distributivity. A measure on a Boolean algebra is 'semi-finite' if every element of the Boolean algebra which has infinite measure has a part which has finite measure. A measure is 'positive' if any element other than the null element has positive (non-zero) measure. One can also prove that the mereology (Boolean algebra) of pointless regions violates countable weak distributivity. (For these results, see Fremlin (2002), Chapters 31 and 32.) In short, one cannot put a countably additive, positive, semi-finite measure on topological gunk.[5]

OK, but perhaps we can reasonably drop one of these three requirements on measures. Dropping semi-finiteness is a non-starter: surely every pointless region of infinite size must contain some pointless region of finite size. How about positivity? Well, pointless regions correspond to closed regular regions. Every non-null pointless region corresponds to a non-empty pointy closed regular region. Every non-empty pointy closed regular region contains a pointy open region of non-zero Lebesque measure. So it also seems a bad idea to drop positivity. The only remaining candidate is to drop countable additivity. Indeed, Jeff Russell (2008) has suggested that one can reasonably do this. But how?

Let us take as our example the one-dimensional continuum: the real line. We begin with a fairly minimal assumption: a pointless region that corresponds to a closed regular pointy interval consisting of all real numbers (inclusively) between real numbers a and b should have measure equal to the 'length' of that interval; that is, the difference between the real numbers that correspond to the endpoints of the interval: $b-a$ (or, at least, a measure that is proportional to the difference $b-a$). Finite additivity immediately entails that any pointless region that corresponds to a fusion of finitely many disjoint such intervals must equal the sum of the lengths of each of these intervals. More interestingly, it entails that, for example, the measure of the Pointless Odd Archipelago must be greater than or equal to the sum of the measures of the Pointless Odd Islands; that is, it must be greater than or equal to 2/6. For if it were anything less, one could find a finite set of Pointless Odd Islands whose measures add up to more than the measure of the entire Pointless Odd Archipelago, and that would violate finite additivity. Similarly, it follows that the measure of the Pointless Even Archipelago must be greater than or equal to 1/6. And this in turn entails that the measure of the Pointless Odd Archipelago must be less than or equal to 5/6.[6] So a very natural minimal assumption about measure imposes interesting constraints on what a finitely additive measure on pointless regions must look like. Even more interestingly, one can show that one can set the measure of the Pointless Odd Archipelago equal to any value between 2/6 and 5/6, and then extend it to a positive semi-finite finitely additive measure on the mereology of pointless regions. (Indeed, one can do this in very many ways. See Russell (2008) and Birkhoff (1967), pp. 185ff.) So one can put a finitely additive measure on the pointless regions; indeed, one can do so in an incredibly huge number of different ways. Therein lies the problem.

---

[5] Another approach to topological gunk would be to take pointless regions to correspond to equivalence classes of regions that differ on 'meagre' sets. A set is 'meagre' if it can be expressed as a countable union of sets that are nowhere dense. However, this algebra of pointless regions also violates weak countable distributivity. See Sikorski (1964), Section 30.

[6] These two measures correspond to the 'Jordan inner measure' of the pointy Odd Archipelago, and the 'Jordan outer measure' of the pointy Odd Archipelago.

It seems rather implausible that Nature has somehow arbitrarily decided which of a huge infinity of finitely additive measures to put on the pointless regions that there are. A possible response would be to say that there is no fact of the matter as to what the true measure is, beyond what is forced by finite additivity and our minimal starting assumption. But this would mean that there is a large collection of regions that has no well-defined measure. Indeed there would be a much larger collection of measureless regions than in the pointy approach, and we can go ahead and construct many of them. That seems objectionable.

Still, it seems to me that this is not the heart of the problem. The main objection to topological gunk in connection with measure is much more straightforward and compelling. The main problem is that on the topological approach to gunk one is ignoring differences that are much too large to be ignored, and the main idea of this topological approach is that differences between pointy regions that differ only on their boundaries are not real differences. This seems a fairly intuitive and reasonable idea when one considers only pointy regions which are islands, or finite collections of such islands, since their boundaries are 'small'; that is, they have measure 0. But as soon as one realizes that certain countable collections of islands, such as the Cantor Archipelago, have boundaries that have non-zero—indeed, arbitrarily large—measure, the whole idea no longer seems plausible. Since such regions can be formed by elementary constructions, and since it seems evident that one cannot ignore arbitrarily large differences, it seems to me that topological gunk is just a misconceived idea. Relatedly, suppose we start on the job of painting blue the islands of a Cantor Archipelago on our wall. Perhaps we can never finish the job, but still, we are never going to use more than half the paint we would need in order to paint the whole wall, and we are never going come even close to painting the whole wall. So why on earth insist that the fusion of all the Cantor islands is the whole wall? One can coherently insist on this, but unless other options are dire it seems extremely implausible to do so.

4.11 Measure theoretic gunk

Let us start with the pointy real number line. As before, we are going to create a pointless space by putting on blurry glasses. On the measure theoretic approach, what we are going to blur out is differences of Lebesque measure 0. In order to do that we first have to restrict ourselves to Lebesque measurable sets. We begin by restricting ourselves to the Borel sets. One gets the collection of all Borel sets on the real line by starting with the collection of all open intervals (open sets of the form (a,b) for any real numbers a and b), and closing up this collection under complementation, countable union, and countable intersection. Now let us put on our blurry glasses and define the measure-theoretic pointless regions R of the measure-theoretic pointless real line to be equivalence classes of Borel sets of the pointy real line that differ up to Lebesque measure 0. (From here on I am going to drop the qualification 'measure-theoretic': when I talk about 'pointless regions' from I will mean 'measure-theoretic pointless regions', unless I explicitly state otherwise.) Note that forming such equivalence classes preserves complementation, countable union, and countable intersection. Indeed, one can show that the algebra of such equivalence classes is a complete Boolean algebra: that is, a standard mereology (with a null region) which is closed under arbitrary fusion (see Sikorski (1964), pp. 73–5).

As in the case of topological gunk, we do not want to *define* measure theoretic pointless regions as equivalence classes of measurable pointy regions that differ up to measure 0. Rather, we want to put down axioms on pointless regions, and then show that pointless regions satisfying these axioms are uniquely representable as equivalence classes of pointy measurable regions that differ up to measure 0. Luckily, this work has already been done for us. Start by assuming that the mereology of pointless regions is a standard 'atomless' mereology with a null region: a complete 'atomless' Boolean algebra. An element of a Boolean algebra is an 'atom' if it has no proper parts other than the null element. An 'atomless' Boolean algebra has no atoms. We then assume that there is a positive, 'separable', countably additive measure on this algebra; that is, that we have a 'separable measure algebra'. A measure algebra is 'separable' if there is a countable collection of pointless regions C, such that C is 'dense' in the full Boolean algebra of pointless regions; that is, such that for any pointless region R and any measure ε, no matter how small, there is a pointless region R′ in C which differs from R by less than measure ε (such that the difference between the two pointless regions has measure less than ε). One can then prove that given any atomless separable measure algebra such that the measure of the maximal element of the algebra (the whole space) is 1, there is a 1–1 isomorphism between it and the algebra consisting of equivalence classes of measurable regions of the pointy real line segment [0,1] that differ up to Lebesque measure 0. That is to say, there is essentially only one atomless separable measure algebra, and it is identical to the algebra of equivalence classes of measurable pointy regions that differ up to Lebesque measure 0. (For more precise definitions and proofs, see Royden (1968), Chapter 15.) So far, so good.

We can put objects in measure theoretic gunk in the same way that we did in topological gunk: namely, by specifying the pointless region that they exactly occupy. Fields are trickier. As before, it would seem most plausible that the value spaces of such fields are also gunky. However, for convenience of presentation I will start with the assumption that the value spaces of fields are pointy. Once again the crucial work has already been done for us, for one can prove the following (see Sikorski (1964), Section 32): there exists a 1–1 correspondence between equivalence classes of pointy 'Borel-measurable' functions *from* pointy real line A *to* pointy real line B that differ on up to Lebesque measure 0 sets of points, and 'σ-homomorphisms' *from* pointy regions on the pointy real line B *to* pointless regions on the pointless real line A. (I have italicized *from* and *to* in order to emphasize that the homomorphisms run in the opposite direction from the pointy functions to which they correspond.) A function is said to be 'Borel measurable' if it sends Borel sets to Borel sets. A mapping h between Boolean algebras is said to be a 'σ-homomorphism' if

1) $h(\neg R) = \neg h(R)$.
2) $h(\vee R_i) = \vee h(R_i)$, for any countable collection $\{R_i\}$.
3) $h(\wedge R_i) = \wedge h(R_i)$, for any countable collection $\{R_i\}$.

That is to say, if we make the very simple and natural assumption that the state of a pointless scalar field in a pointless continuum can be given by a σ-homomorphism from pointy value ranges to pointless regions in space, then we can recover all Borel measurable pointy functions (including highly discontinuous ones) up to differences of Lebesque measure 0. This is a great result. Not only can one recover all the pointy functions that one could reasonably be expected to ever need in physics, one can also only recover these pointy functions up to the kind of differences that one would expect not to correspond to real differences in Nature.

OK, but what if the value space is pointless? Well, let us say that a σ-homomorphism h from pointless values space to pointless space (or pointless spacetime) is a σ-isomosphism if and only if there exists a σ-homormophism h' from pointless space (or pointless spacetime) such that $h' \circ h$ is the identity map on pointless value space, and $h \circ h'$ is the identity map on pointless space (or pointless spacetime). Here, $h' \circ h$ denotes the map that one gets by first using h to map from pointless value space to pointless space, and then using h' to map the result back to pointless value space. ($h \circ h'$ is defined analogously.) One can show that every such σ-isomorphism corresponds to a unique equivalence class of pointy functions that differ on sets of points up to Lebesque measure 0. (See Royden (1968), Chapter 15, theorem 13.) But note that this does not mean that there is a 1–1 correspondence between such σ-isomorphisms and equivalence classes of Borel measurable pointy functions. I will deal with this problem in the next section when I discuss objections to the measure theoretic approach to gunk.

What about topology? We have just put a measure on the atomless mereology of pointless regions, but that tells us nothing about which pointless region is connected to which pointless region. For, loosely speaking, cutting out a segment of the real line, and pasting it somewhere else along the real line does not alter the mereology of the real line, nor the measure theoretic structure of that mereology. So we need to add a topology separately. How could we do that? Well, what we could try to do is to start with the pointy real line, and then use its pointy topology to define a topology on the pointy real line which is invariant under differences of up to Lebesque measure 0. Let us try that.

Let us say that pointy Borel sets A and B are 'connected' if and only if there exists a point p such that any open set containing p has an overlap of non-zero measure both with A and with B. And let us say that pointy Borel set A is 'limited' if and only if for some compact Borel set B we have that A∩Complement(B) has measure 0.

Clearly, these definitions are invariant under differences in regions A and B up to measure 0. So we can use it to define a topology on the pointless regions of the pointless real line. The resulting structure will satisfy Roeper's axioms A_1 through A_9, but it will violate axiom A_{10}. Let me remind you what this axiom says. If R_a is limited, R_b

is not the pointless null region, and R_a is not connected to the complement of R_b then there is a pointless region R_c which is non-null and limited, such that R_a is not connected to the complement of R_c, and R_c is not connected to the complement of R_b.

To see that this axiom fails, consider a Cantor-type pointy set—for instance, the pointy set $B=(0,1)\cap$complement$(\cup S_n)$, where the S_n are the gap-filling sets defined in the previous section. Set B is a measure $\frac{1}{2}$ Borel set, so we can consider the corresponding non-null pointless region R_b to which it corresponds. Now let R_a be the null region. R_a is limited and not connected to the complement of R_b, since the null region is not connected to anything. So there should be a non-null and limited R_c such that R_c is not connected to the complement of R_b. Now the complement of R_b is the union of three pointless regions: $\{-\infty,0\}$, $\cup R_n$, and $\{1,\infty\}$. Now, any pointy non-null open set has an overlap of non-zero Lebesque measure with any pointy set in the equivalence corresponding to this pointless region, so this pointless region is connected to every non-null pointless region. So there cannot be such an R_c.

The problem is the following. The basic idea of axiom A_{10} is that there is a topological notion of pointless region R_1 being 'strictly inside' pointless region R_2. The idea is that R_1 is strictly inside R_2 if R_1 is disconnected from the complement of R_2. And then the idea of 'pointlessness', or the idea of 'non-atomicity', suggests that if R_1 is strictly inside R_3 then there ought to be an R_2 such that R_1 is strictly inside R_2 and R_2 is strictly inside R_3. In particular, for any non-null R there should be a non-null region R' which is strictly inside R. This axiom fails given the way that I have defined connectedness on the measure theoretic approach, since there are Cantor-type non-null regions such that there are no regions that are strictly inside such a Cantor-type region, since the complement of such a Cantor-type region is connected to every non-null region.

Now, one might think that the failure of this axiom shows that we do not really have a *pointless* space. However, the fact that our space is pointless is still unambiguously represented in two different ways:

1) The algebra of regions is non-atomic.
2) Other than the null region, every region has non-zero measure, and for every non-zero measure, no matter how small, there are regions that have that measure.

So I am not terribly worried about the failure of axiom A_{10}. Still, it is interesting to note that the fact that there exists a pointless region R_b corresponding to a pointy Cantor set shows that one should not think that each pointless region can be decomposed into a collection of extended 'solid islands'. The pointless region R_b, for instance, is not so decomposable.

In any case, my suggestion is that a topology for a pointless space is a 'connectedness' and 'limitedness' structure on an atomless separable measure algebra which satisfies axioms A_1–A_9. However, I do not have a representation theorem on offer: I have no idea what the relation is between structures satisfying these axioms and pointy topo-logical spaces—something for a better mathematician than myself to sort out!

And, of course, this is only a beginning. We also, for example, need to be able to add differential structure (vector and tensor fields!) and metric structure (distances!) in order to do modern physics. There is existing work on metric structure that one might be able to use: Gerla and others (see Gerla (1995) and references therein) have given axioms for pointless metric spaces, which put metric structures on certain algebras of pointless regions which induce unique corresponding pointy metric spaces, where our atomless separable measure algebras satisfy the axioms that they put on their algebras of pointless regions. I should note that because of the global nature of their metric they only manage to recover a very small class of metric spaces. This suggests that it might be more fruitful to first put differential structure on atomless separable measure alge-bras, and then define a metric by means of a metric tensor field. As far as differential structure goes, one might be able to use the homomorphisms that I introduced above in order to mimick the way in which Penrose and Rindler put differential structure on pointy spaces by means of scalar functions that play the role of coordinates on patches of the pointy spaces (see Penrose and Rindler (1984), Section 4.1.) Again, consider-ations of time, space, and mathematical competence prevent me from developing these ideas here. In the meantime, however, we already have enough structure in place to make trouble for the measure theoretic approach to gunk.

4.12 Problems for measure theoretic gunk

The first problem for measure theoretic gunk occurs when we assume that the value space of scalar functions is also pointless. We saw that in that case σ-isomorphisms cor-respond to equivalence classes of Borel measurable pointy functions which differ up to Lebesque measure 0. But while all σ-isomorphisms correspond to pointy functions, there are many perfectly normal pointy functions that do not correspond to any σ-isomorphism. Consider, for instance, some pointy function $f(x)$ which first increases and then decreases (see Figure 4.5). The corresponding 'forwards' homomorphism

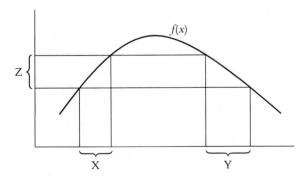

Figure 4.5 Forwards and backwards homomorphisms.

sends pointless region X to pointless region Z. The corresponding 'backwards' homo-morphism sends region Z to the fusion of regions X and Y. So this function does not correspond to two homomorphisms, the composition of which is the identity.

In essence, the functions which correspond to σ-isomorphisms are the monoton-ically increasing functions and the monotonically decreasing functions. One might try to deal with this problem by splitting up functions into their monotonically increasing parts and their monotonically decreasing parts. But that will not deal with a familiar bugbear: namely, functions that are constant over regions of non-zero measure. More-over, it has to be said, this is becoming rather ungainly. What we want to get our hands on are representatives for pointy functions, but these correspond to rather complicated and unnatural elements of (pairs of) gunky spaces. Of course, none of this is a problem if the value space is pointy.

However, even if value space is pointy there is a problem—one that we have already encountered in the case of topological gunk: simple and natural operations on pointy functions, such as point-wise multiplication, do not correspond to simple and natural operations on the corresponding homomorphisms. As a consequence it seems very likely that the fundamental law of physics cannot be stated in a simple way in terms of the fundamental elements of measure theoretic gunky spaces.

Finally, there is something rather unsatisfactory about making use of a global measure —a global notion of the size of regions—before we can put on other structure, such as differential and metric structure. In the first place we would like to be able to make sense of the structure of gunky spaces which do not have a measure or a metric on them. In the second place we would like to be able to introduce a measure as a local volume form, rather than starting off with the assumption that we have a global measure on regions.

On the other hand, it has to be said that the measure theoretic approach to gunk seems much more promising than the topological approach to gunk. The measure theoretic approach does not ignore difference which are fairly obviously too large to be ignored. And, provided that one assumes that value spaces are pointy, one can recover all the pointy functions that one is likely to need in order to do physics.

4.13 Conclusions

The main, obvious, and pitifully weak conclusion has to be that, as yet, it is not clear whether space and time are pointless, but that if they are pointless, then they are more likely to be measure theoretically pointless than topologically pointless. That is a bit of a damp squib. And even that may seem a bit unduly optimistic on the part of pointless spaces. As it stands, we certainly have not found gunky theories that are as simple as the corresponding pointy theories. But, for no good reason, I have the hope that there are gunky theories, along the lines that I have discussed, that are simpler than what I have managed to come up with so far. Not very convincing, I admit. Oh well. Let me end this chapter by discussing a couple of general issues that one might have worried about as we went along.

In the first place, one might have wondered why I did not employ a tactic which I have discussed previously. Why did I not take the view that points exist while also denying that differences (in regions and functions) of up to measure zero are real physical differences? Recall that in Chapter 2 I claimed that it was perfectly coherent to claim that charge values are fundamental quantities, and yet maintain that there are no distinct physical possibilities that differ only by a global charge flip. (This was not my preferred view, but I did claim that it was a coherent view.) And, to look ahead a bit, in the next chapter I will argue that it is quite coherent to maintain that both spacetime and material objects are fundamental, and yet deny that there are distinct physical possibilities that differ only by a global shift of all objects in spacetime. So why not maintain that points exist and are fundamental, and yet deny that measure 0 differences are real, physical differences? That way it would seem that I can have my cake and eat it: a simple mathematical physics accompanied by a denial of the existence of *prima facie* otiose differences.

But the cases are not relevantly analogous. In the case of charge, the reason I was able to maintain that charge values being fundamental did not imply that global charge flips correspond to real differences by denying that there are cross-possible-world facts about identity of charge value (charge set). Similarly, in the next chapter we will see that we can deny that global shifts correspond to real physical differences by denying that there are facts about identity of spacetime points across possible worlds. But we cannot do the analogous thing in the case of measure 0 differences if points are taken to exist. If points exist we cannot plausibly say that a world W_1 in which exactly one spacetime point is red corresponds to the same physical possibility as a world W_2 which is identical to W_1 except that one additional point is red, or that it corresponds to the same physical possibility as a world W_0 in which no point is red, or that it corresponds to the same physical possibility as a world W_3 in which some countable collection of points is red. Whether or not we can identity spacetime points across possible worlds is irrelevant here. On any reasonable way of understanding what physical possibilities are, if spacetime points exist in these physical possibilities, then we can distinguish between a physical possibility in which no points are red, and one in which some measure 0 set of points is red. So we cannot have our cake and eat it. If we are going to claim that differences of measure 0 are otiose, then we had better not have points in our ontology.

Finally, it is interesting to distinguish several motivations for the kind of project that I have examined in this chapter. In the first place one might be motivated by the desire to eradicate differences in possibilities that appear to be otiose differences. As I have said a number of times before, I am wary of being guided in theory choice by intuitions concerning the distinctness of possibilities. But there are motives in the vicinity that seem more epistemologically sound to me: namely, motives of simplicity and ontological parsimony. Something that should already have been obvious, but is brought to the fore in this chapter, is that considerations of simplicity can pull in the opposite direction from considerations of ontological parsimony: getting rid of points complicates our theory, and it is not obvious how the two should be weighed against each other. Relatedly, we should distinguish between two kinds of ontological parsimony. Intuitively speaking, reducing the amount of *fundamental things* that there are does not necessarily reduce the amount of *things* that there are. For instance, if spacetime is pointy, then it seems quite plausible that spacetime points are the fundamental spacetime objects; that is, that (non-point-like) spacetime regions are not fundamental. However, if spacetime is gunky, then there are no plausible candidates for what the fundamental spacetime objects are other than just *all* the (pointless) regions. If that is so, then while it is true that we have *fewer objects* in a gunky spacetime than in the corresponding pointy spacetime, it is also true that we have *more fundamental objects* in gunky spacetime than in pointy spacetime. Unfortunately, this observation muddies the waters even more when it comes to deciding whether or not spacetime is in fact gunky. Oh dear . . .

5

Do space and time exist?

Ye Gods! Annihilate but space and time,
And make two lovers happy.

Alexander Pope

5.1 Introduction

We can see neither space nor time, we cannot smell them, we cannot touch them, we cannot hear them, and we cannot taste them. What, then, are these mysterious entities? Why think they exist? On the other hand, it is hard to see how one can do without space and time. If objects are not situated in space and time, how can there be distances between objects, how can there be time lapses between events, how can things move?

There are two venerable traditions in the philosophy of space and time. One is 'substantivalism', which maintains that space and time (relativistically, spacetime) are objects that exist in addition to ordinary material objects such as tables and chairs. The opposing tradition, 'relationism', rejects the existence of space and time (spacetime) and maintains that all that exists is material objects. According to traditional relationism at each time there are spatial distances between material objects and there are temporal distances between events involving these material objects. But these are just relations that obtain between those objects and those events; there are no further objects, space and time (spacetime), in which those objects and events are situated. How to settle this issue? Well, as usual, the devil is in the details. Let us start with Newtonian physics, and first consider the case of space.

5.2 Leibniz's shifts; an argument against the existence of space

Leibniz, the Continental rival of Newton, gave a famous argument against the existence of space. His argument was as follows. Suppose that space did in fact exist. Now imagine a universe that is exactly the same as ours, except that every material object throughout the history of that universe, is shifted to a different location in space. Say every material object is shifted 5 feet in the direction that the Eiffel tower now points. Such a universe would not differ in any discernible way from the actual universe. Therefore, God could have had no reason to create our universe rather than such a shifted universe. But God has a reason for everything he does. So it cannot be that there is such a choice to be made. Now, if there is no space, if all that exists is material objects, which stand in certain distance relations, then there is no such choice to be made. For, all the distance relations between material objects are the same in the actual universe and in the shifted universe. Thus, if all that exists is material objects, which stand in distance relations to one another, then there are no such two distinct possibilities, and thus there is no choice for God to make. That is, if there is no space in which to shift material objects around, then there simply could not be distinct universes that differ only by a global shift. So God is not Buridan's ass.

Shorn of religious zeal, the argument boils down to this. If space exists, there is a difference between a universe and a shifted universe. But that is a difference without a difference. And why introduce such an elusive difference if you do not need it? Leibniz concluded that space does not exist—that there are only bits of matter which stand in spatial (distance) relations.

5.3 Newton's buckets; an argument for the existence of space

Newton responded to Leibniz's 'shift argument' against the existence of space by presenting an equally famous argument for the existence of space: namely, his 'bucket argument'. Here it is.

Take a bucket, fill it with water, and let it rest for a while. The water surface will be flat. (This is stage 1; see Figure 5.1.) Now start spinning the bucket as smoothly as you can. Initially the water will not have caught up with the bucket, and the surface of the water will remain flat (stage 2). Then, after you have been spinning the bucket for a while, the water will be spinning with the bucket, and the surface of the water will

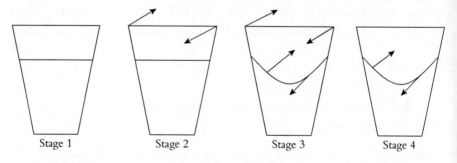

Stage 1   Stage 2   Stage 3   Stage 4

Figure 5.1 Newton's bucket.

have a concave shape (stage 3). Now suddenly stop the bucket. The water will initially keep spinning, and its surface will remain concave (stage 4). Eventually the water will stop spinning, and its surface will be flat again (back to stage 1).

Newton's explanation of the changing shape of the surface of the water is straight-forward. Water, like anything else, moves in a straight line through space unless a force is acting on it. So the water in the bucket, once it is set in motion, would naturally move in a straight line. If it were not for the walls of the bucket this motion would take the water out of the bucket. But the walls of the bucket exert an inward-directed force on the water, which, together with the gravitational force, will lead to a concave water surface.

Newton claims that Leibniz cannot possibly explain the changing shape of the water surface. Consider stages 1 and 3. According to Leibniz there is no such thing as space, and hence no such thing as motion through space. Motion, according to Leibniz, can only be said to exist when some distances between some material objects change. Note that both in stage 1 and in stage 3 there are no distances between material objects that change. In each of those two stages, each part of the water and each part of the bucket remain exactly the same distance from any other part of the water or bucket. So, says Newton, Leibniz cannot possibly explain why in stage 1 the water surface is flat and in stage 3 the water surface is concave.[1] Newton concluded that relationism was sunk. What a nice argument!

So now we have two nice arguments: Leibniz's shift argument against substan-tivalism, and Newton's bucket argument against relationism. Which to adopt? In the next eight sections of this chapter I will discuss a number of varieties of relationism and argue that they all face severe objections. In the last two sections I will return to substantivalism, and defend it.

5.4 Leibnizean relationism and Newtonian particle theories

The nineteenth-century Austrian physicist Ernst Mach claimed that in his bucket argument against relationism Newton was ignoring essential features of the situation that the relationist can use in order to explain the shape of the water surface at each stage. In particular, said Mach, the reason the water surface is concave in stage 3, and yet flat in stage 1, is that in stage 3 the water is rotating *relative to most of the matter in the universe* (the earth, the solar system, the stars, and so on), while in stage 1 it is not rotating *relative to the bulk of the universe*.

---

[1] Essentially the same argument holds regarding stages 2 and 4. The relative motions of all parts of the water and the bucket are essentially the same in these stages. So Leibniz, again, cannot explain why in stage 2 the water surface is flat and in stage 4 it is concave. I say 'essentially' because they are not exactly the same: in stage 2, seen from above, the bucket is rotating counter-clockwise relative to the water, while in stage 4 it is rotating clockwise relative to the water. But it is incredibly implausible that this difference has anything to do with the shape of the water surface. Besides, one can test whether it does: just spin the bucket in the opposite direction, and see whether it makes any difference. It does not.

This explanation is all very well, but it brings with it some troublesome issues. For one thing, notice how non-local such an explanation is: the shape of the surface of the water depends on how it is currently moving relative to matter that is incredibly far away. Also, one would like to know exactly how the curvature of the water's surface depends on its motion relative to the other matter in the universe. For instance, if one imagines removing the stars from our universe, one by one, does the surface gradually become flatter? Or, more practically, suppose one makes a bucket with very thick walls, and one suddenly spins such a bucket filled with water. Does the surface of the water then become a tiny bit concave even before the water starts spinning? Mach never provided a quantitative theory detailing exactly how the curvature of the water's surface depends on its motion relative to other matter, nor, more generally, a quantitative theory of the way in which inertial effects depend on the relative motion of material objects. (Inertial effects are matter's inherent resistance to non-straight, or non-geodesic, motion.)

This, however, has recently been done by Julian Barbour and his collaborators. In fact, we have already encountered his relationist Newtonian particle theory, at the end of Section 1.5. In that chapter we were interested in Barbour's idea that one could formulate a theory according to which time had no structure; but in so doing we also encountered a theory of Barbour's in which the only spatial structure that was assumed consisted of spatial distances at a time. Barbour's theory therefore is nicely compatible with the assumption that space does not exist, and the assumption that the only things that exist are material particles which at each time stand in distance relations. Following standard terminology, I will call a theory which says that space does not exist, and that the only fundamental spatial properties and relations are simultaneous spatial distance relations, a Leibnizean relationist theory. We will later encounter other forms of relationism—ones which, for example, assume that there are fundamental cross-time spatial relations.

What does such a Leibnizean relational theory say about the question that I raised in connection with Ernst Mach? Well, suppose that one has a universe with only a bucket containing some water, where the bucket weighs about the same as the water. In that case, any relative motion will lead to a curvature of the water surface that corresponds to a rate of rotation of the water in Newtonian space at about half the relative rate of rotation. Well, the bucket has a bigger average radius than the water, so this is not quite right, but you get the idea. So this theory does deliver a precise quantitative answer to the question as to how much the water surface will curve depending on the relative motions of all the material parts of the universe. However, as we saw in Chapter 1, the initial value data that one needs in order to determine the evolution of a local isolated system will not be the same as it is for the entire universe: one needs to know what the effective total angular momentum of the local isolated system is in order to get a unique evolution of an initial state of such a local isolated system, and while the angular momentum of the total universe has to be 0 the effective angular momentum of a local isolated system need not be 0. One might respond that the concept of state in a relational theory is holistic anyhow, since it consists of a set of *distances*, which are non-local quantities. However, even granted that this is so, one might still hope that the evolution of the state of a local isolated system would be uniquely determined by all the initial distances among the parts of that local isolated system, all the initial rates of change of these distances, and the masses of the particles in the local isolated system. But, alas, this is not so. Let me now consider two additional objections to Leibnizean relational theories of classical particle mechanics.

First let me discuss the so-called 'hand' argument which is originally due to Immanuel Kant. The basic idea of the argument is very simple. Consider a left-handed glove (one that fits a left hand) and a right-handed glove (one that fits a right hand). Clearly, these two gloves have different shapes. for if their shapes were identical they would fit the same hands. Now consider a universe that has no material objects in it except one of those two gloves. It seems clear that there are two distinct such possible worlds: a world which just contains a left-handed glove, and a world which contains just a right-handed glove. However, it is not hard to figure out that according to relationism there is only one such possible glove-world. For, recall that according to relationism all that exists is material objects which stand in certain distance relations. And the set of all distance relations between all the parts of the left-handed glove is exactly the same as the set of all distance relations between all the parts of the right-handed glove. One can get the one glove from the other by 'mirroring' it, and mirroring does not affect distances. Thus, according to relationism there is only one such possible glove-world. On the other hand (bad pun), according to substantivalism, it would seem that there is a distinction between a world containing just the right-handed glove and a world containing just a left-handed glove. According to substantivalism there exist spatial points in addition to the glove. The right-handed glove cannot occupy (fit) exactly the same set of spatial points as the left-handed glove, so the two worlds must differ in the spatial points that are occupied. Therefore, according to substantivalism there are indeed two distinct possible glove-worlds.[2] Since, intuitively, it seems clear that there are in fact two such distinct possibilities, it seems we have an argument for substantivalism and against relationism.

However, matters are not so simple. In the first place, some people will, upon reflection, come to the opinion that if there were just a single glove in the world, it would indeed make no sense to ask whether the glove is left-handed or right-handed. That is to say, some people will, upon reflection, revise their intuitions, and come to believe that there is only one possible single glove-world rather than two. Indeed, some might have such intuitions right off the bat. This complicates matters, since I do not know how to resolve this conflict of intuitions. Secondly, to complicate matters even further, it is, upon reflection, not so clear that substantivalists should maintain that there are two distinct possible glove-worlds. I claimed above that according to substantivalism

---

[2] According to substantivalism there are infinitely many such glove-worlds, since there are infinitely many different locations that the glove could occupy. But there are two types of glove-world—left-handed types and right-handed types—where worlds of the same type differ just by a glove-shift.

there are two distinct possible glove-worlds because the two gloves must occupy different spatial points in the two possible worlds. But this argument relies on the assumption that one can sensibly speak of the identity or non-identity of spatial points in different possible worlds in a way that is independent of the way the glove is situated in each of these possible worlds. This is an issue I will discuss at length later in this chapter when I re-evaluate the Leibniz shift argument. In fact, we will then find that standard substantivalists (so-called 'sophisticated substantivalists') do not accept that one can identify spatial points across possible worlds. So it seems that such substantivalists will have a hard time defending Kant's hand argument. More importantly, I do not want to discuss this issue in any more detail, since, as you might expect on the basis of previous chapters, I am suspicious of arguments which start from intuitions about what is possible and draw conclusions as to what the fundamental objects and quantities in the actual world are. The best (simplest, most natural) theory of the phenomena is our best evidence for what the fundamental objects and quantities are, and this in turn can be used to guide us concerning what is possible and what is not possible. Having intuitions about what will possibly guide us to what the best theory is, and to what fundamental objects and quantities there are, is putting the epistemological cart before the horse. Let us not do this.

We shall instead turn to a closely related argument against relationism which stands up to more scrutiny. In the 1960s, experiments showed that nature violates parity: certain initial states that develop into certain final states are such that the mirror images of those initial states do not develop into the mirror images of those final states. Such violations have been accounted for within quantum field theory. However, parity violations could in principle also occur in Newtonian particle theories, and yield exactly the same argument against relationism as they do in quantum field theory. They are, moreover, easy to describe within a Newtonian particle physics. So let me present a simple (fictitious) case of a parity violation in a Newtonian context, and then see how it can be used to argue against relationism.

Let us suppose that there are three types of particle: a-particles, b-particles, and c-particles, each of which always travels with constant velocity. That is, these particles do not interact at all. Even when any number of them run into one another, they simply pass through one another.

There is, however, one exception to this rule. If, and *only* if, one a-particle, one b-particle, and one c-particle meet and their respective velocities form a 'right-handed triad' when they meet, then they are snuffed out of existence at that very moment (see Figure 2). Velocities v_a, v_b, and v_c are said to form a 'triad' if they are mutually orthogonal. In order to figure out whether such a triad is 'right-handed' or 'left-handed', imagine having an ordinary screw, pointing the screw in the direction that v_a points, and rotating the screw in the direction that goes from v_b to v_c (by the shortest path). If this is the direction that one screws when one is screwing in an ordinary screw, then v_a, v_b, and v_c form a right-handed triad. If this is the direction that one screws when one is unscrewing an ordinary screw, then v_a, v_b, and v_c form a left-handed triad.

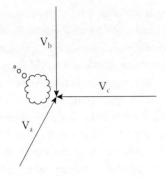
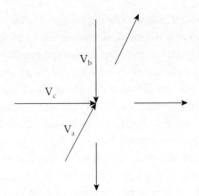

v_a, v_b and v_c form a right-handed triad
The particles cease to exist when they
meet.

v_a, v_b and v_c form a left-handed triad.
The particles pass through one another
when they meet.

Figure 5.2 Parity violation.

Since the particles only cease to exist if they meet with velocities v_a, v_b, and v_c that
form a right-handed triad, they will not cease to exist (they will pass through each
other) if they meet with velocities v_a, v_b, and v_c that form a left-handed triad. Since
a left-handed triad is the mirror image of a right-handed triad, this is a violation of
parity. Now, violations of parity are very surprising. Who would have thought that
the laws of nature treat mirror-image situations differently? Yet experiments show
that they do. The crucial question now is: how can one formulate a theory that entails
such parity violations?

It is easy to see how a substantivalist can, in principle, formulate such a theory.
According to substantivalism, there is space everywhere. A region of space, whether or
not there are ordinary material objects in it, has structure: metric structure, topological
structure, and so on. In order to account for parity violations, substantivalists can adopt
a theory which says that space has 'handedness' structure everywhere. Such a theory
would state that at each point in space there is a structure that distinguishes the right-
handed orthogonal trios of directions from the left-handed orthogonal trios of directions. One can picture such a structure by imagining there to be tiny screws everywhere
in space, which we cannot see, but which trios of particles can 'consult' in order to
decide whether to cease to exist or to pass through one another. It is of course surprising that space has such structure; but then, of course, it is surprising that particles
behave in this way. In any case, it is not difficult for a substantivalist to account in a
simple way for such a surprising phenomenon.

The relationist, however, denies the existence of space, and hence cannot adopt a
theory that talks of the local structure of space. A relationist, moreover, cannot (in
terms of distances) distinguish whether the particles are approaching each other along
a right-handed triad or along a left-handed triad. So how on earth can a relationist

state a parity violating laws of Nature? Well, there is a way in which a relationist can do this. To see how, let me return to left-handed and right-handed gloves. We have seen that a relationist cannot distinguish between a world containing only a right-handed glove and one containing only a left-handed glove. Now consider a world that contains two gloves and nothing else. Clearly, for the same reason as before, according to relationism there is no distinction between a world in which both gloves are right-handed, and one in which both are left-handed. But a relationist can tell the difference between a world in which the two gloves have opposite handedness, and one in which both have the same handedness. The reason for this is that the distances between the parts of two gloves that are both left-handed (or both right-handed) are different from the distances between the parts of two gloves that have opposite handedness. A relationist can use this difference to formulate a parity-violating theory. Such a theory would simply say that all the cases in which particles cease to exist are cases in which those particles were approaching one another along triads of the same handedness, and in all cases in which they approach one another along a triad of the other handedness they just pass through one another. But note how bizarre and non-local such a relationist theory is. Particles, according to such a theory, do not 'consult' the local structure of space in order to 'decide' whether to cease to exist. Rather, they need to 'consult' what other incoming triads of particles, at distant locations and times, are doing, will do, or have done: sets of particles that are far away from each other in space and time need to coordinate their behaviour, so as to make sure that taken altogether they violate parity. To put it less anthropomorphically, according to relationism it would not be locally determined, neither locally in space nor locally in time, whether or not a given incoming triad of particles will cease to exist.

In fact, matters are even slightly worse for a Leibnizean relationist. According to Leibnizean relationism there are only facts about distances between particles at the same time. There are no cross-time spatial distance, no facts of the form 'Particle A at time t_1 is 5 metres from particle B at time t_2'. But if that is so, what on earth could it mean to say that material triad A at time t_1 has the same handedness as material triad B at time t_2. One cannot derive this from cross-time distance relations, since there are none, and to take it as a primitive fact (to assume a primitive cross-time same-handedness relation) flies in the face of the spirit of Leibnizean relationism. An option of last resort would be to make use of the fact that in a world that is rich enough in terms of continuously existing matter, there will be persisting material triads so that one can define the relative handedness of material triads at different times by assuming (by fiat) that persisting material triads retain their handedness during their continuous evolution as long as they do not pass through 'singular' non-handed configurations. Using such an assumed preservation of handedness one will be able to formulate a parity-violating theory for universes that are not too impoverished in terms of their material contents. But it will still be a highly non-local theory that does not seem as plausible as the corresponding substantival theory.

Another option for the relationist would be to assume the existence of material, but invisible, triads of the same handedness everywhere and at all times. These invisible triads could determine how ordinary visible triples of particles behave when they meet. And one might claim that assuming the existence of such invisible triads is no better nor worse than the substantivalist assumption that space everywhere has a handedness structure. The problem with this suggestion is that assuming the existence of invisible matter everywhere where the substantitivalists claims that space exists simply amounts to a rather tortured version of the assumption that space exists. In essence I think this accusation is correct, but I will postpone a more detailed discussion to when we consider the related, but somewhat more natural, idea that the relationist can accept the existence of a field everywhere where the substantivalist posits the existence of space.

Now let me turn to my last objection to Leibnizean relationism. In the context of Newtonian physics, distances between objects are subject to very strong constraints. For instance, one cannot have five equidistant particles. One can have four equidistant particles: namely, particles at the corners of a pyramid, all of whose sides are equally long. But this is the only possible configuration for four equidistant particles in a flat three-dimensional space. Since it is clearly impossible to add to this configuration a fifth particle such that the distance that it is away from each of the four particles is the same as that between these four particles, it follows that one cannot have five equidistant particles. So, given the distances between four particles one is not free to specify the distances between them and a fifth particle.

In fact, it is easy to see why there must be such constraints in a flat three-dimensional space. The locations of N particles in a flat three-dimensional space can be given by $3N$ numbers which are freely and independently specifiable: namely, their locations relative to a Cartesian coordinate system. So the distances between all the particles are determined by $3N$ real numbers.[3] But there are $(N-1)+(N-2) + \ldots 1 = N^2/2$ pairwise distances between N particles. And for large N the number $N^2/2$ is much larger than $3N$, so there are lots of constraints on distances. Moreover, it would seem that there is no simple way to write down those constraints *in terms of a formula which uses only those distances*. The simplest way to express what the constraints are is to say that the distances must be such that they can be expressed in the form $\sqrt{((x_p-x_q)^2+(y_p-y_q)^2+(z_p-z_q)^2)}$; that is, in terms of squares of differences of numbers. This suggests that the distance relations between particles are not fundamental, but that the numbers x_p, y_p, z_p, x_q, y_q, z_q, ... represent the fundamental spatial properties of individual particles. For it is those numbers that appear in the simplest way to state the laws of our theory. However, there are three reasons why this is not a good argument as it stands.

In the first place, it is not true that one cannot write constraints directly in terms of distances which have as a consequence that these distances can be embedded in a Euclidean three-dimensional space. C. L. Morgan, following K. Menger, has proved that there are certain fairly simple constraints on distances which are equivalent to the

---

[3] In fact, somewhat less information would do too, since the distances are invariant under global rotations and shifts; but this does not affect the current argument.

demand for embeddability in an n-dimensional Euclidean space. (Thanks to Gordon Belot for pointing this out to me.) Let me briefly explain what these constraints are, and refer the intrigued to Menger (1974) for further details.

Let x, y, and z be (point-sized) material objects, and $d(x,y)$ the distance between x and y. Let us define $<x,y,z>=\frac{1}{2}((d(x,z))^2+(d(y,z))^2-(d(x,y))^2)$. Next let us define $D(x_0, x_1, \ldots x_n)$ as the determinant of the nxn matrix whose ij-th entry is $<x_i, x_j, x_0>$, where $x_0, x_1, \ldots x_n$ are point-sized material objects. In fact, D is symmetric, so it is a function of sets of material objects (rather than of ordered n-tuples of material objects). Then we can define $\text{Vol}(x_0, x_1, \ldots x_n)=(1/n!)\sqrt{D(x_0, x_1, \ldots x_n)}$. Note that Vol can be a complex number (as opposed to a real number). Now let us say that distance structure of a set of (point-sized) material objects is flat if $\text{Vol}(x_0, x_1, \ldots x_n)$ is real for any (finite) set $(x_0, x_1, \ldots x_n)$. Finally, let us say that the dimension of a flat distance structure is the largest natural number n for which there is a set of n (point-sized) material objects such that $\text{Vol}(x_0, x_1, \ldots x_n)$ is non-zero. Morgan then proved that a distance structure can be embedded in an n-dimensional Euclidean space if and only if the distance structure is flat and of dimension less than or equal to n.

In the second place the argument I gave is not an argument for substantivalism—for the existence of space. Rather, it is an argument that spatial properties are fundamental rather than spatial relations. And in the third place, there is an arbitrariness in the numbers x_p, x_q, y_p, v_q, and so on, which suggests that the numbers do not directly correspond to fundamental features of the world. The resolution of second and third worries lies in an axiomatization of the flat three-dimensional spaces in the style of Euclid. In such an axiomatization one assumes the existence of a space, which contains points and lines as parts. One then lays down axioms which say things such as 'Between any two points there is a unique straight line' and 'Given any line L and a point P not on L there is a line L' through P that is parallel to L', and so on. Tarski has given a particularly nice and rigorous such axiomatization, in which he uses a primitive three-place predicate Between(p,q,r) and a primitive four-place predicate Congruent(p,q,r,s). (For details, see http://en.wikipedia.org/wiki/Tarski%27s_axioms.) Intuitively speaking Between(p,q,r) holds whenever point q lies between p and r on the straight line that runs from q to r, and Congruent(p,q,r,s) holds whenever the straight line between p and q is just as long as the straight line between r and s. More formally, Tarski lays down a number of axioms using these predicates such that it follows that anything satisfying these axioms is a Euclidean space. Tarski proved that if his axioms are satisfied, then all the congruence and betweenness facts can be represented by a coordinatization x,y,z of all the points in space, which is unique up to global rotations, shifts, and mirrorings; that is, up to transformations which leave the distances $\sqrt{((x_p-x_q)^2+(y_p-y_q)^2+(z_p-z_q)^2)}$ invariant. In this way we obtain a very nice explanation of why our choice of coordinates for space and time is partly conventional, and an explanation of the exact extent to which it is conventional. Since such an axiomatization crucially relies on the existence of points, lines, surfaces, and volumes which are not occupied by any material particles, there is no simple or natural Leibnizean relationist equivalent.

In the end, one will have to judge whether a Tarski-style axiomatization is simpler and more plausible than a Morgan-style axiomatization. It seems to me that the Tarski-style axiomatization is simpler and more plausible. But readers can make up their own minds.

To summarise: we have found two decent arguments against Leibnizean relationism in the context of Newtonian particle physics. Leibnizean relationism entails that ungainly and holistic initial value data are needed. And, arguably, the simplest theory of the distances that the relationist theory allows is a theory which postulates the existence of space.

5.5 Relationism and Newtonian field theories

Newtonian field theories are theories which include fields such as gravitational or electromagnetic fields, set in a Newtonian or neo-Newtonian spacetime. Such fields are distributed throughout space at all times.[4] According to standard Newtonian field theories, the value that a field F has at a location is simply a property of this location. This assumes that locations exist, and hence is a substantival theory. However, in line with relationism one could instead suggest that space does not exist, but there exists an object, the field F (or a number of such fields), which has spatial features. Since on the substantivalist picture the field (or fields) fill space (have values everywhere in space) it seems that the relationist now has a surrogate with which he can do everything that the substantivalist can do with space, and so can formulate a satisfactory relationist theory which denies the existence of space. An issue which I will set aside in this section is exactly which spatial relations the relationist will want to avail himself here: only distances at a time like the Leibnizean relationist, or also distances across time? Inertial structure, as in neo-Newtonian spacetime? Other relations and properties? I am setting this issue aside for two reasons. In the first place I will address it in Section 5.8 ('Rich relationism and Newtonian physics'). In the second place, the main worry about a relationism which assumes the existence of an object, or objects, which exist everywhere where the substantivalists posits the existence of space is that such a relationism is tantamount to substantivalism—or at least, has no discernible advantage over substantivalism. It is this worry that I want to discuss in this section, and it can be discussed independently of the question as to which relations the relationists avails himself of in the context of Newtonian field theories.

Let us start with the simple case in which there is only one field F. The first thing our relationist will have to decide is what parts field F has. There are three salient options:

1) It has no parts.
2) It has as many parts as it has values.
3) It has as many parts as the substantivalist claims that space has.

---

[4] The field may have value 0 at various locations, but 0 is just as significant a value as any other value.

It would seem that the easiest way to mimick the substantivalist theory is to adhere to option 3, for then one could simply assume the same theory of the spatial (and temporal) features of field F as the substantivalist assumes that space (and time) has. But this option also most obviously invites the complaint that it is but substantivalism in disguise. The obvious relationist response is that this is not substantivalism in disguise, since, in the first place, he is denying the existence of space, and, moreover, the Leibniz shift argument cannot be brought to bear against him. After all, a Leibniz shift, in the context a field theory, consists of shifting everything—all particles *and fields*—across space, and one can do no such thing if all that exists is a field F (and perhaps particles too), for then there is no space over which to shift the field F.

However, this is not right. On the standard substantivalist picture, the field F is not an object. Rather, it corresponds to a set of quantities—field values—at locations in space (and time), or perhaps better, a set of field-betweennesss and field-congruence relations (or something similar) that hold between triples and quadruples of spacetime points. A Leibniz shift corresponds to a redistribution of such quantities, or such relations, over space and time. So, complains our substantivalist, we can surely do the same thing with the field F that the relationist posits as an object. After all, this field F has point-sized parts, which have the same properties as our parts of space have. One of the properties of a point-sized part of field F is surely its field strength. So surely we can now perform a Leibniz shift by shifting all the field strengths—all the properties of the point-sized parts of the field—in exactly the same way that we can shift field strengths across space on the substantivalist picture.

This, it seems to me, is a fair complaint. One can imagine our relationist objecting: 'No, you cannot shift field values across the parts of a field, because it would not be the same part if it were to have a different field value.' But why could not our substantivalist say the same thing? Why could not a substantivalist claim that it would not be the same spatial location if it had a different field strength? The possibility of a Leibniz shift in the case of space may seem a bit more plausible than in the case of a field. But in the end this difference in plausibility arises merely from the fact that we call it a 'field' rather than 'space'. Well, indeed, we can get out of the Leibniz shift argument by, in effect, stipulating the truth of certain modal facts. But that hardly seems to amount to an interesting rival theory. In any case, I will later argue that the Leibniz shift argument is not a good argument. And once one ceases to care about immunity to Leibniz shifts, to assume that the features of field F include all the features that space and time have on the substantivalist theory does not seem to amount to an interesting alternative to the standard substantivalist theory.

Moreover, it is not as if our relationist, by denying that the parts of the field could have had different field values, thereby has avoided all shift-like problems. For instance, consider some pattern of field value distribution in space and time. There will be many parts of the field which have the same field value. Now consider relocating each part of the field to a new location where the same field value obtains according to the given pattern. The pattern of field values will be the same after the relocation, but the distance relations that obtain between the very same parts of the field will generically be different before and after such a relocation. So it seems we have the kind of difference without a difference that motivates relationists to reject substantivalism. And it seems very hard for the relationist to stipulate that this is not a genuinely distinct possibility, given that he accepts that redistributions of field values over spacetime do constitute distinct possibilities even when they correspond to the same distribution pattern (since, if he would not believe that, he would have no Leibniz-shift argument against substantivalism).

There is another problem that arises for our relationist if we have only one field which is a vector field v. In Chapter 2 we saw what a vector field v is according to standard theory: it is a function from functions from spacetime to the real numbers to functions from spacetime to the real numbers which, for all real numbers α, satisfies:

1) $v(f{+}g)=v(f)+v(g)$
2) $v(\alpha f)=\alpha v(f)$
3) $v(fg)=fv(g)+gv(f)$

But our relationist has no spacetime, and hence, *a fortiori*, no functions from spacetime to the real numbers. Our relationist does have a surrogate for spacetime: the vector field v (and its parts). However, it would be viciously circular to define a vector field as a function from functions from parts of itself to the real numbers to functions from parts of itself to the real numbers. So relationism has a problem if there is only a vector field in the world.[5]

Another issue is what to do if there is more than one field. Is each field an object whose parts stand in distance relations, or is there one privileged field which is an object such that all other fields are represented as properties of the parts of the privileged field? It seems objectionably asymmetric to postulate that there is one privileged field which is the only object. On the other hand, if all fields are objects which have parts that stand in distance relations, then the fact that there are co-location properties between distinct fields, and the fact that all the fields have the same spatiotemporal structure, cries out for an explanation in terms of a single spacetime which they occupy.

Let us now turn to option 2: a field F has exactly as many parts as it has values. It may seem that this is a non-starter, for on the substantivalist picture there will be many locations which have the same field value, and how on earth can a relationist specify the distances that obtain in such a situation when there are no distinct parts corresponding to the distinct locations with the same field values? Well, in a way the answer is simple: the relationist should accept that there are facts of the form 'Field value F=3 is 5 metres from itself and 7 metres from itself and . . .' In this way one can in principle specify all the facts that one needs in order to recover the full distribution of values in

---

[5] As far as I know, Oliver Pooley was the first to present this argument (see his forthcoming, Chapter 3). More generally, Pooley's book is the one to read on the issue of relationism versus substantivalism. It enters into much more depth than I do, and is essential reading for anyone interested in the issue.

a Euclidean space (up to distance-preserving transformations). Now, while I am happy to countenance such facts, odd as they may seem, it will unfortunately be impossible to present a simple theory of the spatial structure of the parts of the field in terms of the fundamental objects and relations that the relationist postulates. The best one can do is to say: all the distance facts must be such that they can be represented as corresponding to a field F which has point-like parts which stand in distance relations that are embeddable in a Euclidean space. Of course, the field values do not in fact have any (proper) parts, and *a fortiori* have no point-like (proper) parts. So the demand is just that they can be so represented. But this means that one cannot give a simple theory of the spatial structure of the field directly in terms of the objects and relations that the relationist countenances.

Still, option 2 does have one advantage over option 3. Since there is only one part corresponding to each field value, one cannot relocate point parts to different locations with the same field value, so option 2 escapes a type of shift objection that can be made against the relationist of option 3.

How about option 1? Well, at best this amounts to a complicated version of option 2. One now needs to assume facts of the form 'The field F has the property that field value *a* is distance *b* from field value *c*', where, of course, field value *a* now is not an object. There seems no hope of deriving a nice theory of the spatial structure of the field in this manner, or a nice theory of the dynamical relation between field values, particle properties, and the spacetime features of the world.

All in all, it seems that relationism in the context of Newtonian field theories at best has no advantage over substantivalism, and at worst has considerable disadvantages.

5.6 Relationism about time in Newtonian physics

One can give a Leibniz-shift-type argument against the existence of time. For one can argue that a fixed global shift of all events forwards in time, or backwards in time, is a difference that makes no difference, and argue that it follows that time does not exist. In addition there are a couple of features of time that make it more amenable to relationism than space. In the first place it is reasonable to assume that every instant is occupied by some particle or field, so that there is not much of a problem about axiomatizing the structure of time using temporal betweenness and congruence relations between events involving matter or fields. In the second place, time is one-dimensional, so there is no problem about distinguishing between one constellation of events and another one which is 'rotated in temporal space' relative to the first one.

Nonetheless, just as parity violations give rise to non-local relationist theory about space, time-reversal violations give rise to non-local relationist theories of time. For suppose that one has a Newtonian theory that violates time-reversal invariance; a Newtonian theory such that there exists a sequence of states S(*t*) such that S(*t*) is allowed by the theory (is a solution to the theory), while the time reverse of S(*t*)—the sequence $S'(t)$ such that $S'(t)=S(-t)$—is not allowed by the theory.[6] Now, temporal distances do not determine temporal directions, since distances are preserved under temporal mirrorings. So, a temporal Leibnizean relationist can only prescribe a temporal asymmetry by claiming that whenever and wherever the relevant temporally asymmetric processes occur, these asymmetries must 'point' in the same direction of time. And that is a non-local, holistic, prescription.

Having said this, which is really the main conclusion of this section, let me now discuss a strange issue that I have skated over. The point is that there is a weird difference between the cases of time and space. Relationists about space claim that there is no such thing as space. If there is no such thing as space, then not only do substantival histories of the world that differ by a constant global spatial shift—the same spatial shift at all times—correspond to the same relational history, it is also the case that substantival histories that differ by different spatial shifts at different times correspond to the same relational history, since they correspond to the same history of distances. Now, if a relationist about time were to really treat the case of time as analogous to the case of space, then he ought to claim that substantival histories that differ by different temporal shifts at different spatial locations correspond to one and the same relational history. To put it another way: relationists about space think that there are matters of fact concerning the distance between simultaneous events, but they do not think that there are matters of fact concerning non-simultaneous events. The analogous relationist view of time would be that there are matters of fact only about temporal distances between events occurring at the same spatial location, but there are no matters of fact concerning the temporal distances between events that do not occur at the same spatial location. Now since, as far as I know, no relationist about time has ever maintained this, let me give a new name to this view, and call it 'strong relationism about time'.

Strong relationism about time seems rather bizarre. For instance, imagine a universe that is like ours, except that at different spatial locations, different temporal shifts are made. Suppose, for instance, that in the spatial region that corresponds to the region in space currently occupied by the Oval Office, everything is shifted 100 years backwards in time, while the rest is left intact. This yields an apparently very strange history: everyone in the Oval Office is always doing the wrong things at the wrong time (as opposed to doing the wrong things at the right time, which is standard procedure in the Oval Office). Consequently, it may seem obvious why nobody has ever suggested strong relationism about time: it is just an absurd idea. Nonetheless, it will turn out to be interesting and instructive to further investigate strong relationism about time.

Let us go over the problem a little more slowly and carefully. Suppose we take the history of a Newtonian universe, and then make different temporal shifts at different locations in space. This yields a very strange universe. Generically, the so-shifted history

---

[6] Some *cognoscenti* will complain that I have not allowed a time-reversal operation on states. This is a somewhat controversial issue that is irrelevant for current purposes. I will discuss it in detail in chapter 7.

will not satisfy the standard Newtonian laws. So perhaps one can rule out strong relationism about time on the grounds that such variably temporally shifted histories will generically violate the standard Newtonian laws. However, if one accepted *that* argument one would thereby immediately rule out ordinary relationism about space. For if one makes different global spatial shifts at different times one also generically produces a history that does not satisfy the standard Newtonian laws, since the so-shifted history will include lots of accelerations (or jumps) that violate the standard Newtonian laws.

In the spatial case the relationist can respond that the fact that such a variably spatially-shifted history will violate the *standard* Newtonian laws does not matter, for such a variable spatial shift will not alter the phenomena. Moreover, variably spatially-shifted histories do not violate the proper *relationist* version of the Newtonian laws. So one can argue that variable spatial shifts are acceptable. Can the strong relationist about time respond in the same manner? If one takes a given history and then applies a variable temporal shift to it, does this change the phenomena? At first sight, it would seem so. After all, once one has performed such varying temporal shifts, different events will be simultaneous, and this surely amounts to a difference in the phenomena if anything does. However, one might counter that it begs the question to simply assert that differences as to which events occur simultaneously must amount to differences in the phenomena, while differences as to which events occur at the same location do not.

Now, you may think that this last claim is insane. So let me try to elucidate how a strong relationist about time could be so insane as to think that making different temporal shifts at different spatial locations could preserve the phenomena. Well, suppose that our strong relationist about time says that the way in which the history of the world determines the phenomena is as follows. The strong relationist history of the world includes all the temporal distances between events that occur at the same location. This consists of an infinite collection of time-lines—one for each spatial point. If you now want to know what the phenomena are in such a world, do the following: align these time-lines in such a way that one produces a spacetime satisfying the standard Newtonian laws, and then read the phenomena off in the way that substantivalists would have you do. If there turn out to be essentially different ways of doing this—multiple ways that correspond to different histories of phenomena—then each of these different histories of phenomena in fact occurs. Now, I admit that it is a rather bizarre idea; but it is not incoherent. Thus, strong relationism about time, according to which there are no facts about temporal distances between non-co-located events, does not appear to be incoherent. Well, if that is right, then why not treat the cases of space and of time in truly analogous fashion by being both a relationist about space and a strong relationist about time?

Well, to put it bluntly, that *would* be incoherent. The reason is simple. Relationists about space claim that the only spatial distance relations that exist are distances at a given time between material objects, or events involving such material objects. They do not admit the existence of spatial distance relations between material objects, and events involving such material objects, *at different times*. However, strong relationism about time denies that there is a matter of fact as to whether spatially separated events *occur at the same time*. So if one is a strong relationist about time, one could not possibly be a relationist about space.

Where does this discussion leave us? It leaves us with the following conclusion. If one is a relationist about space, who allows that different spatial shifts at different times correspond to the same relational history, then one cannot be a strong relationist about time who thinks that different temporal shifts at different spatial locations correspond to the same relational history. And vice versa. Now, it seems more plausible that variable spatial shifts preserve the phenomena than that variable temporal shifts preserve the phenomena. Therefore, the result of this discussion is a rather long-winded justification for the standard view of relationists that variable spatial shifts correspond to the same possibility, whereas variable temporal shifts do not.

5.7 Piggy-back relationism

What I call 'piggy-back relationism' is not a specific relationist theory, but a general method for constructing relationist theories. Nick Huggett has formulated, and defends, a version of this theory, which he calls 'regularity relationism'. (For more details on his exact view, see Huggett (2006) and Pooley (forthcoming).) However, there are details of his account that I will ignore, so I do not want to use his term. I merely wish to point out that the piggy-back relationism is not my invention.

The basic idea of piggy-back relationism is very simple. Let the relationist pick whatever objects and properties and relations he wishes to claim are all the fundamental objects, fundamental properties, and fundamental relations that there are. Then claim that these indeed are all the fundamental things that there are. Call something a relational history if it is a complete specification of all the fundamental objects and their fundamental properties and relations that one takes there to be throughout history. Next, simply decline the project of finding simple laws formulated directly in terms of those fundamental objects and properties and relations. Just state one's favourite substantival theory, and state constraints on how relational histories are allowed to be embedded in substantival histories. One's theory, then, is just the claim that all relational histories which are embeddable in substantival histories which are allowed by one's favourite substantival theory are allowed. That is it. In certain cases it will turn out that the relational history will determine a substantival history that is unique up to shifts, rotations, and mirrorings. In other cases (for example, General Relativistic cases with parts of space devoid of matter) this will not be the case. So be it, says the piggy-back relationist; then there simply is no matter of fact regarding those features of the history of the world.

My only objection to such a theory is that such a theory is not a simple theory. By 'simple' I mean simple in the sense that is important when it comes to evaluating whether a theory is likely to be true, or likely to be approximately true. One can try to be more precise about this sense of simplicity. Cian Dorr (2010) has made a start on the business of characterizing the sense of simplicity that is relevant to epistemology. But to do so in detail, and to justify such an account, is a difficult, and as yet unfinished, project that I do not wish to try to engage in here. Instead let me just present one quick and dirty argument that piggy-back theories are not simple in the epistemologically relevant sense. This argument is that if such theories were to count as simple it would make life too easy for people who want to get rid of objects and properties that they do not like for some whimsical reason. For instance, suppose I were to claim that the world is pretty much as you think it is, except that rocks do not exist. I then go on to claim that the true theory of the world is that there are no rocks, and that the true theory of the world merely says that the things and properties and relations that there are (namely, everything other than rocks and their properties) are embeddable in a non-existing make-belief world which includes rocks and in which your favourite make-belief laws hold. It seems obvious to me that such a theory is not simple in the sense relevant to evaluation how good such a theory is, and that one should not believe that it is true. Theft is theft. Honest toil is honest toil.

5.8 Rich relationism and Newtonian physics

A relationist can choose to recover either more, or less, of the substantival structure of spacetime by increasing, or decreasing, the set of spatiotemporal relations he makes use of. We have seen that the standard Leibnizean relationist about space in the context of Newtonian physics tries to make do solely with the spatial distance relation between simultaneous events. We have seen that this leads to problems, because distances and their rates of change do not determine angular momentum. So why not try increasing one's stock of spatiotemporal relations? Here is a natural suggestion: assume that there are well-defined objective distances between non-simultaneous events.

If there are spatial distances between non-simultaneous events, then it immediately follows that one can speak of the distance between an object at time t and that object at time t'. And that means that there is a fact concerning the absolute speed of an object, for that is just the rate at which an object is moving away from where it is:

$\text{Lim}_{dt \to 0}(\text{distance}(A \text{ at } t+dt, A \text{ at } t)/dt)$

In fact, there are lots of 'absolute speeds' about which there are facts according to the rich relationist. For instance, given that there exists a particle A at a time t_1 and a particle B at a time t_2, there is a fact as to the absolute speed of particle B at time t_2 relative to A's location at t_1:

$d(\text{distance}(B \text{ at } t_2, A \text{ at } t_1))/dt_2$

Moreover, if all of these distances, and rates of changes of distances, are to be embeddable in a Newtonian spacetime, then there are many complicated constraints that are imposed on them. The only simple way to state these constraints is to demand that they are embeddable in a Newtonian spacetime. There is no simple axiomatization of rich relationism in terms of the fundamental objects and quantities of the theory. Rich relationism will of course also have problems with time reversal and parity violations, in the sense that the theory of such violations will be spatially and temporally non-local. All of this means that rich relationism has essentially the same defects as Leibnizean relationism: there is no simple axiomatization of the theory in terms of its fundamental objects and quantities, and the initial value data needed to determine future evolution are ugly and holistic.

Now, of course, I have only considered one simple way of enriching the relations that one can avail oneself of in the context of Newtonian physics. That hardly shows that there is no viable version of rich relationism in the context of Newtonian physics. However, Oliver Pooley (forthcoming, Chapter 3) considers many *prima facie* natural versions of rich relationism. They all suffer from the same problem: no simple axiomatization of the theory in terms of its fundamental objects and quantities, and ugly and holistic initial value data. It seems unlikely that there is a viable form of rich relationism in the context of Newtonian physics.

5.9 Relationism and Special Relativity

According to Leibnizean relationism there is no space, and the fundamental spatial relations are simultaneous distance relations. However, in according to standard Special Relativity, which I called 'Einsteinian relativity' in Chapter 1, there is no frame-independent notion of simultaneity, so one might wonder whether Leibnizean relationism makes sense with respect to Special Relativity. But actually, we already know the answer to this, for in Chapter 1 I sketched Barbour's version of Einsteinian relativity which is Leibnizean relationist. Barbour assumes that there is a unique slicing of spacetime into spaces at times, and then provides a dynamics, in the form of an action principle, for particles and/or fields in it which has as a consequence that the total angular momentum of the universe must be 0, but is otherwise equivalent to standard Special Relativity.

Alternatively, one might respect the idea that there is no privileged notion of simultaneity and adopt a rich relationism according to which the fundamental spacetime relations between events involving matter and fields correspond to the distances in Minkowski spacetime between these events.

The objections to either of these theories are essentially the same as in the Newtonian case. If there are no fields, the problem is that one cannot produce a theory of the spatial and temporal distances (Leibnizean case) or of the spatiotemporal distances (rich case), which is simple when formulated in terms of the fundamental relational objects and quantities. And if there are no fields, then the initial value data needed will be ugly and holistic. If there are fields, then it is not clear what advantage one has over substantivalism other than that one is stipulating that one is not subject to certain shift arguments. It seems hard to come up with a decent such theory if there is only a single vector field. And if there is more than one field, the harmony of the distance relations among the parts of the various fields cries out for an explanation in terms of an underlying spacetime.

In short, prospects for relationism seem just as bleak in the context of Special Relativity as they are in the context of Newtonian physics. How about General Relativity?

5.10 The 'hole' argument

In the context of General Relativity, substantivalists believe in the existence of a curved spacetime and its parts (spacetime regions). The Leibniz shift argument against substantivalism takes a slightly different form in the context of General Relativity. It is known as the 'hole' argument. Despite the fact that this argument does not differ much from the Leibniz shift argument, it has generated a lot of attention in the last twenty years or so, and has been partially responsible for the recent revival of relationism. Let us quickly discuss it.

The reason one cannot straightforwardly use the Leibniz shift argument in the context of General Relativity is simple. According to General Relativity, matter causes local curvature. Thus, if one were to take a spacetime that is consistent with General Relativity, and then shift the matter in this spacetime in some way while keeping its curvature fixed, one would typically obtain a spacetime that is *not* consistent with General Relativity, as the matter and local curvature would no longer be related in the right way. The solution to this problem is also simple: shift the curvature in exactly the same way as one shifts the matter. Technically speaking there is no problem in doing this, since, just as the matter content of a spacetime is representable by tensor fields, the curvature of spacetime is also representable by a tensor field (the metric tensor field), and both of these can be shifted as one pleases. Indeed, in essence the only constraint that General Relativity imposes on such shifts is that one performs them in a smooth manner by a so-called 'diffeomorphism'.

Now, there are many more possible ways to perform such a shift in General Relativity than there are ways of performing Leibniz shifts in Newtonian and Special Relativistic physics (at least when one formulates those theories in terms of a fixed metric). For instance, one possible way of performing such a shift in the case of General Relativity is to pick a relatively small region in spacetime—a 'hole'—and restrict the shift to this region. (Smoothness of the shift then implies that the size of the shift goes to 0 as one approaches the boundary of the hole.) Then choose a time-slice such that the hole is entirely to the future of this time-slice. The state on this time-slice, and the state everywhere prior to it, will be the same in the original spacetime as in the shifted spacetime. This means that the state on the time-slice—indeed, the history of states prior to and including the time-slice—does not determine the state to its future. Thus, according to the hole argument, determinism must fail radically if one is a substantivalist. The hole argument then continues by claiming that it should surely be an interesting question, whose answer depends on the dynamical laws of the theory in question, as to whether ot not determinism holds. In particular, it should not follow directly from one's view of the ontological status of spacetime that determinism fails. Therefore, substantivalism ought to be rejected according to the hole argument. Fine, but what does a relational theory of General Relativity look like?

5.11 General Relativity and relationism

The problem for relationism in the case of General Relativity is that space has metric properties which are determined by the metric tensor field. A tensor field is standardly defined as a linear map from n-tuples of vector fields (and/or co-vector fields) to scalar fields. According to General Relativity there is a metric tensor field (which satisfies a non-trivial dynamical equation) even when there are no particles and no other fields. So the relationist faces essentially the same problems as I indicated concerning a single vector field in the Newtonian and Special Relativistic case.

In the face of these problems, Barbour, in essence, just gives up. He admits that space exists, and that there is a metric tensor at each point in space which is a property of such points. There are two slight wrinkles to his views in the context of General Relativity that I should mention. In the first place, as we saw in Chapter 1, he devises a theory according to which what exists is not a spacetime, but spaces-at-times. But, as we also saw in Chapter 1, he admits that if one considers *classical* General Relativity, as opposed to a quantum version of General Relativity, then a theory according to which spacetime exists, rather than spaces-at-times exist, is more plausible. Secondly, his theory achieves diffeomorphism invariance by stipulating that the states of his spaces at times are equivalence classes of states under diffeomorphisms. But equivalence classes of states of a space are still states (properties) *of a space*. So while his stipulation makes his states diffeomorphism invariant, nonetheless his theory is still committed to the existence of *spaces* at times, and so is still a substantivalist theory.

Does that mean we should give up on relationism in the context of General Relativity? Not quite, yet. John Earman (1989, Chapter 8), using work by Robert Geroch (1972), has suggested a relationist approach to General Relativity. Here is the idea.

Consider a four-dimensional differentiable manifold; that is, a four-dimensional space, consisting of points and regions, which has topological and differential structure. The topological structure determines which lines in the space are continuous and which are discontinuous, what the boundaries of regions are, which regions are disconnected, and so on. The differential structure of a manifold determines which lines are smooth, which lines are n times differentiable, which functions from the manifold to the real numbers are n times differentiable, which functions are smooth, and so on. (In Chapter 8 I will enter into more detail as to what a differentiable manifold is.) Now consider the set of all smooth functions f from a given differentiable manifold M to the real numbers. There will be facts as to which smooth function f is the addition of any given pair of smooth functions g and h, and which smooth function k is the multiplication of any given pair of smooth functions l and m. Now suppose that we are not given a manifold M, but are given the set of all smooth functions on M. It turns out that the addition and multiplication facts among all these functions determines the differentiable manifold M up to diffeomorphism. Let me be a little more precise. We will call a differentiable manifold M plus the set of all smooth functions on M a *realization* of a collection of functions with an addition and multiplication structure; that is, a *realization* of the algebra of functions A, if and only if there is a 1–1 onto mapping from the functions in the algebra A to the smooth functions on M which preserves the addition and multiplication facts. Then one can show that if a differentiable manifold M *realizes* A, then a differentiable manifold M' realizes A if and only if M' is related to M by a diffeomorphism.

Earman's idea now is that the functions are the fundamental objects that exist, not the manifold, and the fundamental relations that obtain are the addition and multiplication relations between the functions. Then one has a theory that is not substantivalist: the fundamental objects are functions, not spacetime and its parts. Moreover, one appears to obtain diffeomorphism invariance of the standard manifold representations of the fundamental facts for free! One can then go on to define vector fields as maps (satisfying the 'Leibniz property') from functions to functions, co-vector fields as (linear) maps from vector fields to functions, and tensor fields as (linear) maps from n-tuples of vector fields and co-vector fields, and develop General Relativistic theories in this manner.

However, things are not so simple. In the first place, while the addition and multiplication facts determine the differential structure of the corresponding manifolds M up to diffeomorphism, it is not clear that one can produce a simple axiomatization of the addition and multiplication facts which determines the corresponding manifolds M to be the four-dimensional differentiable manifolds of General Relativity. Secondly, while an Earman-style theory is not committed to the existence of spacetime, it is committed to the existence of another, huge, space—the space of all functions. Thirdly, and most importantly, this space is also subject to a shift argument. Consider any 1–1 onto mapping of all the functions in an algebra A to the functions in an algebra B which preserves all addition and multiplication facts: an isomorphism from algebra A to algebra B. In so far as one thinks that the substantivalist is committed to thinking that diffeomorpically related manifolds correspond to distinct possibilities, one should think that Earman-style relationists are committed to thinking that isomorphically related algebras correspond to distinct possibilities. But isomorphic differences are just as much differences without a difference as are diffeomorphic differences. Earman is aware of this problem, and therefore says that the possible states correspond to equivalence classes of algebras related by isomorphism. But, of course, if he is allowed to say that, then why are substantivalists not allowed to say the same—that the possible spacetime states are equivalence classes of manifolds under diffeomorphisms. In fact, this is pretty much exactly what so-called 'sophisticated substantivalists' have said. I will discuss this view in more detail in the next section. For now, let us create even more problems for Earman-style relationism.

The analogy between algebra isomorphisms and manifold diffeomorphisms goes even deeper. Let us say that an algebra A realizes a differentiable manifold M if and only if there is a 1–1 onto mapping from the smooth functions on M to the functions in A which preserves facts about addition and multiplication. Clearly, a differentiable manifold M corresponds to an equivalence class of algebras under isomorphism. Just as an algebra determines a differentiable manifold only up to diffeomorphism, a differentiable manifold determines an algebra only up to isomorphism.

Moreover, consider a particular diffeomorphism D which is determined by some smooth 1–1 onto map from all points in M to all points in M. This will determine a corresponding isomorphism I from the algebra of all smooth functions on M onto the algebra of all smooth functions on M. The isomorphism I that corresponds to D will simply send the value of a function f at a point p in M to the point $D(p)$ in M. To see which function $I(f)$ a function f gets mapped to by the I that corresponds to D, just check where all its values are sent in the way that I have just indicated. This determines a mapping of smooth functions which preserves all addition and multiplication facts (since addition and multiplication of functions is *pointwise* addition and multiplication.) So each diffeomorphism D corresponds to a unique isomorphism I. Moreover, there are no other isomorphisms from the algebra A to itself: the only isomorphisms from A to A are maps which shift the values of the functions to new points.[7] In short, the isormorphisms on the algebras are the mirror images of the diffeomorphisms on manifolds. Earman-style relationism is just as subject to the hole argument as substantivalism. Only if one has other good reasons to prefer realism about spaces of functions to realism about spacetime should one contemplate adopting it.

So, is relationism in the context of General Relativity dead? Perhaps. But there is at least one approach to quantum gravity that has some hope of giving rise to a relationist quantum gravity: namely, 'loop quantum gravity' (see, for example, Rovelli (2003)). The fundamental states in loop quantum gravity—the so-called 's-knot states'—are invariant under diffeomorphisms. But to what extent this invariance is achieved by brute force (by taking something like equivalence classes), rather than that the fundamental objects and quantities naturally give rise to an equivalence class of diffeomorphically related representations, is not clear to me. Nor is it clear to me to what extent one should regard these states as states of matter, rather than as states of spacetime. Moreover, loop quantum gravity is as yet too undeveloped for it to be clear how serious a candidate it is for a quantum theory of gravity. But there is hope yet for relationism in the context of General Relativity. But let us now, finally, turn to substantivalism.

---

[7] One cannot change any of the values of functions at the same point without changing some of the addition and multiplication facts. For if one knows all the addition and multiplication facts, one knows which is 1: if you multiply anything by it you get the same thing back. You also know which is 0: if you multiply anything by it you get 0 back. And then all the other values are fixed by the addition and multiplication facts. This, incidentally, shows just how strong addition and multiplication structure is.

5.12 Substantivalism

The only objection to substantivalism that we have encountered are Leibniz's shift argument and its General Relativistic cousin, the hole argument. Let me start by evaluating Leibniz's shift argument. Recall that this argument is just the following: substantivalism implies that two worlds differing only by a global shift of all material objects represent genuinely distinct possibilities, when it seems obvious that they do not. But is this really true? Must any substantivalist really be committed to the claim that global shifts produce genuinely distinct possibilities? The answer is 'no'. To quickly see why, start by imagining that one is a relationist. Then consider a world containing only three material objects: three electrons, A, B, and C. Suppose that A is 3 feet from B, B is 4 feet from C, and C is 5 feet from A. Now, imagine switching these electrons around, so that B is 3 feet from C, C is 4 feet from A, and A is 5 feet from B.[8] Must any relationist now be committed to the claim that such a switching generates a genuinely distinct possibility? It seems intuitively clear that this need not be so. And, *mutatis mutandis*, neither need a substantivalist be committed to the claim that global shifts of material objects generate distinct possibilities. Let me explain this in rather more detail.

David Lewis (1973) has developed a semantics for counterfactual assertions. According to his theory, roughly speaking, a claim of the form 'If X were the case, Y would be the case' is true if, and only if, in the nearest possible world (the one most similar to the actual world) in which X is the case, Y is also the case. Thus, on Lewis's account, whether any particular counterfactual claim is true or false depends on what possible worlds there are, and what the distance relations (similarity relations) are between these worlds. Now, one does not have to think that such possible worlds really exist in order to agree that Lewis's semantics is correct in the sense that it classifies as valid exactly those inferences that we intuitively accept as valid. Let us now see whether Lewis's semantics, combined with realism about space, implies that a shift of all material objects in space generates a distinct possibility.

According to Lewis, no object exists in more than one possible world.[9] Thus, for instance, distinct possible worlds cannot contain the very same electrons. Now, one might ask, if distinct possible worlds cannot contain the very same objects, how can Lewis's semantics make sense of counterfactuals that claim of some object that something would have happened to *that very object* had *that very object* been in some different situation? Well, according to Lewis's semantics, whether such an assertion is true or false depends on the features of a possible world that contains not the object itself, but an object with very similar properties, very similar qualitative features—a 'counterpart' of the object in question. For instance, according to Lewis's theory, when one says something such as, 'If this apple were red instead of green, then I would eat it', the possible world in question does not contain this very same apple, nor does it contain

---

[8] This is a slight modification of an example introduced by Hartry Field (1985, footnote 15).
[9] See Lewis (1973).

me. Rather, it contains an apple that is extremely similar to this apple other than its colour, a 'counterpart' of this apple in that world, and a person very similar to me, my counterpart in that world. And if it is the case that in the most similar world that contains such a counterpart apple my counterpart eats it, then the counterfactual assertion is true.

Now, since no object occurs in more than one possible world, there are no distinct possible worlds that differ by mere 'object-switching'. Mere electron swaps, for example, do not generate distinct possible worlds. In order to generate a distinct possible world one has to alter some of the *qualitative* features of a world. Now consider a Leibniz shift. After the shift, the location to which an object was shifted has exactly the same properties—the same qualitative features—as the location that the object came from originally had. The world and the shifted world are qualitatively identical. Hence, according to Lewis, a Leibniz shift does not produce a distinct possible world. And if one assumes that possible worlds correspond 1–1 to possibilities, then it follows that Leibniz shifts do not generate unwanted new possibilities, and hence they pose no problem for substantivalism. At least, this is what so-called 'sophisticated substantivalists' say in response to the Leibniz shift argument.

But the above is a bit too quick. Lewis himself does not identify possibilities with possible worlds; and according to Lewis, objects can also have counterparts in the very world that they themselves are in. Suppose that Harry is eating tomatoes and Johnny is eating bananas. Suppose that Harry says: 'If I were you and you were me, then I would be eating bananas and you would be eating tomatoes.' On Lewis's semantics this assertion will come out as true if we take Johnny—Johnny in that very world—to be Harry's counterpart, and Harry—Harry in that very world—to be Johnny's counterpart. Moreover, one might quite reasonably claim that Harry eating bananas and Johnny eating tomatoes is a distinct possibility from Harry eating tomatoes and Johnny eating bananas. So merely adopting Lewis's semantics does not imply that there are no distinct possibilities that are qualitatively identical. And the Leibniz shift argument can be run in terms of possibilities (rather than possible worlds), for one can claim that the substantivalist is committed to there being distinct possibilities corresponding to Leibniz shifts, but that clearly there are no such distinct possibilities, so substantivalism is false. In response, the sophisticated substantivalist cannot just appeal to Lewis's semantics; he must also make the stronger claim that there are no distinct possibilities that are qualitatively identical.

Now, this is a controversial claim. One might deny it, for instance, on the grounds of my above example of Harry and Johnny. Moreover, semantics other than Lewis's exist for counterfactual talk, and it is not at all obvious that Lewis's semantics is the best. Nor is it even clear what it is for a semantics to be good. How much does it matter what entities and properties and relations the semantics makes use of (that is, how much do the metaphysical commitments of the semantics matter), how much does it matter whether the semantics corresponds with our intuitive procedures for evaluating the truth and falsity of claims, and how much does it matter that it presents a simple and general account of the linguistic behaviour of (ordinary) people? Now, in fact, it strikes me that in certain respects the semantics of the sophisticated substantivalist is not so good.[10] But surely, whether substantivalism or relationism is true does not depend on such apparently unrelated semantics issues.

Quite so. Suppose, for instance, that one *does not* think that global Leibniz shifts produce genuinely distinct possibilities. Even then one had better not claim that this shows that spatial points do not exist. For if one did, then, analogously, the possibility of electron swaps would show that electrons do not exist. But relationists cannot conclude that electrons do not exist, since electrons are exactly the type of things that relationists *do* think exist. All of this haggling over the distinctness of possibilities, the semantics of counterfactuals, inner world counterparts, and so on, is neither here nor there. The Leibniz shift argument is just not a good argument, for if it were, it would also tell against electrons—indeed, against all objects. Now, some might be willing to bite this bullet. Some might argue that it makes no difference if one swaps all properties and relations among all objects in such a way as to leave the overall pattern of properties and relations the same, and that this implies that there are no objects whatsoever. Well, I would like to see how one then proposes to conceptualize the world instead. My guess is that the best one can do is to use a quantificational logic stripped of constants. And this hardly strikes me as denying the existence of objects. (For more on this issue, see Sider (2006) and Dasgupta (2009).) The more important point is that this no longer has anything to do with substantivalism versus relationism; it is just a view about the existence of objects in general. And that is not the subject of this chapter.

Before going on to the hole argument and accounts of determinism, I should slightly qualify my claim that the Leibniz shift argument is no good whatsoever. I do not deny that it can be good to have a theory which has fewer 'symmetries'—where by a 'symmetry' I mean a transformation which leaves the dynamics and the phenomena invariant. Getting rid of apparent redundancies in one's formalism is indeed, other things being equal, a good thing, for it reduces one's commitments—*but only if it leads to a simpler (empirically adequate) theory*. Arguments of the form 'This theory has a symmetry, therefore it is false' are bad arguments. And we have found relationism wanting in simplicity as compared to substantivalism. OK, let us now turn to the hole argument.

Given the way in which the substantivalist can respond to the Leibniz shift argument, it is not hard to see how the substantivalist can respond to the hole argument. In the first place, one can be a sophisticated substantivalist and claim that diffeomorphisms do not give rise to distinct possibilities. In the second place, one can accept that the existence of hole diffeomorphisms shows that General Relativity is indeterministic,

---

[10] For instance, sophisticated substantivalism has as an almost inevitable consequence that if there is some possible world (some possibility) in which there is only one spacetime point x that is occupied by a material object, then any of x's counterparts in other possible worlds will also be occupied. This amounts to a rather bizarre modal property of that point. Thanks to Gordon Belot for bringing this point home to me. See also Skow (2005).

but deny that this means that spacetime does not exist, on the grounds that the possibility of electron switches would then similarly entail the non-existence of electrons. And thirdly, one can accept that hole diffeomorphisms generate distinct possibilities but deny that this implies that General Relativity is indeterministic. This last point will take a bit of explaining.

Consider the following (somewhat strange and unrealistic) theory, or set of laws of nature, T.[11] The universe will exist for 10 seconds. When the universe starts there will be three towers standing on an infinite flat surface in a three-dimensional Newtonian space. The foundations of the three towers will lie on a straight line, and the middle one will be exactly halfway between the two outside ones. All three towers will have exactly the same qualitative features (same height, shape, colour, and so on). After 5 seconds the middle tower will fall towards one of the outside towers and thereby slightly dent it. Theory T does not specify towards which outside tower the middle tower will fall. That is it. That is all there is to theory T.

Prima facie it seems that T is an indeterministic theory exactly because it does not specify the direction in which the middle tower will fall. It seems that there are two genuinely distinct possibilities, and that theory T is indeterministic since it does not specify which of those possibilities will occur. Notice that the sophisticated substantivalist denies that there are two distinct possibilities, for he maintains that there are no distinct possibilities corresponding to the same arrangement of qualities. So, according to the sophisticated substantivalist, theory T is deterministic. The sophisticated substantivalist might indeed go on to explain why it may seem to us that T is indeterministic. The actual world is asymmetric. Thus, for any object that falls in the actual world, one can generate distinct possible worlds corresponding to any of the angles between 0 and 360 degrees over which one can rotate the direction in which that object is falling. This explains why we are inclined to think that, beginning with any possibility, one can always generate distinct possibilities by rotating the direction of any fall by any angle between 0 and 360 degrees. However, starting with a symmetric world such as the tower world, one just cannot generate a distinct possibility by rotating the fall over 180 degrees; hence, contrary to our initial intuition, T is really a deterministic theory.

While I agree that one can maintain sophisticated substantivalism in the face of this example, let me add one more twist to it, which, to me at least, makes sophisticated substantivalism seem less plausible.[12] Suppose that we add two human beings, each one standing between the middle and one of the two outer towers. When the middle tower falls towards one of the outer towers, the human being standing between the middle tower and that outer tower is crushed. The other human breaths a sigh of relief, and says 'But for the Grace of God, there go I'. And surely he is right; surely it was possible that he could have been crushed, and surely that was a different possibility from what actually happened. So let us consider a different response.

---

[11] This is a variation on an example from Mark Wilson (1993).
[12] Tim Maudlin gave me this example.

Suppose that we accept that T is indeterministic. Does it follow that we should infer from the hole argument that standard, substantival, General Relativity also is indeterministic? If not, the hole argument is still no argument against substantivalism. In fact, Joseph Melia (1999) and Brad Skow (2005, Chapter 2) have argued that according to the most natural account of what it is for a law to be deterministic, theory T is indeed indeterministic, while General Relativity is deterministic. Let me explain.

Melia's and Skow's basic idea is something like the following. Why do we think that the tower world is indeterministic? Well, the earlier qualitative state of the world—the earlier distribution of qualities—determines its later qualitative state—the later distribution of qualities, and hence the earlier distribution of qualities determines a unique distribution of qualities throughout history. But consider one of the towers—call it tower A—at the earlier time. The qualitative state of the world at the earlier time does not determine whether the middle tower will collapse towards *that* tower, tower A. So there is something important that is not determined by T. Melia and Skow claim that in order for a theory to count as deterministic one should not merely demand that the distribution of qualities prior to a time t uniquely determine the distribution of qualities after time t. One should also demand that the distribution of qualities prior to t should determine what happens to any part of the world that exists before t and continues to exist after t. Now, each of the outside towers exists both before and after the collapse of the middle tower, and T does not determine which of them will be dented. So T is not deterministic. This seems plausible. So let's try to apply Melia and Skow's idea to General Relativity, and the hole argument.

Before doing so we need to be a little more general and precise. Consider the following modification of the tower world. Suppose that at the moment of collapse the two outside towers are going to be torn down by some very fast robots (which were hiding in the outside towers), and then be quickly replaced by two new towers in the same location (whereupon the robots self-destruct). So it is one of the two *new* towers that will become dented by the falling debris. If that is so, then we cannot complain that the state of the world prior to the collapse does not determine what happens to each of the outside towers that existed at the earlier time, for those towers are no longer in existence after the collapse. Nonetheless, it seems clear that we should still maintain that this world is indeterministic, for there is an unambiguous fact as to which of the later outside towers succeeded which of the earlier outside towers, and it is not determined by the earlier state of the world which of the later (successor) towers will receive a dent. So we need to ensure that our definition of determinism also allows for that kind of failure of determinism.

In order to present such a definition of determinism let me first define what it is for a mapping M from a part PH of a total history H to another part PH' of another total history H' to count as a 'duplication mapping'. (A part PH of a total history H is just any, non-zero length, stretch of that total history.) A map M from PH to PH' is a 'duplication mapping' if it maps all objects (and their parts) in PH to objects (and their parts) in PH', while preserving all (perfectly natural) qualities and (perfectly natural) relations. (Note that this definition allows *PH* and *PH'* to be identical.) Now let us say that a theory *T* is deterministic if and only if for any total histories *H* and *H'* allowed by *T* and any parts *PH* and *PH'* thereof, any duplication mapping from *PH* to *PH'* can be extended to a duplication mapping from *H* to *H'*.[13]

It is easy to see that theory *T* will not be deterministic according to this definition. Take a collapsing tower history, and consider *PH* to be the history up until a time *t* just before the collapse. Let *PH'* be exactly the same partial history; that is, let it be *PH*. (As noted above, the definition of 'duplication mapping' allows *PH* and *PH'* to be identical.) Now consider the duplication mapping from *PH* to *PH* which maps the middle tower onto itself, but maps each outside tower onto the other outside tower. This duplication map cannot be extended to a duplication mapping from *H* to *H*, for if one continues by mapping the one outside tower onto the other one, then one will end up mapping a tower with a dent onto a tower without a dent, which therefore does not preserve a (perfectly natural) property. And one cannot suddenly switch which outside tower gets mapped to which outside tower without violating the rule that external relations, such as (spacetime) distances and parthood relations, must be preserved under a duplication mapping. So *T* is not deterministic. The same thing goes for the modified example where the towers are quickly destroyed and rebuilt, for if one suddenly switches which tower gets mapped onto which, one will not preserve (spacetime) distances under the mapping. So we produce the intuitively correct verdict that *T*, and its modifications, are indeterministic.

How about General Relativity, and the hole argument? Well, the hole argument provides one with a mapping in a finite region—the hole—which is a duplication mapping. Indeed, if the models are diffeomorphically related, then one can extend this to a duplication mapping everywhere, just by using the hole mapping that generates the hole argument. So the hole argument does not yield indeterminism, according to the just-given definition of determinism. This then, I claim to be the correct response to the puzzle posed by the collapsing towers: according to the most natural definition of determinism, the tower world is indeterministic, but substantival General Relativity is deterministic, so substantivalism is not in trouble.

The upshot of all of this is that substantivalists can respond in many ways to Leibniz's shift argument and the hole argument. Moreover, substantivalism, as it stands, gives rise to simpler and more natural theories than does relationism. So substantivalism wins! But how total can the victory be?

5.13 Supersubstantivalism

Supersubstantivalism is the claim that the only object that exists is spacetime, or, perhaps better: supersubstantivalism claims that there are no material objects and no fields,

---

[13] This definition of determinism was first formulated (though ultimately rejected) by Gordon Belot (1995).

just spaces which have properties. Spacetime regions can have particle properties: namely, masses or mass-densities, charges or charge densities, and so on. Or perhaps better: there are various betweenness and congruence relations (or something similar such as addition relations) that can hold between spacetime points and regions. And spacetime regions can have field features: scalar-field values, vector-field values, tensor-field values, spinor-field values, and so on. Perhaps better: betweenness and congruence relations can hold between points in field value spaces at points in spacetime.

Why believe supersubstantivalism? Here are two arguments in its favour. Argument 1: ontological economy; fewer objects is better than more. Argument 2: supersubstantivalism can explain why parts of objects, or rather what normally are considered to be parts of objects, occupy parts of the regions that the objects occupy, while people who think that there are material objects as well as spacetime have to postulate that parts of objects occupy regions that are parts of the regions that the objects occupy.

This is hardly decisive; but still, these are *prima facie* reasons to favour supersubstantivalism. Spaces rule!

6

Gauge theories and fibre-bundle spaces

These differences shall all rest under gage

William Shakespeare

(I know, I know, the gage mentioned by Shakespeare is a glove, not a gauge; but let us just ignore that.)

6.1 Introduction

In this chapter we will discuss whether one should think that in addition to space-time there are also 'fibre-bundle' spaces. We will also discuss the related question as to whether the standard conception of properties is the correct conception. On the standard conception, a property, such as having a particular colour, is something that distinct objects can have in common. This standard view seems patently correct. For instance, we often recognize objects at different times as being the same object, because the object at earlier times and at later times has many of the same properties. Scientists theorize about the patterns of property distributions—patterns according to which one and the same property is distributed over distinct objects. And what patterns could there be if no objects at distinct places, or at distinct times, ever had a property in common? Indeed, it would seem hard to live in a world in which objects at distinct spacetime locations never have any properties in common. Nonetheless, I am going to argue that there is a large class of properties (though not all)—namely, field values at locations—such that no sense can be made of the idea that the same field value obtains at distinct locations.

I should note that at points this chapter will presuppose some knowledge of some group theory and some differential geometry. A good introduction to the relevant material is presented by Baez and Muniain (1994).

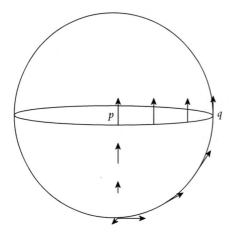

Figure 6.1 Parallel transport.

6.2 Are velocities properties?

Consider vectors in a curved space. Does it make sense to ask whether vectors at two different locations are parallel—are pointing in the same direction? As we saw in Chapter 2, it does not (see Figure 6.1). Dragging a vector from p along two different paths, while always (intuitively) keeping it pointing in the same direction, will result in two different vectors at the South Pole. So there is no path-independent sense to be made of the notion of vectors at distinct locations, such as p and the South Pole, being parallel or not.

However, according to General Relativity it does make sense to ask whether, as one 'drags' a vector along a (smooth) path, this vector changes its direction or remains parallel. Spacetime, according to General Relativity, includes a structure that determines what it is for a vector to be 'parallel transported' along a path, but this does not allow for a non-local path-independent notion of parallelhood of vectors.

The structure that determines what it is for a vector to be parallel transported along a path is known as a 'connection': for any vector at any point and any direction, the connection determines what happens to that vector as one parallel transports it in that direction. Of course, since it tells one how nearby tangent spaces are connected, the connection at a point is not intrinsic to a point, but it is intrinsic to arbitrarily small open neighbourhoods.[1]

With hindsight it also seems more natural to suppose that even in flat spacetimes, such as those of Special Relativity and Newtonian physics, the structure of spacetime

---

[1] There is a sense in which the metric of a spacetime determines the connection between its tangent spaces. That is to say, if one demands, as one normally does, that the inner product of parallel transported vectors remains invariant, then one can show that a metric picks out a unique connection. See, for example, Wald (1984), pp. 34–6. However, the general concept of a connection in gauge theories is that of a connection on a fibre-bundle. Many fibre-bundles have connections without having a metric, so it is important to introduce the concept of a connection independent of that of a metric.

includes a 'connection', which determines what it is to parallel transport a vector along a path. It just so happens that in flat spacetimes the connection is such that when one parallel transports a vector from one point to another, one always ends up with the same vector no matter what path one takes. Indeed, one can take this as a definition of what it is for a spacetime to be flat.[2]

As Tim Maudlin (2002) has pointed out, all of this has consequences for the idea that the velocity of an object is a property of that object. Normally, when one thinks of properties, one thinks that different objects can have the same property. But, as we have just seen, in curved spacetimes it makes no sense to ask whether vectors at different locations are the same. According to General Relativity, velocities are therefore not properties—at least, not properties as traditionally conceived.

6.3 Fibre-bundle substantivalism

The phenomenon of non-comparability of properties at distinct locations in spacetime is not confined to velocities. It is part and parcel a certain type of modern field theory: namely, gauge theories. In the case of velocities there is attached to each point x in spacetime another space, the tangent space at x, where the points in the tangent space at x correspond to all the possible tangent vectors at x. According to General Relativity, the collection of all these tangent spaces—the tangent bundle—has a structure, a 'connection', which determines what happens when you 'drag' (parallel transport) a vector along a path in spacetime. Gauge theories generalize this idea. In this section I will sketch one approach to gauge theories: namely, as a theory of the structure of certain spaces—'fibre-bundle spaces'—which exist in addition to spacetime. This approach I will dub 'fibre-bundle substantivalism'. After that I will discuss an alternative approach to gauge theories, according to which they are theories of certain quantities—so-called 'loop holomonies' or, in certain cases, 'Wilson loops', which are properties of paths in spacetime. This approach, for reasons that will become clear, I will dub 'gauge relationism'. I will end this chapter by arguing that fibre-bundle substantivalism is the better view.

According to the fibre-bundle substantivalist approach to gauge theories there is a space (in fact, a differentiable manifold) attached to each point p in spacetime: the 'fibre' at p. The points of the fibre at a point p in spacetime represent the possible states of a physical field φ at point p. Normally, each fibre at each point in spacetime has the same structure, and normally this includes vector-space structure (so that one can add points in a fibre and multiply them by real numbers, while staying in the fibre). But, in principle, fibres at distinct points in spacetime need not all have the same structure, nor need they be vector spaces, and often they will have more structure than just vector-space structure. In any case, the collection of all the fibres at all points in spacetime,

---

[2] The benefit of taking this as a definition of curvature, rather than defining flatness in terms of a metric, is that it can be applied to fibre-bundles that have no metric structure.

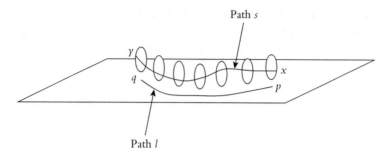

Figure 6.2 A fibre bundle.

with a topology and differential structure on the whole collection, is called a 'fibre bundle'. A set of points in the fibre bundle—exactly one for each point x in spacetime—is called a 'section' of the fibre bundle, and it can be taken to represent a possible state of a field φ throughout spacetime. Bundles can also have a connection structure, where this connection may correspond to another physical field: the 'connection field' A. The connection tells you what it is to parallel transport (drag) a point p in the fibre at a point x in spacetime along some path in spacetime. One can then impose field equations which amount to constraints on the ways in which the field φ and the connection field A can be jointly distributed. Let me illustrate all of this by means of an example.

In Figure 6.2 I have pictured spacetime as a plane, and I have drawn fibres at various points where each fibre has the topological structure of a circle. In this case I have not assumed that the fibres have a vector-space structure. I will return to that issue. The topology and differential structure of the fibre bundle is as pictured. That is to say, think of the circles as all lying in parallel planes in a three-dimensional flat space; the topology and differential structure of the fibre bundle is then the one that comes from the three-dimensional plane in which one can think of the fibres as being embedded. Incidentally, one should think of the fibres—that is, the circles—as 'hovering over' the spacetime plane. One should not imagine that any of the points in the fibres are in the spacetime plane, nor even that any of the points in the fibres are 'closer' or 'further away' from the spacetime plane than any other points in the fibres. Rather, each fibre, in its entirety, is associated with a unique point in the spacetime plane (by means of 'projection mapping'). I have also assumed that the fibre bundle in question has a connection. Figure 6.2 illustrates what happens if one parallel transports a point x in the fibre 'above' p along path l in spacetime to point q in spacetime: x will then be parallel transported along path s in the fibre bundle to point y in the fibre bundle.

Now let me present a reason why one normally assumes that the fibres have a vector-space structure. Consider a spacetime which has the topology of the surface of a sphere, and a fibre bundle 'over it' such that each fibre has the topology of a circle (see Figure 6.3). Suppose that one can picture the topology of the fibre bundle as

Figure 6.3 A fibre bundle without a section.

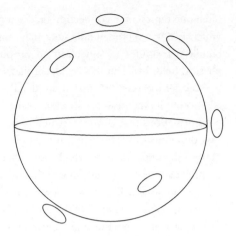

follows: each fibre—that is, each circle—at each point p in spacetime lies in the plane tangent to the surface of the sphere at p. That is to say, think of the points in a fibre at a point p of spacetime as corresponding to all the unit length vectors in the tangent space of p. Then one can picture a continuous line in the fibre bundle as a continuous vector field consisting of unit-length vectors along the corresponding line in space-time. Or, perhaps better, think of each point in the fibre at p as corresponding to a unique direction in spacetime at p. Then a continuous line in the fibre bundle corresponds to continuously varying directions along the corresponding line in spacetime.

   The somewhat surprising thing is that this fibre bundle does not admit of a section. One cannot choose a point in each fibre such that the chosen points vary continuously everywhere (according to the topology of the fibre bundle just indicated). Here is why. Choosing a point in each fibre amounts to choosing a direction everywhere in space-time. Now imagine that there is hair growing at each point on the surface of the sphere, and imagine pointing each hair in the direction to which the chosen point in the fibre corresponds. If one could choose points in the fibre bundle in such a way that the variation in directions is continuous everywhere, then one could 'comb' the hair on the surface of a sphere such that there is no 'parting' anywhere; that is, such that there is no discontinuous change in the direction in which the hair is combed any-where. But, in fact, every possible way of combing the hair on a hairy sphere must have a parting somewhere. So there is no distribution of points in this fibre bundle which is continuous everywhere; this fibre bundle admits of no sections whatsoever. A natural way to avoid this problem is to assume that the fibres have a vector-space structure. For any vector space includes a null vector, and any assignment of the null vector everywhere will be a continuous assignment everywhere. (At least, this will be so if the fibres are 'glued' together such that the null vectors in the different fibres are all connected. I will say more about this below.) Moreover, any continuous deformation of this null section will also be a section. In gauge theories one assumes that physical fields either are sec-tions of vector bundles, or connection fields on such vector bundles. Well, actually, often one represents a connection field as a connection on a so-called 'principal bundle' which is not a vector bundle (and may not admit of a section), where this principal bundle determines a connection on various 'associated' vector bundles in which the physical fields live. But this is a detail that, for the sake of simplicity, I shall ignore.

Now let me present some more details. As I said, each fibre can have structure in addition to its vector-space structure. One can specify such structure by specifying the transformations that leave the structure in question invariant. For instance, consider a two-dimensional vector space. If the only structure is vector-space structure then the group of transformations which leave that structure invariant is the group of linear transformations. But let us suppose that in addition to vector-space structure each fibre also has 'angle-and-length' structure—by which I mean structure that can be given by specifying a representation of the group of rotations on the vector space. The idea here is that rotations leave the angles between vectors invariant and leave lengths invariant, so that one can specify an angle-and-length structure on a vector space by specifying a representation of the group of rotations.[3] Given such a structure, how can we now glue together such fibres so as to arrive at a fibre bundle over spacetime?

Here is a how. We divide up spacetime into overlapping open regions {R} and provide each such region R with a 'local trivialization' of the fibre bundle F_R over R. A 'local trivialization' of a fibre bundle F_R over R consists of two elements:

1) A representation ρ of the group of rotations G on a single, 'standard', fibre F.[4]
2) A 1–1, onto, map φ from F_R to the Cartesian product FxR of the standard fibre F and the region R, such that φ preserves topological, differential, and angle-and-length structure.

Finally, we demand that if a point p of spacetime lies in two overlapping regions R_i and R_j then the two maps φ_i and φ_j which map the fibre above p to the fibre F must be related by a smoothly varying angle-and-length structure preserving transformation. That is, for all points x in the fibre above p we must have that $\varphi_i(x)=\rho(g)\varphi_j(x)$ for some rotation g in G, and g varies smoothly across spacetime.

Note that since the local trivializations include a particular representation ρ of the group of rotations, there is a fact as to which transformation on the standard fibre F corresponds to a particular rotation g. Does this mean that if two points x and y in the fibre above p are related by a rotation g' according to a trivialization φ_1 in a neighbour-

---

[3] One might think that a representation of the group of rotations on a vector space only induce a 'sameness of angle' and 'sameness of length' structure on the vector space, and that this is not sufficient to determine (numerical values of) angles and lengths themselves. However, the numerical values of angles are determined by facts of the form: rotation r repeated n times is the identity. Numerical values of lengths are determined, up to a choice of unit length, by the 'same length' facts, and the numerical ratios of lengths of parallel vectors—the latter being determined by the vector-space structure alone. One might also think that a representation of the group of rotations on a vector space additionally induces a 'same-handedness' structure, since rotations cannot change handedness. However, this structure is already induced by the vector-space structure alone.

[4] A 'representation' of a group G on a vector space F is a group homomorphism ρ from G to the linear transformations of F, such that $\rho(g_1 g_2)=\rho(g_1)\rho(g_2)$ for all g_1 and g_2 in G.

hood of p, then they are related by the same rotation g' according to another trivializa-tion φ_2 in a neighbourhood of p? Let us see. We have $\varphi_1(y)=\rho(g')\varphi_1(x)$. We also have $\varphi_1(x)=\rho(g)\varphi_2(x)$ and $\varphi_1(y)=\rho(g)\varphi_2(y)$ by our compatibility demand on local trivializa-tions on overlaps. Putting the two together we obtain $\rho(g)\varphi_2(y)=\rho(g')\rho(g)\varphi_2(x)$; that is, $\varphi_2(y)=\rho(g^{-1})\rho(g')\rho(g)\varphi_2(x)$. Now the group of rotations in a plane is in fact 'Abelian'—that is, $gg'=g'g$ for all such rotations g and g'—so its representations are also Abelian—$\rho(g)\rho(g')=\rho(g')\rho(g)$, so $\varphi_2(y)=\rho(g^{-1})\rho(g')\rho(g)\varphi_2(x)=\rho(g^{-1})\rho(g)\rho(g')\varphi_2(x)=$ $\rho(g')\varphi_2(x)$. So the answer is 'yes': if two points x and y in the fibre above p are related by a rotation g' according to trivialization φ_1, then they are related by the same rotation g' according to any other allowed trivialization φ_2. But this argument crucially relied on the group of transformations being Abelian. (An example of a non-Abelian group is the group of all rotations in a three-dimensional space—rotations around all possible axes in a three-dimensional space. First rotating around an axis x by, say, 90 degrees, and then around an axis y by, say, 90 degrees, is not the same as first rotating around y by 90 degrees and then around x by 90 degrees.) However, even in the case of a non-Abelian group, two trivializations whose overlap includes a point p cannot differ as to whether a pair of points x and y in F_p are related by *some* transformation in the non-Abelian group. We have just seen a general argument that if two points in a fibre are related by a transformation g' in the non-Abelian group according to local trivial-ization φ_1, then they are related by transformation $\rho(g^{-1})\rho(g')\rho(g)$ according to local trivialization φ_2. And even if this is not identical to $\rho(g')$, it is still an element of the same (non-Abelian) group of transformations.

Note also that my definition is slightly different from the standard textbook defini-tion, in that it assumes that the fibres in the fibre bundle come pre-equipped with an angle-and-length structure and then demands that the local trivializations be angle-and-length structure-preserving. Standardly, one does not assume that each fibre in the fibre bundle comes pre-equipped with an angle-and-length structure. Rather, one induces such a structure on the fibres in the fibre bundles by means of sets of allowed local trivializations. Moreover, standard textbooks do not talk about the structure that corresponds to the group of transformations in question; they just talk about the group of transformations itself.

Now let me define a gauge transformation of our fibre bundle. A gauge transforma-tion $\breve{g}$ is a transformation which maps each fibre of our fibre bundle into itself by means of a transformation which preserves the angle-and-length structure, where this transformation varies smoothly in spacetime; that is, a gauge transformation rotates the points in each fibre, and the rotations vary smoothly across spacetime. (I use the $\breve{g}$ with a breve in order to distinguish gauge transformations in the group of gauge trans-formations $\breve{G}$ from the rotations g in the group of rotations G.) In this manner one can also 'gauge transform' a section of our fibre bundle: one rotates the points of the section by the smoothly varying amounts to obtain a new section. In a moment we will see that one can also gauge-transform certain connections on our fibre bundle; namely, 'rotation-connections'.

A 'rotation-connection', roughly speaking, is a connection D such that if one parallel transports a point x according to D along some line l in spacetime, then relative to any local trivialization the point x just rotates in the standard fibre as you travel along l. Let me present some more details.

A connection is a rule which specifies what it is to parallel transport a point x in the fibre above a point p in spacetime along a path l in spacetime. More precisely, a connection D assigns to each spacetime vector field V a function D_V from smooth sections s in the fibre bundle to smooth sections s' such that for all smooth real-valued functions f on spacetime:

1) $D_V(s+t)=D_V(s)+D_V(t)$
2) $D_V(fs)=V(f)(s)+fD_V(s)$
3) $D_{v+w}(s)=D_V(s)+D_W(s)$
4) $D_{fv}(s)=fD_V(s)$

Here, fs is the section obtained by multiplying s at each point p in spacetime by the real number value of f at that point in spacetime. (The fibres have vector-space structure, so there is a well-defined notion of multiplying section s at point p by a real number.) We call $D_V(s)$ the covariant derivative of s in direction V. A section s is 'parallel transported' along a curve $\gamma(t)$ in spacetime if and only if $D_{\gamma(t)}(s)=0$ everywhere along that curve, where $\gamma'(t)$ is the tangent vector to the curve $\gamma(t)$.[5]

One can show that the above definition is equivalent to a 'local definition'; that is, a connection can equivalently be defined as a map (subject to the analogue of the above axioms) that maps any vector V_p at any spacetime point p and any section s in a neighbourhood of p, to a unique point in the fibre over p.

Next, let us call a 'C$^\infty$-linear map' E from sections of our fibre bundle to sections of our fibre bundle; that is, a map E such that $E(fs)=fE(s)$ for any smooth real valued function f—a 'fibre-bundle endomorphism'. And then let us call a map A from spacetime vector fields V to fibre-bundle endomorphisms, such that $A(fV+gW)=fA(V)+gA(W)$ for all real valued functions f and g, an 'endomorphism valued co-vector field'. So, if you give an endomorphism valued co-vector field a vector field, you obtain an endomorphism, which is a C$^\infty$-linear map from sections to sections. Note that such a map A is not a connection, since it does not satisfy axiom 2 above: $A(V)(fs)=fA(V)(s)$, rather than $A(V)(fs)=V(f)(s)+fA(V)(s)$ as would be required by axiom 2. Now, let D be any connection on our fibre bundle. Then D+A is also a connection, where we define $(D+A)_V(s)=D_V(s)+A(V)s$. In fact, it is precisely the fact that axioms 2 fails for A that has as a consequence that D+A satisfies the above axioms. Moreover, one can show that, given any arbitrary connection D, any other connection D' can be expressed in the form D+A for some endomorphism valued co-vector field A.

Now suppose we have a local trivialization of our fibre bundle in region R and a connection D on R such that for any spacetime tangent vector V at any point in R,

---

[5] Conversely, the facts about parallel transport determine the connection: see http://en.wikipedia.org/wiki/Parallel_transport

$D_V(s)=0$ when according to the local trivialization s does not change location in the standard fibre F if one moves in direction V in spacetime. We then say that connection D 'is flat' relative to this local trivialization. Next we say that D' is a 'rotation-connection' on our fibre bundle if D' everywhere is of the form D'=D+A, where D is flat according to a local trivialization, and for any smooth spacetime vector field V the 'rotation endomorphism' A(V) is a smoothly varying element of the 'Lie algebra' of the group of rotations. The 'Lie algebra' is the set of 'infinitesimal rotations'—the tangent space to the rotation group at the identity. In our case we have a two-dimensional vector space, so we can specify an infinitesimal rotation by a single real number, which corresponds to a 'rate of rotation'. Suppose now that we have a connection D'=D+A, which is a rotation connection. Then suppose that we have a section s such that $D_V(s)=0$. Then $D'_V(s)=A(V)(s)$; that is, s is simply rotating at rate A(V)(s) according to D'. So we can say that D' differs from D by a pure rotation.

Now suppose that D is a rotation-connection. Then we can transform this connection D with any gauge transformation $\breve{g}$ so as to get a new rotation-connection D' by stipulating that $D'_V(s)=\breve{g}D_V(\breve{g}^{-1}s)$ for all vector fields V and all sections s. It immediately follows that $D'_V(\breve{g}s)=\breve{g}D_V(s)$. This says that if one applies a smoothly rotated connection to a smoothly rotated section, the result is the smooth rotation of what one obtains when one applies the original connection to the original section. In particular, if $D_V(s)=0$ then $D'_V(\breve{g}s)=0$.

The above generalizes from vector bundles whose structure corresponds to the rotation group, to vector bundles whose structure is given by other Lie groups. (A Lie group is a group of transformations which has the structure of a manifold, so that it can locally be parameterized by n-tuples of real numbers.) The equations governing a field that is a section in such a vector bundle and a field that determines a connection in that vector bundle can only make use of the structure that the vector bundle has. Such equations will be invariant under gauge transformations: if a connection plus a section is a solution to the equations, then so is the gauge-transformed connection plus section. This is how one manufactures local gauge theories.

In fact, classical electromagnetism takes exactly the form of our example. The electromagnetic 4-potential A corresponds to rotation-endomorphism A on a fibre bundle whose fibres are the complex plane (rotations correspond to multiplications by $e^{i\theta}$). One can then formulate a theory of the free electromagnetic field by imposing equations on the form that this connection can take. One can also assume that the electromagnetic field interacts with a complex scalar field (so that it is not free), whose state is given by a section of the complex plane fibre bundle, or indeed that it interacts with any section of any vector bundle for which the electromagnetic field naturally provides a connection.

Let us now discuss what all of this tells us about metaphysics: what objects and properties should one take there to be? The answer seems obvious. For the same reasons that I gave for the existence of spacetime as an object, one should take fibre bundles (and their parts) to be objects that exist. One might additionally assume the existence of spacetime (and its parts), or, as we shall discuss more exensively in Chapter 8, one might assume the existence only of the fibre bundle and identify spacetime points with the fibres in the fibre bundle. Furthermore, we should take the connections and the sections of these fibre bundles to correspond to fundamental properties of the fibre bundle, the sections corresponding to point local properties of the fibre bundles, and the connections corresponding to neighbourhood local properties of the fibre bundles.

In what sense is it then true that there are no properties as properties are standardly conceived'—that is, as features of which one can ask: 'Does this thing over here have the same property as that thing over there?' Well, consider a field F that corresponds to some section in some fibre bundle. One cannot ask: 'Is the value of F over here the same as the value of F over there?' A section—a global state of field F—is determined by which points in the corresponding fibre bundle are occupied by F. But the geometrical structure of the fibre bundle does not determine facts of the form 'location x in the fibre above spacetime point p corresponds to the same value of F as location y in the fibre above spacetime point q'. That is why it makes no sense to say things such as 'at spacetime point p the field F has the same value as it has at spacetime point q.' But there is still a property that distinct objects can have in common: distinct points in the fibre bundle can have the property in common that they are occupied, or have the property in common that they are unoccupied, or fail to have these properties in common. One can take 'occupation' here to be a fundamental property of a point in a fibre bundle, or one can take it to be a fundamental relation between a field F and a point in a fibre bundle. Parsimony suggests taking it to be a property. But either way, 'being occupied' is an old-fashioned local feature that distant locations can have in common or fail to have in common.

How about the connection field, and how should we understand the connection features of a fibre bundle? Well, we defined a connection D as a function from vector fields V and smooth sections s in the fibre bundle to smooth sections s', where this function has to have certain properties, which I listed above. There are two issues here. In the first place: how should we understand this 'function from bla to bla' talk. In the second place: this definition defines a connection as a global function. To what extent can we understand it as being determined by local facts?

Let us start with the function talk. Traditionally, a function with domain A and range B is nothing but a set of ordered pairs of elements from A and B. So if one accepts set theory—if one accepts that any set of objects is also an object—then a function is just another object. Sections of a fibre bundle are lines in fibre bundles—sets of points, sets of objects—so functions from sections to sections are objects. We saw in Chapter 2 that spacetime vector fields are maps; that is, functions—from functions from spacetime to the real numbers, to functions from spacetime to the real numbers. (And real numbers, in turn, traditionally are understood as sets which one can ultimately build up from the empty set.) So if we take it that real numbers are objects and sets of objects are objects, then vector fields are objects. (In Chapter 8 we will discuss whether we can get rid of real numbers and sets and replace them by purely geometrical objects, but this does not matter for present purposes.) So one can represent any particular connection field D as a relation $D(V,s,s')$ between certain objects—vector fields, sections, and sections—which satisfies certain axioms.

To what extent is D determined by local relations between local objects? Well, one can show that if $D(V,s,s')$ holds—that is, if section s' is the directional derivative of section s in the direction of vector field V—then the location which s' occupies in the fibre above any point p in spacetime depends only on what the vector V_p is of vector field V at location p, and on which points the section s occupies in the fibre bundle in an arbitrarily small neighbourhood of p. So let us say that $D_p(V,s,s')$ if and only if the directional derivative of s at p in direction V_p occupies the location in the fibre at p that s' occupies. So $D_p(V,s,s')$ is a neighbourhood local relation. Now, obviously, $D(V,s,s')$ if and only if $D_p(V,s,s')$ for all p. So D is determined by neighbourhood local relations, which we can take to be the fundamental connection relations. So there will be neighbourhood local relations such that it makes sense to ask: do V, s_1, and s_2 at p stand in the same relation as W, s_3, and s_4 at q; that is, do $D_p(V,s_1,s_2)$ and $D_q(W,s_3,s_4)$ either both hold, or both fail to hold?

So, there are fundamental properties and relations such that distinct, distant, objects and distinct, distant, n-tuples of objects can have them in common. In fact, in classical field theories *all* facts are determined by the facts about these fundamental properties and relations. In particular, in classical field theories one can assume that all thes fundamental objects are points (in spaces), and that all the fundamental properties and relations are occupation properties and relations that specify geometric structure: topological, differential, connection, metric, and so on, structure. (One might think that I have missed out on properties such as masses and charges, but in field theories these are represented by dimensional constants, m and q, which occur in the field equations.) That is to say, it is not the case that gauge theories show that there are no properties and relations as traditionally conceived—that is, as 'universals'—which distinct objects or n-tuples of objects can have in common. On the contrary, it shows that all fundamental properties and relations are universals. However, these universals are occupation properties and geometrical relations rather than the field values that one might initially have taken them to be. And this is just as well. For, as the standard view with which I started this chapter says: it is hard to see how the world could have any interesting structure, how there could be interesting patterns in the world, if there were no properties and relations that distinct things could have in common.

6.4 Gauge relationism

Gauge theories are invariant under gauge transformations: if some history of fields and/or connections is a solution to a gauge theory, then every gauge transformation of that solution is also a solution, just as the Leibniz shifts that we encountered in Chapter 5 are invariances of the equations of motion of Newtonian mechanics. And just as in that case, gauge transformations do not change the phenomena. Moreover, just as in the case of hole diffeomorphisms, one can apply gauge transformations only after some time t, so that fibre-bundle substantivalism appears to entail indeterminism. Gauge relationists claim that gauge-transformation-related fibre-bundle states do not represent genuinely distinct physical possibilities, and that since fibre-bundle substantivalists are committed to these being genuinely distinct physical possibilities, it follows that fibre-bundle substantivalism is false. Gauge relationism, as I will use the term, is the view that there are no fibre bundles, that the states of gauge fields and connection fields do not correspond to geometric features of fibre bundles, but instead correspond to certain properties of paths in spacetime. (For views that are close to what I have dubbed 'gauge relationism', see Belot (1998) and Healey (2007).)

We have seen, in Chapter 5, that I think that such arguments (based on symmetries, indeterminism, and the putative non-distinctness of possibilities) are not convincing. For in the first place one could be a 'sophisticated fibre-bundle substantivalist'; that is, one could accept the reality of fibre bundles and yet deny that there are distinct possible worlds that differ only by a gauge transformation. In the second place one could accept that gauge transformations produce distinct possible worlds, but deny that this violates determinism, given the intuitively correct definition of determinism. And thirdly, arguments based on intuitions about possibilities and their putative distinctness are not to be trusted. Nonetheless, it is interesting to see what alternative account of gauge theories gauge relationists have come up with, and it is interesting to evaluate such an account on its own merits. How simple and natural can such an account be?

Let us return to our example of a rotation connection on a fibre bundle whose fibres are a two-dimensional vector space. First we consider what happens when we drag—parallel transport—a location x in a fibre over point p in spacetime around a loop in spacetime back to p. Well, as we drag it along, the point will rotate according to any allowable local trivialization, and will end up at a point y which is just x rotated through some angle α. Now consider what would have happened if we had started at a different point x' in the fibre above p. Just as x, it will be rotated relative to any allowable local trivialization—indeed, at the same rate relative to any allowable trivialization. So it will also end up at angle α relative to its starting point. In general, we call the map which maps starting points in a fibre above a point p to the corresponding endpoints when they get parallel transported along a loop l according to connection D, the 'holonomy H(D) of loop l with basepoint p'. If D is a G-connection, the holonomy H will be a transformation g which is in the group G. Now let us ask whether holonomies are invariant under gauge transformations of the connection.

It is easy to see that they will be if the group G in question is an Abelian group. Here is the argument. Let us suppose that we have a looped curve $j(t)$, parameterized by parameter t, where $j(0)=j(T)=p$. Suppose we have a connection D and a path $u(t)$ in the fibre bundle over $j(t)$ such that $u(t)$ is parallel transported over $j(t)$. So the holonomy H(D), of loop $j(t)$ with basepoint p, is a linear map which maps $u(0)$ to $u(T)$. Now suppose we gauge transform D by means of gauge transformation $\breve{g}$ to obtain a connection D'. Then H(D') maps $\breve{g}(j(0))u(0)$ to $\breve{g}(j(T))u(T)$ (by our earlier definition of what it is to gauge transform a connection.) But notice that $\breve{g}(j(T))H(D)\breve{g}^{-1}(j(0))$ produces exactly the same map: $\breve{g}(j(T))H(D)\breve{g}^{-1}(j(0))$ $\breve{g}(j(0))u(0)=\breve{g}(j(T))H(D)u(0)=\breve{g}(j(T))u(T)$. So under a gauge transformation, H(D) transforms to $\breve{g}(j(T))H(D)\breve{g}^{-1}(j(0))$. Now

$\breve{g}(j(T))$ and $\breve{g}(j(0))$ are just transformations in the group G, and so is H(D). So if the group is Abelian, one has $\breve{g}(j(T))H(D)\breve{g}^{-1}(j(0))=\breve{g}(j(T))\breve{g}^{-1}(j(0))H(D)=H(D)$. So if the group is Abelian, its holonomies are invariant under gauge transformations. What if the group is not Abelian? Well, then the so-called 'trace' of the holonomy, the 'Wilson loop', is invariant under gauge transformations. The 'trace' of a linear mapping is the sum of the diagonal elements of a matrix representation of the mapping (which is independent of the representation). The reason the Wilson loop is invariant is that when one 'sandwiches' H(D) between $\breve{g}^{-1}$ and $\breve{g}$, one is, in effect, performing a similarity transformation on H(D), and its trace is invariant under such a similarity transformation.

The first question to ask now is whether the holonomies, in the case of Abelian theories, and the Wilson loops, in the case of non-Abelian gauge theories, are a *sufficient* gauge invariant basis; that is, whether they determine *all* the gauge-invariant facts. The answer, basically, is 'yes'. But it will be helpful to provide a little more detail.

In the case of holonomies, one can prove the following reconstruction theorem. Let H be a map from spacetime loops with base-point x to a group of transformations G which satisfies the following constraints:

1) $H(l_1 \circ l_2)=H(l_2)H(l_1)$.
2) If l_1 and l_2 are 'thinly equivalent', then $H(l_1)=H(l_2)$.
3) H is a smooth map.

Then H has a representation as the holonomy of a (principal) fibre bundle with a connection which is unique up to gauge transformations (see Loll (1994)). Here, '$\circ$' denotes the operation of concatenating two loops (going round, the one after the other). To say that H is a smooth map is to say as one smoothly varies the loop in spacetime the group element that it gets mapped to by H varies smoothly. (Since G is a Lie group it comes equipped with a notion of smoothness. One will have to put a topology on the space of loops with base point x, but this can be done in a natural manner.) Two loops are said to be 'thinly equivalent' if and only if you can turn them into the same loop by 'shrinking' parts of each of the two loops in such a manner that during this shrinking process the loop that is being shrunk remains confined to the region that it originally covered. See Figure 6.4 for an example of two thinly equivalent loops: the one loop just goes round the circle from X to X, and the other loop goes round the circle until it hits point Y, then goes out on a line to Z, and then comes back along the same line to Y.

Now, while this is all very nice for the gauge relationist, there are already signs that gauge-invariant quantities are not fundamental. In the first place, a fairly obvious explanation of why conditions 1 and 2 hold is that the map H is, roughly speaking, the integration of a connection around a loop. But gauge relationists deny that there are local connection properties, so they cannot avail themselves of such an explanation. Similarly, it seems strange to have elements of a group G (the holonomies) as one of the fundamental quantities. It is very natural to explain this in terms of a group of

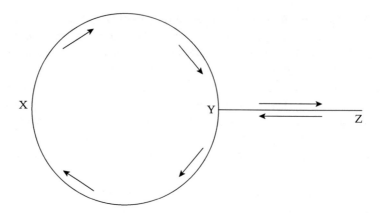

Figure 6.4 Thinly equivalent loops.

transformations G which leaves the structure of an existing space invariant: namely, the structure of the fibre at X. However, gauge relationists deny the existence of these fibres, so cannot avail themselves of such an explanation.

Matters become worse when we turn to Wilson loops (and will become even worse when we turn to dynamics). There is a general reconstruction theorem in the case of Wilson loops. Here it is. Let W map from the space of loops to the complex numbers such that

1) It satisfies the 'Mandelstam identities'.
2) If l_1 and l_2 are 'thinly equivalent', then $W(l_1)=W(l_2)$.
3) $W(l_1)W(l_2)-W(l_1 \circ l_2)=0$.
4) W is a smooth map.

Then there are transformations $g(l)$ in a group G such that $W(l_1 \circ l_2 \ldots \circ l_n)=Tr(g(l_n)\cdot g(l_{n-1}) \cdot \ldots \cdot g(l_1))$; that is, the Wilson loops have a representation as traces of loop holonies. The 'Mandelstam identities' are not simple to state, and I will refrain from doing so (but see, for example, Loll (1994) or Gambini and Pullin (1996) for the gory details). The reason why they are not simple to state is that in essence they state the constraints that are imposed on complex numbers by the fact that they are not arbitrary complex numbers but are the traces of matrices representing linear transformations on a vector space. Of course, if one takes Wilson loops to be the fundamental quantities, one cannot explain these constraints in this manner. They would just be fundamental (structural) laws regarding the fundamental quantities of one's theory.

There are also some specific reconstruction theorems which are useful when one wants to characterize the Wilson loops that correspond to a particular group (SU(n) or SL(2,C) or . . .). Demanding that the Wilson loops correspond to some specific group imposes additional constraints on them. Not only are these additional constraints often quite complex to state, but it is also the case that apart from a few examples it is not generally known how to formulate them. (Again, see Loll (1994).) This means that axioms that are central to gauge theories which are quite simple and easy to state in the framework of fibre-bundle substantivalism, are complex and hard to state on the gauge relationist approach. All of this strongly suggests that the gauge-invariant holonomies and Wilson loops are not the fundamental quantities in gauge theories.

Next let me turn to dynamics: the equations of motion for gauge fields. First we consider free fields. If one thinks that only certain gauge-invariant quantities are fundamental, then the equations of motion ought to be stateable—indeed, ought to be simply and naturally stateable—in terms of these fundamental gauge-invariant quantities. And in some cases this is so. For instance, one can state the equations of the free electromagnetic field in terms of the Maxwell–Faraday tensor $F_{\mu\nu}$. Since the Maxwell–Faraday tensor in turn corresponds to the infinitesimal holonomy of the electromagnetic connection field A, this means that we can state the theory of the free electromagnetic field quite simply and naturally in terms of the gauge-invariant holonomies. However, I know of no argument for the claim that every theory of a free connection field can be stated in a simple and natural way in terms of the holonomies of this connection field. Indeed, Renate Loll (1994, p. 283) cites this as one of the unsolved problems of the loop representation approach to gauge theories.

Now, how about a free field that is not a connection field, but is a field which according to fibre-bundle substantivalism is a section in a fibre bundle? Let us consider the example I used before: a complex scalar field φ, where the structure of the fibres in question is given by the rotation group. If one does not have a connection with which to interact, then the only structure that there is is the rotation structure on each fibre, and the differential and topological structure of the fibre bundle. But this will not allow one to write any interesting dynamical equations, as it is just too little structure with which to do much of interest. The natural response is that one can only write dynamical equations of any interest if there is also a connection D on the fibre bundle.

Indeed. But now we face another issue. In gauge theories the dynamical equations are equations governing a connection field D and a section field φ which are invariant under gauge transformations which act *simultaneously* on the field φ and the connection D. If gauge transformations do not correspond to real changes in the state of the world, as gauge relationists maintain, then the ordered pair $<\varphi, D>$ and the ordered pair $<\breve{g}\varphi, \breve{g}D>$, where $\breve{g}$ is a gauge transformation, represents the same possible state. But that does not mean that the gauge-invariant features of a world which contains both fields are fully given by a gauge equivalence class X of complex scalar field states and a gauge equivalence class Y of connection states. For $<\breve{g}_1\varphi, \breve{g}_2D>$, generically, is not gauge-equivalent to $<\varphi, D>$ for distinct gauge transformations $\breve{g}_1$ and $\breve{g}_2$, even though $\breve{g}_1\varphi$ is gauge-equivalent to φ, and $\breve{g}_2D$ is gauge-equivalent to D. In a way, this makes matters slightly easier for the gauge relationist, for the above means that there are more gauge-invariant features than just those of φ and D separately. Here is an example of such an additional feature: the angle between $\varphi(q)$—that is, the complex scalar field at point q in spacetime—and the result of parallel transporting $\varphi(p)$ along a path γ from p to q (not a loop!) according to connection D, is a gauge-invariant quantity. So gauge relationists can make use of such quantities in their theories.

The crucial question is then the following: can gauge relationists write down simple structural equations which characterize the gauge-invariant quantities they take there to be, and simple dynamical equations which constrain how these quantities are allowed to be distributed in the world, without making use of non-gauge-invariant quantities? So, for instance, gauge relationists are not allowed to use an expression such as $\varphi^\star(b)H(\gamma(a{\to}b))\varphi(a)$ in their equations. For even though the quantity corresponding to that whole expression is gauge-invariant, there occur in that expression quantities which are not gauge-invariant: $\varphi(a)$, the complex scalar field value at a, and $H(\gamma(a{\to}b))$, the holonomy along path γ from a to b. If one really maintains that the fundamental quantities are gauge-invariant, then one should be able to state one's theory as a simple theory purely in terms of those gauge-invariant quantities; one should not need to use terms that are defined in terms of non-gauge-invariant expressions. That is to say, gauge relationists are allowed to introduce a primitive quantity $P(\gamma)$, which, intuitively speaking, is supposed to denote the quantity that fibre-bundle substantivalists denote by $\varphi^\star(b)H(\gamma(a{\to}b))\varphi(a)$, and then impose axioms governing it and the other gauge-invariant quantities in order to arrive at a theory that is empirically equivalent to the standard version of the relevant gauge theory. Unfortunately, it seems very doubtful that simple versions of interacting gauge field theories can be formulated in this manner. See, for example, Gambini and Pullin (1996), Chapters 5 and 6, Loll (1994), and Healey (2007), Chapter 7, Section 4. However, note that these authors, with the exception of Loll, are not worried about using expressions such as $\varphi^\star(b)H(\gamma(a{\to}b))\varphi(a)$. They are concerned only with whether certain expressions denote gauge-invariant quantities, and do not care whether parts of these expressions are expressions that denote non-gauge-invariant quantities.

All in all it seems implausible that gauge theories can be formulated as a simple theory in terms of only fundamental gauge-invariant quantities. Of course, this is not a knock-down argument, and quantized gauge theories—quantum loop gravity in particular—may prove me wrong.

6.5 Conclusions

Gauge theories are best understood as theories about the geometrical and occupation structure of fibre-bundle spaces. This shows that certain features of locations allow only for path-dependent comparisons of these features. However, this does not imply quite as radical a revision of the metaphysics of properties as Tim Maudlin (2002) has suggested. For all fundamental properties and relations are still good old 'universals' which distant locations either have in common or do not have in common.

7

Directions, hands, and charges

Time flies like an arrow. Fruit flies like a banana.

Groucho Marx

7.1 Introduction

In quantum field theory there is a celebrated theorem: the 'CPT' theorem, which says that if we take any possible history of the universe, flip the sign of all charges, reverse the order of all events in time, and then take the spatial mirror image of the constellation of all events, we always end up with another possible history. That is, it says that any relativistic quantum field theory must be invariant under the combined operation of charge conjugation C, spatial parity P, and time reversal T, even though none of those individual invariances need hold. *Prima facie* this is a perplexing theorem. Why does the combination of two spacetime transformations plus a charge-reversing transformation have to be a symmetry of any relativistic quantum field theory? Is there an analogous theorem for classical theories? What does charge conjugation have to do with spacetime symmetries? What, if anything, does the CPT theorem tell us about spacetime structure?

We can derive a hint of an answer to these questions by listening to what Richard Feynman had to say about anti-particles:

A backwards-moving electron when viewed with time moving forwards appears the same as an ordinary electron, except it is attracted to normal electrons—we say it has positive charge. For this reason it is call a 'positron'. The positron is a sister to the electron, and it is an example of an 'anti-particle'. This phenomenon is quite general. Every particle in Nature has an amplitude to move backwards in time, and therefore has an anti-particle. (Feynman (1985), p. 98.)

A natural way to understand this passage is that if one takes a history of a particle and time-reverses it, then one obtains a history of the corresponding anti-particle. That is to say, the idea is that time reversal T *properly understood* includes charge conjugation, and that what standardly is called a CPT transformation really is a PT transformation. This would mean that the CPT theorem, properly understood, is a PT theorem, and that the theorem says that any relativistic world is invariant under spacetime mirroring. This is the idea that I want to examine in this chapter.

In Section 7.2 I will briefly clarify the notion of PT invariance, and explain why one might be interested in such an invariance. In section 7.3 will I examine the PT invariance of classical field theories, and argue that the PT transformation includes charge conjugation. In section 7.4 I will discuss the same with respect to quantum field theories, and then I will end with some conclusions.

7.2 How do quantities transform under PT?

Suppose we describe a world (or part of a world) using some set of coordinates $\{x,y,z,t\}$. A 'passive' PT transformation is what happens to this description when we describe the same world but instead use coordinates $\{x', y', z', t'\}$, where $x'=-x$, $y'=-y$, $z'=-z$, $t'=-t$. An 'active' PT transformation is the following: keep using the same coordinates, but change the world in such a way that the description of the world in these coordinates changes exactly as it does in the corresponding passive PT transformation.[1] Suppose now that we have a theory which is stated in terms of coordinate-dependent descriptions of the world—a theory which says that only certain coordinate-dependent descriptions describe physically possible worlds; that is, are solutions. Such a theory is said to be PT invariant if and only if PT turns solutions into solutions and non-solutions into non–solutions.[2]

Why might one be interested in PT invariance or non-invariance of theories? Because failure of PT invariance tells us something about the structure of spacetime. It tells us that spacetime either has objective spatial handedness, or has an objective temporal orientation, or both. Why? Well, suppose we start with a coordinate-dependent description of a world which some theory allows. And suppose that after we do a passive coordinate transformation the theory says that the new (coordinate-dependent) description of this world is no longer allowed. This seems odd. It is, after all, the same world, just described using one set of coordinates rather than another. How could the one be allowed by our theory, and the other not? Indeed, this does not make much sense unless one supposes that the theory, as stated in coordinate-dependent form, was true in the original coordinates but not in the new coordinates. And that means that according to the theory there is some objective difference between the $\{x,y,z,t\}$ coordinates and the $\{x',y',z',t'\}$ coordinates; that is, the $\{x,y,z,t\}$ coordinates do not

---

[1] Note that there are therefore many distinct PT transformations—one corresponding to each distinct inertial coordinate system. I will assume a flat spacetime throughout this paper, and am not here going to address how to talk about PT in General Relativity. For more on that issue, see Malament (2004) and Arntzenius and Greaves (2007).

[2] If the theory is probabilistic, then the theory is PT invariant if its probabilities are invariant under PT.

stand in the same relation to the objective structure of the world as the $\{x',y',z',t'\}$ coordinates.

In the case of PT this could be because spacetime has an objective temporal orientation, or an objective spatial handedness, or both. Note that failure of PT invariance does not indicate that spacetime has a spacetime-handedness structure, for spacetime-handedness is invariant under PT. It is the four-dimensional analogue of spatial handedness: when one mirrors a single coordinate of a 4-tuple of coordinates, one flips the spacetime-handedness of the coordinate system. So, if one mirrors all four coordinates, as one does in PT, one ends up in a coordinate system of the same spacetime-handedness as the original coordinate system. It is, in fact, more interesting to consider what one should infer if a theory is invariant under PT, but fails to be invariant both under P and under T, since it appears that our world is such. (That is to say, it appears that the world is PT-invariant on the proposed 'Feynman understanding' of what a PT-transformation is, which, in standard terminology means that the world is CPT-invariant.) This indicates that spacetime has a spacetime-handedness, but neither a spatial handedness nor a temporal orientation, since spacetime-handedness is the minimal natural structure which explains the symmetry properties in question. (The fact that some interactions are not invariant when we apply just a P transformation, or just a T transformation, can be explained by the fact that each such transformation changes the spacetime-handedness of the interaction. The fact that all interactions are invariant under a combined PT transformation is explained by the fact that spacetime has neither a spatial handedness structure nor a temporal orientation structure, each of which could be used to construct PT symmetry violating interactions.)

OK, so that is a reason why we should be interested. But how do we go about investigating PT invariance. In particular, how do we know how the quantities occurring in our theories transform under PT? Well, though we often present our theories in coordinate-dependent form, Nature itself, of course, is coordinate-independent. We can use (n-tuples of) numbers to denote locations in spacetime, and we can use (m-tuples of) numbers to indicate the magnitudes and directions of various quantities in spacetime, but Nature itself does not come equipped with numbers. How our numerical representation of a quantity should transform under a change of coordinates depends on the structure of the quantity and on the way in which we have designed our coordinate representation of the quantity in question. Let me illustrate this for a very simple case.

Suppose a vector V at a point p in a three-dimensional Euclidean space is a coordinate-independent quantity which has a magnitude and picks out a direction. We can put Cartesian coordinates $\{x,y,z\}$ on the Euclidean space, and then use these coordinates to numerically indicate the direction and magnitude of V. To be precise: the coordinates on the Euclidean space naturally induce corresponding coordinates on the space of tangent vectors at p. It follows from the vector nature of V that when we, say, switch to coordinates $\{x', y', z'\}$, where $x'=-x$, $y'=-y$, $z'=-z$, then the three numbers representing V will each flip their sign. My point here is simply that one is not free to choose how one's numerical representation of quantities transforms under certain transformations. In particular, one cannot 'make' a theory invariant under some transformation simply by judiciously choosing how the quantities occur in the theory transform. How a quantity transforms is determined by the coordinate independent nature of the quantity in question (together with the way in which we manufacture coordinate representations of it).

7.3 PT in classical field theories

Let us start with a simple case: the classical real Klein–Gordon field—a real scalar field whose field values are invariant under the 'restricted Lorentz transformations'.[3] The Lorentz transformations are the transformations which leave the Minkowski metric invariant. (Well, strictly speaking, these are the Poincaré transformations. The 'Lorentz' transformations are the Poincaré transformations minus the transformations that merely shift everything by a fixed spacetime vector. The difference between the Poincaré transformations and the Lorentz transformations does not matter for purposes of this chapter.) The 'restricted' Lorentz transformations are the Lorentz transformations that are 'continuously connected' to the identity transformation, where the identity transformation is the boring Lorentz tranformation that does nothing. A Lorentz tranformation L is 'continuously connected to the identity' if one can start with the identity transformation, and then change this transformation in a continuous manner so that it is always a Lorentz transformation and ends up being L. The restricted Lorentz transformations include neither P nor T nor PT, since one cannot start with the identity transformation and then change this transformation in a continuous manner such that it always is a Lorentz transformation, and such that it ends up being P, or T, or PT.

We can impose a law of evolution on our scalar field—for example, the Klein–Gordon equation, $(\partial^\mu\partial_\mu+m^2)\phi=0$—and check whether this law of evolution is invariant under the restricted Lorentz transformations. It is. That is to say: if one takes any real scalar field which is a solution of the Klein–Gordon equation, and then applies a restricted Lorentz transformation to it, we always end up with another solution to the Klein–Gordon equation.

How about PT invariance? Well, we first need to know how the Klein–Gordon field transforms under PT. The standard assumption is that it is invariant under PT, by which the field $\phi(t,r)$ transforms into $\phi(-t,-r)$. It immediately follows that the Klein–Gordon equation is invariant under PT. I will later return to the issue as to whether this is the only possible way in which a scalar field could transform under PT. In the meantime, let us turn to another field: the classical electromagnetic field.

---

[3] For the sake of simplicity I am assuming that there are objective, path-independent, facts as to whether the values of the real Klein–Gordon field at two different locations in spacetime are the same. That is to say, I am here ignoring the idea that the Klein–Gordon field configurations correspond to sections on a fibre bundle with a connection on it.

Maxwell's equations for the free electromagnetic field, written in terms of the 4-potential A^μ, is $\Box A^\mu - \partial^\mu(\partial_\nu A^\nu) = 0$. In order to see whether this equation is invariant under PT, we need to know how the 4-potential A^μ transforms when we move it ('actively') from location (t,r) to the PT-related location $(-t,-r)$, or, equivalently, how the coordinate representation of the 4-potential transforms ('passively') when we switch from using coordinates (t,r) to using coordinates (t',r') where $t'=-t$ and $r'=-r$. This depends on what kind of coordinate-independent quantity we take the 4-potential to be. Let us make the simplest assumption: namely, that it is the same kind of quantity as $\partial^\mu\phi(t,r)$—a tangent vector in a four-dimensional spacetime.[4] Now, we know how $\partial^\mu\phi(t,r)$ transforms under active PT. The scalar field ϕ just gets moved to its new location, and this means that its derivatives flip sign. So, $\partial^\mu\phi(t,r)$ transforms to $-\partial^\mu\phi(-t,-r)$. Assuming that $A^\mu(t,r)$ is the same kind of quantity, it follows that $A^\mu(t,r)$ transforms to $-A^\mu(-t,-r)$ under the PT transformation.

It is important to note that this is *not* the standard view of how $A^\mu(t,r)$ transforms under PT. On the standard view, it transforms to $A^\mu(-t,-r)$ under PT. This should strike one as a little bit odd. So, let me give an explanation as to why this is the standard view. The standard view starts with the idea that the *spatial* components of a 4-velocity should flip under time-reversal (in the frame of reference that one is performing the time-reversal), and that the temporal component of 4-velocity should remain the same under time-reversal. The idea here is that if before time-reversal an object has a spatial 3-velocity that indicates that it is travelling from A to B, then after time reversal it should have a spatial 3-velocity that indicates that it is travelling from B to A. Now, obviously, spatial parity P (spatial mirroring) should flip the spatial components of 4-velocity (in the frame of reference that one is performing the parity transformation), and leave the temporal component invariant. Putting the two together, the standard view follows. PT should leave 4-velocities invariant, and merely move them to the PT-related locations in spacetime; that is, under PT each 4-velocity $V^\mu(t,r)$ should transform to $V^\mu(-t,-r)$. And then the idea is that 4-potentials should transform in the same way as 4-velocities transform, so that under PT a 4-potential $A^\mu(t,r)$ transforms to $A^\mu(t,r)$ on the standard view.

The first thing to note about the standard view is that it is not the mathematically natural way for a 4-vector to transform. The mathematically natural way for a 4-vector to transform under *time* reversal is for its *time*-component to flip (while its spatial components remain invariant), rather than that its spatial components flip (and its time-component remains invariant). Now, I do not deny that one can coherently conceive quantities that transform as the standard view has 4-potentials and 4-velocities transform, but these are rather weird and unnatural quantities, and we should not assume odd quantities in nature unless we need to do so. My guess is that the (psychological) explanation of the near universal adoption of the standard view is that we are accustomed to thinking in terms of 3-velocities, and are not used to thinking that

---

[4] Again, for simplicity, I am ignoring the idea that A^μ corresponds to a connection on a fibre bundle.

whether an object is moving from B to A rather than from A to B can be encoded by the temporal component of its 4-velocity rather than the spatial components of its 4-velocity. But whatever one thinks of this explanation, my first argument for the non-standard view that $A^\mu(t,r)$ transforms to $-A^\mu(-t,-r)$ under PT is that the mathematically most natural quantities (which behave like 4-vectors under the restricted Lorentz transformations) transform in this way under PT.

My next argument, which in essence I presented when I introduced my non-standard view, is that spatial and temporal derivatives transform in my way under PT; that is, ∂/∂^μ transforms to $-\partial/\partial^\mu$ under PT. So, in particular, if there is an interaction between a 4-potential (or a 4-velocity) and a scalar field which is governed by an interaction Lagrangian which includes a term such as $(\phi^\star \partial^\mu \phi - \phi \partial^\mu \phi^\star)A_\mu$, then this term will switch signs under PT on the standard view, so that (generically) the interaction will not be invariant under PT, which is odd and undesirable. ($\star$ stands for complex conjugation.) That is to say, my second argument against the standard view is that it has as a consequence that 4-potentials (and 4-velocities, and more generally primitive 4-vectors) transform differently under T (and also under PT) from the way in which gradients of scalar fields transform. This is neither simple nor natural, and leads to difficulty in forming T-invariant (and PT-invariant) interactions between these two types of 4-vectors.

For my third argument I will turn to the 'complex Lorentz transformations'. The set of all ordinary, 'real', Lorentz transformations forms a group of transformations that splits into 4 disconnected components. Parity (the mirroring of all three spatial axes) is a Lorentz transformation. But in the space of all possible Lorentz transformations there is no continuous path that starts out at the identity and ends up at parity. (The pure spatial rotations are all continuously connected to the identity, as are the pure Lorentz boosts, but one cannot reach parity by pure boosts or pure rotations or combinations of the two.) So the real Lorentz group splits into at least two disconnected components: the Lorentz transformations that one can reach via a continuous path from the identity (the 'restricted' Lorentz transformations), and the Lorentz transformations that one can reach via a continuous path from parity. And there is another split—between the Lorentz transformations that include time reversal and those that do not. So the Lorentz group has at least four disconnected components. In fact, one can show that it has exactly four disconnected components.

Now, the Lorentz transformations of 4-vectors can be represented as 4×4 matrices L, with real entries acting on 'columns' of four real numbers representing the 4-vectors, where these matrices have the property that they preserve the Minkowski inner product between the columns. The demand that each L preserves the Minkowski inner product amounts to the demand that $L^{TR}GL=G$, where L^{TR} is the transpose of L, and G is the matrix whose diagonal entries equal 1,−1,−1,−1, and whose off-diagonal entries equal 0. While it is natural to suppose that the matrix L^{PT} representing PT (in some inertial frame of reference) should be the matrix whose diagonal entries each equal −1 and whose off-diagonal entries are 0, this is not the only possible representation of the real Lorentz group. Another possibility, for example, is one in which PT is represented as the identity matrix (though this is not a 'faithful' representation).[5]

However, let us now turn to the complex Lorentz group, which can be introduced abstractly as the so-called 'complexification' of the real Lorentz group. It is easiest to think of the complex Lorentz group in terms of a representation by means of 4×4 matrices with complex entries which preserve the Minkowski inner product, that is, the set of 4×4 complex matrices L such that $L^{TR}GL=G$. Perhaps somewhat surprisingly, the fact is that within the complex Lorentz group, PT *is* connected to the identity. Here is why. The following is a one-parameter subset of the complex Lorentz matrices, where the parameter is t:

$$\begin{pmatrix} \cosh it & 0 & 0 & \sinh it \\ 0 & \cos t & -\sin t & 0 \\ 0 & \sin t & \cos t & 0 \\ \sinh it & 0 & 0 & \cosh it \end{pmatrix}$$

For $t=0$ we find that L_t is the identity. Continuously increasing t to $t=\pi$ we arrive at minus the identity, which is a representation of PT. So, $A^\mu(t,r)$ transforms to $-A^\mu(-t,-r)$ if it transforms as an element of the standard (four-dimensional) representation of the complex Lorentz group. A similar argument establishes that a scalar field which is invariant under the restricted Lorentz transformations must be invariant under PT.

Note that the above argument does not tell us how $A^\mu(t,r)$ transforms under P or T separately; for in the complex Lorentz group, P and T are not connected to the identity. There can be so-called 'pseudo-scalar' fields, 'pseudo-vector' fields, and 'pseudo-tensor' fields, which flip sign under P and under T. Of course, the above argument is not completely compelling, for it depends on the assumption that the fields transform as elements of the standard representation of the complex Lorentz group. All I can say is that this seems a fairly natural and simple assumption to me.

A final, fourth, argument for the claim that $A^\mu(t,r)$ must transform to $-A^\mu(-t,-r)$ under PT, and that a scalar field must be invariant under PT, can be given if one makes the assumption that the only types of quantities that can occur in our theories must be (restricted) Lorentz invariant tensor quantities. Let me begin this argument by indicating how one can manufacture 'pseudo-tensors'—tensors whose sign flips under P and under T—using tensors that are invariant under the restricted Lorentz transformations. Consider the totally anti-symmetric Levi–Civita tensor $\mathcal{E}_{ABCD}$. It is invariant under restricted Lorentz transformations, and can be taken to represent an objective spacetime orientation (spacetime-handedness). One can also use it to manufacture a pseudo-scalar field from four distinct vector fields. Suppose that vector fields V^A, W^B, X^C, and Y^D each flip their time component under time reversal T. Let us take it that spacetime orientation is a geometric, invariant, object represented by $\mathcal{E}_{ABCD}$. Then the pseudo-scalar $\Sigma_{ABCD}\mathcal{E}_{ABCD}V^AW^BX^CY^D$ will transform to $-\Sigma_{ABCD}\mathcal{E}_{ABCD}V^AW^BX^CY^D$

---

[5] A 'faithful' representation of a group (by matrices) is one whereby each distinct element of the group is represented by a distinct matrix.

under T. So in this manner one can manufacture pseudo-scalars whose signs flip under P and T. However, one cannot in this manner manufacture pseudo-scalars whose signs flip under PT. For a proof, see Greaves (manuscript). (The basic idea of this proof is as follows. Any tensor representing a temporal orientation has to have an odd number of spacetime indices; it has to have to have odd rank. But one can show that there are no tensor fields of odd rank that are invariant under the restricted Lorentz transformations.) So $A^\mu(t,r)$ transforms to $-A^\mu(-t,-r)$ under PT.

On the basis of these four arguments let us accept that $A^\mu(t,r)$ transforms to $-A^\mu(-t,-r)$ under PT. It immediately follows that Maxwell's equations for the free electromagnetic field, $\Box A^\mu - \partial^\mu(\partial_\nu A^\nu) = 0$, are invariant under PT.

Let us examine one more example: a complex Klein–Gordon field ϕ interacting with the electromagnetic field. For ease of presentation let me represent the electromagnetic field using both the 4-potential A^μ and the Maxwell–Faraday tensor $F^{\mu\nu}$. The following Lagrangian then gives a dynamics for the interacting fields:

$$L = \partial^\mu\phi \star \partial_\mu\phi - m^2\phi\star\phi - \tfrac{1}{4}(F^{\mu\nu}F_{\mu\nu}) + e^2 A_\mu A^\mu \phi\star\phi - ie(\phi\star\partial^\mu\phi - \phi\partial^\mu\phi\star)A_\mu$$

Is this theory invariant under PT? Well, suppose that under PT the 4-potential $A^\mu(t,r)$ transforms to $-A^\mu(-t,-r)$. The Maxwell–Faraday tensor and the 4-potential are related via the following equation: $F_{\mu\nu} = \partial_\mu A_\nu - \partial_\nu A_\mu$. It follows that the Maxwell–Faraday tensor is invariant under PT. The complex scalar field is invariant under PT, so $\partial^\mu\phi$ flips sign under PT. All of this taken together implies that each of the five terms of the Lagrangian is separately invariant under PT. So the Lagrangian is invariant under PT. So this dynamics is invariant under PT.

It should be obvious from this last example that the PT-invariance of my sample theories is not a coincidence. If one's theory derives its dynamics from a local Lagrangian, where this Lagrangian is a Lorentz-scalar built (by contractions and summations) from tensors, each of which transform as indicated under PT, then this Lagrangian, and hence one's dynamics, will be invariant under PT.

In fact, J. S. Bell (1955) has proved a general classical PT theorem along these lines. Here is a statement of it. Let us suppose that the equations of a theory can be stated in the following form: $F^i(\phi, A^\mu, \ldots, \partial^\nu\phi, \partial^\lambda A^\mu, \ldots) = 0$, where $\phi, A^\mu, \ldots$ are fields which transform as tensors under the restricted real Lorentz transformations (those that are connected to the identity), that the $\partial^\nu\phi, \partial^\lambda A^\mu, \ldots$ are finite order derivatives of the tensor fields, and the F^i are finite polynomials in these terms. Then the equations are invariant under PT, when the representation of PT in some frame is

$$\begin{pmatrix} -1 & 0 & 0 & 0 \\ 0 & -1 & 0 & 0 \\ 0 & 0 & -1 & 0 \\ 0 & 0 & 0 & -1 \end{pmatrix}$$

At this point one might very well ask what all of this has to do with charge conjugation. Well, notice that under the above PT transformation all 4-vectors flip. In particular herefore, any charge-current 4 vector, such as $ie(\phi^\star\partial^\mu\phi-\phi\partial^\mu\phi^\star)$ in the case of the complex Klein–Gordon field, will 'flip over' under PT. So any charge density, which is the first component of a charge-current 4-vector, will flip sign under PT. So the PT transformation, when properly conceived, has as a consequence that the PT-transformed fields behave as if they have opposite charge. So, what standardly is called the CPT transformation should really have been called the PT transformation. This also provides an answer as to how it can be that what is allegedly a combination of two geometrical transformations (PT) and a non-geometrical transformation (C) has to be a symmetry of any quantum field theory. The answer I am suggesting is that what is standardly called the CPT transformation really is a geometric transformation—namely, the PT transformation—and that invariance under PT, and lack of invariance under each of P and T, corresponds to the fact that our spacetime has spacetime-handedness structure, but neither a spatial-handedness nor a temporal orientation.

Note also that one can include classical particles (rather than just fields) in our considerations by making the assumption that the 4-velocities V^μ of particles flip over under PT. We can then, for example, consider an interaction between a charged particle and the electromagnetic field which is governed by the following Lagrangian:

$$L=-\tfrac{1}{4}(\partial_\mu A_\nu-\partial_\nu A_\mu)(\partial^\mu A^\nu-\partial^\nu A^\mu)-qV_\mu A^\mu$$

It is clear that this Lagrangian is invariant under our PT transformation. Moreover, note that if we switch the sign of q and switch the sign of the 4-velocity V^μ, while keeping A^μ invariant, then the Lagrangian is invariant. That is to say: flipping over the 4-velocity of a particle is equivalent to flipping the sign of the charge q. So, again, PT, when properly conceived, includes charge conjugation. (For a more extensive discussion of the classical charged particle case, see Arntzenius and Greaves (2007).)

7.4 PT in quantum field theories when one takes wave-functions as the fundamental quantities

The basic idea of this section is very simple. In quantum field theory, particle states correspond to 'positive frequency' solutions of the corresponding classical field theory, while anti-particle states correspond to 'negative frequency' solutions. Since PT turns positive frequency solutions into negative frequency solutions, PT in quantum field theory turns particles into anti-particles.[6] Now for some details.

Let us start with the classical free complex Klein–Gordon equation: $(\partial^\mu\partial_\mu+m^2)\phi=0$. This equation has plane wave solutions: $\phi_k=exp(ik_\mu x^\mu)$, where $k_\mu k^\mu=m^2$. Any solution $\phi(x)$ is a unique superposition of these plane wave solutions: $\phi(x)=\int f(k)exp(ik_\mu x^\mu)dk$.

[6] Particles which are their own anti-particles correspond to real solutions, which are superpositions of positive and negative frequency complex solutions. One can choose to represent these real solutions by the corresponding positive frequency complex solutions, but this does not affect the fact that time reversal leaves the type of particle invariant.

Relative to a given direction of time, we will call plane wave ϕ_k with positive k^0 a 'positive frequency' plane wave, and a plane wave ϕ_k with negative k^0 a 'negative frequency' plane wave. More generally, any solution that is a superposition of positive frequency plane waves will be called a positive frequency solution, and any solution that is a superposition only of negative frequency plane waves will be called a negative frequency solution. The particle Hilbert space $\mathcal{H}$ of the quantized Klein–Gordon field and the operators on it, can be constructed from the positive frequency solutions to the classical Klein–Gordon equation, and the anti-particle Hilbert space $\mathcal{H}$ can be constructed from the negative frequency solutions to the classical Klein–Gordon equation. Here is how. (In this section I am largely following Geroch (1971). Any errors are all mine.)

Start by assuming that there is a 1–1 correspondence between single-particle Hilbert space states $|\phi\rangle$ and positive frequency solutions $\phi(x)$ to the classical Klein–Gordon equation. The superposition of two Hilbert space state is the Hilbert space state corresponding to the addition of the two corresponding positive frequency solutions; that is, $|\phi_1\rangle + |\phi_2\rangle$ corresponds to positive frequency solution $\phi_1(x) + \phi_2(x)$. Scalar multiplication of a particle Hilbert space state corresponds to scalar multiplication of the corresponding positive frequency solution: $c|\phi\rangle$ corresponds to $c\phi(x)$. The inner product between two particle Hilbert space states is defined as $(|\phi_1\rangle, |\phi_2\rangle) = \int f_1(k) f_2{}^\star(k) dk$. This defines the particle Hilbert space.

The single anti-particle Hilbert space is constructed in analogous fashion, now using the negative frequency solutions, *except* that multiplication of an anti-particle state by a complex number c corresponds to multiplication of the corresponding classical solution with the complex conjugate number of that number: $c^\star$. That is, if $|\phi\rangle$ corresponds to $\phi(x)$, then $c|\phi\rangle$ corresponds to $c^\star\phi(x)$. The inner product between two anti-particle Hilbert space states is defined as $(|\phi_1\rangle, |\phi_2\rangle) = \int f_1{}^\star(k) f_2(k) dk$. This defines the anti-particle Hilbert space.

Since it is important for what follows, let me explain why multiplication by a complex number c of the anti-particle Hilbert space states corresponds to multiplication by $c^\star$ of the corresponding negative frequency solution. Associated with a constant time-like vector field r^a on Minkowski spacetime is an energy operator $\hat{e}$, which acts on solutions of the complex Klein–Gordon equation in the following way: $\hat{e}\phi(x) = -ir^a\nabla_a\phi(x)$. Here, multiplication by i means multiplication of the Hilbert space state $|\phi\rangle$, not (pointwise) multiplication of the (complex) classical field $\phi(x)$. Now, suppose that multiplication of a Hilbert space state did correspond to (pointwise) multiplication of the corresponding solution $\phi(x)$, both for negative frequency solutions and positive frequency solutions. Then the expectation value of $\hat{e}$ for $\phi(x)$ would be $\int r^a k_a f(k) f^\star(k) dk$. This is positive for any k which points in the same direction of time as r, and negative for any k which points in the opposite direction of time from r. That is to say, anti-particles and particles would then have opposite signs of energy. This would be a disaster. In the first place, it is experimentally known that particles and anti-particles have the same sign of energy: they can annihilate and thereby produce energy (particles with non-zero energy), rather than that their total energy is 0. Moreover, in an inter-acting theory, one would beget radical instability: decays into deeper and deeper negative energy states would be allowed which would release unlimited amounts of positive energy. This is no good. We need the energies of particles and anti-particles to have the same sign (though it is perfectly acceptable if what sign that is is a matter of convention.) So we choose the Hilbert space structure of the anti-particle state-space such that $c|\phi>$ corresponds to $c^\star\phi(x)$ for negative frequency solutions $\phi(x)$. For then the expectation value of $\hat{e}$ equals $\int_{M+}r^a k_a f(k)f^\star(k)dk - \int_{M-}r^a k_a f(k)f^\star(k)dk$, where M+ is the positive mass shell, and M− is the negative mass shell; that is, the first integration is over momenta that point in the same direction of time as r, and the second integra-tion is over momenta that point in the opposite direction of time as r. This has as a consequence that the energies of particles and anti-particles have the same sign.

Let me clarify and emphasize one more point. At the beginning of this section I arbitrarily picked some direction of time, and called plane wave solutions 'positive frequency solutions' if their wave-vector pointed in that direction of time. Later I associated particles with positive frequency solutions and anti-particles with negative frequency solutions. And then I said that multiplication of a Hilbert space particle state by a complex number c corresponded to multiplication of the corresponding positive frequency solution by c, while in the anti-particle case it corresponded to multiplica-tion of the corresponding negative frequency solution by $c^\star$. None of this implies that spacetime has a temporal orientation. All I have made use of is that there is a fact of the matter as to whether two time-like vectors point in the same direction of time, or in opposite directions of time. Which direction of time gets called the future, which the past, which solutions get dubbed positive frequency and which negative frequency, which Hilbert space state multiplication corresponds multiplication of the corres-ponding solution by c and which corresponds to multiplication by $c^\star$—all of that can be taken to be a matter of convention. But that the two directions, the two frequency types, and the two particle types are not identical—that is not a matter of convention. Let me now continue with the construction of the full particle and anti-particle Hilbert spaces. (So far we have only the single particle and single anti-particle Hilbert space.)

Given the single particle Hilbert space $\mathcal{H}$, we can build the corresponding Fock space $\mathcal{F}$

$$\mathcal{F} = \mathbb{C} \oplus \mathcal{H}^\alpha \oplus (\mathcal{H}^{(\alpha} \otimes \mathcal{H}^{\beta)}) \oplus \cdots.$$

Here $\mathbb{C}$ is the space of complex numbers, and the $\mathcal{H}^\alpha$, $\mathcal{H}^\beta$ and so on, are simply copies of $\mathcal{H}$. The brackets around the indices indicates the restriction to symmetrical states in the tensor product Hilbert spaces. A typical element of this Fock space is $|\psi> = (\chi, |\chi>^\alpha, |\chi>^{\alpha\beta}, \dots)$. Here, χ is a complex number representing the amplitude of the vacuum state, $|\chi>^\alpha$ is an element of $\mathcal{H}^\alpha$—a one-particle state, $|\chi>^{\alpha\beta}$ is an element of $\mathcal{H}^{(\alpha} \otimes \mathcal{H}^{\beta)}$ —a two-particle state, and so on. Similarly, given the single anti-particle Hilbert space $\underline{\mathcal{H}}$ we can build the corresponding Fock space:

$$\mathcal{F}=\mathbb{C}\oplus\underline{\mathcal{H}}^\alpha\oplus(\underline{\mathcal{H}}^{(\alpha}\otimes\underline{\mathcal{H}}^{\beta)})\oplus\cdots.$$

(Note the underlining of the symbols associated with the anti-particle Hilbert spaces.)

We can then define the particle momentum creation operators $\hat{c}_k$ and $\hat{c}_{-k}$ which, when operating on the vacuum, create a particle in momentum eigenstate $|k>, |-k>$, respectively—that is, create a particle and the corresponding anti-particle, respectively. Similarly, one can define particle momentum annihilation operators $\hat{a}_k$ and $\hat{a}_{-k}$, which, when acting on momentum eigenstate $|k>, |-k>$, respectively, produce the vacuum. Then one can define a Klein–Gordon field operator

$$\hat{\varphi}(x)=\int \hat{a}_k exp(-ik_\mu x^\mu)+\hat{c}_{-k}exp(ik_\mu x^\mu)\,dk$$

and its adjoint:

$$\hat{\varphi}^+(x)=\int \hat{c}_k exp(ik_\mu x^\mu)+\hat{a}_{-k}exp(-ik_\mu x^\mu)\,dk$$

One can then show that these field operators, $\hat{\varphi}(x)$ and $\hat{\varphi}^+(x)$, satisfy the same equation that the corresponding classical fields, $\phi(x)$ and $\phi^\star(x)$, satisfy: namely, the complex Klein–Gordon equation.[7]

Now let us turn to PT. How do quantum states $|\phi>$ transform under PT? We will begin with the single particle states. Well, under PT the corresponding classical solution $\phi(x)$ should transform to $\phi(PTx)$. If we choose our coordinate system x so that PT consists of mirroring in the origin of that coordinate system, then a classical solution $\phi(x)$ transforms to $\phi(-x)$ under this PT transformation. Given that multiplication in the anti-particle Hilbert space by c corresponds to multiplication of the corresponding solution by $c^\star$, this is an anti-linear transformation on the Hilbert space.

How do the field operators transform? Well, a particle state $|k>$ transforms to the corresponding anti-particle state $|-k>$ (given a suitable choice of phases for the momentum states), and vice versa. So $\hat{c}_k$ transforms to $\hat{c}_{-k}$ and vice versa, and $\hat{a}_k$ transforms to $\hat{a}_{-k}$ and vice versa. This, together with the fact that the transformation is anti-unitary means that the field operators $\hat{\varphi}(x)=\int \hat{a}_k exp(-ik_\mu x^\mu)+\hat{c}_{-k}exp(ik_\mu x^\mu)\,dk$ transform to $\int \hat{a}_{-k}exp(ik_\mu x^\mu)+\hat{c}_k exp(-ik_\mu x^\mu)\,dk=\hat{\varphi}^+(-x)$. So $\hat{\varphi}(x)$ transforms to $\hat{\varphi}^+(-x)$ under PT. Similarly, $\hat{\varphi}^+(x)$ transforms to $\hat{\varphi}(-x)$ under PT. But this is exactly how the standard view has it that the Klein–Gordon field operators transform under CPT! So I have argued that what standardly is called a CPT transformation in quantum field theory should really have been called a PT transformation.

Essentially the same story goes for other fields (see Geroch (1971), Arntzenius (forthcoming), and Greaves and Thomas (manuscript) for details, including how this applies to spinor fields). So standard proofs of the CPT theorem amount to proofs that relativistic quantum field theories must be invariant under what I have argued to be the PT transformation.

---

[7] One has to be a bit careful. Strictly speaking, the way I defined the field operators makes no sense. I should have smeared them out with test functions.

The crux of the argument in this section was that under PT the classical Klein–Gordon wave $\phi(x)$ should transform to $\phi(\text{PT}x)$, and hence that the quantum mechanical wave-function transforms as a (complex) scalar field. Now, if the quantum mechanical wave-function, as opposed to the operator field, is the relevant fundamental quantity, then this is justified. However, in Chapter 3 we saw that it is not at all obvious that the quantum mechanical wave-functions should be taken to be the fundamental quantities in quantum theory. In fact, we have seen that one can produce an argument that the operator fields are the relevant fundamental quantities. And then one would be justified in assuming that the scalar operator field $\hat{\phi}(x)$ transforms into $\hat{\phi}(\text{PT}x)$, which is a different transformation from the one we just discussed. Let us take a brief look at what happens when one takes the operator fields to be the fundamental quantities.

7.5   PT in quantum field theories when one takes field operators as the fundamental quantities

Greaves and Thomas (manuscript) have given a very nice proof of a CPT theorem which takes the field operators as the fundamental entities. They begin by assuming that the operator fields transform according to a representation of the universal covering group of the restricted Lorentz transformations. (The universal covering group here is needed in order to include spinor fields. Spinors are not true representations of the restricted Lorentz group; they are 'projective representations' of the restricted Lorentz group. But they are true representations of the universal covering group.) They then show that if one has a set of local differential equations for the operator fields which is invariant under Hermitian conjugation and under the transformations corresponding to the universal covering group of the restricted Lorentz transformations, one can extend this representation to a representation of a covering group ρ of the proper Lorentz transformations, which includes PT, such that the differential equations are invariant under this whole group ρ of proper Lorentz transformations, and hence under PT. They call this a CPT theorem rather than a PT theorem. Why? Well, as we saw above, one way of extending a representation of the restricted Lorentz group to a representation of the proper Lorentz group is by complexifying the representation. However, the representation ρ for which Greaves and Thomas prove invariance of the equations is not equal to this complexification, for it involves an addional Hermitian conjugation of the operator fields. In particular, this means that $\rho(\text{PT})$ sends a scalar field $\hat{\phi}(x)$ to $\hat{\phi}^{+}(\text{PT}x)$ rather than to $\hat{\phi}(\text{PT}x)$. But if one takes the operator fields as fundamental, then the PT transformation should send $\hat{\phi}(x)$ to $\hat{\phi}(\text{PT}x)$, and CPT should send $\hat{\phi}(x)$ to $\hat{\phi}^{+}(\text{PT}x)$. So they are right to call their theorem a CPT theorem rather than a PT theorem. The upshot is that if one takes the field operators as fundamental, then the standard view is right: relativistic quantum field theories must be invariant under CPT, but need not be under PT (nor under any of the components of CPT).

7.6 Conclusions

If wave-functions are the fundamental objects of quantum field theories, then spacetime has a spacetime-handedness structure, but neither a temporal orientation structure nor a spatial-handedness structure. Additionally, non-invariance under the charge conjugation operation implies that the spaces of values of the wave-functions associated with these fields have a complex conjugation structure. On the other hand, if operator fields are the fundamental objects, then spacetime has a spatial-handedness structure and a temporal orientation structure, and the space of operators has a Hermitian conjugation structure. Sorry to have such ambivalent conclusions.

8

Calculus as geometry

Frank Arntzenius and Cian Dorr

Geometry is the only science that it hath pleased God to bestow on mankind.

Thomas Hobbes

Mathematicians are like Frenchmen: whatever you say to them they translate into their own language and forthwith it is something entirely different.

Johann Wolfgang von Goethe

8.1 Introduction

Hello again. I am now going to stop talking in the first person singular, since as you can see from the heading, this chapter is written in collaboration with Cian Dorr. So from now on, when it says 'we', it means Arntzenius and Dorr.[1]

Modern science is replete with mathematics. The idea that an understanding of mathematics is an essential prerequisite to understanding the physical world is expressed in a famous quote from Galileo:

Philosophy is written in that great book which ever lies before our eyes—I mean the universe— but we cannot understand it if we do not first learn the language and grasp the symbols, in which it is written. This book is written in the language of mathematics. (Galilei (1623), p. 197)

The centrality of mathematics to physics has increased immeasurably since Galileo's time, thanks in large part to two mathematical innovations of the seventeenth century: the invention of analytic geometry (principally due to Descartes and Fermat), and the invention of the calculus (principally due to Newton and Leibniz).

First let us consider analytic geometry. We nowadays are used to the idea that geometrical figures correspond to numerical functions and algebraic equations. But this is not how geometry was done before the seventeenth century. Euclid never represented

---

[1] Credit and/or blame for this chapter belongs equally to the two authors.

geometrical figures by numerical functions; he talked of straight lines, triangles, conic sections, and so on, without ever mentioning any corresponding numerical (coordinate) functions characterizing these shapes. It is true that prior to the seventeenth century on occasion real numbers were used in order to represent geometrical figures but there was no systematic use of algebraic equations to represent and solve geometrical problems until the early seventeenth century. It was Descartes and Fermat who first established a systematic connection between geometrical objects on the one hand, and functions and algebraic equations on the other hand, by putting 'Cartesian' coordinates on space, and then using the numerical coordinate values of the locations occupied by the geometrical objects to characterize their shapes. This made a vast supply of new results and techniques available in geometry, physics, and science more generally.

Now let us turn to the calculus. We are also used to the idea that whenever one has a quantity which varies (smoothly) in time, one can ask what its instantaneous rate of change is at any given time. More generally, when one has a quantity which varies (smoothly) along some continuous dimension, we nowadays immediately assume the existence of another quantity which equals the rate of change of the first quantity at any given point along the dimension in question. However, until Galileo, in the early seventeenth century, started to make use of instantaneous velocities, instantaneous rates of change had almost no use in science. Even Galileo himself had no general theory of instantaneous velocities—had no general method for calculating instantaneous velocities given a position development—and at times made incoherent assertions about instantaneous velocities.[2] It took Newton and Leibniz to develop a general theory of instantaneous rates of change, and to develop an algorithm for calculating their values. This theory was the calculus. And of course most of physics—indeed much of modern science—could not possibly have developed without the calculus.

There are two ways in which this incursion of mathematics into physics is worrying. The first worry involves the relations that physical objects bear to mathematical entities like numbers, functions, groups, and so forth. Much of the vocabulary used in standard physical theories expresses such relations: for example, 'the mass in grams of body b is real number r'; 'the ratio between the mass of b_1 and that of b_2 is r'; 'the strength of the gravitational potential field at point p is r'; 'the acceleration vector of body b at time t is v'. Some of these 'mixed' mathematico-physical predicates have standard definitions in terms of others; but in general, some such predicates are left undefined. But there would be something unsatisfactory about this, even if we were completely comfortable with the idea that entities like real numbers are every bit as real as ordinary physical objects. We would like to think that the physical world has a rich *intrinsic* structure that has nothing to do with its relations to the mathematical realm, and that facts about this intrinsic structure explain the holding of the mixed relations between concrete and mathematical entities. The point of talking about real

---

[2] For instance, he gave a fallacious argument that it was impossible for instantaneous velocities to be proportional to distance traversed.

numbers and so forth is surely to be able to *represent* the facts about the intrinsic structure of the concrete world in a tractable form. But physics books say hardly anything about what the relevant intrinsic structure is, and how it determines the mixed relations that figure in the theories. So there is a job here that philosophers need to tackle, if they want to sustain the idea that the truth about the physical world is determined by its intrinsic structure.

The second worry has to do with the very *existence* of mathematical entities—numbers, sets of ordered pairs, Abelian groups, homological dimensions of modular rings, and so on. These things are not part of the physical universe around us. They do not interact with physical objects—or at least, they do not do so in anything like the way in which physical objects interact with one another. Some, including us, consequently cannot shake the suspicion that *mathematical objects do not really exist*.[3] But if they do not exist, should not it be possible, at least in principle, to characterize the physical world without talking about them at all? Here is another job for philosophers: to find alternatives to standard 'platonistic' (mathematical-entity-invoking) physical theories which can do the same empirical explanatory work without requiring any mathematical entities to exist.

We will call the project of responding to the first worry, by showing how all the 'mixed' vocabulary of some platonistic physical theory can be eliminated in favour of 'pure' predicates all of whose arguments are concrete physical entities, the 'easy nominalistic project'. To the extent that we are moved by the second worry, we will want not only to find such predicates, but to write down some simple laws stated in terms of them which presuppose nothing about the existence of mathematical entities. Call this the 'hard nominalistic project'.

There is an influential line of thought (propounded by Putnam (1971) amongst others) that has convinced many philosophers that the second worry, about the very existence of mathematical entities, is misplaced. The idea is that just as the success of theories which entail that there are electrons (for example) gives us good reason to believe that electrons do in fact exist, so the success of theories which entail that there are real numbers gives us the same kind of reason to believe that real numbers do in fact exist.

One concern about this thought is the fact that, whereas we ended up with electron-positing theories as a result of a rather thorough exercise in which these theories were compared with a wide range of rivals which did not posit electrons, and the latter theories were found wanting, scientists have generally invested no effort in even developing alternatives to standard theories that do not posit the same range of mathematical entities, let alone in comparing their merits. Instead, practicing scientists simply take it for granted that they can help themselves to as many mathematical entities as they like—their attitude in this case is utterly different to their attitude towards the positing of physical entities. Because of this, it appears rash to take the fact that all of our currently most empirically successful theories presuppose the existence of certain

---

[3] See Dorr 2007 (section 1) for some attempts to clarify the meaning of this claim.

mathematical entities as a good reason to assume that there are no other equally successful theories that avoid such presuppositions. Since scientists do not seem interested, the task of looking for such theories and comparing them with the usual ones—the hard nominalistic project—falls on philosophers.[4]

There are *prima facie* reasons to be optimistic about this undertaking. For very often, standard mathematical physics invokes mathematical entities that have 'surplus structure' relative to the physical phenomena. For example, when we 'put' a coordinate t on, say, time, we are assuming the existence of a function from a very rich structure—the real line—onto a much less rich structure—time. The rich structure of the real number line includes both an 'addition structure' and a 'multiplication structure': there are facts about which real number you obtain when you add two real numbers, and which real number you obtain when you multiply two real numbers. Time does not have any such structure: it does not make sense to ask which location in time you produce when you 'add' two locations in time, or 'multiply' two locations in time. Or to be more precise: we could *introduce* meanings for 'add' and 'multiply' on which this would make sense; but in order to do this, we would have to make some arbitrary choices which are not in any sense dictated by the nature of the entities we are dealing with, namely, times. (For example, assuming the falsity of the view discussed in Chapter 1, according to which time lacks metric structure, we could institute such meanings by choosing one instant of time, arbitrarily, to call 'zero', and another to call 'one'.) The disparity between the two structures is revealed by the fact that there are many different coordinate functions that are equally 'good'—equally well adapted to the task of representing the kind of structure that time really does have. It is natural to suspect that this detour through an unnecessarily rich structure can be cut out. There has to be some way of characterizing time intrinsically, other than by saying which coordinate functions on it count as 'good'; and once we have settled on a systematic way of doing this, it seems plausible that we would then have a way to say what needs to be said without dragging real numbers into the picture at all.

Even if the hard nominalistic project went as well as we could possibly hope—even if we found some general algorithm for systematically turning any scientific theory into an equally simple, empirically equivalent theory free from all presuppositions about the existence of mathematical entities—some philosophers would remain unmoved. There are some who think it is just obvious that mathematical entities do exist, independent of any detailed results from empirical science. Some say: look, real scientists seem to treat it as obvious that these things exist, since they constantly

---

[4] Dorr (2010) argues that the it is not so hard to find such laws, since given any platonistic theory T, the theory that T follows from the truth about the concrete world together with certain mathematical axioms can provide satisfactory explanations of the phenomena putatively explained by T, without committing us to the actual existence of mathematical entities. However, the task of evaluating such 'parasitic' theories raises tricky epistemological issues. In this chapter, we will be looking for theories which avoid talking about mathematical entities altogether, even in the scope of modal operators. If we can find them, our response to the 'indispensability argument' for the existence of mathematical entities will be on firmer epistemological ground.

presuppose their existence in theorizing about other subject matters, and take no
interest (at least, no professional interest) in the project of coming up with theories
which do not make require such a presupposition; if this attitude is good enough for
them, it should be good enough for us. We will not try to argue anyone out of attitudes
like this. But we will just note a couple of things. First, if it turns out that the kinds
of empirical considerations that might support belief in electrons do not similarly
support the belief that there are mathematical entities, that would be an interesting
epistemological discovery even if it in fact the latter belief is well-justified for some
other reasons. Second, your understanding of platonistic physical theories will be
deeper if you understand when quantification over mathematical entities is merely
playing an expressive role that could equally well have been achieved in some other
way, and when—if ever—it is really essential. And third, even if you think it is completely absurd to suppose that mathematical entities do not exist, you could and should
be interested in the easy nominalistic project of finding some pure predicates which
characterize the intrinsic structure of the physical world upon which the relations
between physical and mathematical entities supervene. And once you have gone this
far, you should care about finding physical laws that are simple when expressed in
terms of your chosen primitive predicates. Even if you do not mind quantifying over
mathematical entities, this could turn out to be a highly non-trivial task, and might
require overcoming many of the same challenges posed by the hard nominalistic
project. For example, you will want to find simple geometric axioms which entail that
the intrinsic structure of space is such as to allow coordinates to be assigned in a way
that respects that structure.

Historically, those who have worried about the existence of numbers, sets, and so
forth have often also worried about the existence of regions of space, time, or spacetime. Other chapters of this book have argued that we really do have good empirical
reason to believe in these entities. Theories that posit them are genuinely simpler, and
for that reason more credible, than theories that do not. So in searching for ways of
doing physics without quantifying over real numbers, sets, functions, and so on, we will
want to pay special attention to the work that geometric entities can do in providing
substitutes for such quantification. It is instructive in this regard to see that two of the
fathers of the mathematization of physics, Galileo and Newton, favoured the 'geo-
metrization' of physics, not the 'arithmetization' of physics. To see that this is what
Galileo thought, let us extend that famous quote from Galileo a little beyond the place
that it is usually ends. Here is how it continues:

...This book is written in the language of mathematics, and the symbols are triangles, circles,
and other geometrical figures, without whose help it is impossible to comprehend a single word
of it; without which one wanders in vain through a dark labyrinth.

Galileo's 'language of mathematics' seems to be the language of *geometry*, not of
arithmetic or algebra. Newton, in turn, was extremely critical of Descartes' analytic
geometry, in which geometry and algebra are joined together:

To be sure, their [the ancients'] method is more elegant by far than the Cartesian one. For he [Descartes] achieved the result by an algebraic calculus which, when transposed into words would prove to be so tedious and entangled as to provoke nausea, nor might it be understood. (Newton (1674–84), p. 317)

Henry Pemberton, who knew Newton well, had this to say:

I have often heared him [Newton] censure the handling of geometrical subjects by algebraic calculations . . . and speak with regret of his mistake at the beginning of his mathematical studies, in applying himself to the works of Des Cartes and other algebraic writers before he had con- sidered the elements of Euclide with that attention which so excellent a writer deserves. (Pemberton (1728))

Newton eventually came to the opinion that the proper way to do calculus was as a geometric theory, by means of his 'synthetic method of fluxions', and was critical of his own earlier 'analytic method of fluxions' which relied on algebraic classifications of curves and numerical power series:

Men of recent times, eager to add to the discoveries of the ancients, have united specious arithmetic with geometry. Benefitting from that, progress has been broad and far-reaching if your eye is on the profuseness of an output, but the advance is less of a blessing if you look at the complexity of its conclusions. For these computations, progressing by means of arithmetical operations alone, very often express in an intolerably roundabout way quantities which in geometry are designated by the drawing of a single line. (Newton (1674–84), p. 421)

Perhaps the above quotes do not quite amount to a ringing endorsement of a full-on attempt to rid physics of all real numbers, sets, functions, groups, and the like. Still, we will take ourselves to be encouraged by Newton and Galileo, and set off on that enterprise. We will start by summarizing, and slightly amending, the one serious attack on the hard nominalistic project that has been made up to now: Hartry Field's nomi- nalization of Newtonian gravitational physics (Field 1980). After that we will attempt to push the project forward by developing a way of nominalizing the theory that lies at the heart of modern calculus and modern physics: the theory of differentiable manifolds.

8.2 Nominalizing Newtonian gravitation

Field undertakes a case study in the hard nominalistic project. He considers a certain physical theory formulated in the standard way (that is, using lots of mathematical entities), and shows how to write down a completely nominalistic successor for this theory, which can do just as good a job as the original theory at explaining the phenomena. The particular physical theory that Field chooses for this case study is a version of Newtonian gravitation. Of course, this theory does not have a hope of being *true*. For one thing, it says that the only form of interaction is by gravitation, and we know perfectly well that this is not the case. So the nominalistic successor theory

Figure 8.1 The Axiom of Pasch.

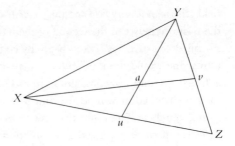

does not actually do a *good* job at explaining all that needs to be explained by a physical theory. But the point of a case study like this is to notice general strategies which we can put to work in finding nominalistic successors for other platonistic physical theories. Ultimately, we would like to consider whole families of theories sharing some general structural features. Then we could formulate general results of the form, 'so long as the phenomena do not require us to reach for mathematical tools beyond those invoked by theories of this class, they can be explained without invoking mathematical entities at all.'

One salient feature of the Newtonian theory chosen by Field is its flat spacetime setting—that of so-called Neo-Newtonian (or 'Galilean') spacetime (see Section 1.2 for an explanation.) The basis of Field's nominalistic physics is an axiomatic characterization of this Neo-Newtonian spacetime, which builds on the axiomatic Euclidean geometry developed by Hilbert (1899) and Tarski (1959), and the axiomatic affine geometry developed by Szczerba and Tarski (1965). This axiomatization uses just three primitive predicates, all of which take spacetime points as arguments: a two-place Simultaneity predicate, a three-place Betweenness predicate, and a four-place 'spatial congruence' predicate 'S-Cong'. ('S-Cong(a,b,c,d)' intuitively means that points a and b are exactly as far apart as points c and d. It is a consequence of the axioms that whenever SCong(a,b,c,d), a and b are Simultaneous and c and d are Simultaneous: this captures the fact that no notion of absolute rest is definable within Neo-Newtonian spacetime.) The axioms that Field uses are essentially nothing more than a modern, rigorous, version of the axioms that Euclid set down more than 2,000 years ago. For example, one of them is the 'Axiom of Pasch': if Between(x,u,z) and Between(y,v,z), then for some a, Between(u,a,y) and Between(v,a,x). Or in words: given a triangle xyz, with a point u on the side xz and a point v on the side yz, there is a point a where the lines uy and vx intersect (see Figure 8.1).

These axioms do not mention real numbers, functions, sets, or anything like that. Like Newton himself, the theory shuns Descartes and imitates Euclid. We will later discuss one of the axioms—a 'richness' axiom that is quite different in character from the other axioms—in a little more detail. But for now, let us push ahead and sketch Field's treatment of the contents of this spacetime.

The particular mathematical version of Newtonian gravity that Field takes as his input has two parts. First, there is a theory about the relations between two spacetime fields: the *mass density field* and the *gravitational potential*. Second, there is a theory about the relations between the second of these fields and the spatiotemporal trajectories of so-called 'test particles'. Let us begin by considering just the first part. In mathematical terms, one would think of both the mass-density field and the gravitational potential as functions from spacetime points to real numbers. Relative to any coordinate system, each such function will correspond to a function from quadruples of real numbers to real numbers. The claim that the theory makes about the relation between these fields can then be expressed as a condition on the latter functions—namely, Poisson's equation:

$$\partial^2\varphi/\partial x^2 + \partial^2\varphi/\partial y^2 + \partial^2\varphi/\partial z^2 = -k\rho$$

Here $\varphi(x,y,z,t)$ is the function from $\mathbb{R}^4$ to $\mathbb{R}$ that represents the gravitational potential and $\rho(x,y,z,t)$ is the one that represents the mass-density field. k is a constant.

This is a good illustration of the challenges involved in both the easy and the hard nominalistic project. To carry out the easy project we would need to explain what it is for a given real number to be the value of the gravitational potential or of the mass-density field at a spacetime point. Moreover, our explanation should do justice to the fact that there is something arbitrary about the use of real numbers in this connection, insofar as the mapping depends on an arbitrary choice of a unit for mass, and of a unit and a zero for the gravitational potential. To carry out the hard project, we will also have to dispense with the extensive quantification over mathematical entities required by this formulation: as things stand, we are quantifying over functions from spacetime points to real numbers (the coordinate functions), over functions from real numbers to real numbers (the coordinate representatives of the fields), and over functions from some such functions to other such functions (since differentiation is standardly explained as 'the' function of this sort satisfying certain properties).

Field's approach is as follows.[5] To talk about the gravitational potential we will use two predicates—GravPotBetweenness and GravPotCongruence—subject to one-dimensional analogues of the axioms for spatial betweenness and congruence discussed earlier. Just as the geometric axioms entail that a unique mapping from points of space to points of $\mathbb{R}^4$ is determined once we settle which points we want to map to <0,0,0,0>, <1,0,0,0>, <0,1,0,0>, <0,0,1,0> and <0,0,0,1>, so the axioms for GravPotBetweenness and GravPotCongruence will let us determine a unique mapping from points of space to $\mathbb{R}$ once we decide on a pair of points which we want to map to 0 and 1 respectively. To talk about the mass density field, we can use a single predicate MassDensitySum—where intuitively MassDensitySum(x,y,z) means that the real number that is the value of the mass density field at z is the sum of those that are its values at x and y—subject to axioms which determine a unique mapping to the real numbers once we have chosen a point (with non-zero mass density) to map

---

[5] Field is not quite explicit about the primitive predicates he wants to use in the case of the mass density field; what we describe is one way of doing it.

to the real number 1. (We use MassDensitySum rather MassDensityBetwenness and MassDensityCongruence because there is an objective fact about which points have zero mass-density, whereas there is no objective fact as to which points have zero gravitational potential, any more than there is an objective fact about which instant of time is the 'zero instant'. This also explains why numerical representations of mass-density are unique up to transformations of the form $m \rightarrow am$, rather than of the form $m \rightarrow am+b$.)

Thinking of the gravitational potential as a fundamental field on a par with mass-density may seem surprising. Since Poisson's equation completely determines the facts about the gravitational potential at each time given the facts about the mass-density field at that time, it is tempting to regard the gravitational potential as nothing more than a device for summarizing certain facts about the distribution of mass-density that have a special relevance when we are trying to figure out how things (in Field's theory, 'test particles') will accelerate at a given point. Someone who was only concerned with the easy nominalistic project could afford to go along with this attitude. But Field is engaged in the hard project: he wants a simple nominalistic *theory* which can do all of the explanatory work of the platonistic theory it replaces. Taking the gravitational potential to be a fundamental scalar field is a crucial part of Field's strategy for doing this. Without it, it is completely unclear how one could express in a nominalistically acceptable way a law determining the net force on each particle as a sum of component forces deriving from all the rest of the mass in the universe. We think Field is thinking in the right way here. As has been emphasized many times in this book, the right way to form views about the fundamental structure of the world is to be guided by the idea that the laws are simple when stated in terms of fundamental predicates. In this way we can be justified in positing fundamental structure that is 'nomologically redundant', in the sense that the facts about part of the structure follow, given the laws, from facts about the rest of the structure. For such redundancy might obtain without there being any simple definition of the redundant predicates in terms of the others.

To state a nominalistic version of Poisson's equation as given above, the central thing we need to be able to do is to take directional derivatives. For instance, we need to give a nominalistic expression which says that the derivative of the gravitational potential φ at spatial point p in direction V equals the derivative of gravitational potential φ at spatial point q in direction W (see Figure 8.2).

How do we say that? Well, in the friendly setting of Euclidean space, a vector V at a point p can be identified with a straight line $p \rightarrow p'$ which runs from p to another point p' (the direction of the line corresponding to the direction of V, and the length of the line corresponding to its magnitude), and a vector W at q can be identified with a straight line $q \rightarrow q'$. If φ were to change at a constant rate along the lines $p \rightarrow p'$ and $q \rightarrow q'$, then directional derivatives of φ at p in direction V and at q in direction W would be equal iff the ratio between the difference in the value of φ between p' and p and the difference in the value of φ between q' and q were equal to the ratio between the lengths of $p \rightarrow p'$ and $q \rightarrow q'$. Of course, generically the potential does not change at a

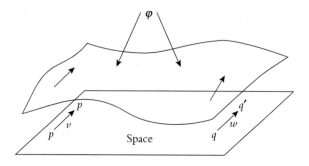

Figure 8.2 Directional derivatives.

constant rate between a point p and a point p' which is a finite distance away. So we need to take limits as we approach closer and closer to p and q, while keeping the ratio and directions fixed. Here is how to express the claim *nearly* nominalistically:

For all points w,x,y,z such that $\varphi(w)-\varphi(x):\varphi(y)-\varphi(z) > 1$, there exist a point p'' Between p and p', and a point q'' Between q and q', such that, for any point p''' Between p and p'' and any point q''' Between q and q'': if $|q{\rightarrow}q'''|{:}|p{\rightarrow}p'''|=|q{\rightarrow}q'|{:}|p{\rightarrow}p'|$, then $\varphi(y)-\varphi(z):\varphi(w)-\varphi(x) < \varphi(p''')-\varphi(p):\varphi(q''')-\varphi(q) < \varphi(w)-\varphi(x):\varphi(y)-\varphi(z)$.

Here $|q{\rightarrow}q'''|{:}|p{\rightarrow}p'''|$ is the ratio of the lengths of lines $q{\rightarrow}q'''$ and $p{\rightarrow}p'''$. The idea is that the directional derivative of φ at p in direction V equals the directional derivative of φ at q in direction W iff for any desired degree of accuracy one can find a point p'' in direction V from p, and a point q'' in direction W from q, such that for any points p''' and q''' in the same directions from p, such that their distances from p and q respectively stand in the same ratio as V to W, the ratio of the difference between values of φ at p and p''' and the difference between values of φ at q and q''' is within that degree of accuracy of 1. The 'degree of accuracy' demand is imposed by saying that it has to be smaller than $\varphi(w)-\varphi(x):\varphi(y)-\varphi(z)$ for any such ratio that is larger than 1, and also larger than its inverse.

The above is not yet expressed in terms of the primitive congruence and betweenness predicates: we have not said how to express claims about the inequality and equality of ratios of lengths of lines and of gravitational potential differences. But it is not surprising that this can in fact be done, given the central role such claims play in Euclid's geometry. (For the details of this, and about how to use these tools to express the more complicated claim about differentiation required to nominalize Poisson's equation, see Field (1980), Chapter 8.) Thus in this case at least, the grounds for optimism we mentioned in Section 8.1 are vindicated. The aspects of calculus that are needed to state the physical theory can be developed using just the geometric structure expressed by the relevant betweenness and congruence predicates, without appeal to the richer structure characteristic of the real number line. The claim quoted above may look dauntingly complex, but in fact the result of unpacking the standard definitions of differentiation in terms of limit, and of limit claims in terms of quantification over epsilons and deltas, results in something formally isomorphic.[6]

So far this is far from being anything like a fully worked out Newtonian gravitational theory. Poisson's equation determines the gravitational potential given the mass density field, but it does nothing at all to constrain the mass–density field. The second part of Field's theory, which concerns particles, gives us something a bit more like what we would have expected, since it tells us how 'test particles' move in response to the gravitational potential. The claim is a version of Newton's second law: the acceleration of each particle p is proportional to the gradient of the gravitational potential at the place where it is, divided by the particle's mass. However, the total package is still manifestly unsatisfactory, in that it says nothing about the relation between the mass-density function and the point particles, and indeed still leaves the former entirely unconstrained. There are various ways in which this particular defect could be remedied. For example, we could replace point-particles with little spheres of constant mass-density, which respond to the gravitational potential as if their masses were concentrated at their centres. Or we could try to get rid of point particles in favour of a fully fledged continuous fluid dynamics. Each of these routes raises some tricky issues. For example, with spherical particles we would need to specify what happens when there is a collision. (The easiest approach is to allow them to pass through each other; but then we will need to take all the particles that may occupy a given point into account when figuring its mass density.) Meanwhile, known theories of continuum dynamics involve lots of unrealistic singularities and discontinuities. However, none of these problems is particularly germane to the nominalistic project.

If we were to stipulate that all the test particles are equally massive, nominalizing the second part of the theory would not raise any new technical difficulties. We could just add one new primitive predicate Occupies, relating the particles to the spacetime points in their trajectories. The resources required to express the differential equation governing Occupation are similar to the ones required for stating Poisson's equation. However, allowing the particles to differ in mass brings in a few more complications, which we will discuss in the next section.

8.3 Richness and the existence of property spaces

Now let us return to the richness axiom that we briefly mentioned in the discussion of geometry above. For the sake of simplicity, let us see how this would work if we were only concerned with a one-dimensional space like time, instead of four-dimensional Neo-Newtonian spacetime. We want to say something about the

---

[6] Moreover, since the nominalistic theory lets us avoid all the complexity attendant on the usual constructions of real numbers (e.g. as Dedekind cuts of rationals, themselves construed as sets of ordered pairs of natural numbers . . .), it seems to us that even setting questions of ontological economy to one side, the nominalistic theory has a substantial advantage in terms of simplicity (when formulated in terms of fundamental predicates).

TimeBetweenness and TimeCongruence facts which entails, modulo standard mathematics, that any two functions from instants of time to real numbers which 'respect' the TimeBetweenness and TimeCongruence facts in certain specified ways are related by a linear transformation. In order to achieve this, our axioms will have to entail that there are *lots* of instants of time. For instance, if (bizarrely) there were only three instants of time *a*, *b*, and *c*, then there would only be one TimeBetweenness fact, and, generically, no TimeCongruence facts other than trivial ones such as TimeCongruent(*a*,*b*,*a*,*b*). Requiring a mapping from the three instants of time to real numbers to respect these facts does very little to constrain it, and certainly does not pin it down up to a linear transformation. And all of this holds, *mutatis mutandis*, for spacetime, mass, mass density, and the gravitational potential.

So, in each case, Field assumes a richness axiom. Here is the basic idea of the richness axiom in the case of time:

Between any two distinct instants lies another distinct instant, and for any instant there are two distinct instants that it lies between.

There are two worries about this axiom as stated. The first is that it is not strong enough to force a representation by the *real* numbers (as opposed to, say, the rational numbers). The second is that in some cases—for example, those of mass and mass-density—the axiom is *too* strong, since there might not be that many distinct masses or mass densities in the world. Field discusses the first worry at length, but largely ignores the second. Let us discuss each in turn.

The above axiom is consistent with a set of temporal congruence and betweenness facts which is representable by the rational numbers. After all, for each pair of rational numbers there is one that lies between them, and each rational number lies between two rationals. But the temporal coordinates that are used in physics are real numbers, not rational numbers. Moreover, ever since Pythagoras it has been known that the ratio between the diagonal of a square and its side is irrational. So it appears that we will need the reals rather than the rationals in order to characterize spatial distances.

Field's response to this worry involves an important new element: namely, quantification over arbitrary *regions* of spacetime as well as points. Given an ontology of regions, and a primitive predicate 'Part' that expresses their structure, one can supplement the above 'density' axiom with something like the following axiom of 'Dedekind completeness':

For all temporal regions R_1 and R_2, if no instantaneous Part of R_1 is Between two instantaneous Parts of R_2, and no instantaneous Part of R_2 is Between two instantaneous Parts of R_1, there is an instant such that whenever b is an instantaneous Part of R_1 and c is an instantaneous Part of R_2, and a≠b and a≠c, then a is Between b and c.

Here is why, intuitively speaking, this forces one to have the real numbers as coordinates. Suppose one had the rationals as coordinates. Now consider the following regions:

R_1: all the instants the square of whose coordinate is smaller than 2

R_2: all the instants the square of whose coordinate is greater than 2

Since no instant of either of these regions is between two instants of the other, our axiom of Dedekind completeness entails that there is an instant between R_1 and R_2. But such an instant cannot consistently be assigned any rational-numbered coordinate. Every rational number is either smaller than $\sqrt{2}$, in which case there are other rational numbers are bigger than it and yet still smaller than $\sqrt{2}$, or larger than $\sqrt{2}$, in which case other rational numbers are smaller than it and yet larger than $\sqrt{2}$. So we need the reals.

This response works only to the extent that our theory entails that there *are* regions like R_1 and R_2. So our theory will need to include some axioms about Parthood which provide for the necessary plenitude of regions. The canonical way of doing this is to adopt 'classical mereology', which can be axiomatized as follows:

M1 ('Reflexivity'): everything is Part of itself.

M2 ('Transitivity'): if x is Part of y and y is Part of z, x is Part of z.

M3 ('Antisymmetry'): if x is Part of y and y is Part of x, $x=y$.

M4 ('Weak Supplementation'): If x is Part of y, then either $x=y$ or y has a Part that has no Part in common with x.

M5 ('Universal Composition'): for any condition φ: if something is φ, then there is a 'fusion of the φs'—something which has every φ as a Part, and each of whose Parts shares a Part with some φ.

M6 ('Atomicity'): everything has a Part with no Parts other than itself.

However, even then there is a problem, associated with the talk of 'conditions' in M5. The problem is a somewhat technical problem in logic. Since this problem is pretty much orthogonal to the main problem in which we are interested in this chapter—namely, the problem of doing calculus, and differential geometry in particular, in a nominalistic way—we will be brief, referring you for further details to Cohen (1983), Field (1985b), and Burgess and Rosen (1997).

One way to interpret claims like M5 is to take them as expressed in something like second-order logic. Or if one wants to use English, one can use plural quantification: 'For any things whatsoever, there is something that has each of them as a Part, and each of whose Parts shares a Part with one of them.' Another approach to axioms like M5 construes them as first-order schemas. On this approach, M5 is shorthand for the infinite collection of axioms we obtain by substituting particular expressions for 'φ'. The question of which of these approaches is preferable involves deep issues in the foundations of logic which we cannot adjudicate here. But both approaches require one to be careful about the sense in which one might regard the total package of nominalistic theory as 'equivalent' to the platonistic theory upon which it was based.

It would be convenient if we could claim that the platonistic theory is *nominalistically conservative* with respect to the nominalistic one, in the sense that every consequence of the platonistic theory in which all quantifiers are restricted to spacetime regions is already a consequence of the nominalistic theory. This would give us a nice simple story about why it is acceptable to use the platonistic theory when making calculations. It would be sufficient for this to be the case if we could prove, from the mathematical axioms, a *representation theorem* to the effect that every model of the nominalistic axioms can be extended to a model of the platonistic theory (with betweenness and congruence defined in the usual ways). However, if we go for the first-order construal of the nominalistic theory, this just is not true. Anyone who has internalized the lessons of Gödel's theorems will readily understand why. Just by being so very strong, the platonistic theory (which, let us suppose, includes something like first-order Zermelo–Fränkel set theory) can prove sentences which express the consistency of the nominalistic theory, whereas by Gödel's second incompleteness theorem, these sentences cannot be proved in the nominalistic theory itself. (Such 'consistency' sentences can be expressed perfectly well in geometric terms. For example, we can construe 'proofs' as certain intricately shaped spacetime regions.)

So, the (first-order) platonistic theory entails nominalistically statable sentences which are not consequences of the (first-order) nominalistic theory. And indeed some of these consequences are extremely plausible, such as the claim that there are no pieces of paper upon which are ink marks that constitute a proof of a contradiction from the axioms of the nominalistic theory. But so what? The claim we wanted to make on behalf of the nominalistic theory was not that it systematizes absolutely everything that it is plausible for us to accept on the subject matter of spacetime and its contents. Rather, the claim was just to the effect that the nominalistic theory does as good a job as the platonistic theory at explaining the experimental data that matter for physics; the point of making this claim was to undercut a certain style of argument for the existence of mathematical entities, to the effect that only by positing them can we adequately explain those data. There are many claims about the physical world that are quite plausible for reasons that have nothing to do with experiments. Someone might argue that we should believe in the existence of an enormous hierarchy of sets on the grounds that this satisfyingly explains these kinds of truths. This strikes us as an odd sort of reason for believing in mathematical entities. In any case, it is very different in character from the one which the nominalization project is designed to undercut.

If we accept the second-order or plural version of the nominalistic theory, and think that we understand a notion of 'semantic consequence' that floats free from derivability in any formal system, then we are free to accept the claim of nominalistic conservativeness, understood as the claim that every semantic consequence of the platonistic theory with appropriately restricted quantifiers is a semantic consequence of the nominalistic theory. On this approach, the platonistic theory really can be thought of as nothing more than a useful computational device for systematizing the semantic consequences of the nominalistic theory—not all of them, but a larger subset than can be derived by applying any ordinary second-order proof theory directly to the nominalistic axioms. The question of whether this notion of semantic consequence can be understood without commitment to mathematical entities raises deep foundational questions which we will not attempt to engage with here.

An aspect of a second-order nominalistic theory that we find more worrying is the following. Once one has a second-order theory of regions, one can state claims in one's language which in effect mean the same thing as claims such as the continuum hypothesis (that is, the hypothesis that there is no cardinality in between that of the integers and that of the real numbers). Claims like this are puzzling—in part because it is hard to see how one could obtain evidence for or against their truth. Many have thought it an attractive feature of nominalism that it lets us avoid positing unknowable facts of the matter about questions such as this. But this alleged advantage is not one that can be retained if we embrace a second-order theory. (One response to the worry holds that although second-order language is intelligible, it is vague enough that claims such as the continuum hypothesis do not get a determinate truth value. But if one takes this view, it is not clear that one can legitimately claim the advantages of simplicity for a theory expressed in such vague terms.)

We will not take a stand about which of the two approaches is the better. None of the problems strike us as devastating. And even if one did think they were devastating, there would still be many reasons to be interested in the details of the nominalization project, insofar as it is illuminating to understand when talk about mathematical entities is merely giving us a way of saying something we could equally well have expressed 'intrinsically', and when it is really essential to the claim being made.

So let us set this first worry aside and turn to the second worry, to the effect that even the 'density' axiom might be *too strong* to be plausibly true of the physical world. Let us consider the case of mass *qua* property of point-particles. Suppose, for example, that there are only finitely many point particles in the world, or at any rate only finitely many equivalence classes under the 'same mass' relation. Then richness axioms about mass will plainly be false. Indeed, unless the facts about mass are especially well-behaved, there will not be anywhere near enough MassSum facts to fix numerical mass values that are unique up to scale transformations. (Note that if the particles are spatially extended and arbitrarily divisible, then there is no such problem: assuming that the mass of a particle is continuously distributed over its parts, any extended particle will then have a continuum of parts with a continuum of distinct mass properties, which will suffice to determine mass values that are unique up to scale transformations.) The same problem may arise if we take mass density as a fundamental quantity. Certainly the laws we have stated do not rule out the hypothesis that the mass–density field is discontinuous, in such a way that the world can be divided into finitely many regions, each of which is of uniform mass density. And it is not completely physically unrealistic to imagine that the world works like that, at least with respect to *some* fundamental quantities.

What should we do, if we want our strategy for nominalization not to break down in such cases? One attitude would be to say: so what?—if that is so, then numerical attributions of mass are in fact much more conventional than we took them to be. This, however, seems to us to be the wrong attitude. After all, we can get good evidence that mass values are not conventional (other than up to rescalings), for we can empirically confirm that the amount of acceleration that a particle undergoes, when it is subject to a non-gravitational force, is proportional to its mass. That is to say, we can read mass values, up to a re-scaling factor, off from the accelerations that objects undergo when subject to certain forces. (Of course, this requires certain assumptions about the magnitudes of forces in certain circumstances, but we can have well-confirmed simple laws regarding this.)

Now, the fact that we can read mass values off accelerations also suggests a remedy to our problem. For one might suggest that mass is not a fundamental quantity, but rather implictly defined by Newton's second law: the mass of particle p at t equals the ratio of the gradient of the potential at the point occupied by p at t to the acceleration of p at t. If the only mass-facts we were concerned with were facts about the mass of Fieldian 'test particles', this would be fine. We could state the laws governing such particles' trajectories as follows: (i) for any particle and any time, the particle's acceleration vector points in the same direction as the gradient of the gravitational potential; (ii) for any particle and any two times t_1 and t_2 at which its acceleration vector and the gradient of the potential are not both zero, the ratio of the magnitudes of these two vectors at t_1 is the same at their ratio at t_2. We know how to say this sort of thing nominalistically. If we wanted to allow the particles to serve as sources of gravity, by generating curvature in the gravitational potential, we can adapt a similar idea: we would then need a law to the effect that for any two particles p and q, the ratio between the 'inertial mass ratio' of p and that of q equals the ratio between the curvature of the gravitational potential around p to that around q.[7]

However, this programme crucially depends on the fact that the quantity in which we are interested (mass) is intimately associated, given the laws, with another quantity (gravitational potential) which, being continuous, is well-behaved from the point of richness axioms. In other theoretical settings, no such fall-back quantities are available. For instance, we could consider a theory of extended particles of varying mass, which move inertially except for elastic collisions. If we did not want to take any facts about the masses of the particles as fundamental, it is very hard to see how we could define them in terms of the other fundamental facts; namely, the facts about the shapes of the particles' trajectories. Well, what we can do is to say that the 'mass function' is the unique function from particles to numbers such that product of it with velocity ('momentum') and the product of it with velocity squared ('kinetic energy') are both conserved. If collisions are common enough, this may pin down a unique function (up to a linear scaling). But this definition is not at all helpful to us if we are looking for laws that are simple when stated in terms of the fundamental predicates. For it is totally unclear what we could say about the particles that would entail that *there is* any function that plays the 'mass' role just described. And it seems obviously unsatisfactory merely to *stipulate* that there is such a function, not on nominalistic grounds—probably we could code up such function talk somehow as talk about spacetime regions—but

---

[7] Ernst Mach (1893) famously argued that mass is implicitly defined by means of its role in the laws. However, since Mach was equally eager to eliminate the gravitational potential in this way, his project leads to difficulties similar to those we discuss in the next paragraph.

because, as has already been remarked on several occasions in this book, this sort of brute existential quantification is not the sort of thing that could be regarded as an explanatorily satisfactory or plausible fundamental theory.[8]

There is another strategy for dealing with this problem, which is less dependent on the details of the physical theory in question. One can assume the existence of a 'mass space', whose structure is given by MassSum relations, subject to the usual axioms, holding between points in mass space. Each particle is then assumed to 'Occupy' a single point in mass space. Note that there can be many points in mass space which are not occupied by anything. One can therefore safely assume that a richness axiom is satisfied, since all that this means is that mass space has points—whether occupied or unoccupied—corresponding to a continuum of distinct mass values. And then it will follow that the mass values of all particles (and all their parts) are determined up to rescalings, no matter how many or how few points in mass space are occupied by particles.[9]

Instead of calling the points of mass space 'points of mass space' and saying that particles 'occupy' them, one could call them 'mass properties' and say that particles 'have' them. We take it that nothing substantive turns on this choice of terminology. Calling them 'properties' might *seem* to make the positing of them less controversial. There are some views in metaphysics according to which we are obliged to posit a realm of properties as part of our fundamental ontology in any case, no matter how physics turns out. If one were to subscribe to such a view, one might see a big difference between thinking of some entities as points in an unfamiliar new kind of 'space', on the one hand, and thinking of them as belonging to the familiar category of properties, on the other hand. But this is not our attitude. As we have tried to make clear by talking (most of the time) about 'predicates' rather than 'properties', we think it is an open question, to be settled on physical grounds, whether we should posit any entities that could by any stretch of the imagination deserve the label 'properties'. And as we will see, it is quite helpful to think of entities like those we are currently contemplating as points in spaces with the same kind of geometrical structure as more familiar spaces.

In fact, the positing of ordinary space or spacetime is essentially the same sort of move as the positing of mass space: the structure of position properties of particles is (arguably, as we have seen in Chapter 5) best given by assuming the existence of a structured spacetime, and then assuming that each particle occupies a particular region in this structured spacetime. So why not similarly assume the existence of mass space, when its structure can so simply and nicely explain the usefulness, and the scale arbitrariness, of the canonical numerical representation of the mass properties of objects,

[8] See Dorr 2010 for some tentative attempts to say something general about this kind of explanatory badness.

[9] The worry about richness can be dealt with in another way, by using the richness of physical space as a surrogate for the richness of the space of possible masses. One could have a primitive predicate such as this: 'the ratio between the mass of particle x and particle y equals the ratio between the distance between points a and b and the distance between points c and d'. See Burgess and Rosen 1997 (section II.A.3.c) for more discussion of this kind of approach, which can arise as part of a systematic recipe for nominalizing a theory by replacing each variable ranging over real numbers with a quartet of variables ranging over points.

and can do so however few distinct mass properties are had by all existing objects? It seems to us that such a posit might not be so hard to justify on the grounds of the theoretical simplicity it yields.

8.4 Differentiable manifolds

Field's case study is a success so far as it goes. But we would like to be able to nominalize more recent physics. In particular, we would like to be able to have a nominalistic way of stating differential equations governing fields and particles in curved spacetimes and vector bundles, since that is how much of modern physics is done. Key to this is the notion of a differentiable manifold. When one does General Relativity, one starts with a differentiable manifold. One can then endow it with metric and affine structure, by means of a metric tensor field (and a compatible connection and volume form); and one can endow it with other kinds of physical properties, in the form of scalar, vector, and tensor fields. When one develops gauge theories, one starts with two differentiable manifolds—the spacetime manifold and the fibre manifold (which are connected via a projection map)—and one posits physically interesting structure in the form of sections of the fibre bundle, a connection on the fibre bundle, and so on. Moreover, differentiable manifolds are the minimal structure that one needs in order to do calculus. That is to say, given just a differentiable manifold (without a metric), there are facts as to which curves in the manifold are differentiable, which are n-times differentiable, which are smooth; there are facts as to which scalar functions on the manifold are differentiable, n-times differentiable, smooth; one can define vectors and vector fields; one can define directional derivatives of scalar functions; one can define differential forms; and so on. With anything less than a differentiable manifold one could not do any of this. One would just have a space with a topology, which, from the point of view of calculus, is useless.

How is a differentiable manifold normally defined? Well, one starts with a topological space M, the 'manifold'. One then divides M into overlapping open patches (regions) P, and provides each patch P with n coordinate functions; that is, for each patch P one provides a continuous, one-to-one map from P to a patch of $\mathbb{R}^n$ (the space of n-tuples of real numbers, with its standard topology). Using these coordinates, various calculus-related notions that can be defined on $\mathbb{R}^n$ get carried back to M. For this procedure to make sense, we need to guarantee that the notions in question behave in a consistent way when the patches overlap. This is achieved by requiring that when patches P_1 and P_2 overlap, then on the overlap, each of the coordinates provided for P_1 must be a C^∞ *function* of the coordinates provided for P_2: that is, for any finite integer m, the coordinates provided for P_1 must be m times differentiable with respect to the coordinates provided for P_2.

Given this condition, we can consistently make definitions such as the following. A function f from the M to $\mathbb{R}$ is *smooth* iff for each coordinate patch, the induced function from $\mathbb{R}^n$ to $\mathbb{R}$ is smooth(C^∞). Likewise, a parameterized curve in M—a

...function from $\mathbb{R}$ to M—is smooth iff for any coordinate patch, each of the real number coordinates of the curve is a C^∞ function from $\mathbb{R}$ to $\mathbb{R}$.

A *vector* v_p at a point $p \in M$ is a map from smooth functions on M to real numbers, such that

(a) $v_p(f+g)=v_p(f) + v_p(g)$
(b) $v_p(\alpha f)=\alpha v_p(f)$
(c) $v_p(fg)=f(p)v_p(g) + v_p(f)g(p)$

(See Section 2.5 above for why such a map, intuitively speaking, corresponds to a vector at a point.) A *covector* at a point p is a linear map from vectors at p to real numbers. And a *tensor of rank j, k* at p is a map that takes j covectors at p and k vectors at p to a real number, and is linear in each of its arguments.

We can define a *smooth vector field* as a function v that maps each point p to a vector at p, in such a way that whenever f is a smooth function, the function whose value at each point p is $v(p)(f)$ is itself smooth. Alternatively, we can simply identify smooth vector fields with the functions from smooth functions to smooth functions which they induce in this way. On this approach, we define a smooth vector field as a function v from smooth functions to smooth functions such that

(a) $v(f+g)=v(f) + v(g)$
(b) $v(\alpha f)=\alpha v(f)$
(c) $v(fg)=fv(g) + v(f)g$

Similarly, a *smooth covector field* can be defined as a 'C^∞-linear map' from smooth vector fields to smooth functions; that is, a function ω such that

(a) $\omega(v_1+v_2) = \omega(v_1)+\omega(v_2)$
(b) $\omega(fv) = f\omega(v)$[10]

And a *smooth tensor field* of rank j, k can be defined as a function that takes j smooth covector fields and k smooth vector fields to a smooth function, and is C^∞-linear in each of its argument. (Alternatively, as with smooth vector fields, we could treat smooth covector and tensor fields 'pointwise', as functions assigning points to covectors or tensors at those points.)

Note that by this definition, covector fields are just tensor fields of rank 0,1. Also, there is a natural correspondence between vector fields and tensor fields of rank 1,0, given in one direction by $t_v(\omega) = \omega(v)$, and in the other by $v_t(f)=t(df)$, where df is the covector field defined by $df(v)=v(f)$. So vector fields too can be regarded as a special case of tensor fields.

In the above we used a single specific set of coordinates for certain specific patches P. Of course, this seems unnecessarily specific, since any set of patches together with coordinate systems which are everywhere smooth with respect to the specific set in question would have resulted in the same characterization of differentiability and

---

[10] Here v_1+v_2 is the vector field defined by $(v_1+v_2)(f) = v_1(f)+v_2(f)$, and fv is defined by $(fv)(g)=fv(g)$.

smoothness, the same vector fields, and so on. Therefore, often textbooks characteriz
a differentiable manifold not by a unique coordinate system for a unique set of patches
but by a maximal equivalence class of coordinate systems and patches which all resul
in the same characterization of differentiability, and so on.

These ways of defining differentiable manifolds are not merely awash in real numbers
functions, sets, sets of sets, and so on; they are also spectacularly unsatisfying from a
foundational point of view. The fact that a given function from a region of physica
spacetime to $\mathbb{R}^n$ is admissible as a coordinate system surely must have some explanation
in terms of the region's intrinsic structure; but the standard approach gives us no clue
about what the relevant intrinsic structure might be like. And surely that intrinsic
structure is something that could be described independently of any division of the
manifold into patches.

There is another way of defining differentiable manifolds that is a little less hamfisted
While it too is replete with mathematical objects, it is more suggestive of directions
for the nominalistic project. In this alternative approach, a differentiable manifold is
defined as a set of points M together with a distinguished set of functions from those
points to the real numbers, which we call the 'smooth' functions. These functions are
required to obey certain characteristic axioms. Here is one version of the axioms (for
an n-dimensional manifold), from Penrose and Rindler (1984), Section 4.1. (Similar
axiomatizations appear in Chevalley (1946), Nomizu (1956), and Sikorski (1972).)

F1 If $f_1, \ldots, f_m$ are smooth functions on M, and h is any C^∞ function from $\mathbb{R}^m$ to $\mathbb{R}$,
   then the function from M to $\mathbb{R}$ whose value for any point p is $h(f_1(p), \ldots, f_m(p))$
   is smooth.

F2 If g is a function from M to $\mathbb{R}$, such that for each $p \in M$ there is an open set O
   containing p, and a smooth function f which agrees with g in O, then g is
   smooth.

F3 For every $p \in M$, there is an open set O containing p, and n smooth functions
   $x_1, \ldots, x_n$, such that (i) given any two points in O, at least one of the functions
   has a different value at the two points, and (ii) for each smooth function f,
   there is a C^∞ function h from $\mathbb{R}^n$ to $\mathbb{R}$, such that $f(p) = h(x_1(p), \ldots, x_n(p))$ for all
   p in O.

Here there is no need to take the notion of an 'open set' in M as a further primitive:
we can define S to be 'open' iff for some smooth h, $S = \{x: h(x) \neq 0\}$.[11]

---

[11] Given the standard topological definition of a 'continuous' function as one such that the inverse
image of any open set is itself open, it follows from this that all smooth functions are continuous. For any
open $O \subseteq \mathbb{R}$, we can find a C^∞ function $h_O: \mathbb{R} \to \mathbb{R}$ that is non-zero at all and only the points in O. If a region
$R \subseteq M$ is the inverse image of O under a smooth function f, then provided O does not contain zero, the
function $h_O \circ f$, which is smooth by F1, is non-zero at all and only the points in R, and so R is open. If O
contains zero but not the whole of $\mathbb{R}$, we can instead consider $h_O \circ (f + \alpha)$, where α is not in O: by F1, $f + \alpha$ is
smooth if f is. If O is $\mathbb{R}$, its inverse image is just M, which is open because constant functions are smooth,
again by F1.

These axioms are equivalent to the standard characterization in terms of coordinate patches. It is easy to verify that when we define smooth functions in terms of coordinates, F1–F3 hold; conversely, for any model of F1–F3, the functions $x_1, \ldots,$ x_n whose existence is required by F3 will play the role of coordinates for patches. So the other notions mentioned above can all be defined in terms of 'smooth function'. And in many cases—for example, the definitions of smooth vector, covector, and tensor fields given above—there is no need to mention coordinates at all in the definitions.

This is far from being a nominalistically acceptable account of differential geometry: an essential role is played not only by real numbers, but by sequences of real numbers; functions whose values are real numbers; functions whose values are such functions; and so on, quite far up into the set-theoretic hierarchy. There is an attitude towards all this which sees the triumph of calculus as a way of doing physics, as developed by Descartes, Fermat, Newton, and Leibniz, as equally a triumph for the ontology of mathematical entities. But if were not persuaded by this attitude when we were considering only Newtonian space, we should remain suspicious in the current, more general setting. Perhaps we can find a way to see the invocation of mathematical ontology in the theory as nothing more than a representational convenience.

8.5 Nominalizing differential geometry

One way for nominalists to approach physical theories stated in the vocabulary of differential geometry involves completely giving up on the idea that the metric is 'just another physical tensor field'. On this approach, one would (staying close to the approach that worked for Field in flat spacetime) characterize the geometric structure of spacetime using predicates that in the mathematical setting would be defined in terms of the metric (for example, sameness of length). Differential structure would simply be a consequence of this richer metric structure. For several reasons, we are unsatisfied with this kind of approach.

First, what if the physical theory we are trying to nominalize speaks of a space with a differential structure but no metric—a fibre bundle space, for example? Given the wide range of uses which physics has found for the concepts of differential geometry, we risk losing a lot of important generality if we only know how to nominalize theories about spaces with metrics.

Second, we do not know how to state simple axioms on predicates like 'geodesic line segment' and 'same length' which entail that space can be endowed with a differential structure and a metric in such a way that the primitive facts about geodesics and sameness of length behave as if they were defined in terms of that mathematical structure. (Of course, this will not matter to those who only care about what we have been calling the 'easy' nominalistic project, of finding some predicates of concrete physical objects which pin down the mathematical structure in which we are interested.[12])

Third, a special-purpose reconstruction of metric facts does not suggest any general method of nominalizing arbitrary physical tensor fields. Field (1980) uses quantification over pairs of points as a surrogate for quantification over vectors—essentially, vectors at p are represented as straight line segments starting at p, the length of the line segment being proportional to the magnitude of the vector. But this representation breaks down in general curved spaces. On a sphere, if you head out in a straight line from any point you eventually return to where you started. So there are not enough geodesic line segments emanating from a point to represent all the vectors there. There may be other, more complicated, 'codings' which avoid this difficulty. But the more complex the coding, the less simple the laws will look when the fundamental predicates are taken to apply to the objects which serve as surrogates for vectors under the coding.

Fourth, simplicity matters. The formalism of differential geometry allows for very simple and elegant ways of stating physical theories. Nominalistic theories which treat differential structure merely as an ancillary to metric structure risk sacrificing these virtues.

Our aim in the rest of this chapter will be to investigate the prospects for a nominalistic treatment of differential geometry, and of physical theories stated in differential-geometric terms, that stays closer to the mathematics, in treating differential structure as something independent of metric structure. In the next section we will consider whether this can be done while staying within the usual nominalistic ontology of spacetime points and regions. After that, we will turn to approaches which in one way or another go beyond this ontology.

8.6 Can we make do with points and regions?

This section will consider whether we can find what we need for nominalization of differential geometry within the usual nominalistic ontology of spacetime points and regions. We will start with the 'easy' nominalistic project: as we will see, even this turns out to be rather tricky. While it is possible to pin down the differential structure of spacetime, and physical tensor fields, using predicates of spacetime points and regions, the only ways we have found of doing this are quite ungainly. This ungainliness might well motivate even philosophers who have no scruples about mathematical entities to

---

[12] Mundy (1992) shows that the structure of a manifold carrying a metric (of any signature) can be determined by means of a three place 'Betweenness' predicate and a four-place 'Congruence' predicate. (Figuring out what to mean by 'between' in a curved spacetime is non-straightforward.) In his 1992 he seems to be concerned only with the 'easy' nominalistic project. In Mundy 1994 (pp. 92–3), he writes 'I also have some explicit axiom systems using these two primitives, but they are too complex to state here'—this is the sort of thing required by the 'hard' nominalistic project, although the remark about complexity suggests that Mundy's way of doing things will not look attractive by our standards.

posit concrete objects other than spacetime points and regions. And things look even worse from the point of view of those who, like us, care about the hard nominalistic project. We have found no way to state simple axioms using predicates only of space-time points and regions which capture the differential structure of spacetime, let alone some fully worked out physical theory about physical tensor fields on spacetime. And given the awkwardly artificial-looking character of the predicates with which we would have to work, we are not optimistic that this can be done.

We can first note that there can be no hope of pinning down the differential struc-ture of spacetime using only predicates of spacetime *points*. In a differentiable manifold with no additional structure, not only are any two points indistinguishable; any n-tuple of points all of which are distinct is indistinguishable from any other such n-tuple (that is, there is a diffeomorphism which maps each element of one n-tuple onto the corresponding element of the other n-tuple). So no non-trivial relations among points are determined by the geometric structure. By contrast, once we allow our primitive predicates to apply to regions, there are plenty of reasonable-looking candidates. For one thing, differentiable manifolds have topological structure, so it would be natural to begin with a predicate expressing topological openness (or some other topological concept interdefinable with openness).[13] And the differential structure of the space determines many other distinctive properties of regions. For example, there is the notion of a *smooth line*, or more generally, of a *smoothly embedded m-dimensional sub-region* of an n-dimensional differentiable manifold. Mathematically, a smooth line is a one-dimensional region such that for each of its points we can find a coordinate patch in which the region in question is one of the coordinate axes. Similarly, a smoothly embedded m-dimensional region is one each of whose points has a coordinate neigh-bourhood within which the region in question contains all and only those points whose last $n-m$ coordinates are zero. These look like appealing candidates to be the primitive predicates in a nominalistic treatment of differential geometry.

Unfortunately, the facts about which regions of a manifold are smoothly embedded are not sufficient to determine its differential structure. This is obvious for a one-dimensional manifold: in that case, the smoothly embedded 0-dimensional manifolds are just nowhere-dense collections of points, and the smoothly embedded one-dimensional manifolds are just the open regions, so the facts about embedded regions give us nothing beyond the topological structure. One might reasonably hope that things would work out better in higher-dimensional manifolds. After all, in a two-dimensional manifold, the facts about which lines count as smoothly embedded contain an enormous amount of information about the differential structure of the manifold, going far beyond its topological structure. But it turns out that this hope

---

[13] Taking 'Open' as primitive does not, however, look very appealing from the point of view of the hard nominalistic project: we don't know of any simple 'intrinsic' axioms which can express that a topological space is 'homeomorphic to $\mathbb{R}^n$', or which express that a space can be divided into patches each of which is homeomorphic to $\mathbb{R}^n$ (as must be the case in an n-dimensional manifold).

is misplaced: the facts about which regions in a manifold are smoothly embedded are *never* enough to pin down its differential structure. This can be seen most easily by thinking about differential structures which fail to be equivalent only at a single point. We can construct an example using the function Φ from $\mathbb{R}^2$ to $\mathbb{R}^2$, where $\Phi(<x,y>) = <x(x^2+y^2), y(x^2+y^2)>$. ($\Phi$ is just a natural generalization to $\mathbb{R}^2$ of the function $x \rightarrow x^3$ on the x axis: it moves points outside the unit circle further out, and points inside the unit circle further in, while leaving (0,0) and points on the unit circle alone.) We can use Φ to put a non-standard differential structure D' on $\mathbb{R}^2$: D' counts a function f as smooth iff $f \circ \Phi$ is smooth according to D, where D is the standard differential structure on $\mathbb{R}^2$. Since Φ is itself C^∞, every function that is smooth according to D is also smooth according to D'. But because the inverse of Φ (given by $\Phi^{-1}(<x,y>)=<x/(x^2+y^2)^{1/3}, y/(x^2+y^2)^{1/3}>$ when $<x,y> \neq <0,0>$, and $\Phi^{-1}(<0,0>)=<0,0>$) fails to be C^∞ at $<0,0>$, some functions that are smooth according to D' are not smooth according to D.[14] D and D' differ *only* at $<0,0>$, in the sense that any coordinates for a patch that does not include $<0,0>$ are admissible according to D iff they are admissible according to D'. This means that if any line were smooth according to the one structure but not the other, the lack of smoothness would have to occur at $<0,0>$. But in fact, D and D' agree about which lines are smooth at $<0,0>$. While the Φ-induced 'blowing up' of the neighbourhood of $<0,0>$ makes a difference as regards what counts as a smoothly paramaterized *curve* through $<0,0>$, it does not affect the smoothness of lines, since each curve that is smooth according to one differential structure can be reparameterized so as to make it smooth according to the other. (See Appendix A for details).[15]

So, it looks like we are going to have to be more creative in our efforts to fully characterize the differential structure of spacetime using some predicates applying to spacetime regions. If predicates of 'nice' regions such as embedded submanifolds are not giving us what we need, we had better start thinking about predicates of 'nasty' regions. For example, we might think of having a primitive predicate 'Rational', which applies to a region R iff there is some smooth function f that takes rational-number values at all and only the points in R. This gives us a finer-grained grip on the structure of the space than we get just by being told which $n-1$-dimensional surfaces are smoothly embedded: the facts about Rationality also tell us what counts as a smooth way of 'stacking up' smoothly embedded surfaces. Are the facts about Rationality enough by themselves to determine the differential structure of the manifold? The answer is 'no' for a one-dimensional manifold.[16] We are not sure of the answer in the case of a manifold of more than one dimension. However, we do have something that

---

[14] Thus for example the function $f(<x,y>) = x/(x^2+y^2)^{1/3}$, $f(<0,0>)=0$ is not smooth according to D but is smooth according to D', since $f \circ \Phi(<x,y>) = x(x^2+y^2)/(x^2(x^2+y^2)^2+y^2(x^2+y^2)^2)^{1/3} = x(x^2+y^2)/((x^2+y^2)^3)^{1/3} = x$).

[15] Special thanks to Sam Lisi for giving us this counterexample, and to Teru Thomas for helping us to understand why it is in fact a counterexample.

[16] For example, the Rationality facts in the standard differential structure on $\mathbb{R}$ will be the same as in a non-standard structure according to which f is smooth iff the function g is smooth in the standard sense, where $g(x)=f(x)$ when $x \leq 0$ and $g(x)=f(2x)$ when $x>0$.

ve know works in manifolds of more than one dimension. Consider a three-place predicate $\text{Diag}(R_1, R_2, R_3)$, given by the following mathematical condition:

or some smooth functions x and y and open region O such that x and y are two of the coordinates of an admissible coordinate system which maps O onto a convex open subset of $\mathbb{R}^n$: R_1 comprises exactly the points in O where x is rational, and R_2 comprises exactly the points in O where y is rational, and R_3 comprises exactly the points in O where $x=y$.

We can show (see Appendix B) that in a manifold of dimension at least two, the facts about Diag determine the differential structure.

This is good news for those who only care about the easy nominalistic project, and are not too fussy about having artificial-looking primitives. But it is of no obvious use for the hard nominalistic project: we have no idea how to write down some simple axioms involving 'Diag' which guarantee that the Diag facts behave in such a way as to be generated by some differential structure. Well, of course we could just have an axiom that *says* 'there is a differential structure on the set of spacetime points such that $\text{Diag}(R_1, R_2, R_3)$ holds exactly when the above condition obtains according to that differential structure'. But first, this involves quantification over mathematical entities, which we are trying to avoid. And second, even if one did not mind this, the existentially quantified form of this axiom is something we have learned to be suspicious of. Saying that *there is* a differential structure from which the Diag relation can be generated is like saying that *there is* an assignment of masses and charges to particles that fits with the pattern of their accelerations, or like saying that *there is* a way of assigning a velocity field to the points within some homogeneous sphere in such a way that such-and-such laws are obeyed. As we keep on saying, this is not the sort of thing we are looking for when we look for simple laws.

Still, maybe we are just being dim—maybe there is some lovely set of primitives and axioms that we have not thought of, that has exactly the desired effect of capturing the differential structure of spacetime without recourse to any unorthodox ontological posits. So let us continue our investigation of the easy nominalistic project, and see what further predicates of spacetime points and regions we might need to introduce in order to characterize the physical fields that make the world an interesting place rather than a mere void. We have already encountered the tools we need for a nominalistic treatment of physical scalar fields, and these can be characterized using appropriate FieldSum, or FieldBetweenness and FieldCongruence, predicates. But physical theories also talk about other kinds of tensor fields; how are we to capture these? As we have seen, the standard mathematical treatment of these entities places them quite high up in the set-theoretic hierarchy. If we want even to be able to talk about these fields nominalistically, we will need to find some nominalistic surrogates for vectors and covectors at points. Given such surrogates, we could hope to capture, say, a physical covector field Ω using a three-place predicate '$\Omega(v_1) = \Omega(v_2) + \Omega(v_3)$', where v_1, v_2 and v_3 are (surrogates for) vectors at points, not necessarily the same point. Similarly, a physical tensor field T of rank 1,1 would be captured by a six-place predicate

Figure 8.3 A vector surrogate.

'$T(v_1,\omega_1)=T(v_2,\omega_2)+T(v_3,\omega_3)$', which holds only when v_1 is a vector(-surrogate) at certain point, ω_1 is a covector(-surrogate) at that point, and so on.[17]

As we saw, Field uses straight line-segments emanating from a point as his surrogate for vectors at that point. But in the present context, this option is not available to us since we do not have notions of straightness or length to work with—we are hoping to treat the metric as just another tensor field, rather than crafting some special-purpose accounts of metric notions like straightness and length. Fortunately, classical mereology is strong enough to provide us with other entities which can more directly and naturally play the role of vectors and covectors at points.

Before we see how this can be done, let us first see how we could proceed if we were allowed to help ourselves not only to regions, but to countably infinite ordered *sequences* of points. In that case, we could take the infinite sequences of points converging to p as our surrogates for the vectors at p. (See Figure 8.3).

This works because intuitively, vectors are things with 'directions' and 'rates'. We can make sense of the question of whether two sequences of points approach p from the same direction; and when they do approach from the same direction, we can make sense of the question how much faster one approaches than the other. To be more precise, recall that the essential job description of a vector at p is to be something which, given a smooth function f as input, returns a real number, 'the directional derivative of f with respect to that vector'. When σ is a sequence of points $<\sigma(1)$, $\sigma(2),\ldots>$ converging to p, define the directional derivative of f with respect to σ, which we will call $\sigma[f]$, as $\lim_{n\to\infty} n(f(\sigma(n))-f(p))$. (Essentially, what we are doing here is treating the nth point of σ as if it were the point $\gamma(1/n)$ on a curve γ such that $\gamma(0)=p$, and taking the directional derivative of f along γ.) It is straightforward to show that when $\sigma[f]$ and $\sigma[g]$ are both defined, the defining rules of a directional derivative at p are satisfied:

  (a) $\sigma[f+g]=\sigma[f]+\sigma[g]$
  (b) $\sigma[af]=a\sigma[f]$
  (c) $\sigma[fg]=f(p)\sigma[g]+g(p)\sigma[f]$

Of course, many different sequences of points will serve as surrogates for the same vector at p, in the sense that they yield exactly the same directional derivative for each smooth function. Intuitively, two sequences correspond to the same vector when they

---

[17] For a physical vector field V, we might think of simply using a one-place predicate which applies to a vector-(surrogate) at p iff it is the value of V at p. But this would give us no way of accomodating the idea that there is an arbitrariness involved in the choice of units for a vector field, which is physically plausible in many cases. One easy way to represent a physical vector field while allowing for such arbitrariness is to use a 3-place predicate '$\omega_1(V) = \omega_2(V)+\omega_3(V)$' taking covector(-surrogates) as arguments.

P   HLS[2]   HLS[1]

Figure 8.4 A half-line sieve HLS with home point p.

approach p at the same rate and from the same direction. This will happen whenever two sequences share a terminal segment, and it can also happen even if the sequences have no points in common. This multiplicity in the representation of vectors is not a worry in so far as we are only looking for some entities which can serve as arguments for some primitive predicate representing a physical covector field, or tensor field of rank $0, k$. We can simply claim that whenever two sequences are equivalent in this way, they are intersubstitutable with respect to the relevant predicates. Similarly, there are ill-behaved sequences which converge to a point but do not correspond to any vector at that point, because they approach the point too densely or too irregularly for the directional derivative of each smooth function to be defined. But we could simply claim that the relevant physical predicates do not apply to these ill-behaved sequences.

Among the well-behaved sequences of points converging to p, the differential structure of the space will let us introduce relations corresponding to the structure of a vector space. We can say that σ_1 'represents the sum of σ_2 and σ_3' iff for any smooth function f, $\sigma_1[f] = \sigma_2[f]+\sigma_3[f]$. Similarly, for any real number α, σ_1 'represents the result of multiplying σ_2 by α' iff for any smooth function f, $\sigma_1[f] = \alpha\sigma_2[f]$. Of course, since the relation between well-behaved sequences and vectors is many-one, there are many different sequences that represent the sum of two given sequences, or that represent the result of multiplying a given sequence by a real number. Since we are currently only dealing with the easy nominalistic project, there is no need to take these relations as primitive. The facts about which functions are smooth are determined by the facts about the Diag relation, and the facts about which sequences are well-behaved, and which represent sums and multiples of which, are determined by the facts about which functions are smooth.

So in an ontology enriched with the capacity to build infinite sequences, finding surrogates for vectors would be easy. And it turns out that sequences are unnecessary: their work can be done equally well by certain regions. Let a 'half-line-sieve' HLS with 'home point' p be a topological line which has countably many point-sized holes, such that the holes converge to p from one side only. (See Figure 8.4.)

More precisely, a region HLS is a half-line-sieve with home point p iff

(a) Cl(HLS) (the topological closure of HLS) is a non-self-intersecting *topological line* (i.e. a connected region such that there are at most two points the deletion of which fails to yield a disconnected region).

(b) The holes of HLS—that is, the points that are not part of HLS but are part of Cl(HLS)—are infinite in number.

(c) In Cl(HLS), p is not between any two of the holes of HLS. That is, for any two of the holes of HLS, there is a connected part of Cl(HLS) that includes them but does not include p.

(d) Any open region containing p includes all but finitely many of the holes of HLS.[18]

See Figure 8.2 for a picture of a half-line sieve. (Note that we have drawn HLS as a straight line (with holes), since that is easiest to draw, but no significance is attached to this. Being a half-line-sieve with home point p is a purely topological relation between regions and points.)

Clause (iv) ensures (given a reasonably well-behaved topology—to wit, a Hausdorff space) that each half-line sieve has a unique home point. Moreover, there is a natural ordering on the holes of any half-line sieve HLS. q comes before r in this ordering iff every continuous path within Cl(HLS) from q to the home point of HLS passes through r. Since by (iv) each half-line-sieve HLS at p has only finitely many holes outside any open region that includes p, each hole can have only finitely many predecessors in this ordering. Thus HLS must have an *outermost* hole—one such that in Cl(HLS), all the other holes of HLS are between it and the home point of HLS. Call this hole 'HLS[1]'. Similarly, HLS[2] is the second-to-last hole of HLS; HLS[3] is the third-to-last hole, and so on. Thus each half-line-sieve with home point p encodes an infinite sequence of points converging on p. When HLS encodes a sequence of points σ, we let the directional derivative of f with respect to HLS, HLS[f], be the same as $\sigma[f]$ as defined above.

Mereology and topology also provide entities suited to serve as surrogates for *covectors* at points. Again, we will first show how to proceed in an ontology enriched with infinite sequences, and then show how to encode the relevant sequences as single regions. Our approach will codify a common heuristic thought according to which covectors at a point are like collections of $n-1$-dimensional surfaces near that point. (See Figure 8.5.)

Our initial surrogate for a covector at p will be an infinite sequence, $\rho = <p, O, P_1, P_2, \ldots>$, where O is a simply connected, regular open region containing p, and the P_i are pairwise disjoint, connected regions, each of which contains just enough points to

---

[18] Note that the above definition requires us to have a predicate which means that a region contains at most finitely many points. Intuitively speaking such a predicate seems nominalistically acceptable: to say that there are finitely many points in a region need not commit us to the existence of numbers, or any other mathematical entities. We could add 'contains finitely many points' to our list of primitive predicates. Or to be more flexible, we could have 'contains at least as many points as' as primitive, and define 'R contains finitely many points' as 'no proper part of R contains at least as many points as R'. If we want to write down axioms which ensure that these new primitive predicates behave in the way we want, we will be confronted with puzzles similar to those discussed in section 8.3 with respect to first- and second-order formulations of richness axioms. But these puzzles are going to arise in any case for the hard nominalistic project. Another possible route is to define such cardinality predicates in topological terms. In a well-behaved manifold of dimension at least two, when R and S are disjoint regions each of whose points has an open neighbourhood that contains none of their other points, R contains at least as many points as S iff there is a region that contains both R and S, every maximal connected part of which contains exactly one point of R and at most one point of S. And we can extend this to non-disjoint regions by taking disjoint regions as intermediaries.

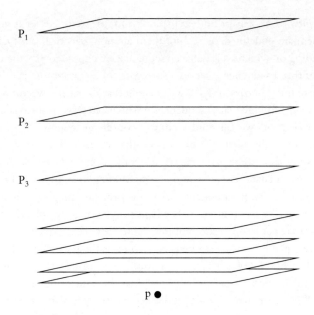

P_1

P_2

P_3

p ●

Figure 8.5 A covector surrogate.

split O in two. That is, O\$P_i$ (the fusion of parts of O that do not overlap P_i) is disconnected, while for every point q in P_i, O\(P_i\$q$) is connected. (In an n-dimensional
manifold, this ensures that the P_i are $n-1$-dimensional.) We also require that the P_i get
closer and closer to p from one side. That is, (i) whenever $j>i$, getting from P_i to p while
staying on a connected path within O requires passing through P_j, and (ii) every open
region containing p should intersect all but finitely many of the P_is.

The essential job of a covector at p is to yield a real number when given a vector at
p as input. So what we need to do with our sequences ρ is to say what it is for a real
number to be the result of applying ρ to σ, when σ is a well-behaved infinite sequence
of points converging to p—a surrogate for a vector at p. We will start by using $\rho=<p,$
$O, P_1, P_2, \ldots >$, to define a function which maps each point q in O to a natural number,
which we will write as $\rho[q]$. When every continuous path from q to p passes through
one of the P_i, $\rho[q]$ is the number of surfaces P_i in ρ that lie 'outside' q—that is, for
which there is a path from p to q in O that does not pass through P_i. Otherwise, $\rho[q]=0$.
We will use this to define $\rho[\sigma]$, where σ is one of the well-behaved sequences that
serve as surrogates for vectors at points. Let 'σ_-' name any well-behaved sequence that
'represents the result of multiplying σ by -1'. As we saw above, for each well-behaved
σ this operation is well-defined (though not unique). Then we let $\rho[\sigma]$ name which-
ever of the following quantities is non-zero:

$$\rho^+[\sigma] = \lim_{n \to \infty} n/(\rho[\sigma[n]])$$
$$\rho^-[\sigma] = -\lim_{n \to \infty} n/(\rho[\sigma_-[n]])$$

(We define $\rho[\sigma]$ to be zero if both $\rho^+[\sigma]$ and $\rho^-[\sigma]$ are zero; we let it go undefined if both of them are undefined, or both of them are non-zero, or if $\rho^-[\sigma]$ takes different values depending on which well-behaved sequence we choose to play the role of '$-\sigma$'.)

The idea is that a sequence ρ serves a surrogate for a covector ω_p at p iff whenever σ is a surrogate for v_p, $\rho[\sigma] = \omega_p(v_p)$. We can show that for each covector ω_p, there is at least one (in fact, infinitely many) sequences ρ which can serve as surrogates for ω_p. For given any covector ω_p, we can find a convex coordinate system x, y ... on an open neighbourhood O of p such that ω_p is $d_p x$—that is, for any vector v_p at p, $v_p(x) = \omega_p(v_p)$—and such that $x(p)=0$ and $x(q)=1$ for some q in O. Given such a system of coordinates, we can take the sequence ρ_x corresponding to ω_p to be $\{p, O, x=1, x=1/2,$ $x=1/3, x=1/4, \dots \}$. The requirement that the coordinates map O to a convex set in $\mathbb{R}^n$ means that each of the regions $x=1/n$ is just big enough to split O in two, as the definition of a covector-surrogate requires. Note that when $x(q)$ is positive, $\rho_x[q]$ is approximately equal to $1/x(q)$—to be precise, $\rho_x[q]$ is the greatest whole number less than or equal to $1/x(q)$. $\rho_x[q]$ is zero when $x(q)$ is zero or negative. Because of this, it follows from the definitions of $\rho_x[\sigma]$ and $\sigma[x]$ that these quantities are equal.[19]

We can call ρ 'well-behaved' if $\rho[\sigma]$ is defined for every well-behaved σ. (Of course, not every ρ meeting the given topological conditions is well-behaved: the surfaces may crowd in on p too densely or too irregularly.) When ρ_1, ρ_2, and ρ_3 are well-behaved sequences of surfaces, we can say that 'ρ_1 represents the sum of ρ_2 and ρ_3' iff $\rho_1[\sigma] = \rho_2[\sigma]+\rho_3[\sigma]$ for every well-behaved σ, and we can say that 'ρ_1 represents the result of multiplying ρ_2 by α' iff $\rho_1[\sigma] = \alpha\rho_2[\sigma]$ for every well-behaved σ.

So, given the ability to form sequences, there is no trouble cooking up entities which can play the role of covectors at points. And it turns out that with a bit of trickery, we can find single regions which can serve as codes for the relevant sequences of surfaces. The idea is simple: we will code $<p, O, P_1, P_2, P_3, \dots >$ as the result of mereologically subtracting p and all the P_is from O. Call the result of doing this O−: a region with one point-sized hole and infinitely many $n-1$-dimensional 'cracks'. We can recover O from O− as the interior of its closure (recall that O was required to be a regular open region). We can recover p itself as the only disconnected *point* in O\O−. (This will work provided our manifold is at least two-dimensional, so that the P_i are not points.) The P_i are just the remaining maximal connected parts of O\O−. Finally, we need to recover the numerical indices on the P_i. This can be done because of the requirement that the relation 'every path from P_i to p in O must pass through P_j' holds exactly when $i<j$. Let us call the kind of region that can be derived in this way from

---

[19] Let σ and σ_- be some well-behaved sequences of points converging to p such that $\sigma[x]$ and $\sigma_-[x]$ are well-defined and $\sigma_-[x] = -\sigma[x]$. It is easy to see that if $\sigma[x] = \lim_{n\to\infty} nx(\sigma[n])$ is positive, it must be equal to $\rho_x[\sigma] = \lim_{n\to\infty} n/\rho[\sigma[n]]$. For if the former limit is positive, then the points of σ must eventually settle into the region of O where x is positive; but within that region, $x(\sigma[n])$ and $1/\rho[\sigma[n]]$ are approximately equal. For the same reason, if $\rho_x^+[\sigma]$ is positive, it must be equal to $\sigma[x]$. Similarly, if $\sigma[x]$ is negative, it must be equal $\rho_x^-[\sigma] = \lim_{n\to\infty} n/\rho[\sigma_-[n]]$, and if the latter quantity is negative, it must be equal to $-\sigma_-[x]=\sigma[x]$. Finally, if $\sigma[x]$ and $\sigma_-[x]$ are zero, both $\lim_{n\to\infty} n/\rho[\sigma[n]]$ and $\lim_{n\to\infty} n/\rho[\sigma_-[n]]$ must be well-defined and equal to zero. For if it is true that for every positive ε we can find an n such that $-\varepsilon<x(\sigma[m])<\varepsilon$ for all $m>n$, it must also be true that for every positive ε we can find an n such that $-\varepsilon<1/\rho[\sigma[m]])<\varepsilon$ for all $m>n$.

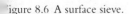

Figure 8.6 A surface sieve.

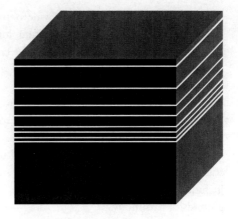

an appropriate $<p, O, P_1, P_2, P_3, \ldots >$ a 'surface sieve'. (See Figure 8.6 for a picture.) Surface sieves, then, can serve as surrogates for covectors at points within an ontology of spacetime regions. Any physical tensor field can thus be taken as determined by some appropriately polyadic predicate applying to half-line sieves and surface sieves.

If you only care only about the easy nominalistic project of finding pure relations among concrete objects in terms of which the mixed predicates that appear in platonistic physical theories can be defined, then you may feel satisfied at this point. However, we have found no way to carry out the hard nominalistic project (of stating simple nominalistically acceptable laws) within the confines of an ontology of spacetime points and regions. When we attempt to describe the distinctive behaviour of our Diag relation, to characterize the 'well-behaved' half-line sieves and surface-sieves, or to say what it is for two half-line sieves to 'correspond to the same vector' or for two surface sieves to 'correspond to the same covector', we constantly run up against the need to quantify over *functions* on the manifold—entities for which we have no nominalistic surrogates. It appears that the hard project can only be carried out if we somehow enrich the ontology. In the next section we will consider one especially simple way to do this.

Note that even if you do not agree with us about the importance of the hard nominalistic project, you might find this investigation interesting. For as you have probably noticed, the ways we have found of recovering the vocabulary of a platonistic physical theory from primitive predicates applying to points and regions seem a bit cheesy and artificial. Even if you do not care about nominalism, you may find it unsatisfying to have to accept such predicates as primitive. If so, it will be worth seeing whether an enriched ontology can provide a more elegant way of doing things.

8.7 Differentiable structure via scalar-value space

Since our expressive difficulties involved the need to quantify over functions from spacetime points to real numbers, the obvious strategy to consider is to enrich the ontology in such a way as to provide nominalistic surrogates for such functions. I[n] this section we will do this by positing, for each spacetime point, a miniature one[-] dimensional space—a 'scalar-value line'—endowed with a rich structure making it i[n] effect a copy of the real line. We will call the collection of all the points on all thes[e] scalar-value lines 'scalar-value space'. One option would be to regard points in scalar[-] value space as further entities disjoint from spacetime points, with a primitive relatio[n] determining a mapping from the former to the latter. Alternatively, we could simpl[y] identify the spacetime points with the scalar-value lines themselves. For we are sti[ll] going to be helping ourselves to classical mereology—so as well as all the points o[f] scalar-value space, our ontology will contain arbitrary regions of scalar-value space[,] including the scalar-value lines themselves. We will choose the latter approach, on th[e] grounds of parsimony.

To work out this approach rigorously, we will need to say what the structure i[s] which determines a natural equivalence relation of 'belonging to the same scalar-value line', and makes each of these lines 'work like a copy of the real numbers'. We can bor[-] row here from any of the many known axiomatizations of the theory of real numbers[.] Since we have mereology, we have regions within each scalar-value line, which wil[l] work like *sets* of real numbers; so we will want to look at second-order axiomatization[s] of the real numbers. The axiomatization we will choose owes much to one develope[d] by Tarski (1936), although we will not avail ourselves of all of his ingenious simplifica[-] tions. Besides the primitive predicate 'Part' from mereology, it has one three-place primitive predicate Sum, and two one-place primitive predicates Positive and Unit. The Sum relation holds only within each scalar-value line: in fact, we will officially define a scalar-value line as a maximal region such that whenever x and y are atomic parts of it, there is a z which is an atomic part of it such that $Sum(x,y,z)$. The axioms we need are as follows.

First, we have some axioms for 'Sum', according to which it gives each scalar-value line the structure of an Abelian group.

A1 If $Sum(x,y,z)$, then x, y and z lack proper parts (are scalar-value points).

A2 If $Sum(x,y,z_1)$ and $Sum(x,y,z_2)$ then $z_1 = z_2$ (Functionality).

A3 If $Sum(x_1,x_2,y_1)$ and $Sum(x_2,x_3,y_2)$ then for some y_3, $Sum(x_1,x_3,y_3)$ (scalar-value lines do not overlap).

A4 If $Sum(x,y,z)$ then $Sum(y,x,z)$ (Commutativity).

A5 If $Sum(a,b,c)$, $Sum(c,d,e)$ and $Sum(b,d,f)$, then $Sum(a,f,e)$ (Associativity).

A6 If a is atomic, then there is a b ('minus a') such that whenever $Sum(a,b,z)$ and a and c belong to the same scalar-value line, $Sum(c,z,c)$. (Existence of additive inverses.)

We will henceforth allow ourselves to use standard arithmetical notation to talk about scalar addition, writing '$a+b=c$' instead of $Sum(a,b,c)$, and so on. 'z is a zero' will abbre[-] viate 'z lacks proper parts and whenever $Sum(z,x,y)$, $x=y$'. Of course, we have many zeroes—one in each scalar-value line.

Second, we have axioms for 'Positive'. To state these axioms it will help to have some definitions: '$x<y$' abbreviates 'there is a Positive z such that $Sum(x,z,y)$)'; '$x\leq y$' means '$x=y$ or $x<y$'; for regions X and Y, 'X<Y' means that for any atomic parts x and y of X and Y respectively, $x<y$; and similarly for 'X$\leq$Y'. In these terms, the axioms say that $\leq$ is a Dedekind-complete, dense, total order on each scalar-value line.

P1 Everything Positive lacks proper parts.
P2 If x and y are Positive, $x+y$ is Positive ('< is transitive').
P3 Whenever x is Positive, $-x$ is not Positive. ('$\leq$ is antisymmetric').
P4 Whenever x is atomic and not zero, either x or $-x$ is Positive ('$\leq$ is total').
P5 If x is Positive, there exist Positive y and z such that $Sum(y,z,x)$ ('$\leq$ is dense').
P6 If X<Y, then there is a z such that X$\leq z$ and $z\leq$Y ('$\leq$ is Dedekind complete').

Finally, we have two axioms about Units:

U1 Every scalar-value line contains exactly one Unit.
U2 Every Unit is Positive.

Note that we need not take multiplication as primitive: using quantification over regions, it can be defined in terms of Sum, Positive, and Unit.[20] Also, note that in this theory it makes perfectly good sense to ask whether two points in different scalar-value lines are 'equal in value' (correspond to the same real number). For we can think of all the zeroes as equal in value and all the Units as equal in value; and this extends to other points in a uniquely natural way.[21] Appendix C shows that, assuming standard mathematics, the above axioms determine a unique one-to-one mapping π_l from the real numbers to points in each scalar-value line l, with the properties that $\pi_l(\alpha+\beta)=\pi_l(\alpha)+\pi_l(\beta)$, $\pi_l(\alpha)$ is Positive iff $\alpha>0$, and $\pi_l(\alpha)$ is a Unit iff $\alpha=1$.

A *scalar field* will be a special kind of region in scalar-value space—one which overlaps each scalar-value line at exactly one point. Given the structure of the scalar lines, there is a natural correspondence between scalar fields so defined, and functions from

---

[20] The definition uses Eudoxus's method of ratios. First we define what it is for a region R of a scalar line to be 'x-spaced', when x is Positive: R is x-spaced iff x is part of R, and every atomic part of R is Positive, and whenever y and z are parts of R such that $y<z$, $y+x$ is a part of R and $y+x\leq z$. Next we define 'a:$b \leq c$:d' in the case where a and b are both Positive and on the same scalar-value line, and c and d are both Positive and on the same scalar-value line: this means that whenever we have regions A, B, C and D which are respectively a-spaced, b-spaced, c-spaced and d-spaced, and A and C contain equally many points, and B and D contain equally many points, and no point in B is greater than every point in A, then no point in D is greater than every point in C. 'a:$b = c$:d' means 'a:$b \leq c$:d and c:$d \leq a$:b'. This lets us define multiplication of Positive scalar-value points: '$a\underline{x}b = c$' means that a:$u = c$:b, where u is the Unit in the same scalar-value line as a. Finally we extend this definition in the obvious way to the case where a, b and c are not all Positive: '$ab = c$' means 'either $a\underline{x}b = c$ or $-a\underline{x}-b = c$ or $-a\underline{x}b = -c$ or $a\underline{x}-b = -c$ or c and at least one of a and b are zero'. (We have helped ourselves here to the notion of two regions containing equally many points. See note 18 above for further discussion.)

[21] We can define 'equal in value' using the Eudoxan definition of 'a:$b = c$:d' from note 20: a and b are equal in value iff either a and b are both zeroes, or a and b are both Positive and a:$u_1 = b$:u_2 (where u_1 is the Unit in a's scalar-value line and u_2 is the Unit in b's scalar-value line), or a and b are both negative and $-a$:$u = -b$:u.

the manifold to the real numbers. But our 'scalar fields' are regions in a concrete space, not mathematical constructs.

This fundamental ontology does not merely contain many collections of entities isomorphic to the real numbers. It also contains some entities we might think of as uniquely natural candidates to *be* the real numbers; namely, the *constant* scalar fields— those scalar fields any two points of which are equal in value. The notions of addition and multiplication of scalar-value points can be extended to constant scalar fields in an obvious way. Because of this, one might doubt whether this fundamental ontology properly deserves to be thought of as 'nominalistic'. But let us not get hung up on the label. The project is to look for an ontologically parsimonious, simple theory of the world; we should not be ashamed to take inspiration from mathematics in working out such a theory. We have entities that behave just like the real numbers; indeed, we also have entities—namely, the *fusions* of constant scalar fields—that behave like sets of real numbers. But we are still far from having to accept the full set-theoretic hierarchy. This seems to us like a genuine theoretical gain.

Since we now have scalar fields in the ontology, there is a very obvious strategy for charaterizing the differential structure of the space: we will simply introduce a new, one-place primitive predicate 'Smooth', taking scalar fields as arguments. For as we saw in Section 8.4, there is a natural mathematical characterization of a differentiable manifold as a set together with a distinguished class of 'smooth' functions from that set to the real numbers; our nominalistic theory of Smooth scalar fields can be developed in analogy to this characterization. What we need to do now is show how to state some axioms that guarantee that 'Smooth' behaves as it should; that is, that the facts about which scalar fields are Smooth uniquely determine a differentiable structure in the mathematical sense (assuming standard mathematical axioms).[22] Basically, we are just going to adapt axioms F1–F3 from Section 8.4, replacing talk of functions with talk of scalar fields. The technical challenges we face in doing this are first, reconstructing quantification over *finite sequences* of functions/scalar fields; and second, saying nominalistically that one scalar field 'can be represented as a C^∞ function of' a given sequence of scalar fields. The trick we use to respond to both challenges involves using mereological fusions of scalar fields as proxies for certain sets of scalar fields—namely, those sets where all the scalar fields involved are continuous, and no two of them overlap. (In that case, the members of the relevant set can be recovered as the parts of the fusion that are continuous scalar fields.)

---

[22] The precise status of this representation theorem will depend on the logical issues discussed in Section 8.3. If we use second order logic to formulate the mereological axiom of universal composition, then it will be true that the conjunction of the nominalistic axioms and (second order versions of) the set-theoretic axioms has as a semantic consequence that there is a unique differentiable structure that fits in the natural way with the Smoothness facts. In a first-order setting, the truth in the vicinity will be a bit more complex, but the dialectical situation will in any case be the same as was discussed in Section 8.3 *vis-à-vis* Field's theory.

To state the axioms we will need some more defined predicates, as follows:

- 'R is a spacetime region': every scalar-value line that overlaps R is part of R.
- 'c is the value of f at p' ($f[p] = c$'): c is a constant scalar field, f is a scalar field, p is a scalar-value line (a spacetime point—remember that we are identifying them with scalar-value lines), and c, f, and p have a part in common.
- 'R is a basic open spacetime region': for some Smooth scalar field h, R contains all and only those scalar-value lines at which the value of h is non-zero.
- 'R is an open spacetime region': R is composed of basic open spacetime regions (every part of R shares a part with some basic open region that is part of R).[23]
- 'f is a continuous scalar field': f is a scalar field, and for any constant scalar fields a and b, the fusion of spacetime points p such that $a[p]<f[p]<b[p]$ is an open spacetime region.
- 'R is bounded': for every continuous scalar field f there are constant scalar fields a and b such that for point p in R $a[p]<f[p]<b[p]$.
- 'F is a multifield': F is a fusion of non-overlapping, continuous scalar fields. (That is, every part of F overlaps some continuous scalar field that is part of F, and no two continuous scalar fields that are part of F overlap.)
- 'f is a component of F': f is a continuous scalar field that is part of F.
- 'f is fixed by F in O': f is a scalar field, and F is a multifield, and whenever two spacetime points p and q in O are such that every component of F takes the same value at p and q, f takes the same value at p and q.
- 'g is the partial derivative of f in coordinate h of F in O': f and g are scalar fields, and F is a multifield, and O is an open spacetime region, and h is a component of F, and f and g are both fixed by F in O, and for each point p in O, and each constant scalar field ε, there is a non-zero constant scalar field δ such that: for any q in O, if every component of F other than h takes the same value at p and q, and $h[p]-\delta<h[q]<h[p]+\delta$, then $g[p]-\varepsilon<(f[q]-f[p])/\delta<g[p]+\varepsilon$. (This looks daunting, but it is really just a transcription of the usual definition of a partial derivative.)
- 'f is C^∞ relative to F in O': f is a continuous scalar field, and f is a component of some multifield G such that whenever g is a component of G and h is a component of F, there exist g', α, β such that: α and β are constant scalar fields, and α is non-zero, and g' is continuous, and g' is the first derivative of g with respect to coordinate h of F in O, and $\alpha g'+\beta$ is part of G.

What is going on this last definition is this. If we had arbitrary sets of scalar fields to work with, we could define 'f is C^∞ relative to set S in O', as 'there is a countable set H of continuous scalar fields which contains f, and is closed under the operation of taking partial derivatives in O with respect to members of S'. The fact we are appealing to is that when O is *bounded*, the existence of such a set H is equivalent to the existence

---

[23] It turns out that given the axioms all open regions are basic open regions (see Penrose and Rindler 1984).

of a countable set of continuous scalar fields G *no two of which overlap* (and which is thus representable by a multifield), such that whenever a scalar field g is in G, and g' is the partial derivative of g with respect to some member of S in O, then some function of the form $\alpha g' + \beta$ (where α is non-zero) is in G. For on a bounded O, all the members of H will be bounded, so we can choose the αs and βs in such a way as to ensure that they do not overlap.

With these definitions in place, we can state our nominalistic versions of F1–F3:

FN1   If F is a multifield with finitely many components each of which is Smooth, and f is C^∞ relative to F in every bounded open region O, then f is Smooth.

FN2   If f is a scalar field and if for each spacetime point p there is an open region O containing p, and a Smooth scalar field g which coincides with f in O, then f is Smooth.

FN3   For each spacetime point p there exists a bounded open region O containing p, and a multifield X composed of n Smooth scalar fields, such that (i) X does not take the same values at any two points of O, and (ii) every Smooth scalar field is C^∞ relative to X in O.

If we were being really careful we would at this point prove a representation theorem showing that any model of FN1–FN3 corresponds to a differentiable manifold in the sense of F1–F3. But since the axioms are so close, this is routine, and we will not try your patience with more details.

OK, that is it. We have shown how to say that the world has the structure of an n-dimensional differentiable manifold, without making use of sets, sets of sets, and so on. All we have done is posit a scalar-value space whose structure is given by a few simple axioms, stated using just five primitive predicates: Part, Sum, Positive, Unit, and Smooth.

8.8 Physical fields in scalar-value space

However, this is not the end of the matter. We want to be able to describe not just a featureless void but an interesting manifold with physical fields (and perhaps particles too, but that is not difficult). Let us start with the simplest physical fields: namely, scalar fields. If we were dealing with a physical scalar field that had a 'preferred' unit value, this would just be a matter of introducing a corresponding primitive one-place predicate that picks out exactly one of the scalar fields as 'physically distinguished' or 'occupied'. But more commonly, talk of physical scalar fields turns out to involve some arbitrary choices. It is a matter of convention when to say that the field 'has value 1' at a point of spacetime; in some cases, it may also a matter of convention when to say that the field 'has value 0' at a point of spacetime. If so, we will want our primitive predicate to give us a way of describing the physical field without making these conventional choices. The easiest way to achieve this is to keep a one-place primitive predicate 'Occupied' of scalar fields, now governed by a law according to which whenever s_2 is non-zero constant multiple of s_1 (or if the field lacks a non-arbitrary zero point, whenever s_2 is the sum of a non-zero constant multiple of s_1 and a constant), then s_2 is Occupied iff s_1 is. Another, less stipulative way to avoid arbitrary choices of units is one we have encountered before: namely, to employ primitive 'FieldAddition' (or 'FieldBetween' and 'FieldCongruence') relations whose relata are spacetime points. Given laws guaranteeing the relevant richness assumption (guaranteeing, for example, that the field varies continuously), this would let us define what it is for a scalar field to be 'occupied', and it would be a theorem rather than an axiom that scalar fields that differ only by a constant multiple (or by a constant multiple and the addition of a constant) are alike as regards occupation.

Note that we do *not* need to assume a separate ontology of 'field value points' corresponding to each physical scalar field. No matter how many physical scalar fields there are, we can characterize their behaviour using predicates of regions in our single scalar-value space.

Now let us turn to physical vector fields. There are at least three ways in which one could incorporate a physical vector field into the current approach.

In the first place one could be old-fashioned, and think of a vector field V in terms of its coordinate representations relative to local coordinate systems. For instance, in a four-dimensional spacetime manifold, a vector field V in a region R can be represented by a quadruple of four components v_1, v_2, v_3, v_4 relative to coordinate system x_1, x_2, x_3, x_4 for R. These components are different relative to different coordinate systems: relative to coordinates y_1, y_2, y_3, y_4, the components of V are:

$$v'_1 = v_1(\partial y_1/\partial x_1) + v_2(\partial y_1/\partial x_2) + v_3(\partial y_1/\partial x_3) + v_4(\partial y_1/\partial x_4)$$
$$v'_2 = v_1(\partial y_2/\partial x_1) + v_2(\partial y_2/\partial x_2) + v_3(\partial y_2/\partial x_3) + v_4(\partial y_2/\partial x_4)$$
$$v'_3 = v_1(\partial y_3/\partial x_1) + v_2(\partial y_3/\partial x_2) + v_3(\partial y_3/\partial x_3) + v_4(\partial y_3/\partial x_4)$$
$$v'_4 = v_1(\partial y_4/\partial x_1) + v_2(\partial y_4/\partial x_2) + v_3(\partial y_4/\partial x_3) + v_4(\partial y_4/\partial x_4)$$

In the current approach this conception can be used in the following way. Our physical vector field V is characterized by a (2N+1)-place relation $V(v_1, \ldots, v_n, x_1, \ldots, x_n, R)$ such that if $x_1, \ldots, x_n$ are Smooth scalar functions which coordinatize R, then there are unique smooth scalar functions $v_1, \ldots, v_n$ such that $V(v_1, \ldots, v_n, x_1, \ldots, x_n, R)$. Moreover, the above rule of transformation applies: if $V(v_1, \ldots, v_n, x_1, \ldots, x_n, R)$, then $V(v'_1, \ldots, v'_n, y_1, \ldots, y_n, R)$ iff $v'_v = (\partial y_v/\partial x_\mu)v_\mu$.[24]

The disadvantage of this approach is that it takes as a mere law something that cries out for further explanation. Why should there be primitive relations V that take that number of arguments, and why should the first block of n arguments transform as they do relative to the second block of n arguments?

The second approach is the obvious one. As we saw in Section 8.4, mathematically a smooth vector field can be characterized as a map v from smooth functions to smooth functions which satisfies the following three rules:

[24] Differential geometry afficionados: we are ignoring the usual top and bottom indexing convention.

(a) $v(f+g) = v(f)+v(g)$

(b) $v(\alpha f) = \alpha v(f)$ (for any real number α)

(c) $v(fg) = fv(g)+gv(f)$

This suggests that the primitive predicate we use to characterize a particular physica[l] vector field should be a two-place relation $V(r, s)$ between scalar fields, subject to th[e] following laws:

V1 If $V(r, s)$ and $V(r, t)$ then $s=t$

V2 For every Smooth r there exists a Smooth s such that $V(r, s)$

V3 If $V(r, s)$ and $V(t, u)$ then $V(r+t, s+u)$

V4 If $V(r, s)$ and α is a constant scalar field, then $V(\alpha r, \alpha s)$

V5 If $V(r, s)$ and $V(t, u)$, then $V(rt, ru+st)$

This approach is much simpler than the previous approach. One can use it to explai[n] what the components of a vector field relative to a set of coordinates are, and why the[y] transform as they do: see Chapter 2, or any textbook on differential geometry, for suc[h] an explanation.

The first and second approaches both pick out a *particular* vector field as physically special, without any need for an arbitrary choice of unit. There are ways one coul[d] avoid this unwanted specificity. For example, one could modify the second approac[h] by replacing its two-place predicate $V(r, s)$ with a four-place predicate $V\star(r_1, s_1, r_2, s_2)$. with the intuitive meaning 'for some choice of units, the physical vector field maps r_1 to s_1, and in those units it maps r_2 to s_2'. However, these modifications seem a bit artificial. It would be nicer if the multiplicity of mathematical representations of the physical vector field arose naturally, as it does in the case of scalar fields represented by betweenness and congruence relations.

The third approach to characterizing a physical vector field is to use a primitive predicate whose arguments are nominalistic surrogates for vectors and/or covectors at points. In Section 8.6 we saw that some such surrogates—namely half-line sieves and surface sieves—can be found in any ontology that includes arbitrary fusions of space-time points. Unsurprisingly, the rich ontology of scalar-value space gives us many new options for constructing such surrogates—for example, we could represent a vector at a spacetime point p as a line in scalar-value space corresponding to a function from real numbers to spacetime points, which maps zero to p. (As with half-line sieves, many such lines will represent the same vector at p.) The approach to representing a physical vector field (without a natural unit) developed in Section 8.6 was to use a three-place predicate $V(\omega_1, \omega_2, \omega_3)$ whose arguments are surface sieves (or some other surrogates for covectors at points), with the intuitive meaning that $\omega_1(V)=\omega_2(V)+\omega_3(V)$. The challenge was to express the laws governing this predicate in a nominalistically acceptable way. Given the ontology of scalar-value space, this challenge can be met. We can say what it is for a given constant scalar field to be the directional derivative of a scalar field according to a half-line sieve; thus we can say what it is for a half-line sieve to be 'well-behaved' (it must assign a directional derivative to every Smooth scalar field) and for two half-line sieves to 'correspond to the same vector' (they assign the same directional derivative to every Smooth scalar field). Given this, we can say what it is for a surface sieve to be 'well-behaved' (it assigns a value to every well-behaved half-line sieve), and what it is for two surface sieves to 'correspond to the same covector' (they assign the same value to any two half-line sieves that correspond to the same vector). So we can state laws such as this: whenever surface sieves χ_1, χ_2, and χ_3 correspond to the same covectors as surface sieves ω_1, ω_2, and ω_3, and $V(\chi_1, \chi_2, \chi_3)$, then $V(\omega_1, \omega_2, \omega_3)$.

The first and third of these approaches generalize straightforwardly to physical covector fields and physical tensor fields of arbitrary rank. In the first approach these will be represented using primitive predicates taking large numbers of arguments ($n^{j+k}+n+1$ arguments for a tensor field of rank j, k in an n-dimensional manifold), subject to stipulative transformation laws. In the third approach, these will be represented by predicates taking half-line sieves and surface sieves, or some other surrogates, as arguments ($3j+3k$ arguments for a tensor field of rank j, k without natural unit). The second approach, by contrast, has no natural analogue for covector fields or general tensor fields. For while the ontology of scalar-value space gives us nominalistic surrogates for scalar functions, it does not contain any natural nominalistic surrogates for vector and covector *fields*. Half-line sieves and surface sieves are surrogates for vectors and covectors at points, not vector and covector fields. So it gives us no way to base a nominalistic account of a physical covector or tensor field on the standard mathematical construction of such entities as functions taking vector and covector fields as arguments.

As it happens, this is no problem as regards tensor fields of rank $j, 0$. For while we defined these officially as functions taking j smooth covector fields as arguments, they can just as well be treated analogously to vector fields; that is, as functions taking j smooth *functions* as arguments, which behave like vector fields in each argument:

(a) $T(\ldots, f+g, \ldots) = T(\ldots, f, \ldots) + T(\ldots, g, \ldots)$
(b) $T(\ldots, \alpha f, \ldots) = \alpha T(\ldots, f, \ldots)$ (for any real number α)
(c) $T(\ldots, fg, \ldots) = f T(\ldots, g, \ldots) + g T(\ldots, f, \ldots)$

(Essentially, we are using the smooth functions $f_1, \ldots, f_j$ as surrogates for the corresponding covector fields $df_1, \ldots, df_j$. It is easy to show that the action of the tensor field on an arbitrary sequence of covector fields is determined by its action on these special covector fields.) So we can represent any physical tensor field of rank $j, 0$ as an $j+1$-ary relation among scalar fields.

What about a physical tensor field of rank j, k where $k>0$? Without vector fields in the ontology, there is no general way to treat these as relations among scalar fields, short of the first, brute-force approach using coordinate representations. However, the physical theories in which we are interested generally feature a metric, which is a physical tensor field g of rank $0, 2$ with the special property of being *non-degenerate*. Any tensor field T of rank $0, 2$ determines a linear mapping Φ_T from vector fields to covector fields, via the equivalence $\Phi_T(v_1)(v_2)=T(v_1,v_2)$: to say that g is non-degenerate is to say that the mapping Φ_g is a bijection. Given this mapping, any tensor field T of rank j, k can be represented as a tensor field $T^\#$ of rank $j+k, 0$. To apply $T^\#$ to a sequence of $j+k$ covector fields, we turn the last k of them into vector fields using Φ_g^{-1}, and then apply T. (This is the operation generally known as 'index raising'.) So if we are dealing with the usual form of physical theory involving a metric, the method of representing physical tensor fields of rank $j, 0$ discussed in the previous paragraph gives us everything we need to represent any physical tensor field. (This includes the metric itself, which we can represent using a three-place predicate $G(f_1, f_2, f_3)$ of Smooth scalar fields, with the mathematical meaning that $g^\#(df_1, df_2)=f_3$, or equivalently $g(\Phi_g^{-1}(df_1), \Phi_g^{-1}(df_2))=f_3$.)

So, we have seen several reasonable strategies for supplementing the basic theory of scalar-value space with primitive predicates corresponding to physical tensor fields. Now we should say something about how we can express in a nominalistically acceptable way the tensor *equations* which play the role of dynamical laws in physical theories expressed in the language of differential geometry. These equations are identities between tensor fields; but the tensor fields being identified are generally defined in terms of other, more basic physical tensor fields. These definitions can be formalized using the following four operations, which build new tensor fields out of old ones:

(a) *Permutation*. We can permute the arguments of one tensor field to get another. For example, if we have a $0, 2$ tensor field T_{ab}, we can apply permutation to get a new $0, 2$ tensor field T_{ba} defined by $T_{ba}(v_1,v_2)=T_{ab}(v_2,v_1)$.

(b) *Addition*. Given tensor fields T and T' both of rank j, k, $T+T'$ is a tensor field defined by $(T+T')(\omega_1,\ldots,\omega_j,v_1,\ldots,v_k)=T(\omega_1,\ldots,\omega_j,v_1,\ldots,v_k)+T'(\omega_1,\ldots,\omega_j,v_1,\ldots,v_k)$.

(c) *Tensor product*. Given tensor fields T and T' of ranks j, k and j', k' respectively, we can form a new tensor field $T \otimes T'$ of rank $j+j', k+k'$, defined by

$$T \otimes T'(\omega_1,\ldots,\omega_{j+j'},v_1,\ldots,v_{k+k'})=T(\omega_1,\ldots,\omega_j,v_1,\ldots,v_k)T'(\omega_{j+1},\ldots,\omega_{j+j'},v_{k+1},\ldots,v_{k+k'})$$

(In abstract index notation, we write T and T' as $T^{a_1\ldots a_j}_{b_1\ldots b_k}$ and $T'^{c_1\ldots c_{j'}}_{d_1\ldots d_{k'}}$, and $T \otimes T'$ is $T^{a_1\ldots a_j}_{b_1\ldots b_k}T'^{c_1\ldots c_{j'}}_{d_1\ldots d_{k'}}$).

(d) *Contraction*. Given a tensor field $T=T^{a_1\ldots a_{j+1}}_{b_1\ldots b_{k+1}}$ of rank $j+1, k+1$, we can form a new tensor field $\mathscr{C}T$ of rank j, k by 'contracting the last upper argument of T with its last lower argument'. In abstract index notation, $\mathscr{C}T$ can be written as $T^{a_1\ldots a_k c}_{b_1\ldots b_k c}$. In a system of local coordinates $x_1,\ldots,x_n$,

$$\mathscr{C}T(\omega_1,\ldots,\omega_j,v_1,\ldots,v_k)=\Sigma_{1\leq i\leq n}T(\omega_1,\ldots,\omega_j,dx_i,v_1,\ldots,v_k,\partial/\partial x_i)$$

(We could also allow ourselves a more general contraction operation which can target arguments other than the last one of each sort. But this gives us nothing essentially new, since we can always use permutation to move the arguments we want to contract into the last place.)

In our nominalistic treatment, these operations for building new tensor fields out of basic ones will correspond to logical operations which build new logically complex predicates—or what comes to the same thing in conventional logical notation, namely, logically complex *open sentences*—starting with the primitive predicates representing basic tensor fields. Suppose we follow the second strategy discussed above, in which physical tensor fields of rank $j, 0$ are represented using $j+1$-ary predicates of scalar fields, using the metric to avoid ever having to talk about tensor fields of rank j, k with $k>0$. If tensor fields T and T' of rank $j, 0$ are represented nominalistically by open sentences $\Phi(f_1, \ldots, f_j, f_{j+1})$ and $\psi(f_1, \ldots, f_j, f_{j+1})$, a physical law given mathematically in the form 'T=T'' corresponds to the nominalistic statement $\forall f_1, \ldots, f_{j+1}(\Phi(f_1, \ldots, f_{j+1})$ iff $\Psi(f_1, \ldots, f_{j+1}))$. So all that remains is to find operations on open sentences corresponding to the four tensor-building operations given above. This is completely straightforward for permutation, addition and tensor product. For example, if we have an open sentence $\Phi(f_1, f_2, f_3)$ representing a tensor field of rank $2, 0$, the permutated tensor field will be represented by the open sentence $\Phi(f_2, f_1, f_3)$. If we have open sentences $\Phi(f_1, \ldots, f_j, f_{j+1})$ and $\Psi(f_1, \ldots, f_{j'}, f_{j'+1})$ representing tensor fields of rank $j, 0$, their sum (in case $j=j'$) is represented by the open sentence '$\exists g \exists h (\Phi(f_1, \ldots, f_j, g) \wedge \psi(f_1, \ldots, f_j, h) \wedge f_{j+1}=g+h)$', while their tensor product is represented by the open sentence '$\exists g \exists h (\Phi(f_1, \ldots, f_j, g) \wedge \psi(f_{j+1}, \ldots, f_{j+j'}, h) \wedge f_{j+j'+1}=gh)$' (where multiplication of scalar fields is defined as in n. 20).

Finally, we need to represent contraction—or rather, the combined operation of 'lowering an index using the metric and then contracting' (or equivalently, 'contracting the last two indices with the metric'), which stands in for it in the current system where we only have predicates corresponding to tensors of rank $j, 0$. This is a bit more complicated.

First, let $D_k(O, x_1, \ldots, x_n, h, j)$ stand for the claim that $x_1, \ldots, x_n$ coordinatize the open region O, and throughout O, $j=\delta/\delta x_k(h)$: we have already seen how to express this nominalistically. Then the open sentence $\Theta_k(O, x_1, \ldots, x_n, g_1, \ldots, g_n)$ defined as follows:

$$\forall h \forall j (D_k(O, x_1, \ldots, x_n, h, j) \leftrightarrow \exists f_1 \ldots f_n(G(x_1, h, f_1) \wedge \ldots \wedge G(x_n, h, f_n) \wedge$$
$$j=g_1 f_1 + \ldots + g_n f_n)$$

means that 'in O, $\partial/\partial x_k(h)=\Sigma_i g_i g^\#(dx_i, dh)$', or equivalently, '$\partial/\partial x_k(h)=g^\#(\Sigma_i g_i dx_i, dh)$'—or in other words, '$\Sigma_i g_i dx_i$ is what we get when we use the metric to 'lower' the vector field $\partial/\partial x_k$ into a covector field'. So, finally, if we have a predicate $\Phi(f_1, \ldots, f_{j+3})$ representing a tensor field T of rank $j+2, 0$, the following complex predicate $\mathscr{C}\Phi(f_1, \ldots, f_{j+1})$ represents the result of contracting the last two arguments of T with the metric:

$\forall O,p,x_1,\ldots,x_n,g_{11},\ldots,g_{1n},\ldots,g_{n1}\cdots,g_{nn},\alpha_{11},\ldots,\alpha_{1n},\ldots,\alpha_{n1},\ldots,\alpha_{nn}\ (x_1\ldots x_n$

coordinatize $O \wedge \Theta_1(O,x_1,\ldots,x_n,g_{11},\ldots,g_{1n}) \wedge \ldots \wedge \Theta_n(O,x_1,\ldots,x_n,g_{n1},\ldots,g_{nn}) \wedge$

$\Phi(f_1,\ldots,f_j,x_1,g_{11},x_1,\alpha_{11}) \wedge \ldots \wedge \Phi(f_1,\ldots,f_j,x_1,g_{1n},x_n,\alpha_{1n}) \wedge \ldots \wedge \ldots \wedge$

$\Phi(f_1,\ldots,f_j,x_n,g_{n1},x_1,\alpha_{n1}) \wedge \ldots \wedge \Phi(f_1,\ldots,f_j,x_n,g_{nn},x_n,\alpha_{nn}) \wedge p$ a point of $O \to$

$(f_{j+1}[p] = \alpha_{11}[p] + \ldots + \alpha_{nn}[p])$

In a similar way, we can define a complex predicate $\mathscr{C}_{\alpha\beta}\Phi(f_1,\ldots,f_{j+1})$ which represents the result of contracting the αth and βth arguments of T with the metric.[25]

This gives us a mechanical way of expressing any tensor equation as a quantified claim using our primitive predicates. For an example, take Einstein's equation for vacuum general relativity,

$$R_{acb}{}^c = -g_{ab}g^{de}R_{dce}{}^c$$

where R is the Riemann tensor, with rank 3,1. We first rewrite this so that all indices except for those on the metric are upper indices: $R^{acbd}g_{cd} = -g^{ab}R^{cdef}g_{df}g_{ce}$. When Φ is our five-place predicate representing R^{abcd} and G is our primitive predicate representing g^{ab}, we can rewrite this as

$$\forall f_1,f_2,f_3(\mathscr{C}_{13}\Phi(f_1,f_2,f_3) = -1 \otimes G \otimes \mathscr{C}_{12}\mathscr{C}_{13}\Phi(f_1,f_2,f_3)).$$

Turning this abbreviation into a sentence expressed using primitive vocabulary is then just a matter of repeatedly applying the above definitions of contraction and tensor product.[26]

The laws we get by applying this algorithm are somewhat more complicated than we need to be. As we have set things up, every application of the contraction operation will introduce a fresh battery of quantifiers over coordinate systems $x_1,\ldots,x_n$ and the components $g_{11},\ldots,g_{nn}$ of the metric relative to these coordinate systems. This can be avoided by having just one such battery of quantifiers at the beginning, and recycling the same variables every time we need to do a contraction. This does something to mitigate the feelings of artificiality that may be prompted by laws generated in accordance with the above algorithm.

In some ways of developing the mathematics, the contraction operation is defined without mentioning coordinate systems at all. Most commonly, the contraction

---

[25] It is easier to define contraction if we adopt the third approach, representing tensor fields as predicates of half-line sieves and surface sieves. Given that we can say that a half-line sieve at a point equals $\partial/\partial x_i$, and that a surface sieve at a point equals dx_i, we can just mimic the mathematical definition of contraction given above, without having to drag in the metric.

[26] The Riemann tensor is not itself primitive. It is commonly defined in terms of the *spacetime connection*: but the task of representing the connection using a nominalistically acceptable predicate raises new difficulties which we want to postpone for now. However, there is also a way of defining the Riemann tensor directly from the metric. This definition uses differentiation relative to coordinates; given that our formulation of the laws already involves a universal quantification 'for all O, and for all scalar fields $x_1\ldots x_n$ which coordinatize O ...', nominalizing this definition raises no new problems, although the length of the definition would make writing it out nominalistically a laborious exercise.

operation $\mathscr{C}$ is said to be the unique linear function from tensors of rank $j+1, k+1$ to tensors of rank j, k with the property that for any vector field v and covector field ω, $\mathscr{C}(T \otimes v \otimes \omega) = \omega(v)T$: one can show that there is exactly one such function. This approach gives a way of glossing the content of tensor equations in which no mention ever needs to be made of coordinate systems. But it involves a kind of quantification—over functions from tensor fields to tensor fields—that is simply not available in a nominalistic framework. Within that framework, there seems to be no way to avoid bringing coordinate systems in at some point. Some philosophers of physics, who have been schooled to think that it is of paramount importance to avoid ever having to talk about coordinates, will think that this is a problem. But we think that the measure of complexity introduced by the quantifiers we use in characterizing contraction is a small price to pay for the advantage of not having to posit tensor fields, and functions among tensor fields, as entities in the fundamental ontology.

There is one way for coordinate systems to show up in putatively fundamental laws that we agree is very problematic: namely, when a law takes the form of an *existential* quantification over coordinate systems—for example, if one characterized the facts about spatial betweenness and congruence by saying that *there is* a system of coordinates in which these relations take such-and-such form. But this especially problematic character is not due to the fact that the laws in question mention coordinate systems: other kinds of existentially quantified laws (for example, 'there is an assignment of masses such that Newton's laws hold') are bad in the same way. Since our laws involve only *universal* quantification over coordinate systems, at least when simplified in the manner suggested above, we do not see any special reason to think ill of them.[27] Of course, it would be nicer not to have quite so many universal quantifiers out in front, but in the present ontology we see no way of avoiding this.

The conclusion of this section is that by positing the rich structure of scalar-value space, nominalists can give a workable account of the differential-geometric structure of spacetime, within which it looks to be a fairly trivial task to formulate nominalistically acceptable versions of physical theories written in the language of differential geometry.

8.9 Differential structure via vector bundles

Positing scalar-value space makes it easy to nominalize differential geometry and physical theories based in it. But it is worth seeing whether we can get by without positing a space with such a rich structure for which we have no motivation independent of the nominalistic project. As we saw in Chapter 6, gauge field theories play an important role in modern physics, and the success of such theories provides motivation for 'fibre-bundle substantivalism'. Scalar-value space is in fact a special case of a fibre

---

[27] Section 6 of Dorr 2010 makes much of this contrast between existential and universal quantification.

bundle over spacetime, insofar as it contains a miniature space (a fibre) corresponding to each point of spacetime. In fact it is a vector bundle, since the points of each fibre carry a natural vector-space structure (that of the real number line). But scalar-value space has several special features that vector bundles need not have. First, the fibres of a vector bundle need not be one-dimensional. Second, there is generally no distinguished 'unit' in a fibre. And third, there is in general no non-arbitrary way to make sense of the question whether points in different fibres are 'equal in value'. But as we will see in this section, the relatively impoverished structure of a vector bundle is still enough to characterize differential structure, both of the underlying manifold and of the vector bundle itself. The rich, real-number-like structure of scalar-value space turns out to be superfluous.

The first task in giving a nominalistic account of a vector bundle is to characterize the vector-space structure on each fibre without helping ourselves to real numbers. This can be done in various ways. One easy way has just the two primitive relations 'Sum' and 'SameDirection', where SameDirection(v_1, v_2) has the intuitive meaning that for some $\alpha > 0$, $v_1 = \alpha v_2$) The axioms for Sum are just the Abelian group axioms A1–A6 from Section 8.7. For SameDirection, what we basically want to do is to adapt axioms P1–P6 by replacing the one-place primitive predicate 'Positive(x)' with the two-place primitive predicate 'SameDirection(v, x)', while restricting the quantifiers to *multiples* of a given non-zero v. Here we define a 'multiple' of v as anything of the form $b-c$, where SameDirection(v, b) and SameDirection(v, c). Making these transformations to P1–P6 (with some small adjustments to allow zero vectors to bear the SameDirection relation to themselves) gives us SD1–SD6:

SD1 If SameDirection(v, x), then v and x lack proper parts.
SD2 If SameDirection(v, x) and SameDirection(v, y), SameDirection($v, x+y$).
SD3 If v is non-zero and SameDirection(v, x), then not SameDirection($v, -x$).
SD4 Whenever x is a non-zero multiple of v, either SameDirection(v, x) or SameDirection($v, -x$).
SD5 For any v, there exist x and y such that $x+y=v$ and SameDirection(v, x) and SameDirection(v, y).
SD6 If X and Y are fusions of multiples of v and X$<_v$Y, then there is a multiple z of v such that X$\leq_v z$ and $z\leq_v$Y.

The predicates '$<_v$' and '$\leq_v$' in SD6 are defined just like '$<$' and '$\leq$' were, substituting 'SameDirection(v, x)' for 'Positive(x)'.

To capture the claim that the fibres are vector spaces, we will need three more axioms:

SD7 SameDirection is an equivalence relation.
SD8 SameDirection($-v_1, -v_2$) whenever SameDirection(v_1, v_2).
SD9 If SameDirection($v+w, x$), then for some y and z such that $y+z=x$, SameDirection(v, y) and SameDirection(w, z).

The key to seeing that these axioms pin down the structure of a vector space is notic-ing that if we choose any non-zero v, interpret 'Positive(x)' as 'SameDirection(v, x)' and 'Unit(x)' as '$x=v$', and restrict all quantifiers to multiples of v, we get back axioms P1–P6 and U1–U2, which as we have already seen, suffice to characterize the structure of the real numbers. So in each model of A1–A6 and SD1–SD9, each non-zero v generates a particular isomorphism π_v between the real numbers and the multiples of v, such that $\pi_v(v)=1$, $\pi_v(x)+\pi_v(y)=\pi_v(x+y)$, and $\pi_v(x)>0$ iff SameDirection(v, x). When $\pi_v(\alpha) = x$ (where α is a real number) or x and v are both zero, we can write '$x = \alpha v$'. And we can show (see Appendix D for the proof) that scalar multiplication, so defined, satisfies the defining properties of scalar multiplication in a vector space, namely

(a) $1v = v$
(b) $(\alpha+\beta)v = \alpha v+\beta v$
(c) $\alpha(\beta v) = (\alpha\beta)v$
(d) $\alpha(v+w) = \alpha v+\alpha w$

Of course, there is no uniquely natural way to define multiplication of vectors in a vector space. However, we can still make sense, in the same way as before (see n. 20), of the claim that $a{:}b{=}c{:}d$ (whenever a is a multiple of b and c is a multiple of d, not necessarily in the same fibre as a and b). We can think of this as a relativized notion of multiplication, writing '$a\times_v b{=}c$' to mean 'either $a{:}v{=}c{:}b$ or b and c are both zero'. In general, every relation that we could define among points in a scalar-value line can be carried over to the points in a fibre in a general vector bundle by giving it an extra parameter, to be filled by a non-zero vector v, serving as an arbitrarily chosen unit.

A *section* of the vector bundle will be the counterpart of a scalar field in scalar-value space: a region that overlaps each fibre at exactly one point. When s is a section and p is a fibre (a spacetime point), $s[p]$ will denote the intersection of s and p. The Sum and SameDirection relations, and other relations defined in terms of them, can be general-ized to sections: Sum(s_1,s_2,s_3) iff Sum($s_1[p],s_2[p],s_3[p]$) for each p, and SameDirection(s_1,s_2) iff SameDirection($s_1[p],s_2[p]$) for each p. Again, while there is no uniquely natural way to define multiplication of sections, we can make sense of multiplication when relativ-ized to a nowhere-zero section s_0 which serves as an arbitrary unit: $s_1\times_{s_0} s_2 = s_3$ iff for each p, either $s_1[p]{:}s_0[p]{=}s_3[p]{:}s_2[p]$ or $s_2[p]$ and $s_3[p]$ are both zero. Similarly, while we cannot make natural sense of the notion of a 'constant' section, we can say that s_1 is a 'constant multiple' of s_0, or 'constant relative to the choice of s_0 as unit': this is true when for any p and q, $s_1[p]{:}s_0[p]{=}s_1[q]{:}s_0[q]$. (If spacetime has an interesting shape there may be no nowhere-zero Smooth sections; but this is not a problem, since our 'unit' section s_0 does not have to be Smooth.)

As in the case of scalar-value space, the other primitive we will use capturing dif-ferential structure is a one-place predicate Smooth, applying now to sections. Our aim is to write down some axioms for Smoothness from which it follows that the space can indeed be given the mathematical structure of a vector bundle. The key insight we will rely on in order to do this is the fact that *pairs* of sections s, s_0 such that s_0 is nowhere zero and s is a multiple of s_0 can be used as surrogates for scalar fields. We say that s_1 is a *smooth multiple* of s_0 iff for every spacetime point p, there exists an open spacetime region O containing p, and Smooth sections s_2 and s_3, such that $s_1(q):s_0(q)=s_3(q):s_2(q)$ for each q in O. 'Open spacetime region' is defined essentially as before: a 'basic open region' is one that contains all and only the points where some Smooth section is non-zero, and an open region is one composed of basic open regions. Given this, all of the definitions in the bulleted list on p. 247 can be carried over to the context of a vector bundle by introducing an extra argument place, to be filled by a nowhere-zero section s_0 serving as an arbitrary unit, replacing 'is a scalar field' with 'is a multiple of s_0', and replacing 'is Smooth' with 'is a smooth multiple of s_0'. So, for example, we can define what it is for s_1 to be continuous taking s_0 as unit; what it is for R to be a multi-field taking s_0 as unit; what it is for s_1 to be the partial derivative of s_2 in coordinate s_3 of R in O taking s_0 as unit; etc. Given these definitions, it is a straightforward matter to adapt axioms FN1–FN3 into the present setting, as follows:

SN1 For any nowhere-zero s_0, if S is a multifield relative to s_0 with finitely many components each of which is a smooth multiple of s_0, and s_1 is C^∞ relative to S and s_0 in every bounded open region O, then s_1 is a smooth multiple of s_0.

SN2 If s is a section, and for each spacetime point p, there is an open region O containing p, and a Smooth section t that coincides with s on O, then s is Smooth.

SN3 For each nowhere-zero s_0, and each spacetime point p, there is a bounded open set O containing p, and a region S that is a smooth multifieldrelative to s_0 composed of n smooth multiples of s_0, such that (i) relative to s_0, S does not take the same values at any two points in O, and (ii) every smooth multiple s_1 of s_0 coincides in O with some section that is C^∞ relative to S and s_0 in O.

These axioms are not yet enough to say all we want to say about the Smooth sections. For example, they are consistent with the claim that some fibres contain points that are not part of any Smooth section. But we can finish the job by adding three more axioms:

SN4 If s_1 is Smooth and s_2 is Smooth, then s_1+s_2 is Smooth.

SN5 If s_1 is a smooth multiple of s_2, and s_2 is Smooth, then s_1 is Smooth.

SN6 For every point p in M, there exists an open region O containing M, and m Smooth sections $s_1, \ldots, s_m$, such that (i) every Smooth section coincides on O with some sum of smooth multiples of $s_1, \ldots, s_m$, and (ii) at every spacetime point q in O, $s_1[q], \ldots$ and $s_m[q]$ form a basis at q.

(Here m is the dimensionality of the fibres. $v_1 \ldots v_m$ 'form a basis' for a fibre iff every point in the fibre is a sum of a multiple of $v_1 \ldots$. and a multiple of v_m, and none of the v_i is a sum of multiples of the others.) SN6 tells us that we are dealing with a *locally trivial*, m-dimensional vector bundle. For the m-tuples of Smooth sections which exist according to SN6 do the work of a *local trivialization* on O (see section 6.3), in that they determine a unique, linear mapping between the points of any fibre within O and the points of any other fibre within O. We define this mapping by expressing a point v in fibre p as a sum of multiples of $s_1[p], \ldots$ and $s_m[p]$, and letting the image of v in fibre q be the sum of the corresponding multiples of $s_1[q], \ldots$ and $s_m[q]$. This means we can treat any of the fibres within O as a 'standard fibre'.

Provided that the dimension m of the fibres is greater than 0 (so that there exist nowhere-zero sections—not necessarily Smooth ones, of course), SN1–SN3 work just as FN1–FN3 did to fix a differential structure on spacetime. Once we have introduced the operation of scalar multiplication, we can define a function f from points of spacetime real numbers to be 'smooth' iff for some sections s_1, s_0 such that s_1 is a smooth multiple of s_0, $s_1[p] = f(p)s_0[p]$ for each spacetime point p. And the smooth functions so defined will satisfy axioms F1–F3, so we know that they uniquely determine a differential structure on spacetime. This is not all we want: a vector bundle is itself a certain kind of differentiable manifold, so if we want the right to call the structure we have just been talking about a 'vector bundle', we need to make sure that our primitive relations suffice to determine a unique differential structure on the set of all points in all fibres as well as on the set of all points of spacetime. But this is straightforward to show.[28]

Given this, we have all the structure definitive of a vector bundle: a base manifold (spacetime), a fibre bundle manifold, a projection map π from points of the latter to points of the former (namely, the function that maps each v to its fibre); and a vector space structure on each set of points which have the same image under π.[29]

---

[28] By SN6, every spacetime point has a spacetime neighbourhood O within which we can find a basis of Smooth sections $s_1 \ldots s_m$. Since we have a differential structure on spacetime, any such O has a subset O⁻ still containing p, such that there is a sequence of scalar functions $x_1 \ldots x_n$ which form an admissible coordinate system on O⁻. Having chosen $x_1 \ldots x_n$ and $s_1 \ldots s_m$, we use them to define a coordinate system on the vectors in fibres in O⁻. Each point v in the fibre over a spacetime point q in O⁻ has a unique expression of the form $\alpha_1 s_1[q] + \ldots + \alpha_m s_m[q]$, so we let the coordinates of v be $x_1(q), \ldots, x_n(q), \alpha_1, \ldots, \alpha_m$. Now we just need to check that any two coordinate systems defined in this way are smoothly related in their region of overlap. That is, if we choose a different coordinate system $y_1, \ldots, y_n$ and basis of smooth sections $t_1 \ldots t_m$ on an open region O⋆ overlapping O⁻ to define coordinates $y_1, \ldots, y_n, \beta_1, \ldots, \beta_m$ on the fibres of O⋆, then each of the coordinate functions $y_1, \ldots, y_n, \beta_1, \ldots, \beta_m$ can be expressed as a smooth function of $x_1, \ldots, x_n, \alpha_1, \ldots, \alpha_m$. For $y_1, \ldots, y_n$ this is straightforward: we already have a differential structure on spacetime, and we know that $x_1 \ldots x_n$ and $y_1, \ldots, y_n$ are both admissible coordinate systems on O⁻∩O⋆, so each y_i must be expressible as $f_i(x_1, \ldots, x_n)$, where f_i is C∞. For $\beta_1, \ldots, \beta_m$, we use clause (i) of SN6. Since each s_i is Smooth and $\{t_i\}$ is a basis of Smooth sections on O⁻∩O⋆, each s_i can be represented in O⁻∩O⋆ as $\gamma^i_1 t_1 + \ldots + \gamma^i_m t_m$, where $\gamma^i_1 \ldots \gamma^i_m$ are smooth functions. So if a point v in the fibre over q can be expanded in the $s_i[q]$ basis as $\alpha_1 s_1[q] + \ldots + \alpha_m s_m[q]$, it can be expanded in the $t_i(q)$ basis as

$$(\alpha_1\gamma^1_1 + \alpha_2\gamma^2_1 \ldots + \alpha_m\gamma^m_1)t_1[q] + \ldots + (\alpha_1\gamma^1_m + \alpha_2\gamma^2_m \ldots + \alpha_m\gamma^m_m)t_m[q]$$

But since the γ^i_j are smooth, each of them can be expressed as $g^i_j(x_1, \ldots, x_n)$, where g^i_j is C∞. So β_i can be expressed as a smooth function of $x_1, \ldots, x_n, \alpha_1, \ldots, \alpha_m$ as follows:

$$\beta_i = \alpha_1 g^1_i(x_1, \ldots, x_n) + \alpha_2 g^2_i(x_1, \ldots, x_n) \ldots + \alpha_m g^m_i(x_1, \ldots, x_n)$$

Thus each of the β_i is a C∞ function of $x_1, \ldots, x_n, \alpha_1, \ldots, \alpha_m$, as required.

[29] Moreover, π is obviously a smooth map (as required by the definition of a fibre bundle), since each our admissible coordinate systems for the fibre bundle include admissible coordinate systems on spacetime points.

For applications in physics, we would normally want a vector bundle whose fibre have a structure richer than that of a mere vector space. For example, the main example in Chapter 6 dealt with bundles whose fibres have further structure ('angle-and-length structure') in addition to vector-space structure, in virtue of which the group of permutations which preserve all of the structure of the bundle (the gauge group) is a subgroup of the group of all permutations which preserve its vector-space structure.

Adding this to the current nominalistic picture would be a straightforward matter of picking some appropriate new primitive predicate applying to points in fibres. For angle-and-length structure, we could have a four-place primitive predicate 'the inner product of v_1 and v_2 is the same as the inner product of v_3 and v_4'.[30]

So far, so good. Now, what about adding some physical fields to this setting? The most obvious kind of physical field we can add is a physically distinguished section of the vector bundle. We can do this with a one-place primitive predicate picking out the 'Occupied' section. By contrast to the analogous strategy for incorporating a physical scalar field in the setting of scalar-value space, this does not in any sense build in a 'preferred unit' for the field in question. The arbitrariness of units is fully captured by the fact that there is no privileged system of coordinates on the fibres, and thus no privileged way to represent our physically distinguished section as an n-tuple of real-number valued functions on spacetime.

As regards spacetime tensor fields, we essentially have the same options that were discussed in Section 8.8 in the context of scalar-value space, since pairs of sections, one of which is a multiple of the other, can do all the work of a scalar field. Each of these options can be generalized in an obvious way to account for the kinds of hybrid tensor fields that occur in gauge field theory, such as section-valued and endomorphism-valued covector fields. For example, we might represent a section-valued covector field by means of a relation mapping half-line sieves to points in the fibre over their home point.[31]

As was discussed in Chapter 6, there is one other kind of physical field that plays a very important role in physical theories which use fibre bundles: namely, a *connection*. Mathematically, a connection on a vector bundle can be defined as a function D that takes a smooth spacetime vector field v and a section s and yields another section $D_v(s)$, in such a way that

(a) $D_v(s_1 + s_2) = D_v(s_1) + D_v(s_2)$
(b) $D_v(fs) = v(f)s + fD_v(s)$

---

[30] One might also consider positing some other fibre bundles in addition to the vector bundle that is used in characterizing the differential structure of spacetime. These additional fibre bundles might have quite different kinds of structure in place of vector space structure: for example, they could be 'principal' bundles which carry a group structure rather than a vector space structure. However we will not investigate this further, since we see no straightforward physical motivation for a substantivalist attitude towards such bundles.

[31] Similarly, an endomorphism-valued covector field, such as the electromagnetic field, can be represented as a three-place relation that takes a half-line sieve and a point in its home fibre, and yields another such point.

(c) $D_{v+w}(s) = D_v(s)+D_w(s)$

(d) $D_{fv}(s) = fD_v(s)$

for any smooth sections s, s_1 and s_2, smooth function f and smooth vector fields v and w). Since our current nominalistic ontology does not contain any single entities corresponding to vector fields, it is not so clear how to endow it with a connection. There are various options we could explore, including the following.

(i) As we noted in Section 8.7, a smooth vector field in an n-dimensional spacetime manifold can be represented by a $2n+1$-ary relation whose arguments are an open region and $2n$ Smooth scalar fields, the latter n of which coordinatize the given region. In a vector bundle, we can achieve the same effect with a $2n+2$-ary relation whose arguments are an open region, a section s_0 that is nowhere zero within that region, and $2n$ smooth multiples of s_0. This gives us a 'brute force' way to nominalize a connection using a $2n+4$-ary predicate whose first $2n+2$ arguments represent the vector field v and whose last two arguments stand respectively for s and $D_v(s)$.

(ii) While we do not have entities corresponding to vector fields, we have plenty of good nominalistic surrogates for vectors at points, for example the half-line sieves of Section 8.6. A connection in the sense defined above determines a mapping d_{v_p} from vectors at a spacetime point p and smooth sections to points in the fibre over p. Conditions (c) and (d) entail that whenever smooth vector fields v and w coincide at p, $D_v(s)$ and $D_w(s)$ must also coincide at p; so we can without ambiguity define $d_{v_p}(s)=D_v(s)(p)$ where v is any smooth vector field whose value at p is v_p. Moreover, two distinct connections D and D′ will always determine distinct such functions d and $d′$. So we could talk about a connection nominalistically using a three-place predicate whose arguments are first, some nominalistic surrogate for a vector at a spacetime point (e.g. a half-line sieve); second, a smooth section; and third, a point in the fibre at the given spacetime point.

But how are we to write down laws using such a predicate which guarantee that it does indeed behave in the right way to generate a connection? We want to say, essentially, that when we smoothly vary v_p (either holding p fixed or allowing it to vary), $d_{v_p}(s)$ will also vary smoothly. And how do we say that? We could fall back here on the trick from the first approach, of representing vector fields by their coordinate representations. We can say something like this: for every open region O, nowhere-zero section s_0, smooth multiples $x_1, \ldots, x_n$ of s_0 which encode a coordinate system on O, smooth multiples $v_1, \ldots, v_n$ of s_0, Smooth section s, and section $s′$, if for every point p in O, when v_p is the vector(-surrogate) at p whose coordinate representation relative to $x_1, \ldots, x_n$ is $v_1(p)\partial/\partial x_1 + \ldots + v_n(p)\partial/\partial x_n$, $s′[p]=d_{v_p}(s)$, then $s′$ is Smooth. This is not the world's most elegant law, but at least on this strategy the primitive predicate itself does not need a large number of argument places.

(iii) The mathematical representation of a connection as a function from vector fields and sections to sections is at some remove from the intuition to which people (such as the author of Chapter 6) appeal in introducing the concept of a connection.

According to this intuition, the essential job of a connection is to give us a notion of what it is to 'parallel transport' a point in the fibre over p along a smooth path from to q, yielding a point in the fibre over q. We could take this intuitive explanation as the basis for our nominalistic treatment. Specifically, we could represent a connection using a single, one-place predicate 'Parallel' applying to certain regions in the fibre bundle, subject to at least the following axioms:

PT1　If Parallel(R), then R is a smooth path (embedded one-dimensional submani-fold) in the fibre bundle, which intersects each fibre at most once.[32]

PT2　For each smooth path λ in spacetime, and each point in each fibre over λ there is a Parallel path through that point whose projection into spacetime is λ.

PT3　Two distinct Parallel paths R and S which have the same projection into spacetime cannot share any points.

PT4　If R, S and T are Parallel and have the same projection into spacetime, then for any spacetime points p and q that they intersect, $R[p]+S[p]=T[p]$ if $R[q]+S[q]=T[q]$.

PT5　If R and S are Parallel and have the same projection into spacetime, then for any spacetime points p and q that they intersect, SameDirection(R$[p]$,S$[p]$) iff SameDirection(R$[q]$,S$[q]$).

These axioms are not yet enough to determine that we are dealing with a *bona fide* notion of parallel transport corresponding to a connection. What remains to be said is something to the effect that as we smoothly vary the spacetime path, we will smoothly vary the result of parallel transporting a given point in a fibre along that path. How could we say something like that? One strategy is to fall back on quantification over coordinate systems again, defining the $2n+4$-ary predicate that was taken as primitive in the first approach in terms of Parallel, and then saying in these terms that operating with the connection on a smooth vector field and a smooth section yields a smooth section. This is feasible, since we have nominalistic surrogates for curves in the sense of functions from real numbers to spacetime points, and we can say that such a curve is an 'integral curve' of a given vector field expressed in coordinate terms. So we can define '$D_v(s)=t$' as 'for any integral curve λ of v, $t[\lambda(0)] = \lim_{h \to 0} (s[\lambda(0)]-$the result of parallel transporting $s[\lambda(h)]$ back along λ to $\lambda(0))/h$'. But probably this is unnecessarily indirect: there may be some more straightforward way to express the smoothness con-straint on Parallel paths. For instance, while we do not have nominalistic surrogates for *all* smoothly parameterized families of smooth paths in spacetime, we do have nominalistic surrogates for *some* such families, namely those in which the paths are the intersections of the level sets of $n-1$ smooth functions, restricted to some open space-time region. So we can express something like this: if F is such a family, and J is a

---

[32] Alternatively, we could allow Parallel paths to loop back on themselves. But this would make other claims, such as PT4, more awkward to state.

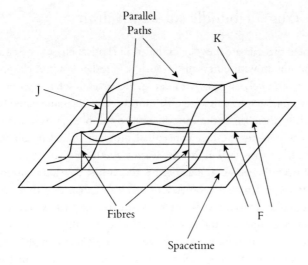

Figure 8.7 A smoothness requirement.

smooth path through the fibre bundle whose projection into spacetime intersects each member of F at most once, and K is a path through the fibre bundle whose projection into spacetime is smooth, and for each point of K, there is a Parallel path which contains some point of J and whose projection into spacetime is a member of F, then K itself is smooth. (See Figure 8.7.)

We conjecture that this should be enough to capture the smoothness requirement on parallel transport, but we are not sure how to show this.

Once we have settled on an approach to representing a connection, it should be a fairly straightforward exercise to write down nominalistic versions of the equations which characterize gauge field theories, such as the Yang–Mills equation. At the very least, we know we can do everything in terms of components, with an initial universal quantification over coordinate systems (both in spacetime and in the fibre bundle). Once we have a way of defining the polyadic predicate which expresses the connection in coordinate terms, we can use it to define other predicates, e.g. one corresponding to the curvature of the connection (an endomorphism-valued two form, F); we can then perform various tensorial operations involving these predicates using the techniques sketched in Section 8.8. Another option is to exploit the metric to turn all the relevant tensors into ones of rank j, 0, which can be represented in a coordinate independent way using predicates of smooth scalar fields (or smooth multiples of a given nowhere-zero section).

So to conclude this section: the independently-motivated ontology of fibre-bundle substantivalism provides not only the resources for a nominalistic account of differential structure, but also provides a range of plausible strategies for nominalizing interesting physical theories, including gauge field theories.

8.10 Tangent-bundle substantivalism

Since gauge field theories are the state of the art in classical physics, we could stop here the task of coming up with nominalistic versions of other kinds of classical theories is to some extent of merely antiquarian interest. However, insofar as we are not dealing with the question how to nominalize quantum theories, the same could be said of this whole chapter; as discussed in the Introduction to this book, it is in the nature of the philosophy of physics to consider conceptual problems raised by outdated physical theories in the hope that we will thereby learn something that continues to be of use in the light of new discoveries. It is a safer bet that future developments in physics will preserve a role for differential geometry of some sort than that they will preserve a role for fibre bundles. Thus it may be an interesting intellectual exercise to think about how we might best approach the task of nominalizing a theory like vacuum general relativity, in which the notion of a fibre bundle has no obvious application.

Of course, there is a sense in which any physical theory that uses the basic apparatus of differential geometry is a fibre-bundle theory. For these theories will talk about vector fields, covector fields, and other kinds of tensor fields. And each of these entities has a mathematical representation as a section of a fibre bundle. For example, a vector field on a n-dimensional manifold M can be identified with a section of the tangent bundle TM, a $2n$-dimensional manifold each of whose points can be identified with a tangent vector at some point of M. Similarly, a covector field can be identified with a section of the cotangent bundle $T\star M$, and a tensor field of rank j, k can be identified with a section of the tensor product bundle $TM^j \otimes T\star M^k$. However, it is unlikely that it would occur to anyone who was not concerned with the question of nominalism to adopt a substantivalist attitude towards any of these bundles. Rather, they would typically be thought of as mere mathematical constructs, rather than as collections of fundamental concrete entities like spacetime points. While Chapter 6 of this book argued that such an attitude is extremely problematic in the case of the bundles that feature in gauge field theory, those arguments do not carry over to spaces like the tangent bundle. But now that we *are* concerned with nominalism, we might think of revising this attitude. As we have seen, we can characterize the differential structure of spacetime nominalistically provided that we take a substantivalist attitude towards some richer space, certain regions of which can serve as surrogates for functions from spacetime points to real numbers. So one avenue worth exploring is that of adopting the substantivalist attitude towards one or more of the bundles mentioned above.

Suppose we choose the tangent bundle. What would be involved in developing a nominalistic tangent-bundle substantivalism? We already know how to describe a vector bundle, so our task is to identify some additional structure which can explain why it should be natural to identify the points in a vector bundle with tangent vectors at points in spacetime. There are several workable ways to do this.

(i) The mathematical job of a vector at a point is to assign a number (a directional derivative) to each smooth scalar function. We could capture this idea in the present framework using a primitive four-place predicate Derivative(x, s_0, s_1, s_2), where x is a point in the fibre bundle, s_0 is a nowhere-zero section, s_1 is a smooth multiple of s_0, and s_2 is a constant multiple of s_0, with the intuitive meaning '$x(s_1{:}s_0) = s_2{:}s_0$'. We would need axioms on this relation guaranteeing, for example, that if Derivative(x, s_0, s_1, s_2) and Derivative(y, s_0, s_1, s_3), then Derivative($x+y, s_0, s_1, s_2+s_3$).

(ii) As we have seen, there are plenty of composite entities that can serve as representatives of vectors at points—half-line sieves, for example. One could express the distinctive 'vector' nature of the points in the tangent bundle by means of a primitive binary relation of 'correspondence' between points in the tangent bundle and half-line sieves. This would be a one-many relation, with a basic axiom guaranteeing that when half-line sieves H_1 and H_2 are 'equivalent', v corresponds to H_1 iff v corresponds to H_2. (Half-line sieves are equivalent iff they assign the same directional derivative to each smooth function: we can express this nominalistically using our usual device of replacing quantification over smooth functions with quantification over smooth multiples of a nowhere-zero section s_0.)

This approach might seem oddly indirect. If we already have entities in the ontology to play the role of vectors at points, what do we gain by adding new entities (points in the tangent bundle) that play the same role? The answer is that we now have entities that play the role of vector *fields* (sections of the tangent bundle). Since half-line sieves are themselves spread out in spacetime, mereological sums of them are not going to work as surrogates for vector fields. (In a one-dimensional space it is obvious that if we have some half-line sieves such that every point in the space is the home point of one of them, their fusion will be the whole space; and thinking about this makes it clear that the problem is not going to go away in higher-dimensional spaces.)

(iii) We could also capture the distinctive character of the tangent bundle using primitive predicates applying to sections rather than points. Mathematically, the job of a smooth vector field is to yield a smooth scalar function as output when given one as input: we could capture this using a four-place relation D(s, s_0, s_1, s_2) holding between a Smooth section s, a nowhere-zero section s_0, and smooth multiples s_1 and s_2 of s_0, with the intuitive meaning that $s(s_1{:}s_0)=s_2{:}s_0$. Slightly more elegantly, we could have a primitive predicate LieBracket(s_1, s_2, s_3). In the usual construction of vector fields as functions from smooth scalar functions to smooth scalar functions, the Lie bracket $[v_1, v_2]$ of vector fields v_1 and v_2 is the vector field defined by $[v_1, v_2](f) = v_1(v_2(f)) - v_2(v_1(f))$. Although the functions $v_1(v_2(f))$ and $v_2(v_1(f))$ are not vector fields (since they do not generally satisfy the Leibniz product rule: $v_1(v_2(fg)) \neq v_1(v_2(f))g + fv_1(v_2(g)))$, it is straightforward to show that their difference is a vector field.[33] So the Lie bracket defines a distinctive structure on the sections of the tangent bundle. In fact, the Lie bracket relation fully pins down the correspondence between sections of the tangent bundle and vector

---

[33] *Proof:* $[v_1, v_2](fg) = v_1(v_2(fg)) - v_2(v_1(fg))$

$= v_1(fv_2(g) + gv_2(f)) - v_2(fv_1(g) + gv_1(f))$

$= fv_1(v_2(g)) + v_2(g)v_1(f) + gv_1(v_2(f)) + v_2(f)v_1(g) - fv_2(v_1(g)) - v_1(g)v_2(f) - gv_2(v_1(f)) - v_1(f)v_2(g)$

$= fv_1(v_2(g)) + gv_1(v_2(f)) - fv_2(v_1(g)) - gv_2(v_1(f)) = f[v_1, v_2](g) + g[v_1, v_2](f)$.

fields in the standard sense. We use the fact that $[v,fv] = v(f)v$.[34] If we are given f in the form of a ratio of two vector fields $v_1:v_0$, we can thus specify $v(f)$ as the ratio of $[v,fv]$ to v (where fv is the vector field such that $fv:v = v_1:v_0$). By plugging this definition o $v(f)$ back into the definition of $[v_1,v_2]$ as $v_1(v_2(f))-v_2(v_1(f))$, we can formulate an axiom involving the primitive LieBracket predicate that captures everything that makes the tangent bundle distinctive among vector bundles.[35]

Tangent-bundle substantivalism makes the task of nominalizing physical theories more straightforward in certain respects. First, it gives us a new option for representing physical tensor fields of rank j, k with $k>0$. As we saw in Section 8.8, tensor fields of rank j, 0 can be represented using relations among scalar fields, and we can formulate physical theories in such a way that we only ever need to talk about tensor fields of this sort, by appealing to the correspondence between covector fields and vector fields generated by the metric. If we have vector fields in the ontology, there is no need to rely on this trick: instead, we can represent a physical covector field in the obvious way, as a relation that maps each smooth vector field to a 'smooth function' (that is, a pair of vector fields, one of which is a smooth multiple of the other). In general, a tensor field of rank j, k will take j 'smooth functions' and k smooth vector fields and yield a 'smooth function'—or to be exact, given an arbitrary nowhere-zero vector field s_0, it will take j smooth multiples of s_0 and k smooth vector fields that need not be multiples of s_0, and deliver another smooth multiple of s_0.

Given the ability to represent tensor fields of all ranks, we can simplify Section 8.7's algorithm for turning tensor equations into nominalistic laws. The predicate that represents the contraction of a tensor field will no longer need to involve quantification over scalar fields $g_{\alpha\beta}$ representing the components of the metric in a given coordinate system: instead, we can simply take over the standard mathematical definition of contraction. We will still need quantification over coordinate systems to state this, however. If one were absolutely determined to avoid mentioning coordinates at all in the treatment of contraction, we see no alternative but to take a substantivalist attitude not just to the tangent bundle, but to the tensor bundles of rank j, k for all j and k, or at least as many of these bundles as are used in the physical theory we are trying to nominalize. In that case, one could have a primitive 'Contraction' predicate that relates each point in the tensor bundle of rank $j+1$, $k+1$ to a point in the tensor bundle of rank j, k, subject to certain axioms. But it strikes us as wrongheaded to engage in so much ontological inflation just for the sake of avoiding ever having to quantify over coordinates, especially since such quantification seems in any case to be inescapable in the axioms which characterize differentiable manifolds (for example, in axiom F3, or its nominalistic versions FN3/SN3).

---

[34] $[v,fv](g)=v((fv)(g))-(fv)(v(g))=v(f\cdot v(g))-f\cdot v(v(g))=v(f)v(g)+f\cdot v(v(g))-f\cdot v(v(g))=v(f)v(g)$

[35] Here is what the axiom in question looks like in non–primitive notation: If $v_3:[v_1,v_2] = v_3:v_1 = v_4:v_2$ and $v_6:v_1 = [v_2,v_4]:v_2$ and $v_7:v_2 = [v_1,v_3]:v_1$, then $[[v_1,v_2],v_5]:[v_1,v_2] = [v_1,v_6]:v_1 - [v_2,v_7]:v_2$. This can certainly be simplified quite a lot, but we will not go into the details.

One other nice thing about tangent-bundle substantivalism is that it gives us several natural ways of introducing a primitive predicate representing a connection on the tangent bundle—all the strategies for representing connections on general vector bundles considered in Section 8.8 work just as well when the vector bundle is the tangent bundle. Since the spacetime connection is fully determined by the metric, it is not indispensable to have a primitive predicate which represents it. However, having such a predicate will probably allow for simpler formulations of the laws, and will certainly allow our nominalistic versions of the laws to follow their platonistic counterparts more closely.[36]

If we are not dealing with a gauge field theory, so that we do not have any independent motivation for substantivalism about some other vector bundle, the special properties of the tangent bundle make it an especially attractive candidate to provide the vector bundle structure we need for capturing the differential structure of spacetime. Even if we are trying to nominalize a gauge field theory, so that we have an independent reason to be substantivalists about some other vector bundle, it might be worth taking a substantivalist view of the tangent bundle in addition, in view of the simplifications in the statements of physical laws which this would allow. The relative merits here depend on delicate issues about the trade-off between simplicity in the statement of laws and ontological economy, concerning which we have no firm general views.

8.11 Further possible simplifications

As we have developed the ontology of fibre-bundle substantivalism, sections are mereological fusions: the atoms of the mereology are points in fibre bundles. This is not the most ontologically economical way of proceeding. We can make the ontology smaller by throwing away the points, and instead taking the *sections* as the atoms of the mereology.[37] The work previously done by *spacetime points* considered as certain fusions of fibre-points could be taken over by certain special sections, or fusions of sections. For example, we might identify a spacetime point with the fusion of all sections that are zero at that point. Two sections s_1 and s_2 'have the same value' at a spacetime point iff $s_1 - s_2$ is part of that spacetime point.[38] Since we have not just Smooth sections to play

---

[36] See note 26. Even without the ontology of tangent bundle substantivalism, we might consider representing a connection using a polyadic primitive predicate of scalar fields—something like 'the covariant derivative with respect to grad f_0 of g_1 grad $f_1 + \ldots + g_4$ grad $f_4 = h_1$ grad $f_1 + \ldots + h_1$ grad f_4' (where grad f is $\Phi_g^{-1}(df)$). Or our primitive predicate could express a function from a quadruple of scalar fields (representing a coordinate system) to the components of the connection with respect to those coordinates (the Christoffel symbols). However, tangent bundle substantivalism makes it possible to use primitive predicates that are less artificial-looking, and have fewer argument places.

[37] Dorr (2011) considers this approach in a bit more detail.

[38] We can pick out the fusions that are spacetime points in this schema as the 'maximal ideals'—fusions with the property that (i) whenever two sections are part of them, their sum is part of them, and (ii) whenever s_1 and s_2 are part of them, any other sections s_3 and s_4 such that $s_1 : s_2 = s_3 : s_4$ are also part of them, and (iii) which are not parts of any other fusions satisfying (i) and (ii), except for the fusion of all sections.

with, but also highly un-Smooth sections (for example, sections that are zero every where except for one spacetime point, which can do almost all the work previousl done by the points of fibre bundles), it would not be a technically difficult matter t rewrite the axioms in such a way as to work in this alternative ontological scheme.

On this approach, the primitive predicates can all be taken to be predicates c mereological atoms. Because of this, a further simplification becomes available, i which we get rid of the mereological element of the theory altogether and have noth ing but sections in the fundamental ontology. For this to work, we will need to b tolerant of something like plural or second order quantification: this will be needed i order to take over the crucial work that quantification over 'multifields' played in th statement of axioms SN1 and SN3 (in particular, in defining what it is for one sectio to be a 'C^∞ relative to' certain other sections). If such quantification is legitimate, the quantification over mereological fusions of sections is redundant from the point o view of the project of nominalizing physics. (Some think that mereological fusion 'come for free', so that there is nothing to be gained by abandoning them. W disagree.)[39]

Having eliminated everything except for sections (and perhaps fusions of sections) from the ontology, it is tempting to venture even further, by eliminating all the non-smooth sections in addition. For the special case of smooth sections in scalar-value space, this kind of ontology has been considered under the name 'Einstein Algebras' by Robert Geroch (1972) and under the name 'Leibniz Algebras' by John Earman (1989, sect. 9.9). However, the challenges facing such an approach are daunt-ing. If we cannot quantify over all sections, how can we nominalistically express the content of axiom F1; that is, that 'C^∞ functions of smooth sections are smooth'? If we had access to all the resources of set theory, we could reconstruct such quantification using quantification over ordered pairs of spacetime points and sections, where points are in turn constructed as sets of sections. And if we were completely blasé about using higher-order logic, we could do something similar within that framework, which might arguably be counted as nominalistic. But this would take us quite far from the kind of nominalization project in which we have been engaged in this chapter.

8.12 Conclusions

The strategies we have presented allow for the nominalization of a wide range of modern theories in fundamental physics. There is still work to be done, since we have

---

[39] By contrast, in order to replace quantification over mereological fusions of fibre-points with plural or second-order quantification, one would need to allow for primitive predicates (such as 'Smooth') to take plural or second-order arguments: we would speak of *some points* as 'collectively' Smooth in a way that doesn't require there to be such a thing as the 'collection' of those points. The question whether primitive predicates of this sort are even intelligible raises deep foundational issues. Even if one regarded them as intel-ligible, one might still think that they introduced a kind of complexity which we would be better off avoid-ing by introducing something like mereology.

not said anything in this chapter about the nominalization of quantum theories. However, it seems to us that the main problem here is simply the one that was discussed in Chapter 3: that of finding a satisfactory account of what quantum theories are telling us about the fundamental structure of the world. We want to be able to understand these theories not just as pragmatic devices for predicting the outcomes of experiments, but as accounts of what there is, fundamentally speaking, and of the pattern of fundamental properties and relations. Once one has given a clear and satisfactory account of the fundamental structure of the world according to quantum theory, we foresee no distinctively new obstacles to the project of nominalizing such an account. For example, one view takes the wavefunction over configuration space as a straightforward representation of the fundamental structure of the world. On this view, the fundamental ontology includes entities standing in some geometric relations that make it natural to think of them as 'points of configuration space', and standing in some other relations that pick out a function from them to the complex numbers as 'the wave-function' (or to be more precise, that pick out a certain small equivalence class of functions from them to the complex numbers as 'legitimate choices of wave-function').

The techniques required for nominalizing classical field theories should extend quite easily to theories of this sort. Other accounts of the fundamental ontology of quantum theories will involve a similarly 'substantivalist' attitude towards other high-dimensional spaces: the Hilbert space, the space of operators, or some interesting subspaces of the space of operators such as the space of field-configuration operators. Again, with such a richly structured domain of concrete entities to work with, nominalization seems unlikely to be very difficult. The dialectical situation seems quite similar to the case of classical gauge field theories: the richly structured ontology of concrete objects which makes nominalization feasible can be motivated quite independently of any commitment to nominalism, simply by the demand for a satisfactory account of the concrete facts upon which the phenomena supervene.

One might think that, for example, a Hilbert space is a paradigm mathematical object, so that no theory positing such a thing could count as genuinely 'nominalistic'. But as we have already said, we do not want to quibble about the label. We are simply interested in the question which entities exist, and how they are structured. We take it that our best theories of the phenomena are our best guide to answering this question, and that a parsimonious, simple theory is more likely to be true than a complex, rich theory. Since the mathematical realm, as conceived by those who believe in it, contains instantiations of more or less every possible structure, *any* answer we might come up with will have the feature that according to it, the structure of the concrete world is isomorphic to that of some (putative) mathematical entity.

It may strike some readers that the theories we have been developing are much more complex than familiar platonistic ones, so that even by our own standards, we should be willing, for the sake of having simple laws, to embrace the mathematical ontology those theories require. We disagree: much of the complexity of platonistic

theories is hidden behind a hierarchy of definitions, which practitioners rarely have
any need to consult.

But even if it is true that there are some additions to the ontology we have been
advocating that can be justified by gains in simplicity, we think it is a mistake to think
of mathematical ontology as an all-or-nothing deal. Otherwise we might as well have
thrown in the towel at the point when Sumerians first discovered how to use abacuses
to keep track of the size of their herds! Mathematics is a stupendously useful tool.
It describes and systematizes a vast array of possible structures, any one of which we
might find ourselves having reason to ascribe to part of the real world. We should feel
free to avail ourselves of these options, without fearing that once we start doing so, we
will somehow end up having to believe that every one of those structures is instantiated somewhere in reality.

Appendices

Appendix A: Different differential structures that generate the same embedded subregions

Let D be the standard differential structure on $\mathbb{R}^2$. Let D' be the non-standard structure
such that a function f is smooth according to D' iff $f \circ \Phi$ is smooth according to D,
where $\varphi(<x,y>)=<x(x^2+y^2), y(x^2+y^2)>$. We will show that for any set S, S is the image
of a smooth embedding of a one-dimensional manifold into D iff S is the image of a
smooth embedding of a one-dimensional manifold into D'. Since D and D' disagree
only at $<0,0>$, it suffices to consider curves $\gamma: (-1,1) \rightarrow \mathbb{R}^2$ with $\gamma(0)=<0,0>$ and $\gamma'(0)$
non-zero (as required for γ to be an embedding).[40]

Lemma 1: A curve γ (function from $\mathbb{R}$ to $\mathbb{R}^2$) is smooth according to D' iff $\Phi^{-1} \circ \gamma$ is
smooth according to D.

Proof: A curve is smooth iff its composition with any smooth function is smooth. But
if f is smooth according to D', it is of the form $g \circ \Phi^{-1}$ with g smooth according to D. So
γ is smooth according to D' iff $f \circ \Phi^{-1} \circ \gamma$ is smooth according to D for every smooth f.
This entails that $\Phi^{-1} \circ \gamma$ is smooth (taking f to be the identity function), and since composition of smooth functions preserves smoothness, it is also entailed by $\Phi^{-1} \circ \gamma$ being
smooth.

Corollary: If γ is smooth according to D', it is smooth according to D.

Lemma 2: Suppose $\gamma(t)$ is a function from $[-1,1]$ to $\mathbb{R}^2$ such that $\gamma(0)=<0,0>$ and $\gamma'(0)$
is non-zero. Then if γ is smooth according to D, $\gamma(t^3)$ is smooth according to D'.

Proof: We will show that $\Phi^{-1}(\gamma(t^3))$ is smooth according to D; this is sufficient for $\gamma(t^3)$
to be smooth according to D' by Lemma 1.

---

[40] This proof is essentially due to Teru Thomas.

Let $\gamma(t) = \langle f(t), g(t)\rangle$. Since $\gamma'(0)$ is non-zero, we know that either $f'(0)$ or $g'(0)$ s non-zero; without loss of generality, let us suppose $f'(0)$ is non-zero. Then when $\neq 0$,

$$\Phi^{-1}(f(t^3)) = \langle f(t^3)/((f(t^3))^2+(g(t^3))^2)^{1/3}, g(t^3)/((f(t^3))^2+(g(t^3))^2)^{1/3}\rangle$$

Define $f\star(t) = f(t^3)/t^3$ when $t\neq 0$, $f\star(0) = 6f'(0)$; $g\star(t)=g(t^3)/t^3$ when $t\neq 0$, $g\star(0)=6g'(0)$. Then when $t\neq 0$,

$$\Phi^{-1}(f(t^3)) = \langle t{\cdot}f\star(t)/((f\star(t))^2+(g\star(t))^2)^{1/3}, t{\cdot}g\star(t)/((f\star(t))^2+(g\star(t))^2))^{1/3}\rangle$$

To show that this is smooth at 0, it is sufficient—since the product of two smooth functions is smooth, and the quotient of two smooth functions is smooth wherever the denominator is non-zero, and any power of a smooth function is smooth wherever that function is non-zero—to show that $f\star$ and $g\star$ are smooth at 0, and that $f\star$ is non-zero at 0 (since in that case $(f\star(t))^2$ must be positive at 0, and hence so must $(f\star(t))^2+(g\star(t))^2)$ and $((f\star(t))^2+(g\star(t))^2))^{1/3}$).

To show that $f\star$ and $g\star$ are smooth at 0, we use the fact—which can be verified by manipulating the epsilon-delta definition of differentiation—that if the first two derivatives of a smooth function $h(t)$ vanish at 0, then the function j defined by $j(t)=h(t)/t^3$, $j(0)=h'''(0)$ is also smooth at 0. The first two derivatives of $f(t^3)$ and $g(t^3)$ do vanish at 0, since

$$d/dt\, f(t^3)|_0 = 3f'(t^3)t^2|_0 = 0$$
$$d^2/dt^2\, f(t^3)|_0 = 9f''(t^3)t^4+6f'(t^3)t|_0 = 0$$

and similarly for g. And the third derivative of $f(t^3)$ and $g(t^3)$ are respectively equal to $6f'(0)$ and $6g'(0)$, since

$$d^3/dt^3\, f(t^3)|_0 = 27f'''(t^3)t^6+36f''(t^3)t^3+18f''(t^3)t+6f'(t^3)|_0 = 6f'(0)$$

and similarly for g. This tells us that $f\star$ and $g\star$ are smooth at 0; also, since $f'(0)\neq0$, we have that $f\star(0)$ is non-zero, as required.

Corollary: for any set S, if according to D, S is the image of a function $\gamma{:}[-1,1]\to\mathbb{R}^2$ with $\gamma(0)=\langle0,0\rangle$ and $\gamma'(0)$ non-zero, then this is also the case according to D', and conversely.

Appendix B: 'Diag' determines differential structure

In this appendix we will show that if we have differential structures D and D' on a topological manifold of dimension at least two, and they agree on the extension of the predicate $\mathrm{Diag}(R_1,R_2,R_3)$ defined as follows:

For some smooth functions x and y and open region O such that x and y form part of an admissible coordinate system mapping O onto a convex open subset of $\mathbb{R}^n$: R_1 comprises exactly the points where x is rational, and R_2 comprises exactly the points where y is rational, and R_3 comprises exactly the points where $x=y$, then D=D'.

Lemma: If f and g are continuous functions on an open region O, and for every x, the subregions $f=x$ and $g=x$ of O are connected, and the points in O where the value of f is rational are exactly those where the value of g is rational, then there is a continuous function h: $\mathbb{R} \rightarrow \mathbb{R}$ such that $f=h(g)$.

Proof: Suppose we had two points a and b in O such that $g(a)=g(b)$ but $f(a) \neq f(b)$. Let r be a rational number between $f(a)$ and $f(b)$. Since f is continuous, every path from a to b must pass through a point where $f=r$. Since the region where $g=g(a)$ is connected, no path from a to b has to pass through a point where the value of g is anything other than $g(a)$. But g is rational whenever $f=r$. So $g(a)$ must be rational. So $f(a)$ and $f(b)$ must be rational. But then there is some irrational number x between $f(a)$ and $f(b)$. Since f is continuous, every path from a to b has to pass through a point where $f=x$. But g is irrational whenever $f=x$. So every path from a to b has to pass through a point where g is irrational. This cannot be the case, since $g(a)=g(b)$ is rational the set of points where $g=g(a)$ is connected.

Lemma 4: Suppose D is a differentiable structure, and x and y form part of a convex coordinate system on an open region O that is admissible according to D. Let R_1 comprise the points where x is rational and R_2, the points where y is rational. Then for any region R_3, Diag(R_1,R_2,R_3) iff for some diffeomorphism f on the real line, R_3 comprises the points where $y=f(x)$.

Proof: Left-to-right: if Diag(R_1,R_2,R_3), there is a D-admissible convex coordinate system x',y' such that x' is rational exactly in R_1, y' is rational exactly in R_2, and $x'=y'$ exactly in R_3. Since x and x' both form parts of convex coordinate systems on O, both are continuous, and their level sets within O must all be connected. So by Lemma 3, x' must equal $g(x)$ for some g: $\mathbb{R} \rightarrow \mathbb{R}$. Similarly, y' must equal $h(y)$ for some h: $\mathbb{R} \rightarrow \mathbb{R}$. Since x' and y' are part of an admissible coordinate system, g and h must be diffeomorphisms. Since R_3 comprises the points where $y'=x'$, it comprises the points where $y=h^{-1}(g(x))$; so $h^{-1} \circ g$ is a diffeomorphism f as required.

Right-to-left: suppose f is a diffeomorphism on the real line, and R_3 comprises the points where $y=f(x)$. If x and y form part of a convex coordinate system on O that is admissible according to D, so do $x'=f(x)$ and y. (Applying f to one coordinate while leaving the others alone maps convex regions to convex regions.) Since R_3 comprises the points where $x'=y$, Diag(R_1,R_2,R_3).

Theorem: Suppose we have two differentiable structures D and D', an open region O, and two functions x', y' which according to D' are part of a coordinate system mapping O onto an convex open subset $\mathbb{R}^n$. Let R_1 be the region where x' is rational and R_2 the region where y' is rational. Choose some diffeomorphism d from the range of x' to the range of y', and let R_d comprise the points in O where $y'=d(x')$. Then by Lemma 4, Diag(R_1,R_2,R_d). So there are continuous functions x, y that are part of a convex coordinate system on O that is admissible according to D, such that x is rational exactly in R_1, y is rational exactly in R_2, and $x=y$ exactly in R_d. Since x and x' are both arts of convex coordinate systems, the regions of the form $x=r$ and $x'=r$, for rational umbers r, are exactly the maximal connected subregions of R_1. So by Lemma 3, there ust be some continuous function g on the real numbers, such that $x'(p)=g(x(p))$. By ne same reasoning, there must be a continuous function h such that $y'(p)=h(y(p))$. Note that since R_d comprises the points where $x=y$, i.e. where $x'=g(h^{-1}(y'))$, and Diag(R_1,R_2,R_d), the right-to-left direction of Lemma 4 tells us that the function $g \circ h^{-1}$, which gives us R_d as a function in the y',x' coordinates, is a diffeomorphism.

Now, let f be any diffeomorphism from the real line to itself. Let R_f be the set of points where $y=f(x)$. By the left-to-right direction of Lemma 2, Diag(R_1,R_2,R_f). But R_f is also the set of points where $y' = h(f(g^{-1}(x')))$. So by the right-to-left direction of Lemma 2, this function $h \circ f \circ g^{-1}$, which gives us R_f as a function in the x', y' coordinates, must be a diffeomorphism. Since we have already established that $g \circ h^{-1}$ is a diffeomorphism, and the composition of two diffeomorphisms is itself a diffeomorphism, it follows that $g \circ h^{-1} \circ h \circ f \circ g^{-1} = g \circ f \circ g^{-1}$ is a diffeomorphism.

Since f was arbitrary, we have established that the function g which gives us x' as a function of x has the following interesting property: whenever f is a diffeomorphism, $g \circ f \circ g^{-1}$ is. We can establish the converse using exactly similar reasoning, but now going n the opposite direction (from the primed to the unprimed coordinate functions). So we are now in a position to apply the following result, due to Floris Takens (1979):

Let $\Phi: M_1 \to M_2$ be a bijection between two smooth n-manifolds such that $\lambda: M_2 \to M_2$ is a diffeomorphism iff $\Phi^{-1} \circ \lambda \circ \Phi$ is a diffeomorphism. Then Φ is a diffeomorphism.

Take $M_1 = M_2 = \mathbb{R}$ and $\Phi = g^{-1}$, it follows from this that g is a diffeomorphism. Analogous reasoning shows that h (which gives y' as a function of y) is a diffeomorphism.

So we have established that the coordinates x', y', which are admissible according to differential structure D', are also admissible according to differential structure D. This means that in general, any convex coordinatization of an open neighbourhood that is admissible according to D' is admissible according to D. And the reverse is true too (by isomorphic reasoning). But if so, D and D' must be the same differential structure: for if any coordinate system were admissible according to one but not the other, some of its restrictions to convex regions of $\mathbb{R}^n$ would have to be admissible according to the one but no the other, admissibility being a local matter. So from the assumption that D and D' agree about the extension of Diag, we have deduced that they are the same differential structure.[41]

Appendix C: Adequacy of our axioms for scalar-value lines

In this appendix we will sketchily prove the following representation theorem: in any model of M1−M5 (second-order classical mereology+atomicity), A1−A6 ('addition is an abelian group on each scalar-value line') and P1−P6 (repeated below), and every

---

[41] Thanks to Andrew Stacey for pointing us to the Takens result and explaining its relevance to our question.

scalar-value line l in that model, there is a unique function π_l from the real numbers to points in u's scalar-value line such that $\pi_l(\alpha+\beta)=\pi_l(\alpha)+\pi_l(\beta)$, $\pi_l(\alpha)$ is Positive iff $\alpha>0$, and $\pi_l(\alpha)$ is a Unit iff $\alpha=1$. And this π_l is one-to-one.

P1 Everything Positive lacks proper parts

P2 If x and y are Positive, $x+y$ is Positive (i.e. '$<$ is transitive', where '$x<y$' means '$x-y$ is Positive'.)

P3 Whenever x is Positive, $-x$ is not Positive. ('$\leq$ is antisymmetric')

P4 Whenever x is atomic and not zero, either x or $-x$ is Positive. ('$\leq$ is total')

P5 If x is Positive, there exist Positive y and z such that $\text{Sum}(y,z,x)$. ('$\leq$ is dense')

P6 If $X<Y$, then there is a z such that $X\leq z$ and $z\leq Y$. ('$\leq$ is Dedekind complete' $X<Y$ means 'whenever x is an atomic part of X and y is an atomic part of Y $x<y$'.)

We will need a lemma:

Lemma 5: For every x, there is exactly one y such that $y+\ldots+y$ [m terms]$=x$.

Proof: Let S be the fusion of points s such that $s+\ldots+s\leq x$, and B the fusion of b such that $b+\ldots+b>x$. S$<$B, since if $x>y$, $x+\ldots+x>y+\ldots+y$ by P2. So by P6 there is a z such that S$\leq z$ and $z\leq$B. Now, suppose that $z+\ldots+z>y$. Then by P5, there is a w such that $0<w<z+\ldots+z-y$. By repeated applications of P5, $w=w_1+\ldots+w_m$ for some Positive $w_1,\ldots,w_m$. Let w_i be the smallest of $w_1,\ldots,w_m$; then $w_i+\ldots+w_i\leq w$. So $(z+\ldots+z)-(w_i+\ldots+w_i)\geq(z+\ldots+z)-w>y$. Hence $z-w_i$ belongs to B, contradicting our assumption that $z\leq$B. The possibility that $z+\ldots+z<y$ can be ruled out by similar reasoning, leaving $z+\ldots+z=y$ the only possibility by P4. Could there be some other z' such that $z'+\ldots+z'=y$? No: if $z+\ldots+z=z'+\ldots+z'$, then $(z-z')+\ldots+(z-z')$ is zero, which by P2 could not happen if $z-z'$ or $z'-z$ were Positive.

We are now in a position to prove our representation theorem.

(i) Existence. We start by defining π inductively for integers, by requiring that $\pi_l(1)$ be the unique Unit of l, and that $\pi_l(n+m)=\pi_l(n)+\pi_l(m)$ and $\pi_l(n-m)=\pi_l(n)-\pi_l(m)$. When α is a rational number of the form n/m (where m is positive), we let $\pi_l(\alpha)$ be the point z such that $z+\ldots+z$ [m terms]$=\pi_l(n)$, which exists by Lemma 5. This extension of π will obviously still respect the addition facts. Finally, when α is irrational, we let $\pi_l(\alpha)$ be the point z such that $X\leq z$ and $z\leq Y$, where X is the fusion of points $\pi_l(n/m)$ where $n/m<\alpha$, and Y is the fusion of points $\pi_l(n/m)$ where $n/m>\alpha$. By P6, there is such a z. Showing that on this definition $\pi_l(\alpha)+\pi_l(\beta)=\pi_l(\alpha+\beta)$ comes down to showing that whenever $x<y$, $x<\pi_l(n/m)<y$ for some n and m. For this, we use P6 to show that every Positive z is greater than some point of the form $\pi_l(1/m)$, and then argue inductively that if so, some point of the form $\pi_l(n/m)$ must occur between any two points whose difference is at least z.

(ii) Uniqueness. Suppose π_l and ρ_l both meet the specified conditions. By induction, $\pi_l(n)=\rho_l(n)$ for each integer n. If α is a rational number n/m (m positive), we have that

$\tau_i(\alpha)+\ldots+\pi_i(\alpha)$ [m terms]$=\pi_i(n)=\rho_i(n)=\rho_i(\alpha)+\ldots+\rho_i(\alpha)$; but if $\pi_i(\alpha)<\rho_i(\alpha)$, P2 tells us that $\pi_i(\alpha)+\ldots+\pi_i(\alpha)<\rho_i(\alpha)+\ldots+\rho_i(\alpha)$ and hence $\pi_i(\alpha)+\ldots+\pi_i(\alpha)\neq\rho_i(\alpha)+\ldots+\rho_i(\alpha)$ (by P3). And since π_i and ρ_i both respect the ordering facts, they must also agree on the points they assign to irrational numbers, again using the fact that any two points are separated by some point of the form $\pi_i(n/m)$.

(iii) One-to-oneness: First, since $\pi_i(\alpha)+\pi_i(\beta)=\pi_i(\alpha+\beta)$, $\pi_i(0)+\pi_i(0)=\pi_i(0)$, so $\pi_i(0)$ is zero. We first show that $\pi_i(\alpha)$ is not zero for any other α. First, $\pi_i(\alpha)+\pi_i(-\alpha)$ is zero for every α, so $\pi_i(-\alpha)=-\pi_i(\alpha)$, so it suffices to show that $\pi_i(\alpha)$ is not zero for any Positive α. Suppose otherwise. Then for some m, $m\alpha\geq1$; so, arguing inductively, and appealing to the fact that π_i respects ordering facts, $\pi_i(\alpha)+\ldots+\pi_i(\alpha)$ [m terms]$\geq\pi_i(1)$. But $\pi_i(1)$ is the Unit of l, which is Positive by U2; so by P2 $\pi_i(\alpha)+\ldots+\pi_i(\alpha)$ is Positive. This cannot happen if $\pi_i(\alpha)$ is zero, by P3.

Suppose then that $\pi_i(\alpha) = \pi_i(\beta)$. Then $\pi_i(\alpha)-\pi_i(\beta)$ is zero, so $\pi_i(\alpha)+\pi_i(-\beta)$ is zero, so $\pi_i(\alpha-\beta)$ is zero, so $\alpha-\beta$ is zero by the result we just proved. So $\alpha=\beta$, proving that π_i is one-to-one.

Appendix D: Nominalistic treatment of vector spaces

In this appendix we prove a representation theorem: in any model of axioms M1−M5 (classical mereology), A1−A6 ('addition is an abelian group on each fibre') and SD1−SD9 (given in Section 8.9, and repeated here for convenience), there is a unique way of assigning each fibre the structure of a vector space over the real numbers, in such a way that SameDirection(x,y) iff $x=\alpha y$ for some positive real number α.

SD1 If SameDirection(v, x), then v and x lack proper parts.

SD2 If SameDirection(v, x) and SameDirection(v, y), SameDirection($v, x+y$).

SD3 If v is non-zero and SameDirection(v, x), then not SameDirection($v, -x$).

SD4 Whenever x is a non-zero multiple of v, either SameDirection(v, x) or SameDirection($v, -x$).

SD5 For any v, there exist x and y such that $x+y=v$ and SameDirection(v, x) and SameDirection(v, y).

SD6 If X and Y are fusions of multiples of v and X$<_v$Y, then there is a multiple z of v such that X$\leq_v z$ and $z\leq_v$Y.

SD7 SameDirection is an equivalence relation.

SD8 SameDirection($-v_1, -v_2$) whenever SameDirection(v_1, v_2).

SD9 If SameDirection($v+w, x$), then for some y and z such that $y+z=x$, SameDirection(v, y) and SameDirection(w, z).

Here 'x is a multiple of y' means 'for some z_1 and z_2 SameDirection(y, z_1) and SameDirection(y, z_2) and $x=z_1+z_2$'.

Lemma 6: $x+\ldots+x = y+\ldots+y$ only when $x=y$.

Proof: Suppose $x+\ldots+x = y+\ldots+y$. If x is zero, then $x+\ldots+x = y+\ldots+y$ is zero. But then y must be zero, since otherwise we would have SameDirection(y,y) by SD7, and hence SameDirection($y,y+\ldots+y$) by SD2, and hence SameDirection($y,-(y+\ldots+y)$) contradicting SD3. Similarly, if y is zero, x must be. So we can assume that neither x nor y is zero. Then by SD2, SameDirection($x,x+\ldots+x$) and SameDirection($y,y+\ldots+y$). So by transitivity (SD7), SameDirection(x,y). Then since $x-y$ is a multiple of x SD4 tells us that either SameDirection($x,x-y$) or SameDirection($x,y-x$) or $x=y$. But if SameDirection($x,x-y$), SD2 implies that SameDirection ($x,(x+\ldots+x)-(y+\ldots+y)$) which is ruled out by SD3, since $(x+\ldots+x)-(y+\ldots+y)$ is zero. The possibility that SameDirection($x,y-x$) is ruled out in the same way, leaving $x=y$ as the only remaining possibility.

Lemma 7: x is a multiple of y iff either SameDirection(y,x), or SameDirection($y,-x$), or x is zero.

Proof: Left to right: immediate from SD4. For the right to left direction, there are three cases to consider: (i) If SameDirection(y,x), then SameDirection($y,x+x$) by SD2, so x is a multiple of y since $x=(x+x)-x$. (ii) If SameDirection($y,-x$), then SameDirection($y,-x+-x$) by SD2, so x is a multiple of y since $x=x-(-x+-x)$. (iii) if x is zero, then x is a multiple of y since $x=y-y$ and SameDirection(y,y) by SD7.

Lemma 8: 'is a multiple of' is an equivalence relation on non-zero points.

Proof: Reflexivity: Since SameDirection(x,x), x is a multiple of x by Lemma 7. Symmetry: If x and y are non-zero and x is a multiple of y, then by Lemma 7 either SameDirection(y,x) or SameDirection($y,-x$). In the first case, SameDirection(x,y) by SD7, so y is a multiple of x by Lemma 7. In the latter case, SameDirection($-x,y$) by SD7 and SameDirection($x,-y$) by SD8, so y is a multiple of x by Lemma 7. Transitivity: suppose y is a multiple of x and z is a multiple of y, and all are non-zero. By Lemma 7, either SameDirection(y,z) or SameDirection($y,-z$), and either SameDirection(x,y) or SameDirection($x,-y$). If SameDirection(x,y), then by SD7 either SameDirection(x,z) or SameDirection($x,-z$), so z is a multiple of x. If SameDirection($x,-y$), then by SD8 SameDirection($-x,y$), so by SD7 either SameDirection($-x,z$) or SameDirection ($-x,-z$), so by SD8 either SameDirection($x,-z$) or SameDirection(x,z), so by Lemma 7, z is a multiple of x.

Lemma 9: If w is not a multiple of v, x_1 and x_2 are multiples of v, y_1 and y_2 are multiples of w, and $x_1+y_1 = x_2+y_2$, then $x_1=x_2$ and $y_1=y_2$.

Proof: If $x_1+y_1 = x_2+y_2$, then $x_1-x_2 = y_2-y_1$. If x_1-x_2 is zero, then $x_1=x_2$ and $y_1=y_2$ and we are done. So suppose $x_1-x_2 = y_2-y_1$ is non-zero. x_1-x_2 is a multiple of v since x_1 and x_2 are; y_2-y_1 is a multiple of w since y_1 and y_2 are. Since 'multiple' is transitive on non-zero vectors by Lemma 8, it follows that v is a multiple of w contradicting our assumption.

Theorem: In any model of the axioms, whenever v is non-zero, there is a unique function π_v from real numbers to vectors with the properties that (a) $\pi_v(1)=v$,

b) $\pi_v(\alpha+\beta)=\pi_v(\alpha)+\pi_v(\beta)$, and (c) SameDirection$(v,\pi_v(\alpha))$ iff $\alpha>0$. And this function is one-to-one.

Proof: From the theorem of Appendix C, noting that P1–P6 and U1–U2 are true when we restrict all quantifiers to multiples of v, interpret 'Positive(x)' as 'SameDirection(v,x)' and 'Unit(x)' as '$x=v$'.

Theorem: The operation '$x=\alpha v$' defined by 'either v is non-zero and $\pi_v(\alpha)=x$, or v is zero and $x=v$' satisfies the axioms for scalar multiplication in a vector space:

(i) $1v = v$

(ii) $(\alpha+\beta)v = \alpha v+\beta v$

(iii) $\alpha(\beta v) = (\alpha\beta)v$

(iv) $\alpha(v+w) = \alpha v+\alpha w$

Proof: (i) and (ii) are immediate from the properties (a) and (b) of π_v. For (iii), there are four cases to consider.

Case 1: v is zero; then both sides are zero.

Case 2: v is non-zero and $\beta=0$. Then $v=(1+\beta)v=v+\beta v$, so βv is zero, so $\alpha(\beta v)$ is zero. And $(\alpha\beta)v = 0v = (1-1)v=v-v$, which is also zero.

Case 3: v is non-zero and $\beta>0$. Then SameDirection$(v,\beta v)$ by (c). By SD7, for any x, SameDirection(v,x) iff SameDirection$(\beta v,x)$. So $0<\pi_v(x)$ iff $0<\pi_{\beta v}(x)$. And more generally, $\pi_v(x)\le\pi_v(y)$ iff $\pi_{\beta v}(x)\le\pi_{\beta v}(y)$. Also, by Lemma 8, the multiples of v are exactly the multiples of βv. We know that $\pi_{\beta v}$ is the one and only additive function from the multiples of βv to the reals such that $\pi(\beta v)=1$ and $\pi_{\beta v}(x)\le\pi_{\beta v}(y)$ whenever $x\le_{\beta v}y$. But we have just seen that the function $f(x):= \pi_v(x)/\beta$ has exactly these properties. So in general, $\pi_{\beta v}(x) = \pi_v(x)/\beta$. In other words, $x=\alpha(\beta v)$ iff $x = (\alpha\beta)v$.

Case 4: v is non-zero and $\beta<0$. Then SameDirection$(v,-\beta v)$. By SD7 and SD8, for any x, SameDirection(v,x) iff SameDirection$(\beta v,-x)$. So $0<\pi_v(x)$ iff $0<\pi_{\beta v}(-x)$ which is true iff $\pi_{\beta v}(x)<0$. More generally, $\pi_v(x)\le\pi_v(y)$ iff $\pi_{\beta v}(y)\le\pi_{\beta v}(x)$. Also, by Lemma 8, the multiples of v are exactly the multiples of βv. Thus as in Case 3, the function $f(x):= \pi_v(x)/\beta$ has exactly the properties that we know are unique to $\pi_{\beta v}$.

For (iv), we have to go through seven cases.

Case 1: v is zero. Then $\alpha(v+w) = \alpha w = v+\alpha w = \alpha v+\alpha w$.

Case 2: v is non-zero and w is a multiple of v. Then for some β, $w=\beta v$. So $v+w = v+\beta v = (1+\beta)v$ (by (i) and (ii)); and thus $\alpha(v+w) = \alpha((1+\beta)v) = (\alpha+\alpha\beta)v$ (by (iii)) $= \alpha v+(\alpha\beta)v$ (by (ii)) $= \alpha v+\alpha(\beta v)$ (by (iii)) $= \alpha v+\alpha w$.

Case 3: v is non-zero, w is not a multiple of v, and α is a positive integer. Then we can use (ii) to argue that $\alpha(v+w) = (v+w)+ \ldots+(v+w) = (v+ \ldots+v)+(w+ \ldots+w) = \alpha v+\alpha w$.

Case 4: v is non-zero, w is not a multiple of v and α is a negative integer. Then $\alpha(v+w)=-\alpha(-v-w)$ (by (ii) and (iii)) $= -\alpha(-v) -\alpha(-w)$ (by Case 3) $= \alpha v+\alpha w$ (by (ii) and (iii)).

Case 5: v is non-zero, w is not a multiple of v, and $\alpha=\beta/\gamma$, where β is a non-zero integer and γ is a positive integer. Then $\alpha(v+w)+\ldots+\alpha(v+w)$ [γ terms]$=\beta(v+w)=\beta v+\beta w$ (by Cases 3 and 4)$=(\alpha v+\ldots+\alpha v)+(\alpha w+\ldots+\alpha w)=(\alpha v+\alpha w)+\ldots+(\alpha v+\alpha w)$. But by Lemma 6 this can only happen if $\alpha(v+w)=\alpha v+\alpha w$.

Case 6: v is non-zero, w is not a multiple of v, and α is positive and irrational. By SD9 (this is our first appeal to SD9!), there are β and γ such that $\alpha(v+w) = \beta v+\gamma w$, and this β and γ are unique by Lemma 9. Suppose δ is some positive rational number less than α. Then SameDirection($\alpha(v+w),(\alpha-\delta)(v+w)$), and hence SameDirection($v+w,(\alpha-\delta)(v+w)$). By (ii), $(\alpha-\delta)(v+w) = \alpha(v+w)-\delta(v+w) = \beta v+\gamma w-\delta v-\delta w$ (using Case 5) $= (\beta-\delta)v+(\gamma-\delta)w$. So we have SameDirection($v+w,(\beta-\delta)v+(\gamma-\delta)w$). But by SD9, $(\beta-\delta)v+(\gamma-\delta)w$ must in that case be the sum of a positive multiple of v and a positive multiple of w. And by Lemma 9 again, $(\beta-\delta)v$ and $(\gamma-\delta)w$ are the *only* multiples of v and w which sum to $(\beta-\delta)v+(\gamma-\delta)w$. So $\beta-\delta$ and $\gamma-\delta$ are both positive: so $\delta<\beta$ and $\delta<\gamma$. By parallel reasoning, whenever δ is a rational number *greater* than α, $\delta>\beta$ and $\delta>\gamma$. It follows that $\alpha=\beta=\gamma$, and so $\alpha(v+w)=\alpha v+\alpha w$.

Case 7: v is non-zero, w is not a multiple of v, and α is negative and irrational. Then $\alpha(v+w) = -(-\alpha)(v+w)=-((-\alpha)v+(-\alpha)w)$ (by Case 6) $= -(-(\alpha v)+-(\alpha w)) = \alpha v+\alpha w$.

Bibliography

Albert, D. (1996). 'Elementary Quantum Metaphysics', in J. T. Cushing et al. (eds.), *Bohmian Mechanics and Quantum Theory: An Appraisal*. Dordrecht: Kluwer, pp. 277–84.

—— (2000). *Time and Chance*. Cambridge: Harvard University Press.

—— (manuscript). 'Physics and Narrative.'

Arntzenius, F. (1994). 'Space-like Connections', *British Journal for the Philosophy of Science*, 45: 201–7.

—— (2000). 'Are There Really Instantaneous Velocities?', *The Monist*, 83(2): 187–208.

—— (2004). 'Is Quantum Mechanics Pointless?', *Philosophy of Science*, 70(5): 1447–58.

—— (forthcoming). 'The CPT Theorem', in C. Callender (ed.). *The Oxford Handbook on Time*. Oxford: Oxford University Press.

—— and Greaves, H. (2007). 'Time Reversal in Classical Electromagnetism', http://philsci-archive.pitt.edu/archive/00003280/

Baez, J. and Muiniain, J. P. (1994). *Gauge Fields, Knots and Gravity*. Singapore: World Scientific.

Barbour, J. (1999). *The End of Time*. Oxford: Oxford University Press.

—— and Bertotti, B. (1982). 'Mach's Principle and the Structure of Dynamical Theories', *Proceedings of the Royal Society of London*, A 282: 295–306.

——, Z. Foster and N. Ó Murchadha (2002). 'Relativity without relativity', *Classical and Quantum Gravity* 19, pp. 3217–3248.

Bell, J. S. (1955). 'Time Reversal in Field Theory', *Proceedings of the Royal Society of London. Series A, Mathematical and Physical Sciences*, 231, No. 1187: 479–95.

Belot, G. (1995). 'New Work for Counterpart Theorists: Determinism', *British Journal for the Philosophy of Science*, 46: 185–95.

—— (1998). 'Understanding Electromagnetism', *British Journal for the Philosophy of Science*, 49: 531–55.

Birkhoff, G. (1967). *Lattice Theory*. Providence, RI: Colloquium Publications.

Bogolubov, N., Logunov, A., and Todorov, I. (1975). *Introduction to Axiomatic Quantum Field Theory*. London: W. A. Benjamin.

Böhm, A. (1978). *The Rigged Hilbert Space and Quantum Mechanics*. Berlin: Springer.

Brighouse, C. (1997). 'Determinism and Modality', *British Journal for the Philosophy of Science* 48: 465–81.

Burgess, J. and Rosen, G. (1997). *A Subject with No Object*. Oxford: Clarendon Press.

Burton, W. K. (1955). 'Equivalence of the Lagrangian Formulations of Quantum Field Theory Due To Feynman and Schwinger', *Il Nuovo Cimento*, 1(2): 355–7.

Butterfield, J. (2004). 'On the Persistence of Homogeneous Matter', http://philsci-archive.pitt.edu/archive/00001760

Callender, C. (2000). 'Shedding Light on Time', *Philosophy of Science*, 67: S587–99.

Chevalley, C. (1946). *Theory of Lie Groups*. Princeton: Princeton University Press.

Cohen, S. (1983). 'Conservativeness and Incompleteness', *The Journal of Philosophy*, 80(9): 521–31.

Dasgupta, S. (2009). 'Individuals: an Essay in Revisionary Metaphysics', *Philosophical Studies*, 145(1): 37–67.

Deutsch, D. and Hayden, P. (2000). 'Information Flow in Entangled Quantum Systems', arX: quant-ph/9906007

Dorr, C. (2007). 'There Are No Abstract Objects', in T. Sider, J. Hawthorne, and D. Zimmerma (eds.). *Contemporary Debates in Metaphysics*, pp. 32–64. Malden, MA: Wiley–Blackwell.

—— (2010). 'Of Numbers and Electrons'. *Proceedings of the Aristotelian Society*, 110: 133–81.

—— (forthcoming). 'Physical Geometry and Fundamental Metaphysics', *Proceedings of th Aristotelian Society*.

Earman, J. (1986). *A Primer on Determinism*. Dordrecht: Reidel.

—— (1989). *World Enough and Space-time*. Cambridge, MA: MIT Press.

Feynman, R. (1948). 'Space-time Approach to Non-relativistic Quantum Mechanics', *Reviews ‹ Modern Physics*, 20: 367–87.

Field, H. (1980). *Science Without Numbers*. Oxford: Blackwell.

—— (1985a). 'Can We Dispense with Space-time?', in *PSA 1984*, vol. 2, ed. P. Asquith an P. Kitcher. East Lansing, MI: Philosophy of Science Association.

—— (1985b). 'On Conservativeness and Incompleteness', *The Journal of Philosophy*, 82(5 239–60.

Fremlin, T. (2002). *Measure Theory*, vol. 3. Published by the author. Available at http://www.essex ac.uk/maths/staff/fremlin/mtsales.htm

Friedman, M. (1983). *Foundations of Space-Time Theories*. Princeton: Princeton University Press.

Galilei, G. (1623). *Il Saggiatore*, in *Opere*, vol. 6.

Gambini, R. and Pullin, J. (1996). *Loops, Knots, Gauge Theories and Quantum Gravity*. Cambridge Cambridge University Press.

Gerla, G. (1990). 'Pointless Metric Spaces', *The Journal of Symbolic Logic*, 55(1): 207–19.

—— (1995). 'Pointless Geometries', in F. Buekenhout (ed.), *Handbook of Incidence Geometry* Amsterdam: Elsevier Science.

Geroch, R. (1971). *Special Topics in Particle Physics*. Unpublished lecture notes, University of Texas at Austin.

—— (1972). 'Einstein Algebras', *Communications in Mathematical Physics*, 26: 271–5.

Greaves, H. (manuscript). 'Towards a Geometrical Understanding of the CPT Theorem.'

—— and Thomas, T. (manuscript). 'CPT theorem.'

Greiner, R. and J. Reinhardt (1996), *Field Quantization*. Berlin: Springer.

Guicciardini, N. (2002). 'Analysis and Synthesis in Newton's Mathematical Work', in *The Cambridge Companion to Newton*, ed. I. B. Cohen and G. E. Smith. Cambridge: Cambridge University Press, pp. 308–28.

Halvorson, H. (2001). 'On the Nature of Continuous Physical Quantities in Classical and Quantum Mechanics', *Journal of Philosophical Logic*, 30: 27–50.

—— and Clifton, R. (2001). 'No Place for Particles in Relativistic Quantum Theories?', http:// xxx.arXiv.org/abs/quant-ph/0103041

—— and Müger, M. (2006). 'Algebraic Quantum Field Theory', in *Philosophy of Physics*, ed. J. Butterfield and J. Earman. Amsterdam: Elsevier, pp. 731–922.

Healey, R. (2007). *Gauging What's Real*. Oxford: Oxford University Press.

Hilbert, D. (1899). The Foundations of Geometry. 10th rev. edn. (1968), trans. Leo Unger. La Salle, Illinois: Open Court.

Howard, D. (1985). 'Einstein on Locality and Separability', *Studies in History and Philosophy of Science, Part A*: 16(3): 171–201.

Huggett, N. (2006). 'The Regularity Account of Relational Spacetime', *Mind*, 115(457): 41–73.

Iwai, T. (1999). 'Classical and Quantum Mechanics of Jointed Rigid Bodies with Vanishing Total Angular Momentum'. *Journal of Mathematical Physics*, 40: 2381–422.

Lewis, D. (1973). *Counterfactuals*. Oxford: Blackwell.

—— (1986a). *On the Plurality of Worlds*. Oxford: Blackwell.

—— (1986b). *Philosophical Papers*, vol. 2. Oxford: Oxford University Press.

—— (1999a). *Paper in Metaphysics and Epistemology*. Cambridge: Cambridge University Press.

—— (1999b). 'Zimmerman and the Spinning Sphere', *Australasian Journal of Philosophy*, 77(2): 209–12.

Loewer, B. (1996). 'Humean Supervenience', *Philosopical Topics*, 24(1): 101–27.

Loll, R. (1994). 'Gauge Theory and Gravity in the Loop Formulation', in J. Ehlers and H. Friedrich, *Canonical Gravity: from Classical to Quantum*. Berlin: Springer.

Mach, E. (1893). *The Science of Mechanics*. La Salle, IL: Open Court.

Malament, D. (1995). 'Is Newtonian Cosmology Really Inconsistent?', *Philosophy of Science*, 62: 489–510.

—— (2004). 'On the Time Reversal Invariance of Classical Electromagnetic Theory', http://philsci-archive.pitt.edu/archive/00001406/

Maudlin, T. (1990). 'Substances and Spacetimes: What Aristotle Would Have Said to Einstein', *Studies in the History and Philosophy of Science*, 21: 531–61.

—— (2007). 'Suggestions from Physics for Deep Metaphysics', in *The Metaphysics within Physics*. Oxford: Oxford University Press, Chapter 3.

—— (manuscript). 'New Foundations for Physical Geometry.'

Melia, J. (1999). 'Holes, Haecceitism and Two Conceptions of Determinism', *British Journal for the Philosophy of Science*, 50: 639–64.

Menger, K. (1928). 'Untersuchungen uber allgemeine Metrik', *Math. Ann.* 100, pp. 113–41.

Morgan, C. L. (1974). 'Embedding Metric Spaces in Euclidean Space', *Journal of Geometry*, 5(1): 101–7.

Mundy, B. (1992). 'Space-time and Isomorphism', *Proceedings of the 1992 Biennial Meeting of the Philosophy of Science Association*, vol. 1. East Lansing, MI: Philosophy of Science Association, pp. 515–27.

—— (1994). 'Quantity, Representation and Geometry', in P. Humphreys (ed.), *Patrick Suppes: Scientific Philosopher*, vol. 2. Berlin: Springer, pp. 59–102.

Myrvold, W. (2003). 'Relativistic Quantum Becoming', *British Journal for the Philosophy of Science*, 54(3), 475–500.

Needham, T. (1997). *Visual Complex Analysis*. Oxford: Oxford University Press.

Newton, I. (1674/1689). *The Mathematical Papers of Isaac Newton*, vol. 4, ed. D. T. Whiteside (1964). New York: Johnson Reprint Corporation.

Nomizu, K. (1956). *Lie Groups and Differential Geometry*. Tokyo: Mathematical Society of Japan.

O' Raifeartaigh, L. (1997). *The Dawning of Gauge Theory*. Princeton: Princeton University Press.

Pemberton, H. (1728). *A View of Sir Isaac Newton's Philosophy*. London: S. Palmer.

Penrose, R. and Rindler, W. (1984). *Spinors and Space-Time*, vol. 1. Cambridge: Cambridge University Press.

Peskin, M. and Schroeder, D. (1995). *An Introduction to Quantum Field Theory*. Reading, MA: Perseus Books.

Pooley, O. (2001). 'Relationism Rehabilitated? II: Relativity', http://philsci-archive.pitt.edu/archive/00000221/

—— (forthcoming). *The Reality of Spacetime*. Oxford: Oxford University Press.

Putnam, H. (1971). *Philosophy of Logic*. New York: Harper and Row.

Roeper, P. (1997). 'Region-based Topology', *Journal of Philosophical Logic*, 26: 251–309.

Rovelli, C. (2003). *Quantum Gravity*. Cambridge: Cambridge University Press.

Royden, H. (1968). *Real Analysis*. London: Macmillan.

Russell, J. (2008). 'The Structure of Gunk: Adventures in the Ontology of Space', in *Oxford Studies in Metaphysics*, vol. 4, ed. D. Zimmerman. Oxford: Oxford University Press, pp. 248–74.

Savitt, S. (2000). 'There's No Time Like the Present (in Minkowski Space-time)', *Philosophy of Science*, 67: S563–74.

Sider, T. (2001). *Four-dimensionalism*. Oxford: Oxford University Press.

—— (2006). 'Bare Particulars', *Philosophical Perspective*, 20: 387–97.

Sikorski, R. (1964). *Boolean Algebras*. Berlin: Springer.

—— (1972). *Introduction to Differential Geometry*. Warszawa: Polish Scientific Publishers.

Skow, B. (2005). *Once Upon a Spacetime*. PhD thesis. http://web.mit.edu/bskow/www/research/onceuponaspacetime.pdf

—— (2010). 'Extrinsic Temporal Metrics', in D. Zimmerman (ed.), *Oxford Studies in Metaphysics*, vol. 5. Oxford: Oxford University Press.

Skyrms, B. (1983). 'Zeno's Paradox of Measure', in R. S. Cohen and L. Laudan (eds.), *Physics, Philosophy and Psychoanalysis*. Dordrecht: Kluwer, pp. 223–54.

—— (1993). 'Logical Atoms and Combinatorial Possibility', *The Journal of Philosophy*, 90(5): 219–32.

Tarski, A. (1936). *Introduction to Logic and to the Methodology of the Deductive Sciences*. Fourth edition (1994), ed. J. Tarski. Oxford: Oxford University Press.

Takens, F. (1979). 'Characterization of a Differentiable Structure by its Group of Diffeomorphisms', *Bol. Soc. Bras. Mat.*, 10(1): 17–26.

—— (1959). 'What is Elementary Geometry?', in L. Henhin, P. Suppes and A. Tarski (eds.) *The Axiomatic Method with Special Reference to Geometry and Physics*. Amsterdam: North-Holland, pp. 16–29.

Teller, P. (1995). *An Interpretive Introduction to Quantum Field Theory*. Princeton: Princeton University Press.

Tomonaga, S. (1946). 'On a Relativistically Invariant Formulation of the Quantum Theory of Wave Fields.' *Progress of Theoretical Physics*, 1(2): 1–13.

Tumulka, R. (2006). 'A Relativistic Version of the Ghirardi–Rimini–Weber Model', arXiv: quant-ph/0508230

Wagon, S. (1985). *The Banach-Tarski Paradox*. Cambridge: Cambridge University Press.

Wald, R. (1984). *General Relativity*. Chicago: University of Chicago Press.

—— (1994). *Quantum Field Theory in Curved Spacetime and Black Hole Thermodynamics*. Chicago: Chicago University Press.

Wallace, D. (2001). 'Emergence of Particles from Bosonic Quantum Field Theory', http://arxiv.org/abs/quant-ph/0112149

—— (2010). 'The Emergent Multiverse', PhD thesis, Oxford University.

—— and Timpson, C. (2007). 'Non-locality and Gauge Freedom in Deutsch and Hayden's Formulation of Quantum Mechanics', *Foundations of Physics*, 37(6): 951–5.

————— (forthcoming). 'Quantum Mechanics on Spacetime, I: Spacetime State Realism', *British Journal for the Philosophy of Science*.

Will, C. (1981). *Theory and Experiment in Gravitational Physics*. Cambridge: Cambridge University Press.

Wilson, M. (1993). 'There's a Hole and a Bucket, Dear Leibniz', *Midwest Studies in Philosophy*, XVIII. Minneapolis, MN: Minnesota University Press, pp. 202–41.

Index

4/P